THE STORY THUS FAR

Long ago, in the "Warring States" era of Japan's Muromachi period, dog-like half demon Inuyasha attempted to steal the Shikon Jewel—or "Jewel of Four Souls"—from a village. The village priestess, Kikyo, put a stop to his thievery with an enchanted arrow. Pinned to a tree, Inuyasha fell into a deep sleep, while mortally wounded Kikyo took the jewel with her into her funeral pyre. Years passed...

In the present day, Kagome, a Japanese high school girl, is pulled down into a well and transported into the past. There she discovers trapped Inuyasha—and frees him.

When the Shikon Jewel mysteriously reappears, demons attack. In the ensuing battle, the jewel *shatters*!

Now Inuyasha is bound to Kagome with a powerful spell, and the grudging companions must battle to reclaim the shattered shards of the Shikon Jewel to keep them out of evil hands...

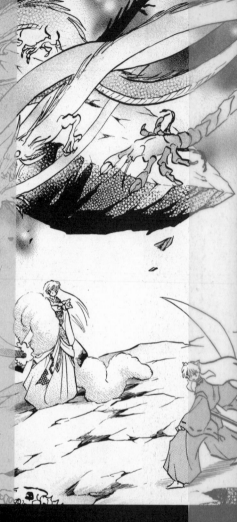

LAST VOLUME Sesshomaru battles Shishinki, the demon his father stole the Meido Zangetsuha from. Turns out Sesshomaru's blade Tenseiga was fashioned *from* Tetsusaiga. When Inuyasha joins the fight, the two blades finally form a full circle! Realizing his only role was to perfect the Meido Zangetsuha for Inuyasha, Sesshomaru takes out his frustration on Totosai.

   Meanwhile, Naraku attempts to reclaim the Shikon shard inside Kohaku by tainting it with his miasma. But Sango drives Naraku off with her restored Hiraikotsu, now imbued with miasma-dispelling power.

CHARACTERS

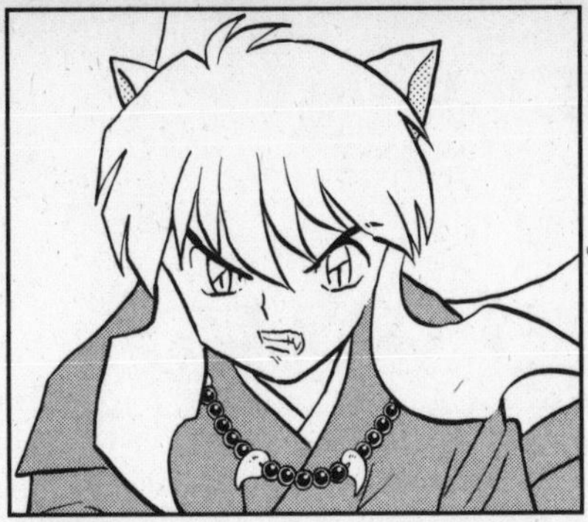

INUYASHA
Half-demon hybrid, son of a human mother and demon father. His necklace is enchanted, allowing Kagome to control him with a word.

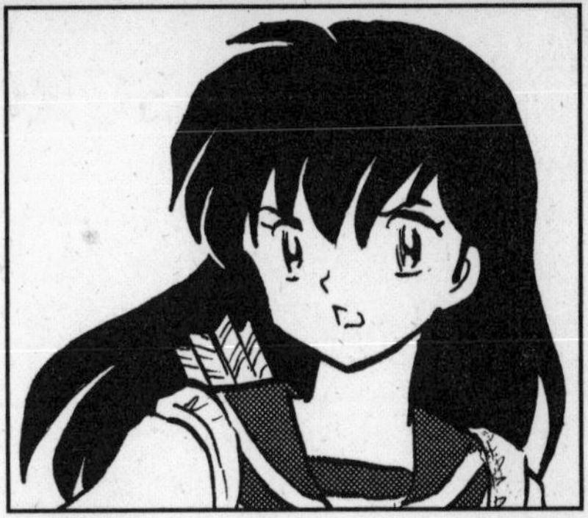

KAGOME
Modern-day Japanese schoolgirl who can travel back and forth between the past and present through an enchanted well.

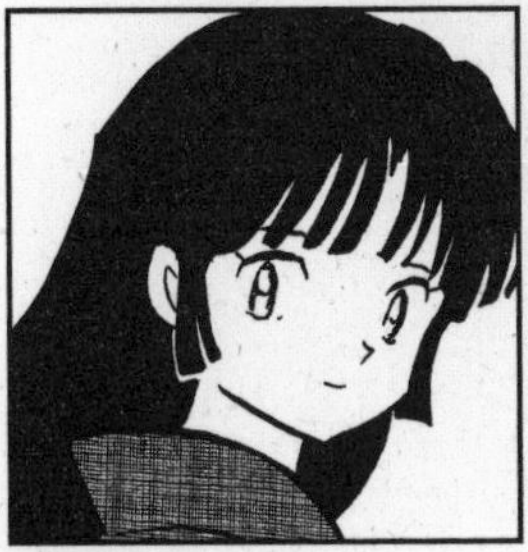

SANGO
A demon slayer from the village where the Shikon Jewel originated.

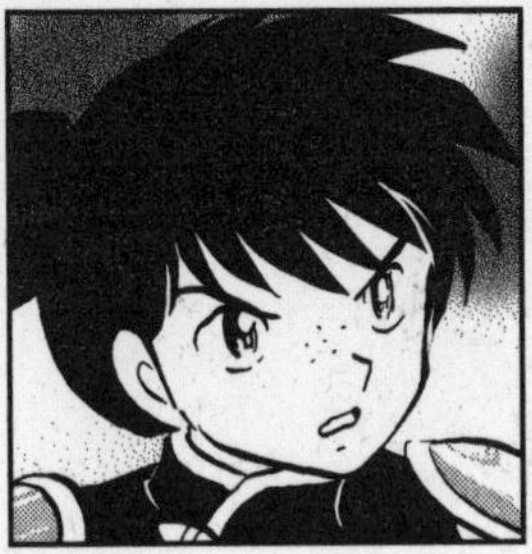

KOHAKU
Naraku used Kohaku as a puppet. Kohaku is trying to redeem himself.

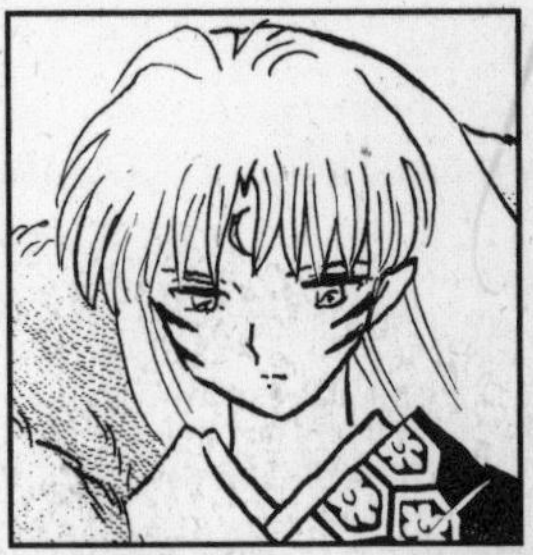

SESSHOMARU
Inuyasha's completely demon half brother. Sesshomaru covets the sword left to Inuyasha by their demon father.

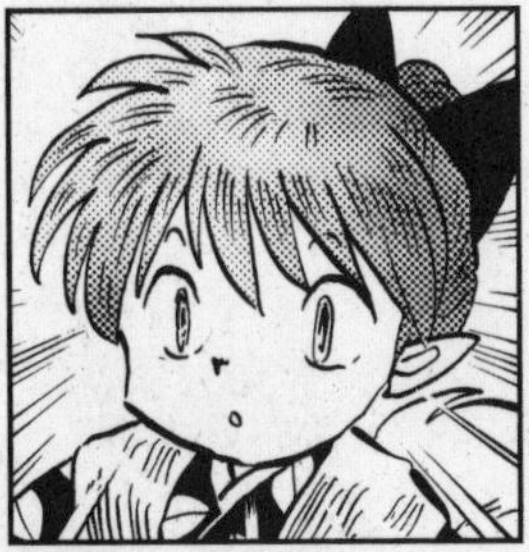

SHIPPO
A tactless fox demon who can perform a little, usually inept, magic.

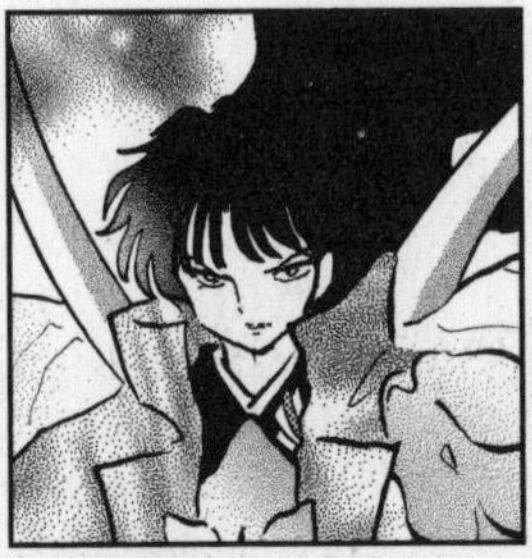

NARAKU
Enigmatic demon mastermind behind the miseries of nearly everyone in the story. He has the power to create multiple incarnations of himself from his body.

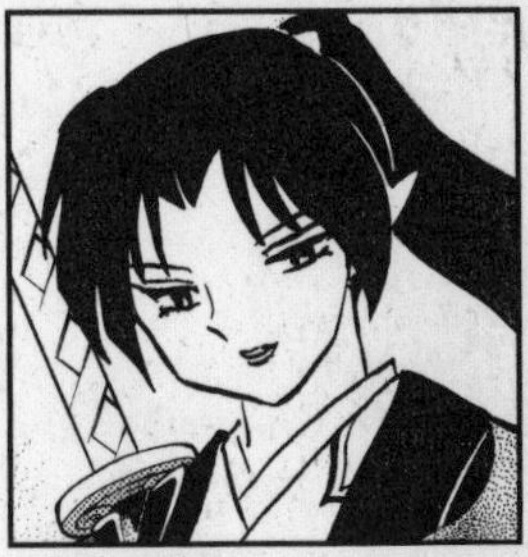

BYAKUYA
A powerful sorcerer and master of illusions created by Naraku.

SCROLL 1

THE ENCHANTED SHARD

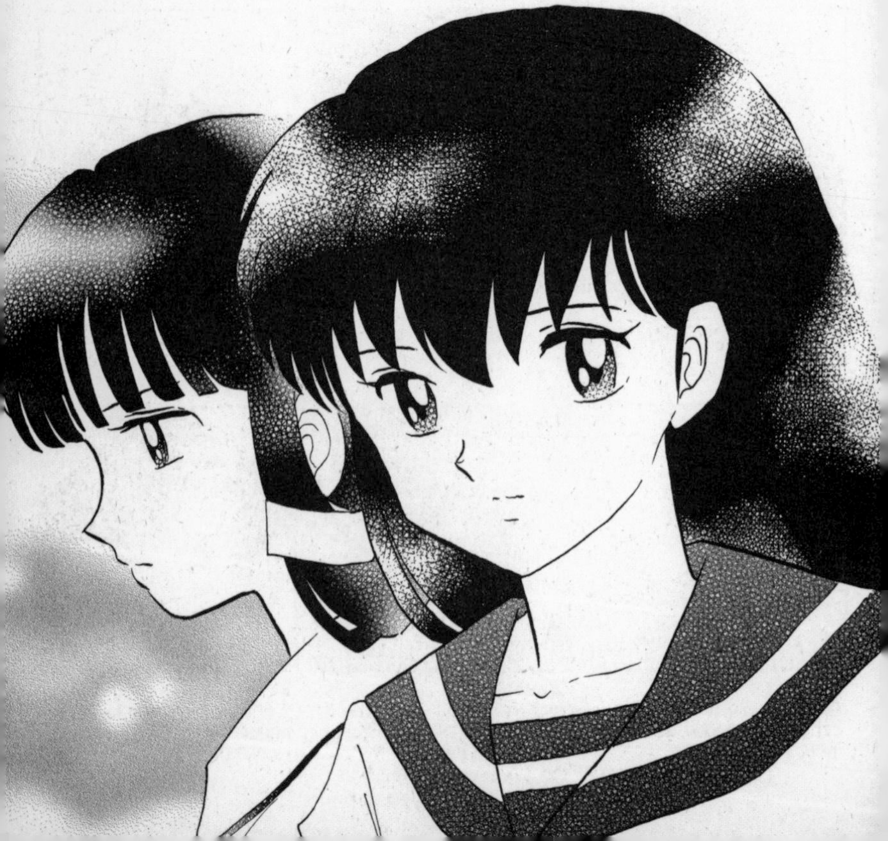

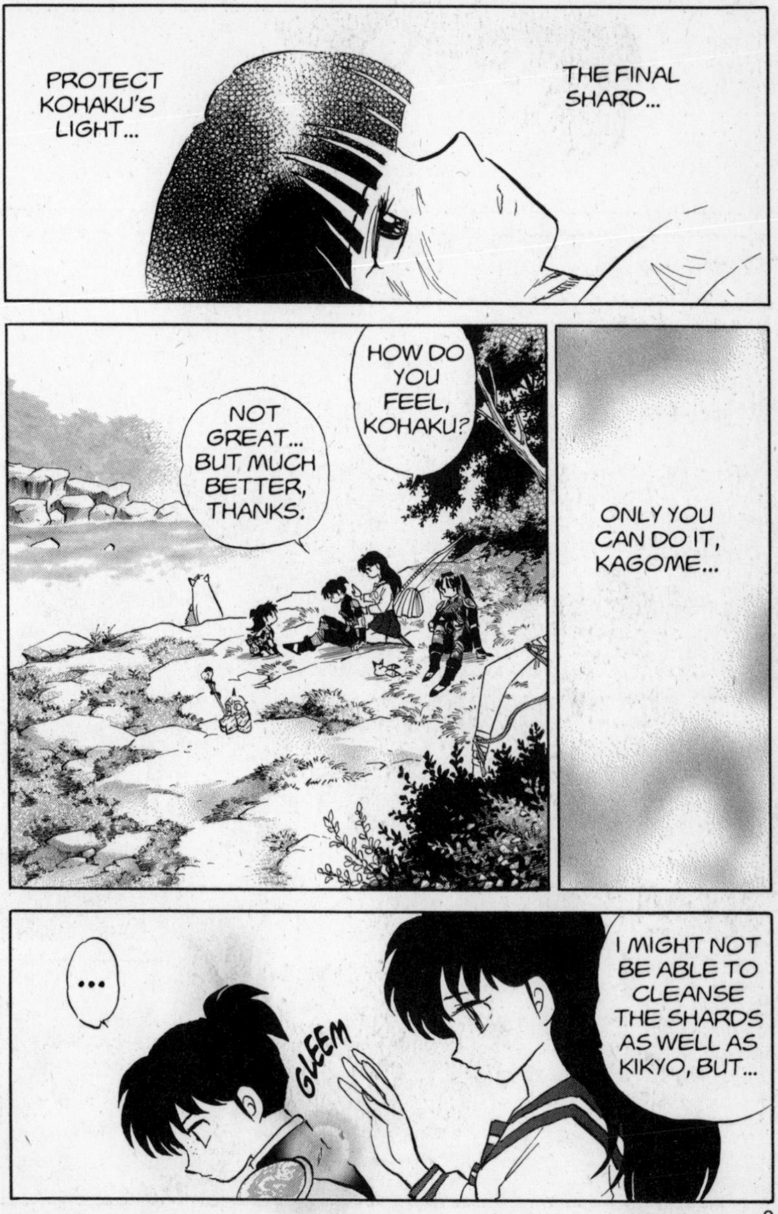
THE FINAL SHARD...
PROTECT KOHAKU'S LIGHT...
ONLY YOU CAN DO IT, KAGOME...
HOW DO YOU FEEL, KOHAKU?
NOT GREAT... BUT MUCH BETTER, THANKS.
I MIGHT NOT BE ABLE TO CLEANSE THE SHARDS AS WELL AS KIKYO, BUT...
GLEEM
...

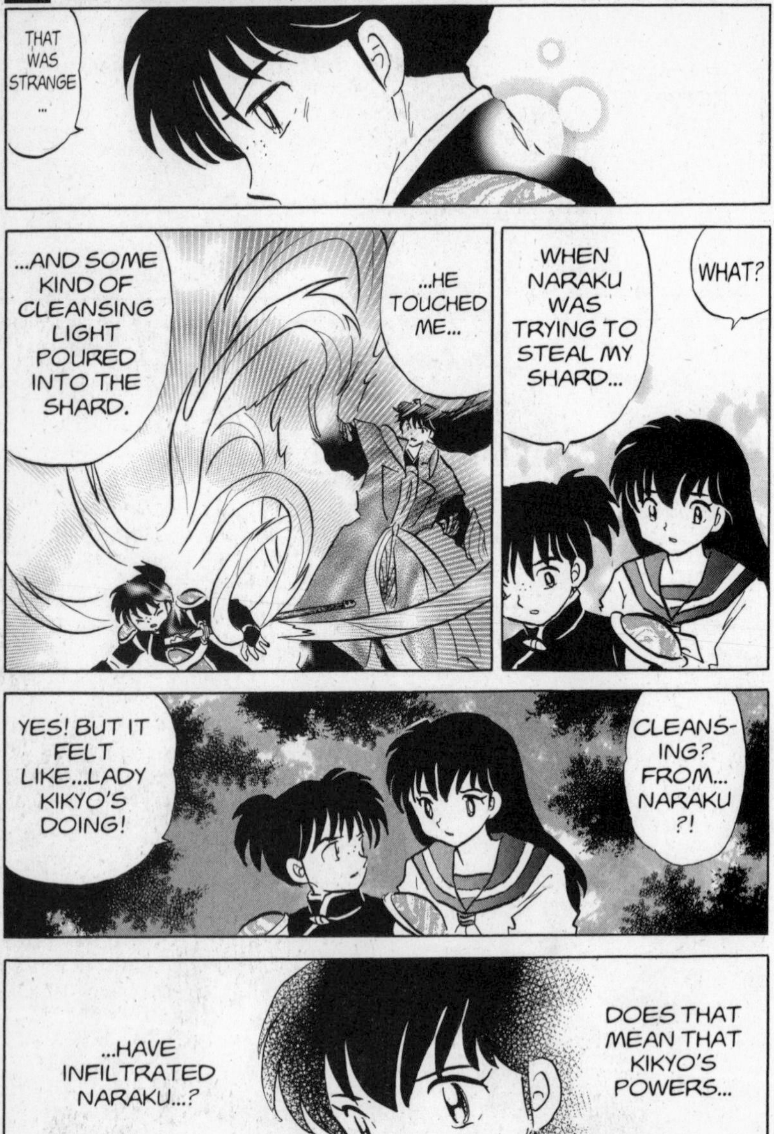
THAT WAS STRANGE ...
WHAT?
WHEN NARAKU WAS TRYING TO STEAL MY SHARD...
...HE TOUCHED ME...
...AND SOME KIND OF CLEANSING LIGHT POURED INTO THE SHARD.
CLEANS-ING? FROM... NARAKU ?!
YES! BUT IT FELT LIKE...LADY KIKYO'S DOING!
DOES THAT MEAN THAT KIKYO'S POWERS...
...HAVE INFILTRATED NARAKU...?

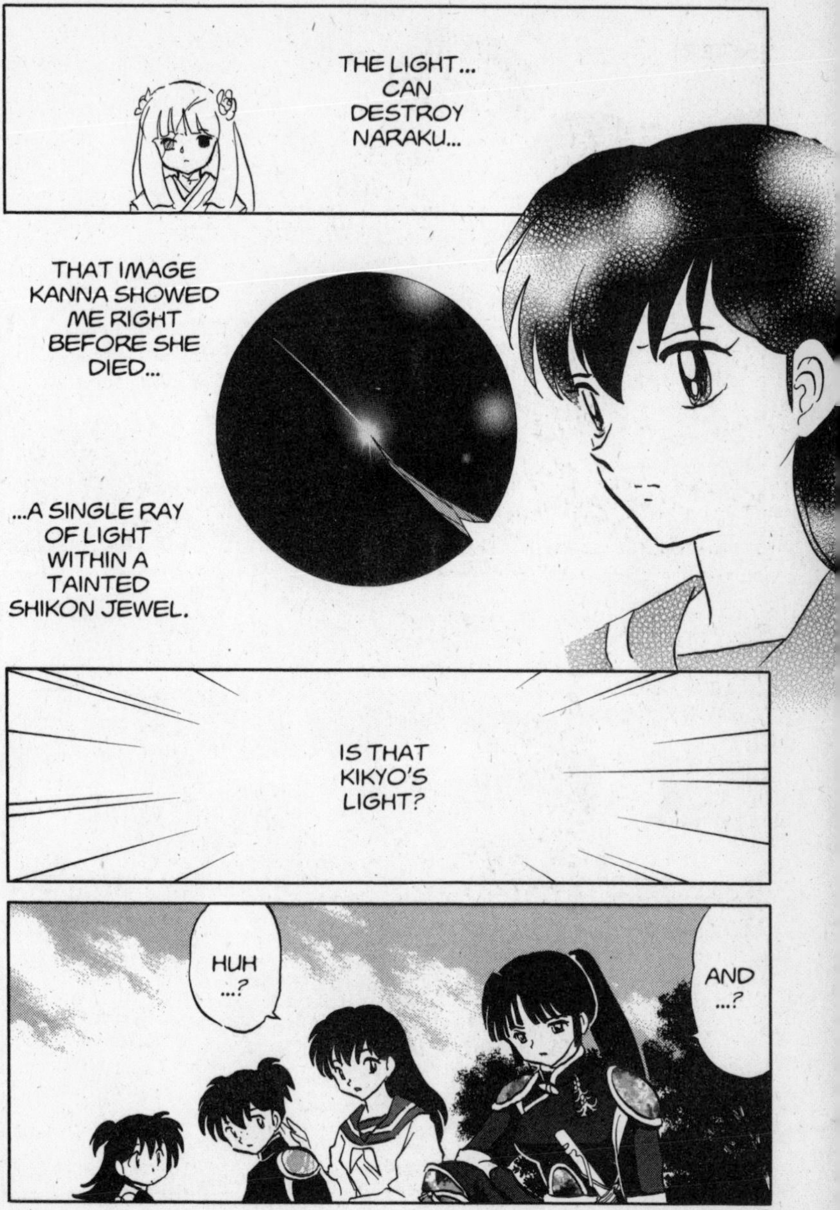
THE LIGHT... CAN DESTROY NARAKU...
THAT IMAGE KANNA SHOWED ME RIGHT BEFORE SHE DIED...
...A SINGLE RAY OF LIGHT WITHIN A TAINTED SHIKON JEWEL.
IS THAT KIKYO'S LIGHT?
AND ...?
HUH ...?

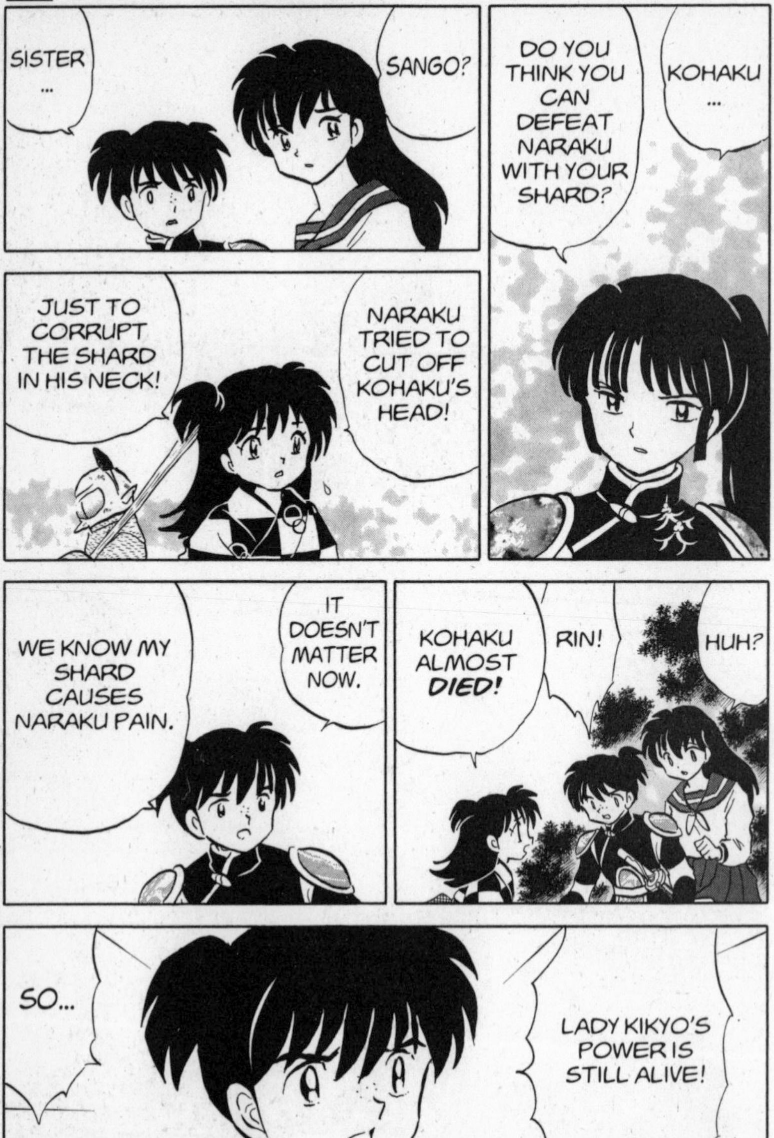
KOHAKU ...
DO YOU THINK YOU CAN DEFEAT NARAKU WITH YOUR SHARD?
SANGO?
SISTER ...
NARAKU TRIED TO CUT OFF KOHAKU'S HEAD!
JUST TO CORRUPT THE SHARD IN HIS NECK!
HUH?
RIN!
KOHAKU ALMOST *DIED!*
IT DOESN'T MATTER NOW.
WE KNOW MY SHARD CAUSES NARAKU PAIN.
LADY KIKYO'S POWER IS STILL ALIVE!
SO...

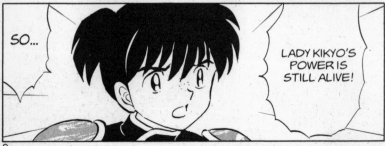

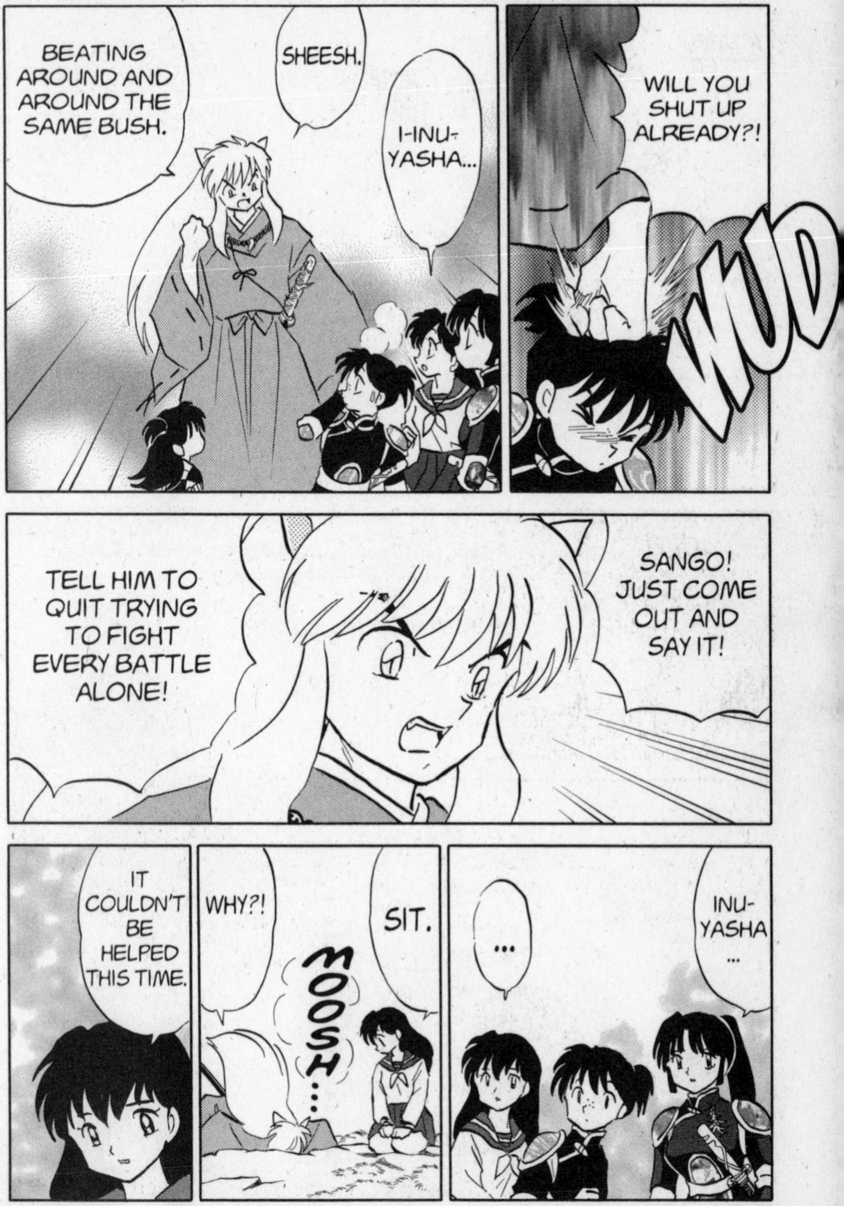
WILL YOU SHUT UP ALREADY?!
WUD
I-INU-YASHA...
SHEESH.
BEATING AROUND AND AROUND THE SAME BUSH.
SANGO! JUST COME OUT AND SAY IT!
TELL HIM TO QUIT TRYING TO FIGHT EVERY BATTLE ALONE!
INU-YASHA ...
...
SIT.
MOOSH...
WHY?!
IT COULDN'T BE HELPED THIS TIME.

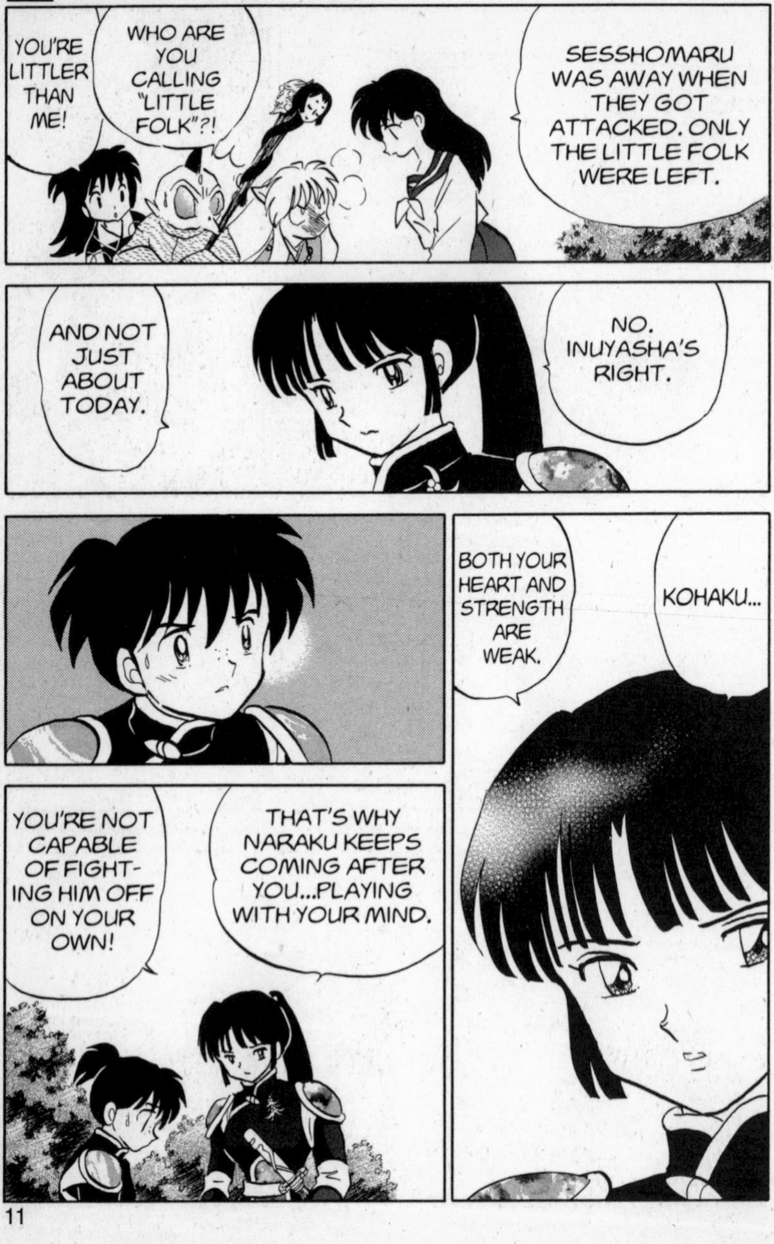
SESSHOMARU WAS AWAY WHEN THEY GOT ATTACKED. ONLY THE LITTLE FOLK WERE LEFT.
WHO ARE YOU CALLING "LITTLE FOLK"?!
YOU'RE LITTLER THAN ME!
NO. INUYASHA'S RIGHT.
AND NOT JUST ABOUT TODAY.
KOHAKU...
BOTH YOUR HEART AND STRENGTH ARE WEAK.
THAT'S WHY NARAKU KEEPS COMING AFTER YOU...PLAYING WITH YOUR MIND.
YOU'RE NOT CAPABLE OF FIGHT-ING HIM OFF ON YOUR OWN!

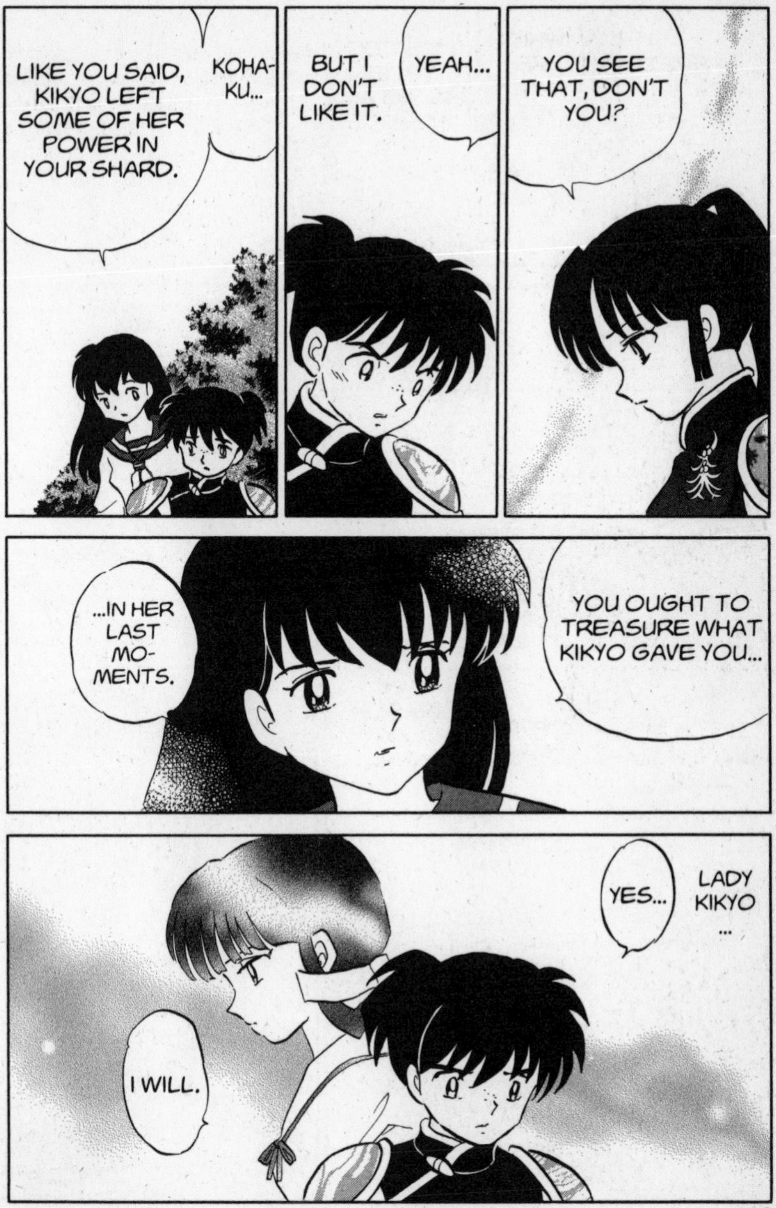
YOU SEE THAT, DON'T YOU?
YEAH...
BUT I DON'T LIKE IT.
KOHA-KU...
LIKE YOU SAID, KIKYO LEFT SOME OF HER POWER IN YOUR SHARD.
YOU OUGHT TO TREASURE WHAT KIKYO GAVE YOU...
...IN HER LAST MO-MENTS.
LADY KIKYO ...
YES...
I WILL.

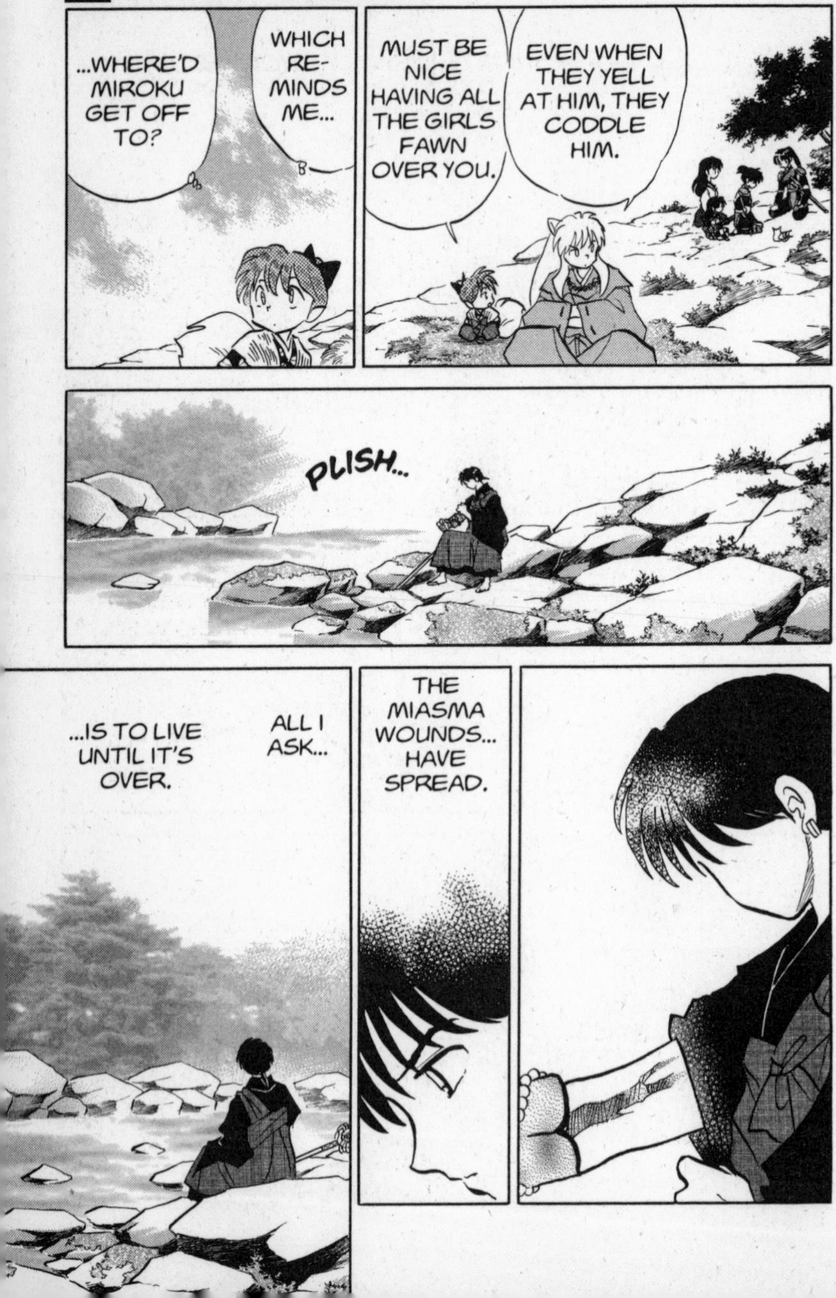
EVEN WHEN THEY YELL AT HIM, THEY CODDLE HIM.
MUST BE NICE HAVING ALL THE GIRLS FAWN OVER YOU.
WHICH RE-MINDS ME...
...WHERE'D MIROKU GET OFF TO?
PLISH...
THE MIASMA WOUNDS... HAVE SPREAD.
ALL I ASK...
...IS TO LIVE UNTIL IT'S OVER.

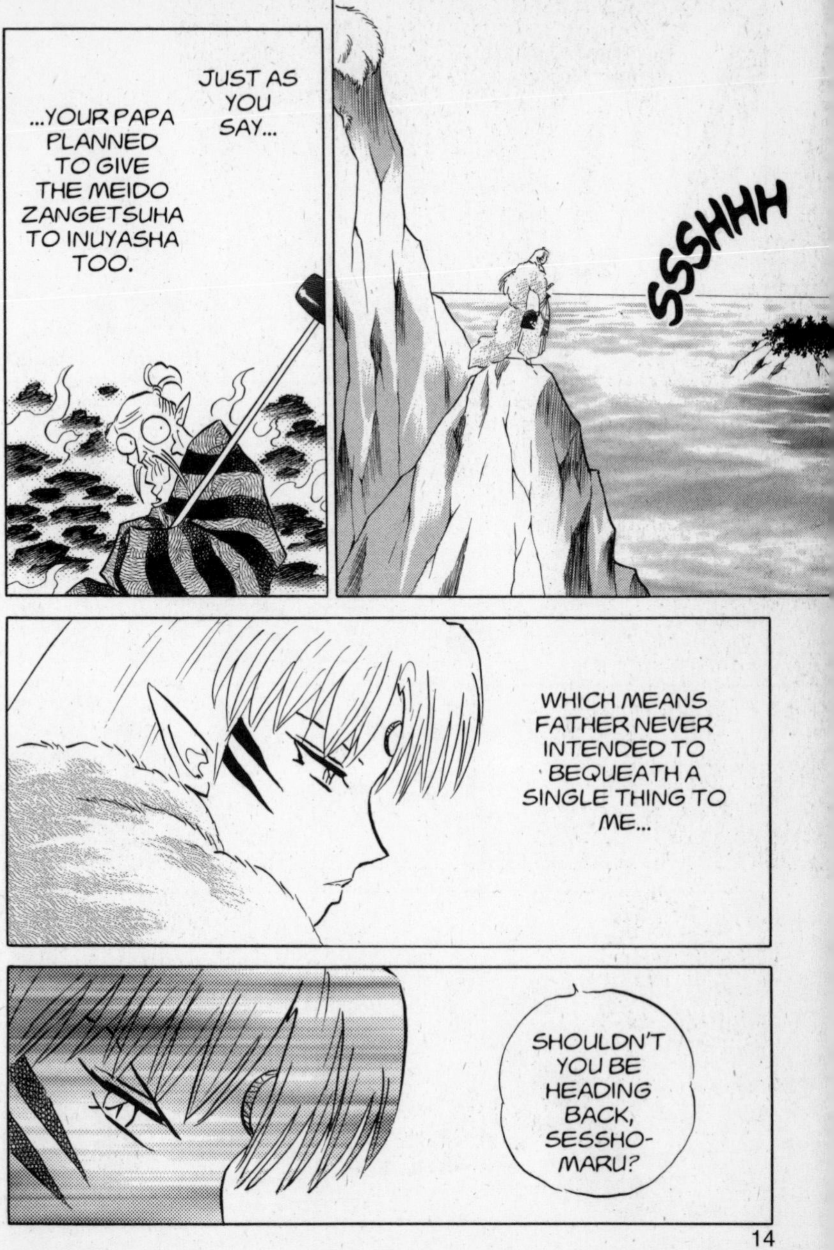
SSSHH
JUST AS YOU SAY...
...YOUR PAPA PLANNED TO GIVE THE MEIDO ZANGETSUHA TO INUYASHA TOO.
WHICH MEANS FATHER NEVER INTENDED TO BEQUEATH A SINGLE THING TO ME...
SHOULDN'T YOU BE HEADING BACK, SESSHO-MARU?

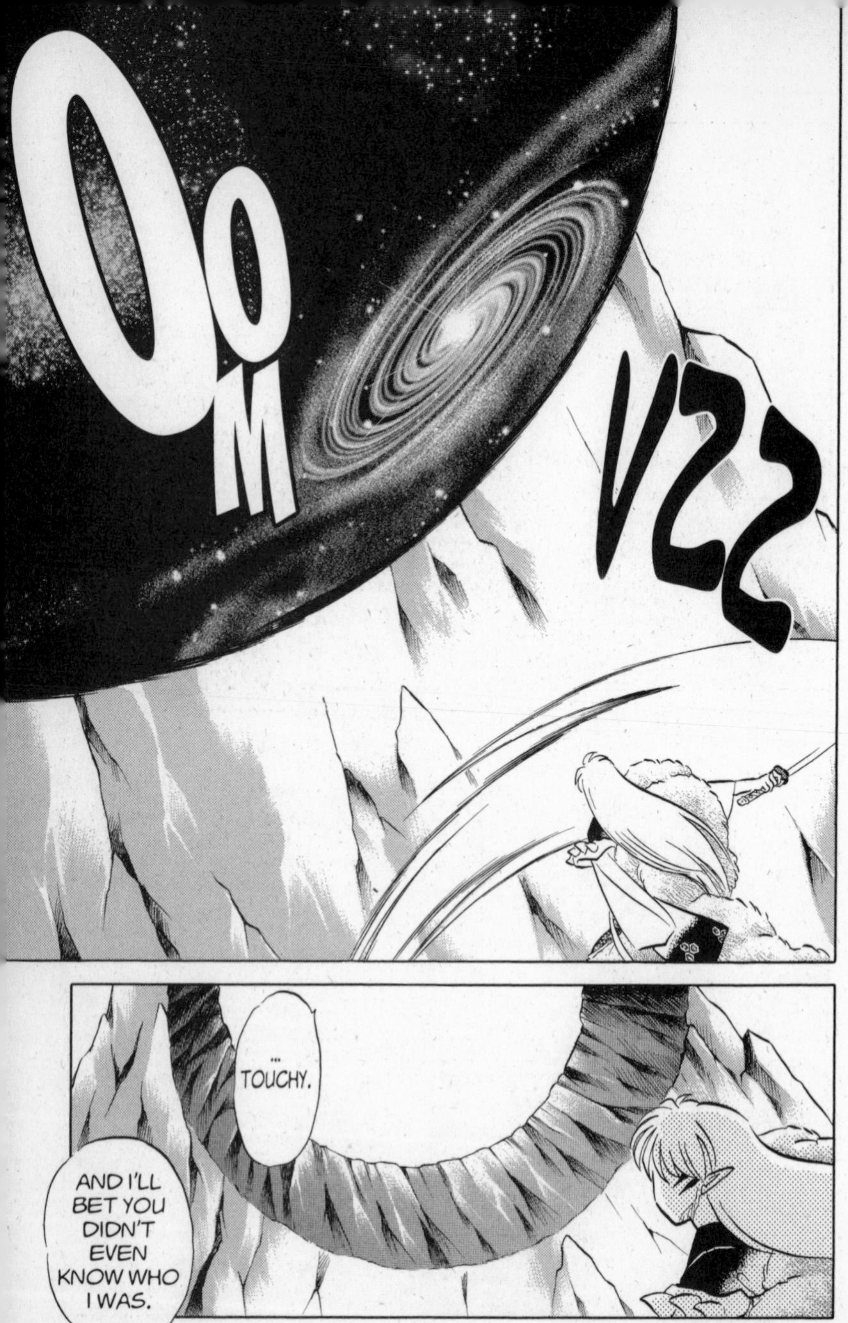
OOM
VZZ
...TOUCHY.
AND I'LL BET YOU DIDN'T EVEN KNOW WHO I WAS.

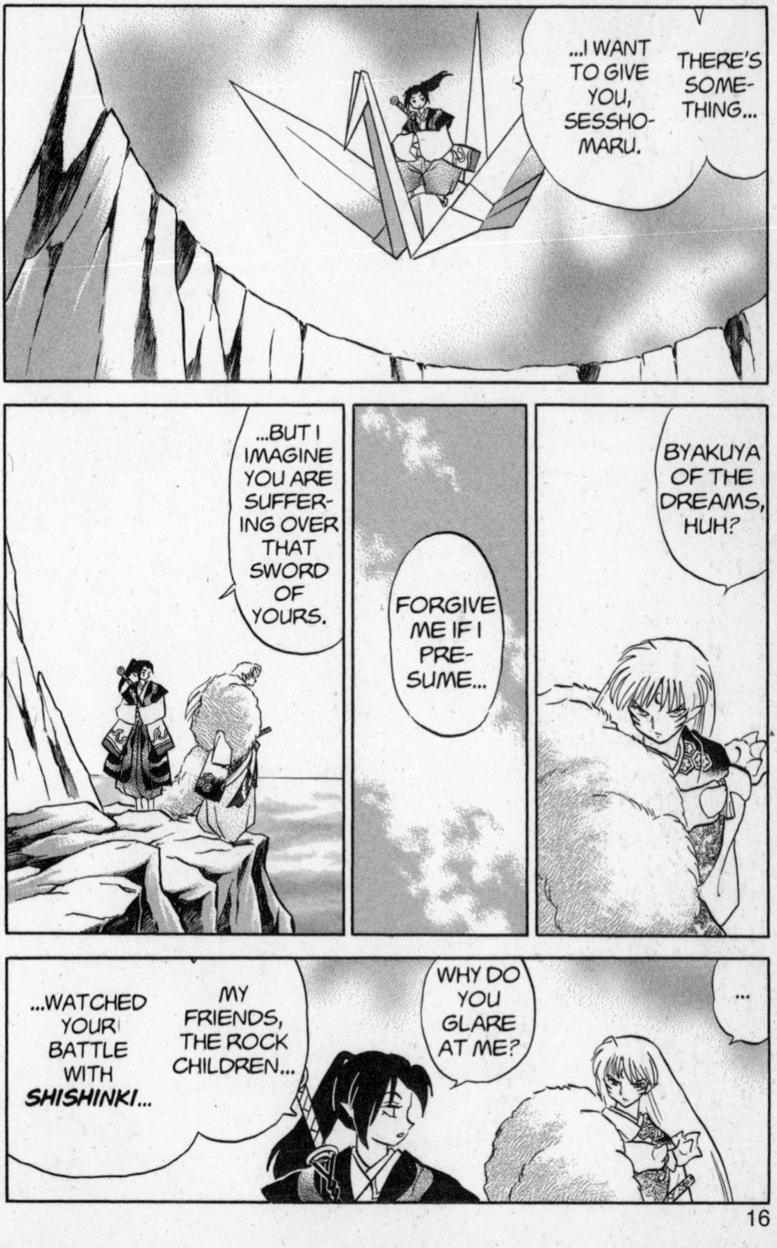
THERE'S SOMETHING...
...I WANT TO GIVE YOU, SESSHOMARU.
BYAKUYA OF THE DREAMS, HUH?
FORGIVE ME IF I PRESUME...
...BUT I IMAGINE YOU ARE SUFFERING OVER THAT SWORD OF YOURS.
...
WHY DO YOU GLARE AT ME?
MY FRIENDS, THE ROCK CHILDREN...
...WATCHED YOUR BATTLE WITH **SHISHINKI**...

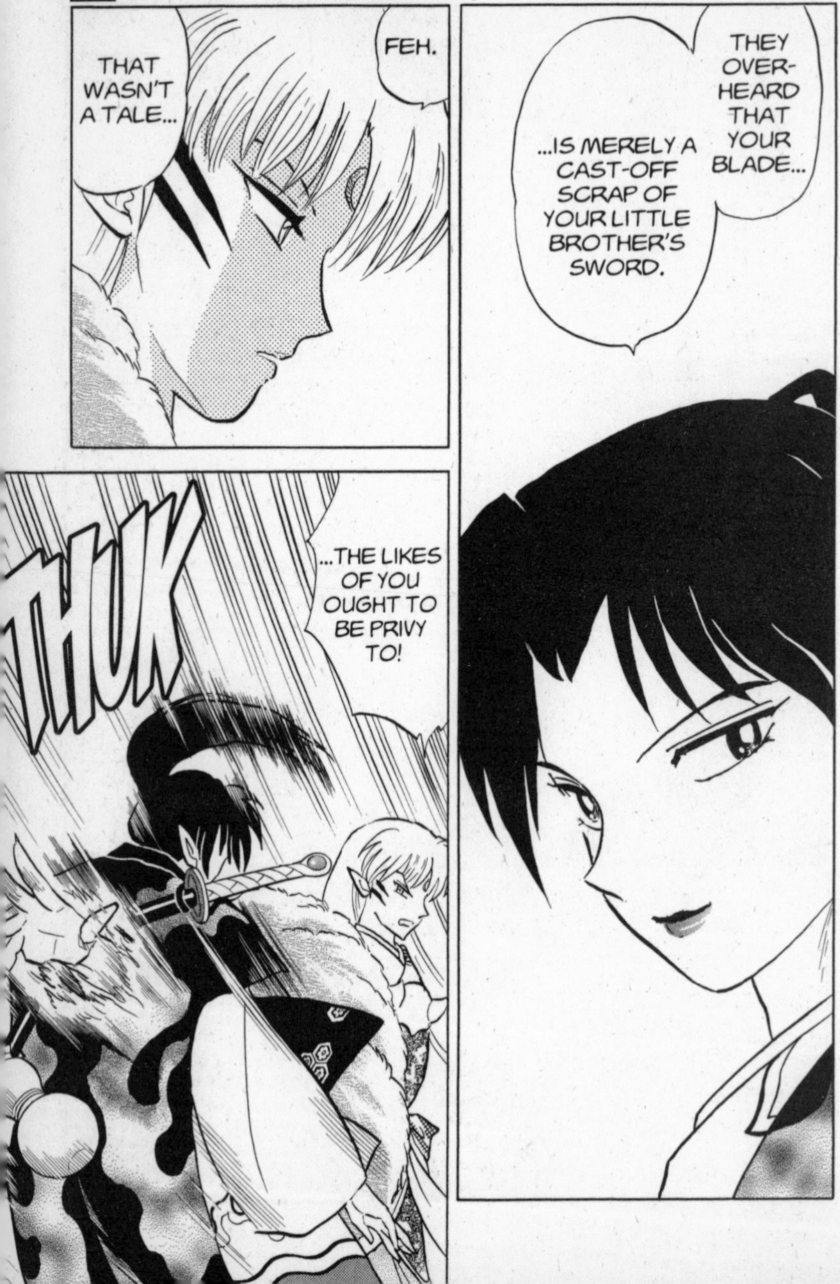
THEY OVER-HEARD THAT YOUR BLADE...
...IS MERELY A CAST-OFF SCRAP OF YOUR LITTLE BROTHER'S SWORD.
FEH.
THAT WASN'T A TALE...
THUK
...THE LIKES OF YOU OUGHT TO BE PRIVY TO!

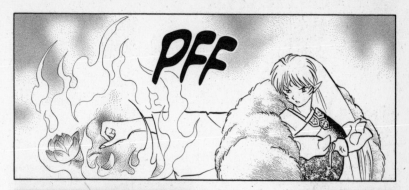

PFF

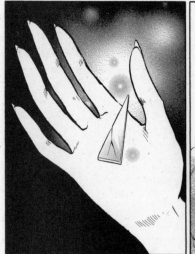

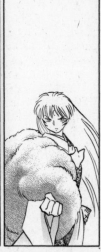

NOW DON'T SAY *I* NEVER GAVE YOU ANYTHING, SESSHO-MARU.

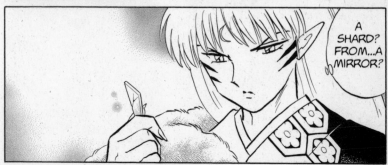

A SHARD? FROM...A MIRROR?

18

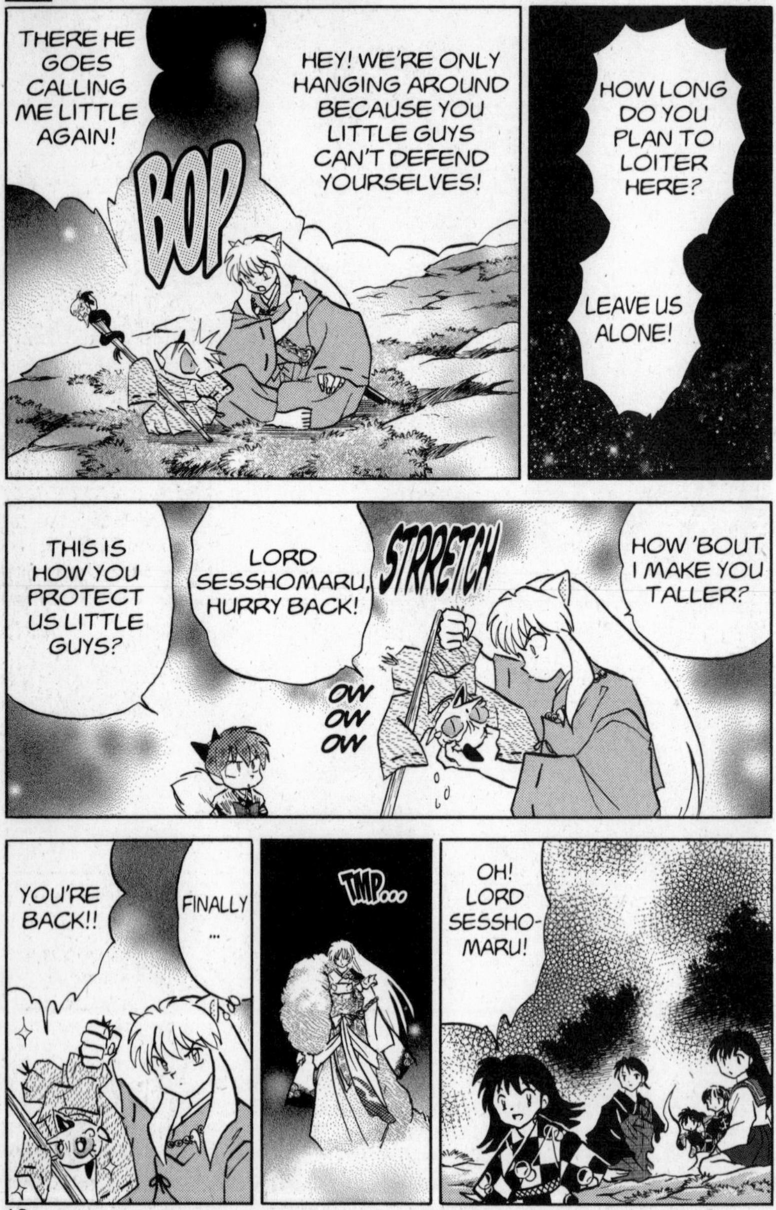
HOW LONG DO YOU PLAN TO LOITER HERE?
LEAVE US ALONE!
HEY! WE'RE ONLY HANGING AROUND BECAUSE YOU LITTLE GUYS CAN'T DEFEND YOURSELVES!
THERE HE GOES CALLING ME LITTLE AGAIN!
BOP
HOW 'BOUT I MAKE YOU TALLER?
STRRETCH
OW OW OW
LORD SESSHOMARU, HURRY BACK!
THIS IS HOW YOU PROTECT US LITTLE GUYS?
OH! LORD SESSHO-MARU!
TMP...
FINALLY ...
YOU'RE BACK!!

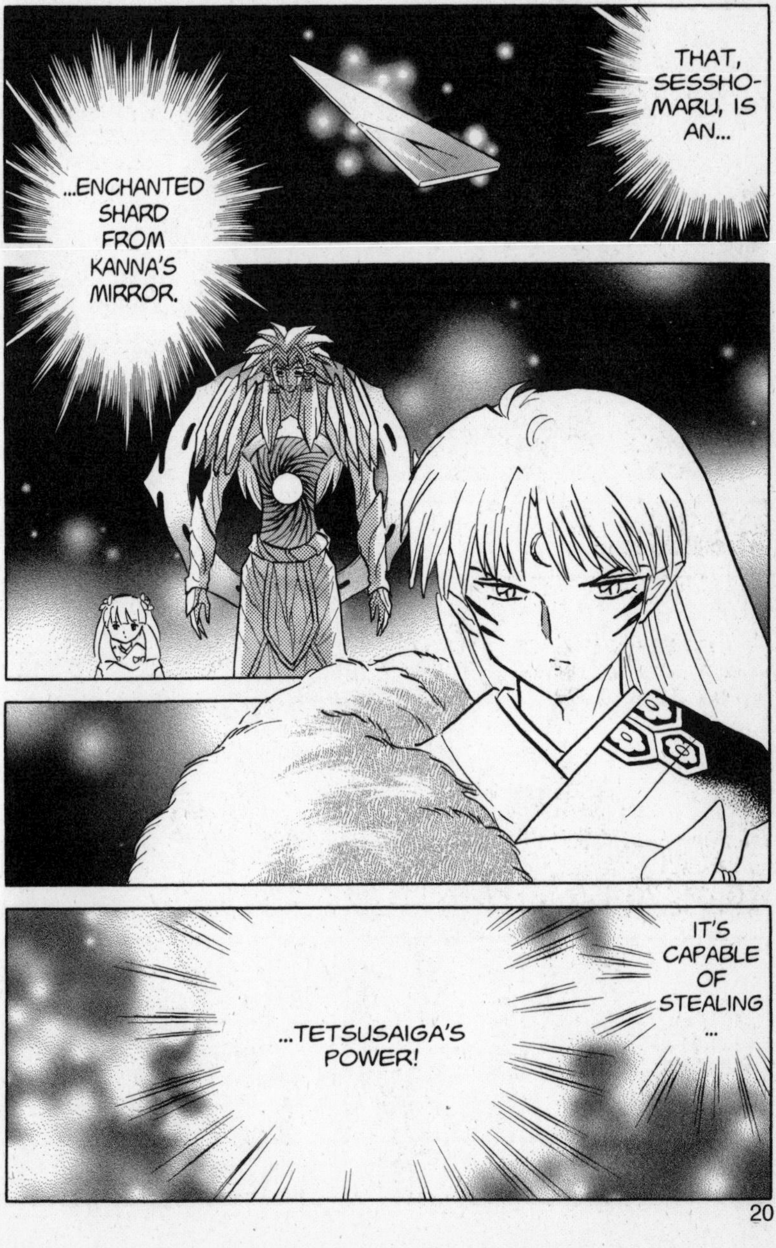
THAT, SESSHO-MARU, IS AN...
...ENCHANTED SHARD FROM KANNA'S MIRROR.
IT'S CAPABLE OF STEALING ...
...TETSUSAIGA'S POWER!

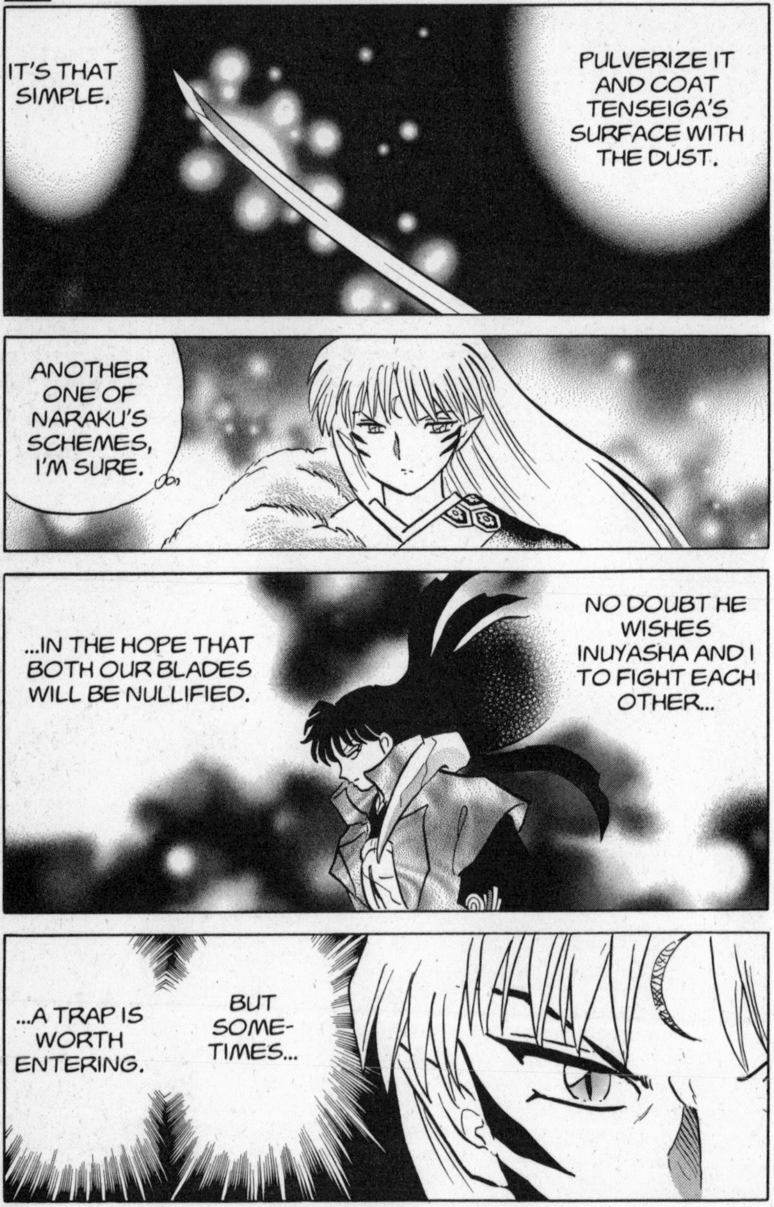
PULVERIZE IT AND COAT TENSEIGA'S SURFACE WITH THE DUST.
IT'S THAT SIMPLE.
ANOTHER ONE OF NARAKU'S SCHEMES, I'M SURE.
NO DOUBT HE WISHES INUYASHA AND I TO FIGHT EACH OTHER...
...IN THE HOPE THAT BOTH OUR BLADES WILL BE NULLIFIED.
BUT SOME-TIMES...
...A TRAP IS WORTH ENTERING.

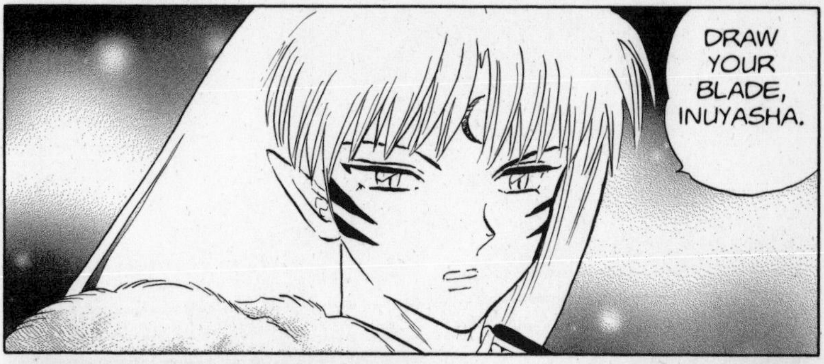
DRAW YOUR BLADE, INUYASHA.

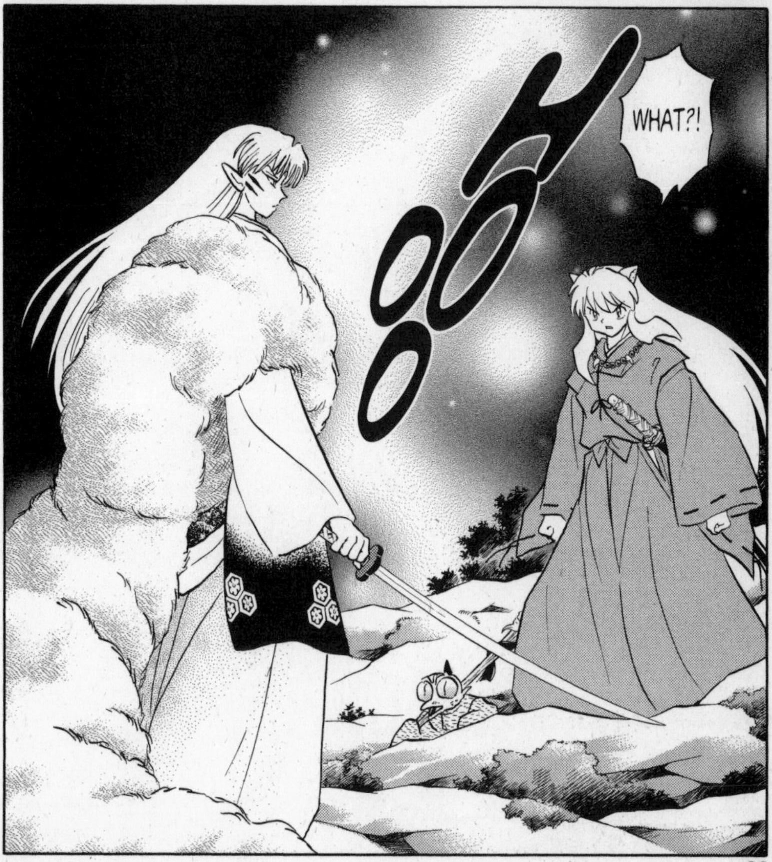
WHAT?!

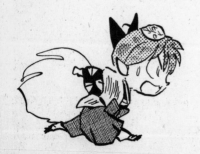

SCROLL 2

THE TRUE HEIR

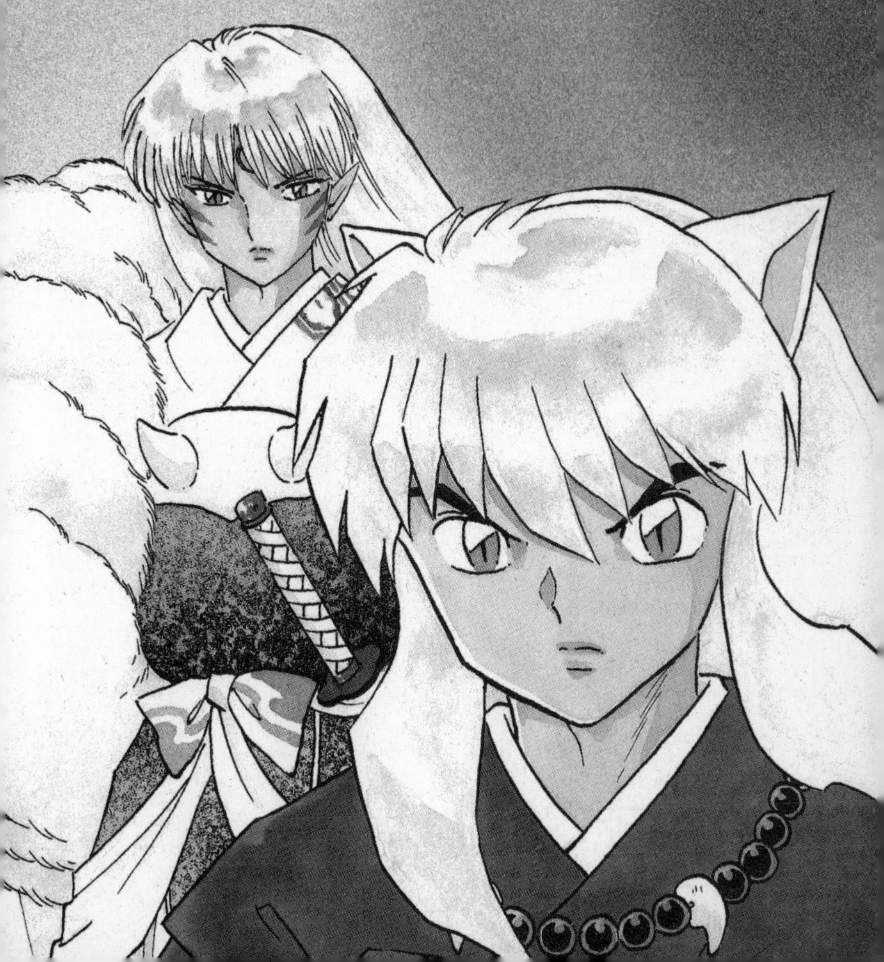

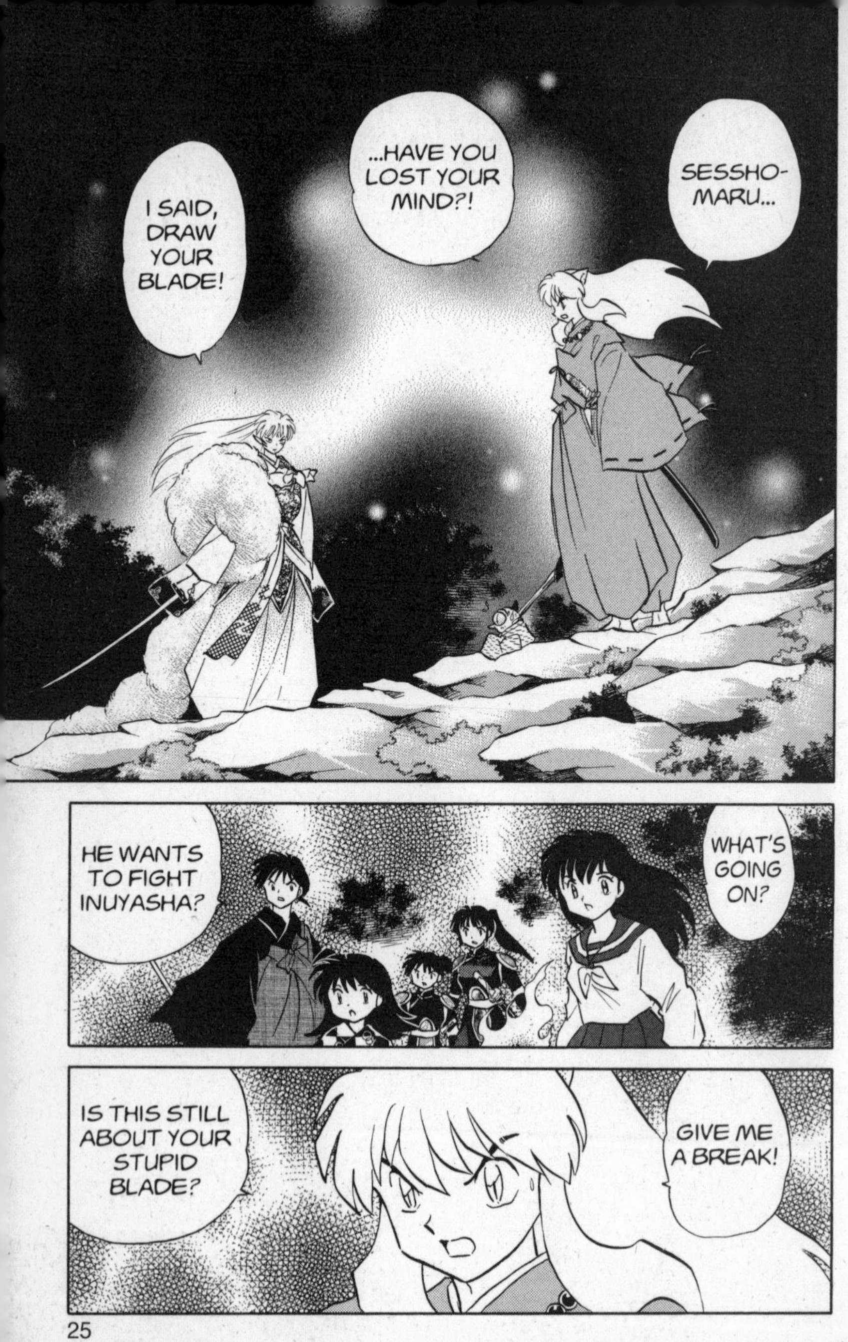
SESSHO-MARU...
...HAVE YOU LOST YOUR MIND?!
I SAID, DRAW YOUR BLADE!
WHAT'S GOING ON?
HE WANTS TO FIGHT INUYASHA?
GIVE ME A BREAK!
IS THIS STILL ABOUT YOUR STUPID BLADE?

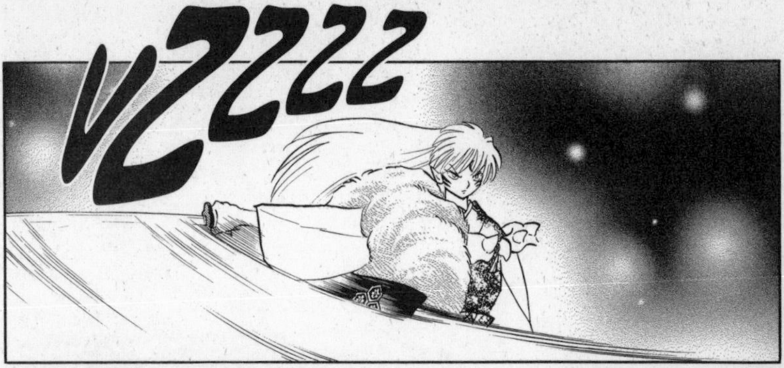
VZZZZ
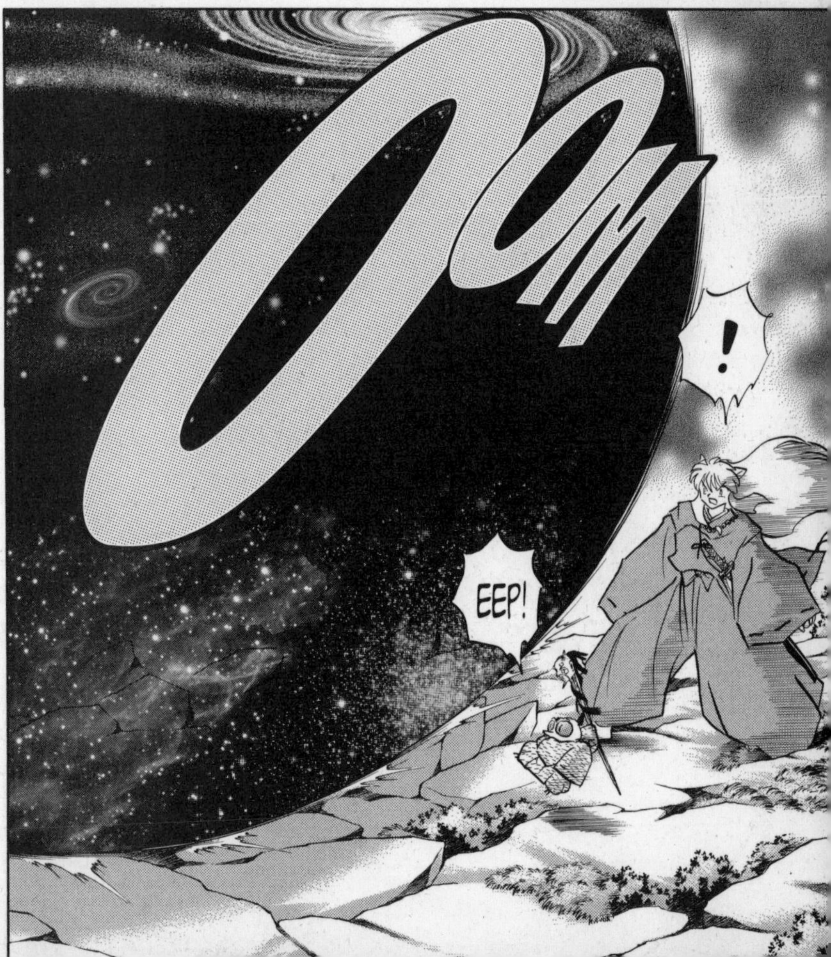
OOM
!
EEP!

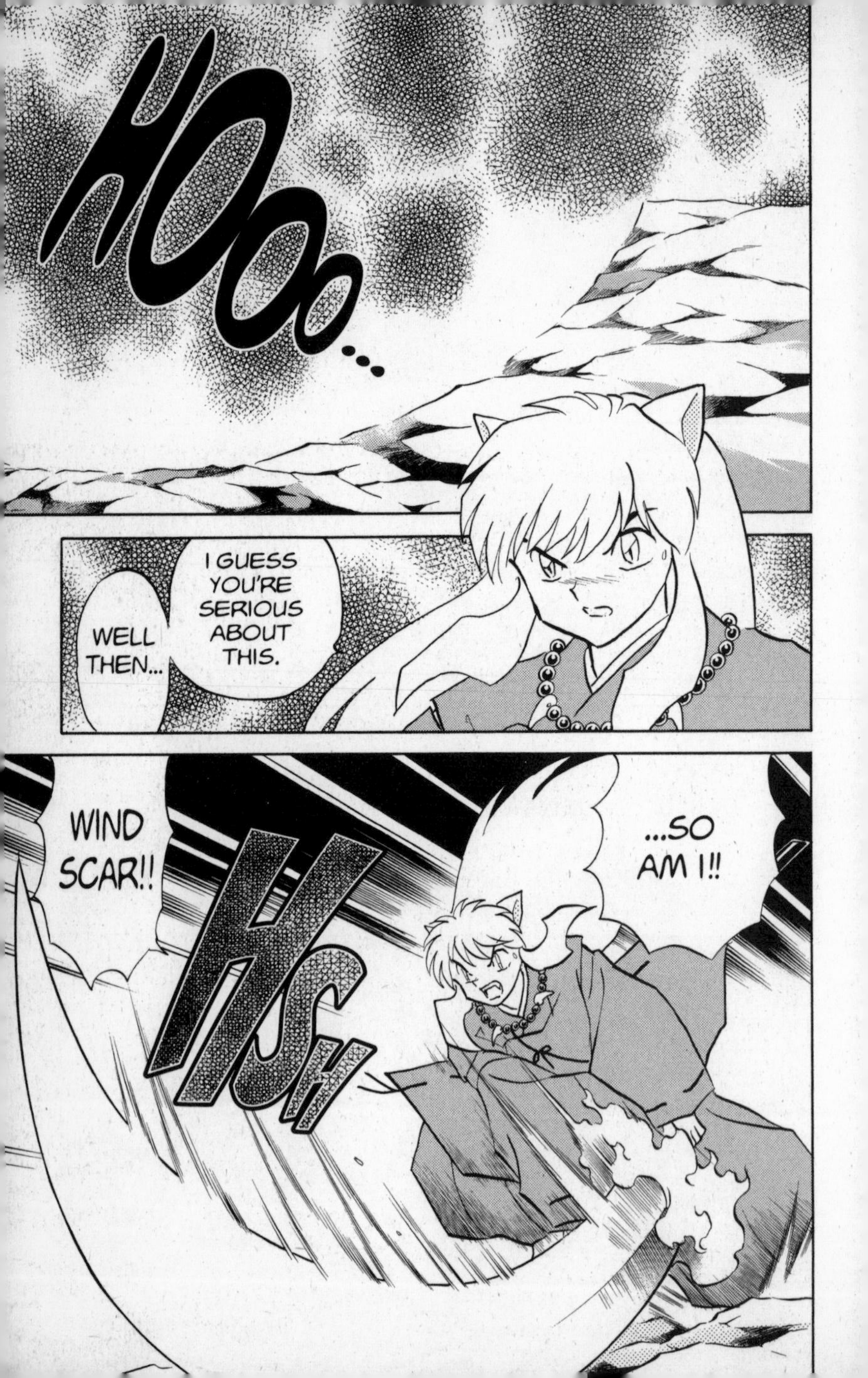
HOOO...
I GUESS YOU'RE SERIOUS ABOUT THIS.
WELL THEN...
...SO AM I!!
WIND SCAR!!
HSH

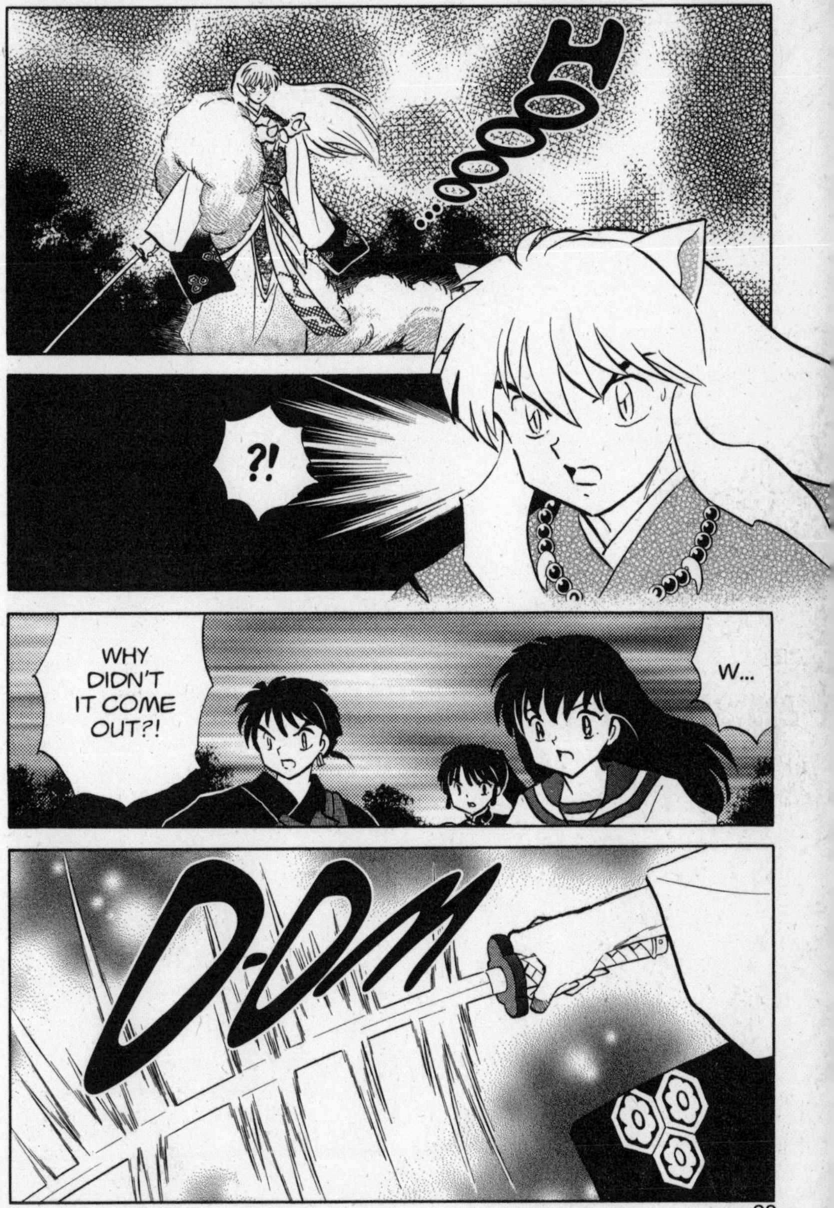
...OOOOOH
?!
W...
WHY DIDN'T IT COME OUT?!
D-DM

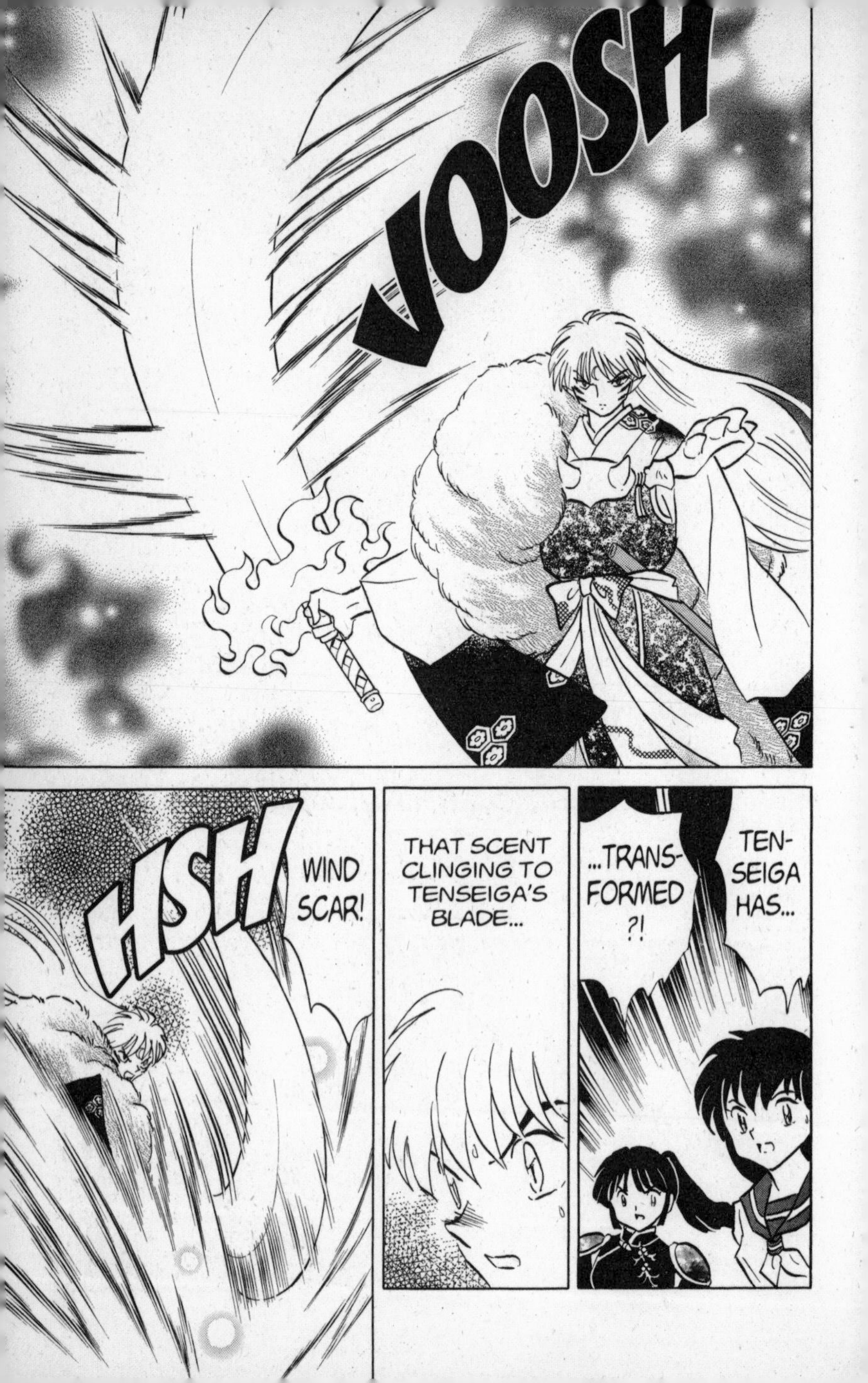
VOOSH
TENSEIGA HAS...
...TRANSFORMED ?!
THAT SCENT CLINGING TO TENSEIGA'S BLADE...
WIND SCAR!
HSH

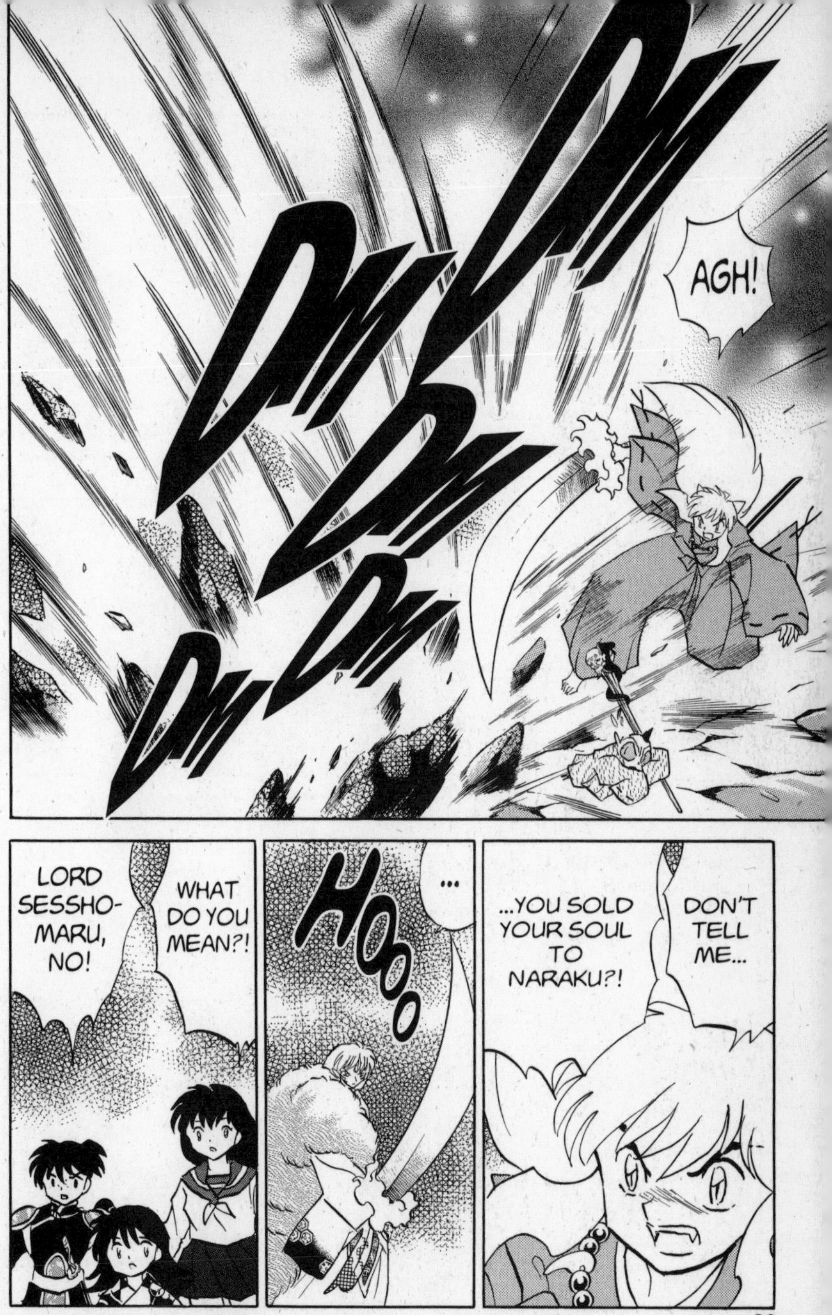
AGH!
DON'T TELL ME...
...YOU SOLD YOUR SOUL TO NARAKU?!
...
HOOO
WHAT DO YOU MEAN?!
LORD SESSHO-MARU, NO!

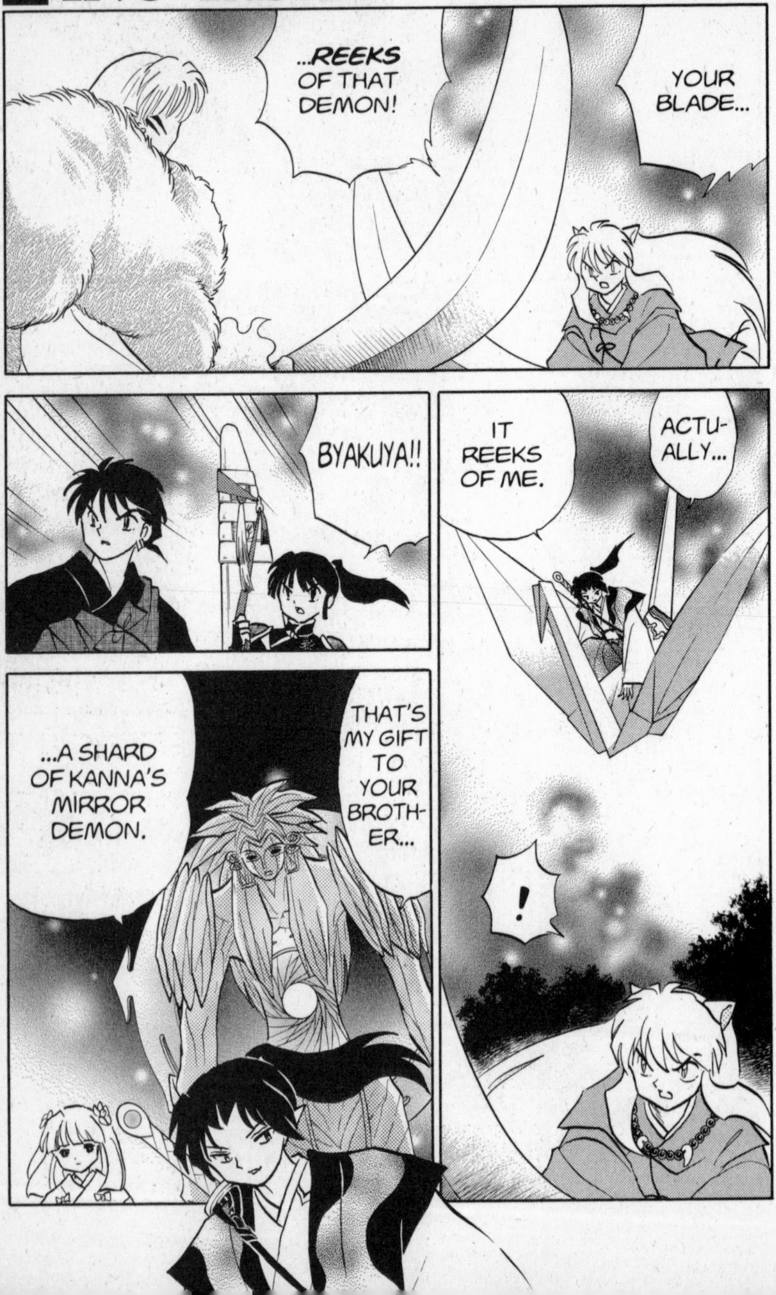
YOUR BLADE...
...REEKS OF THAT DEMON!
ACTU-ALLY...
IT REEKS OF ME.
!
BYAKUYA!!
THAT'S MY GIFT TO YOUR BROTHER-ER...
...A SHARD OF KANNA'S MIRROR DEMON.

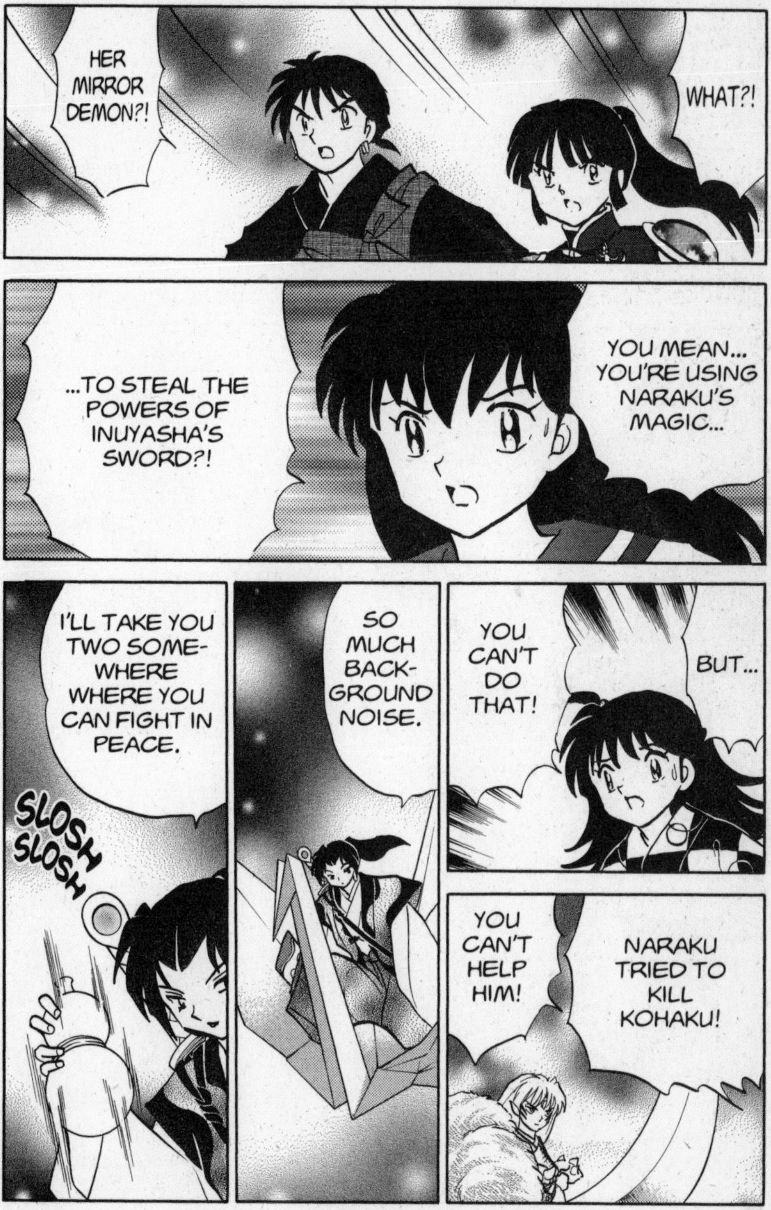
WHAT?!
HER MIRROR DEMON?!
YOU MEAN... YOU'RE USING NARAKU'S MAGIC...
...TO STEAL THE POWERS OF INUYASHA'S SWORD?!
BUT...
YOU CAN'T DO THAT!
NARAKU TRIED TO KILL KOHAKU!
YOU CAN'T HELP HIM!
SO MUCH BACK-GROUND NOISE.
I'LL TAKE YOU TWO SOME-WHERE WHERE YOU CAN FIGHT IN PEACE.
SLOSH SLOSH

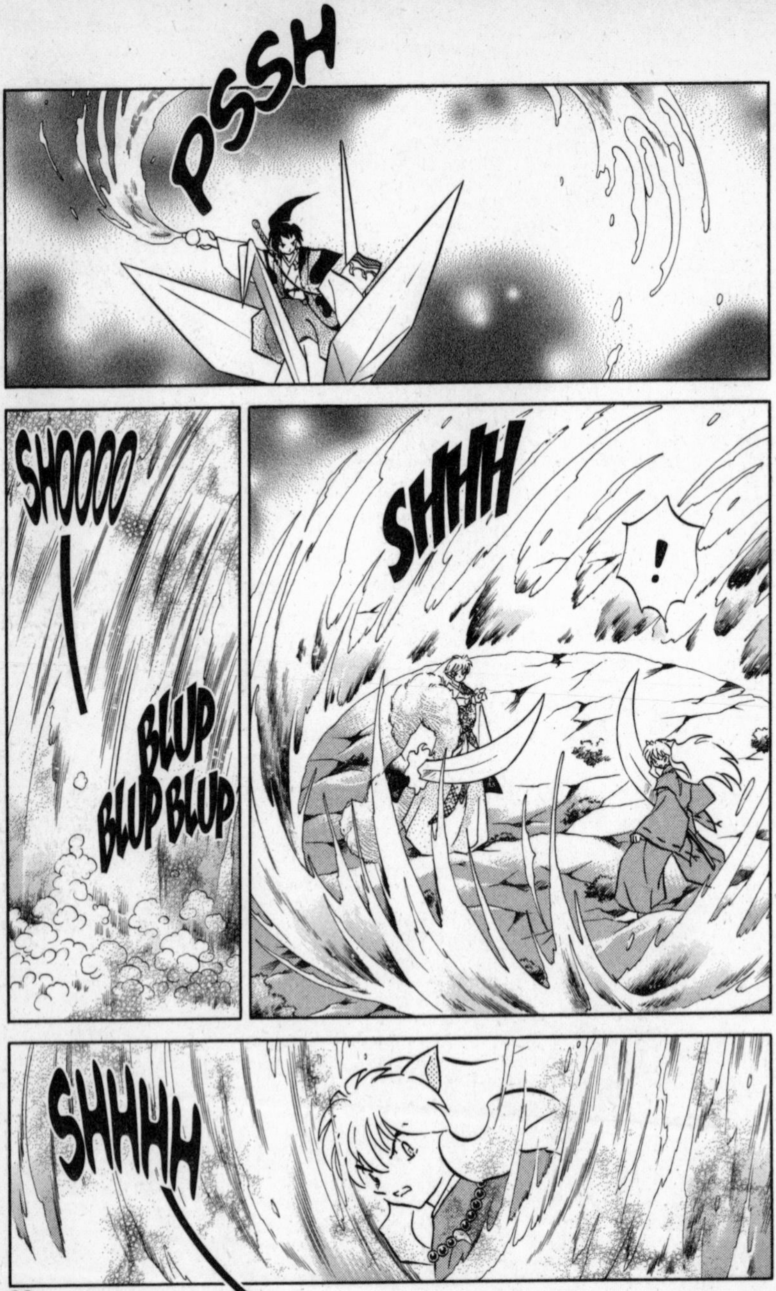
PSSH
SHHH
!
SHOOO
BLUP BLUP BLUP
SHHHH

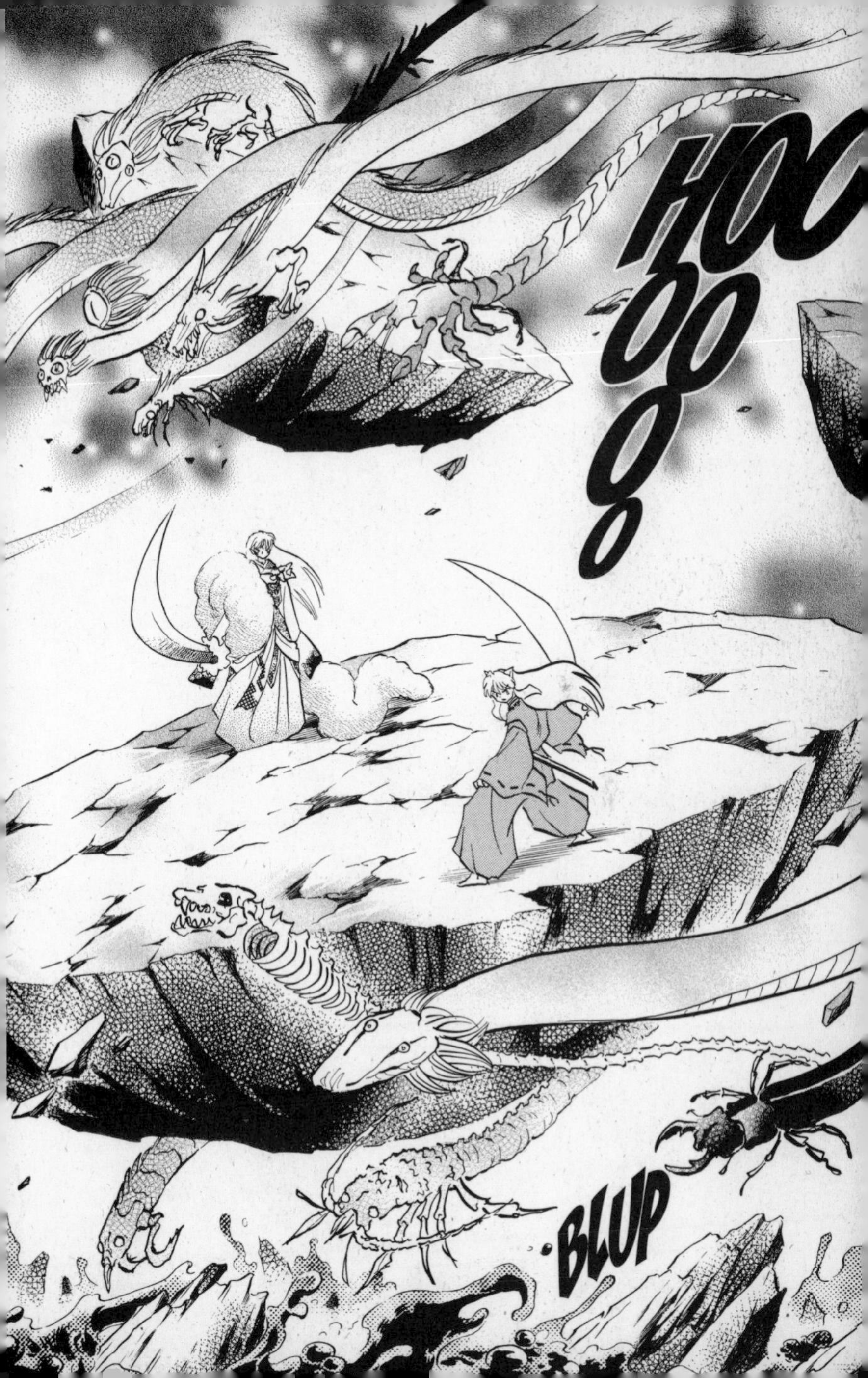

HOOOO
BLUP

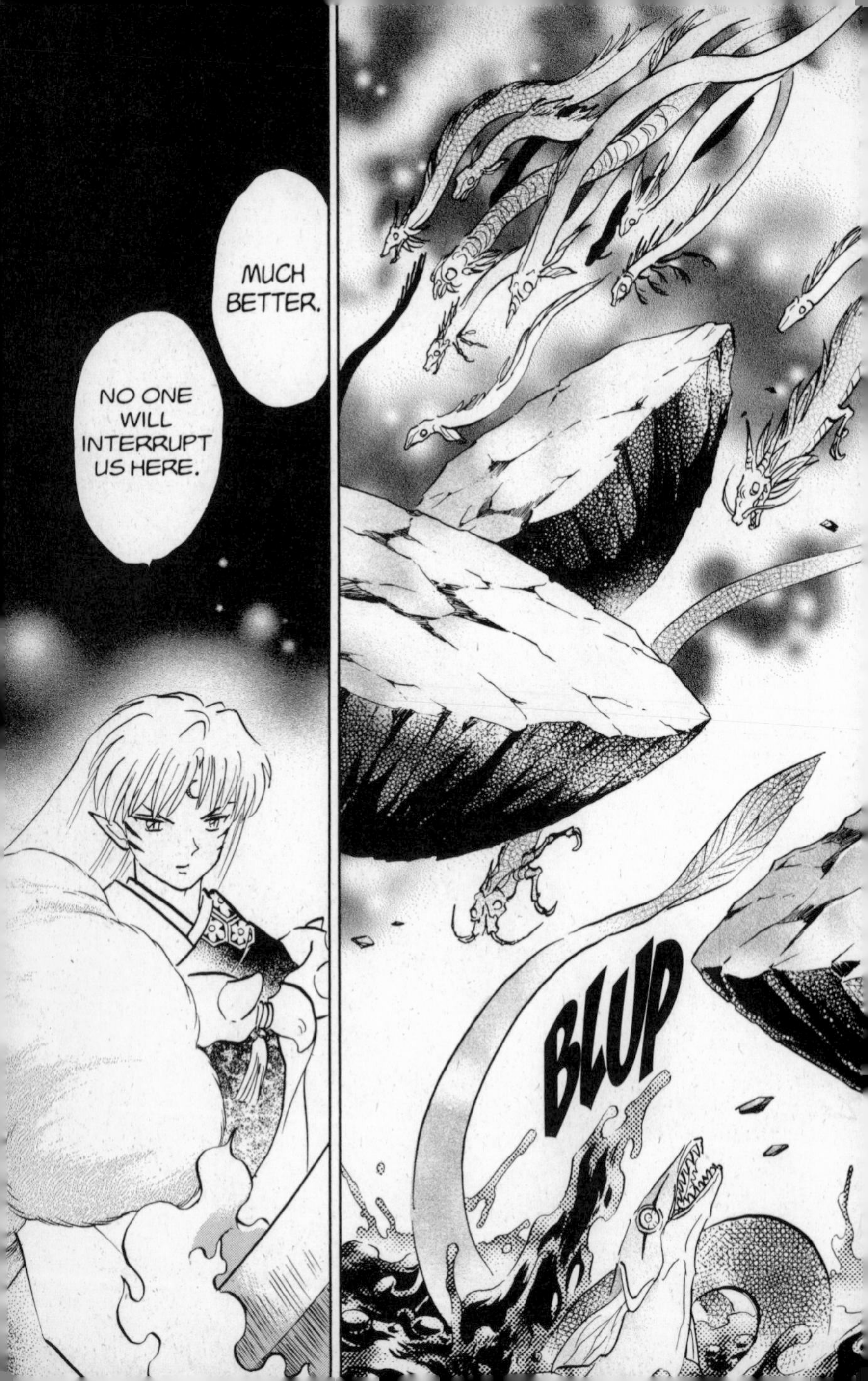
BLUP
MUCH BETTER.
NO ONE WILL INTERRUPT US HERE.

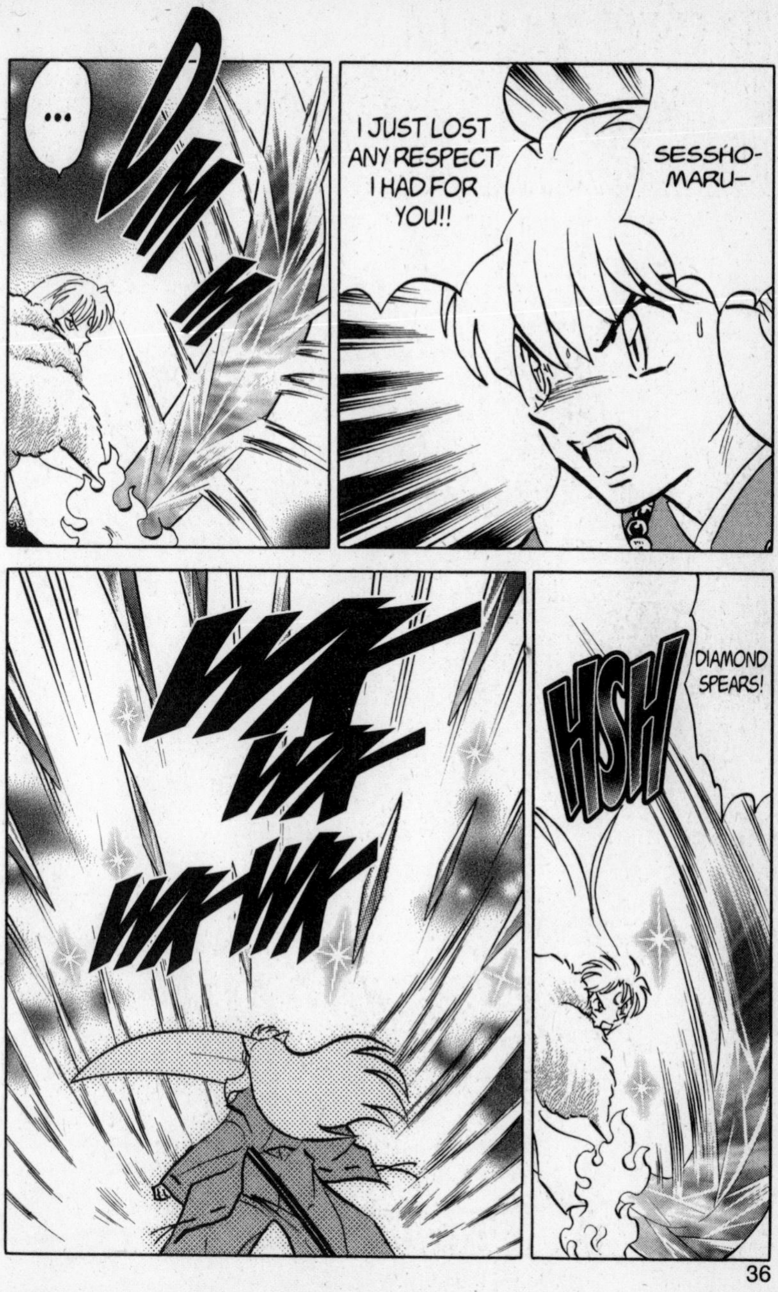
SESSHO-MARU—
I JUST LOST ANY RESPECT I HAD FOR YOU!!
...
DIAMOND SPEARS!
HSH!

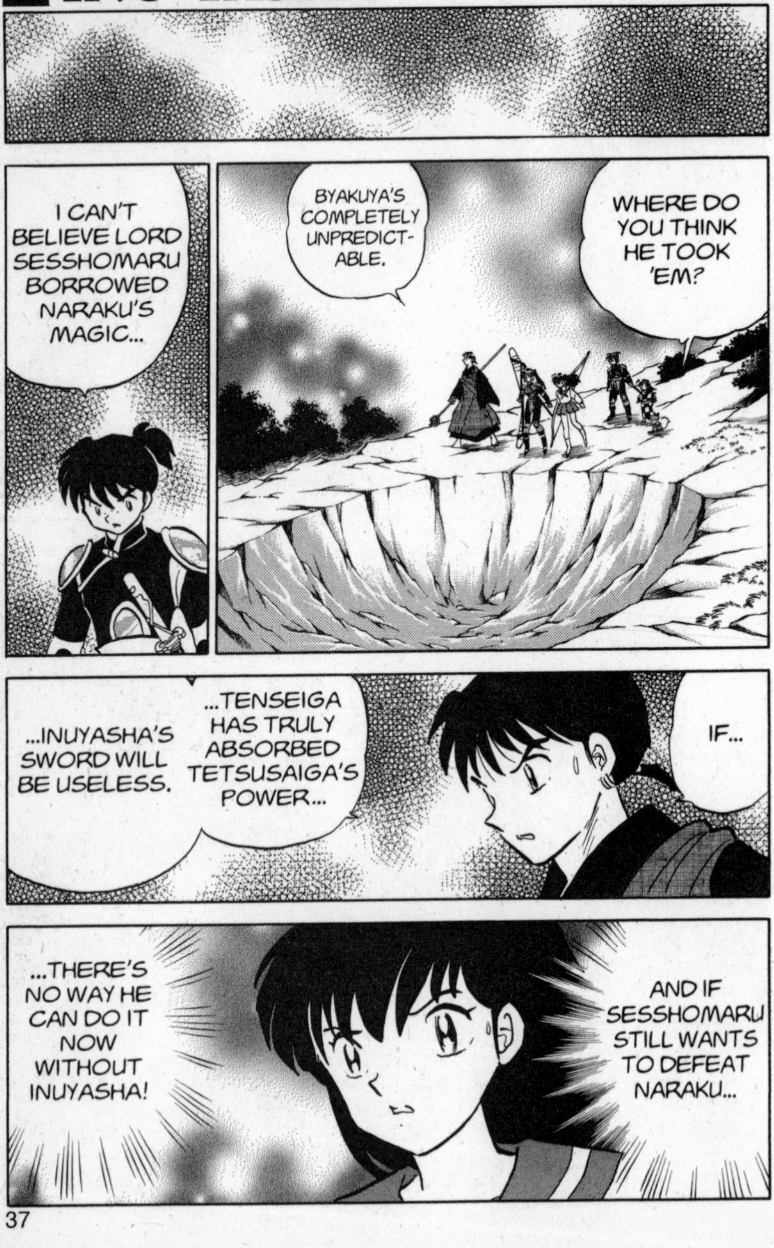
WHERE DO YOU THINK HE TOOK 'EM?
BYAKUYA'S COMPLETELY UNPREDICT-ABLE.
I CAN'T BELIEVE LORD SESSHOMARU BORROWED NARAKU'S MAGIC...
IF...
...TENSEIGA HAS TRULY ABSORBED TETSUSAIGA'S POWER...
...INUYASHA'S SWORD WILL BE USELESS.
AND IF SESSHOMARU STILL WANTS TO DEFEAT NARAKU...
...THERE'S NO WAY HE CAN DO IT NOW WITHOUT INUYASHA!

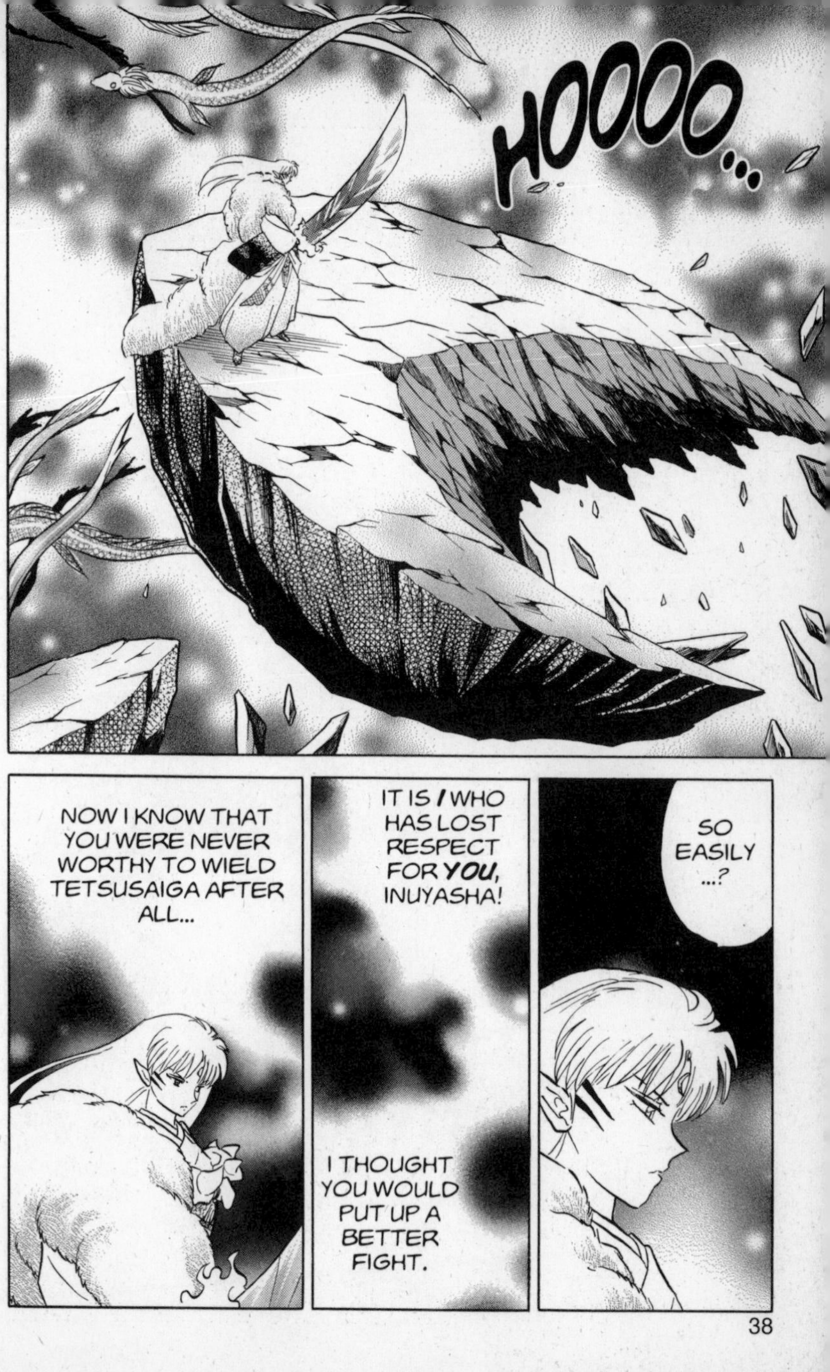
HOOOO...
SO EASILY ...?
IT IS I WHO HAS LOST RESPECT FOR YOU, INUYASHA!
I THOUGHT YOU WOULD PUT UP A BETTER FIGHT.
NOW I KNOW THAT YOU WERE NEVER WORTHY TO WIELD TETSUSAIGA AFTER ALL...

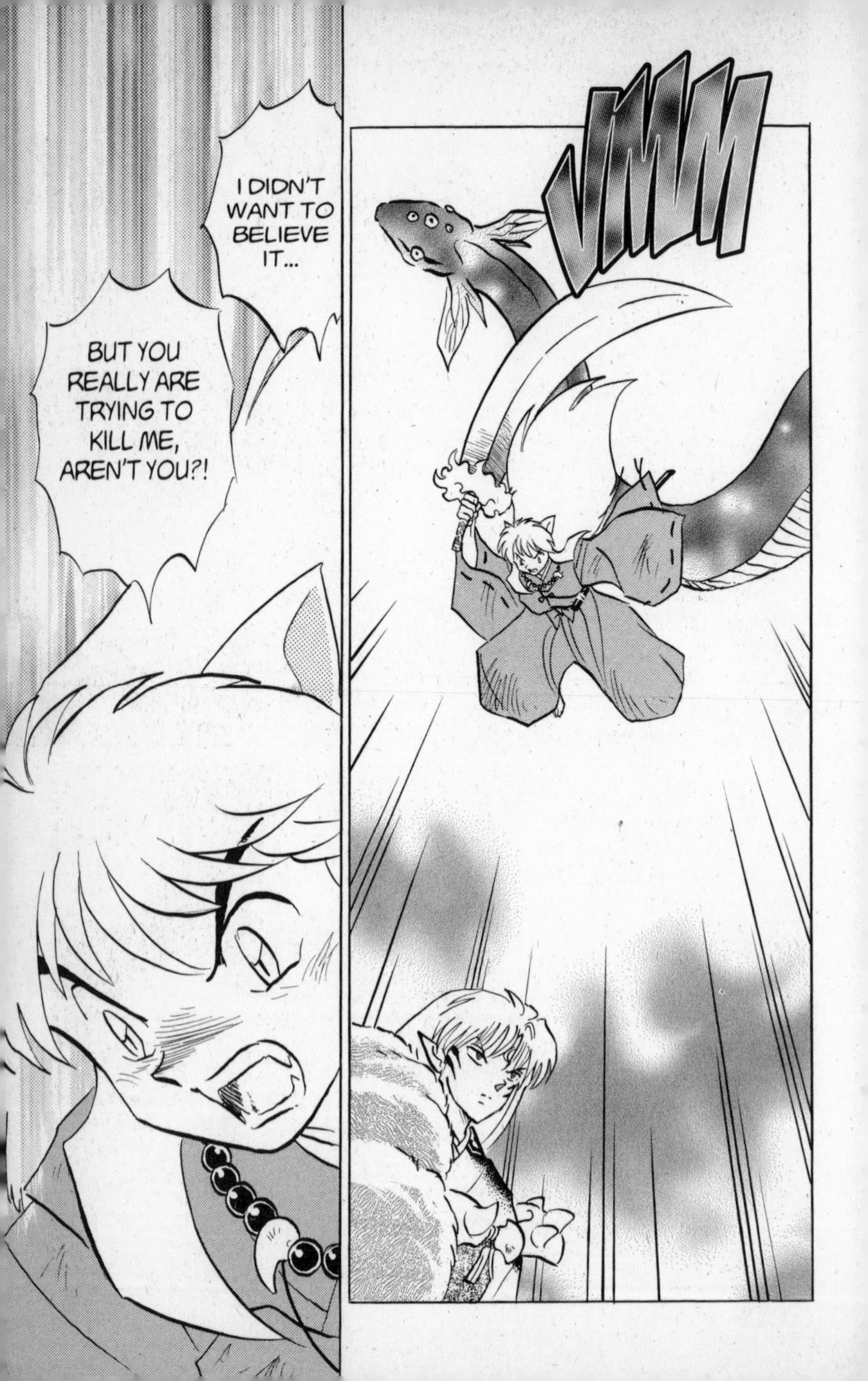
JMM
I DIDN'T WANT TO BELIEVE IT...
BUT YOU REALLY ARE TRYING TO KILL ME, AREN'T YOU?!

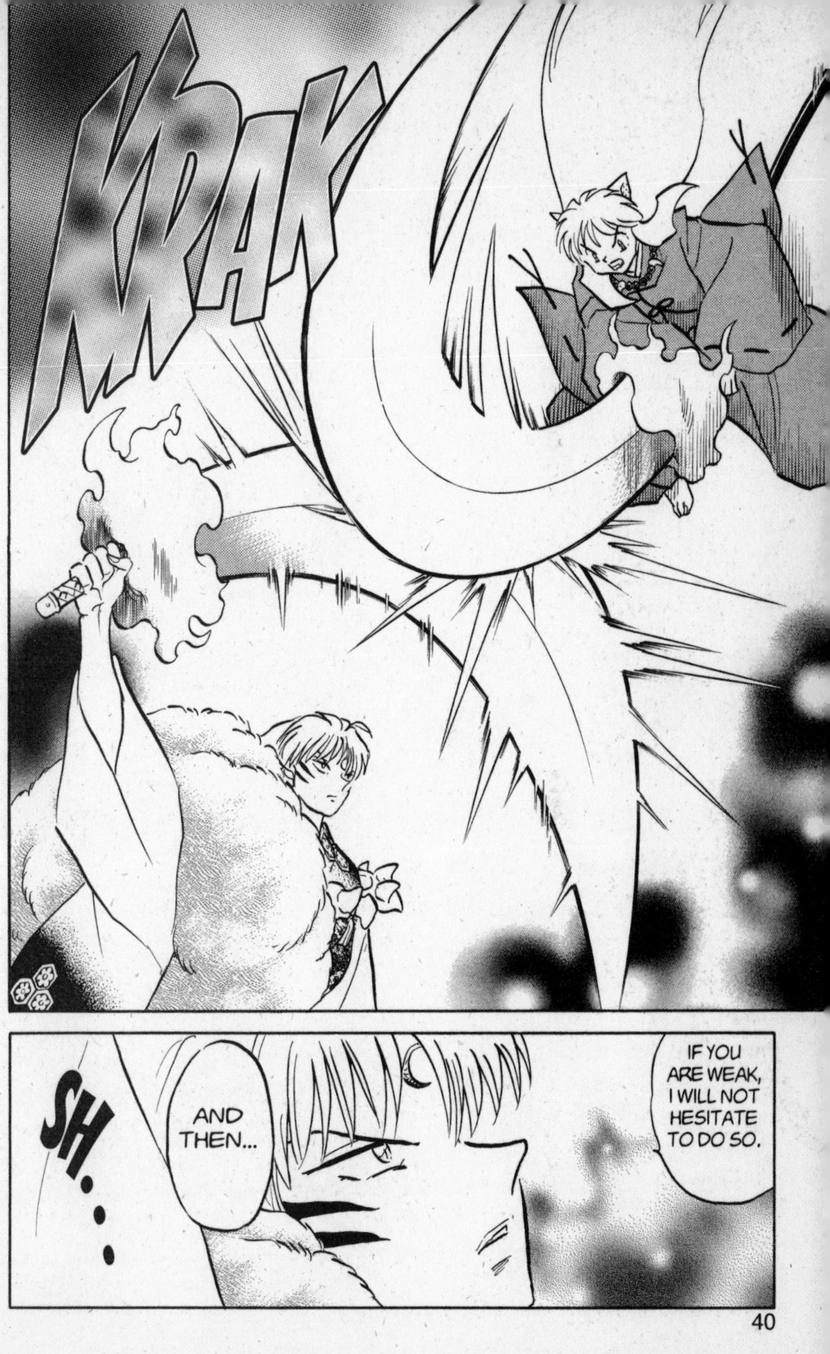
WHAK
IF YOU ARE WEAK, I WILL NOT HESITATE TO DO SO.
AND THEN...
SH...

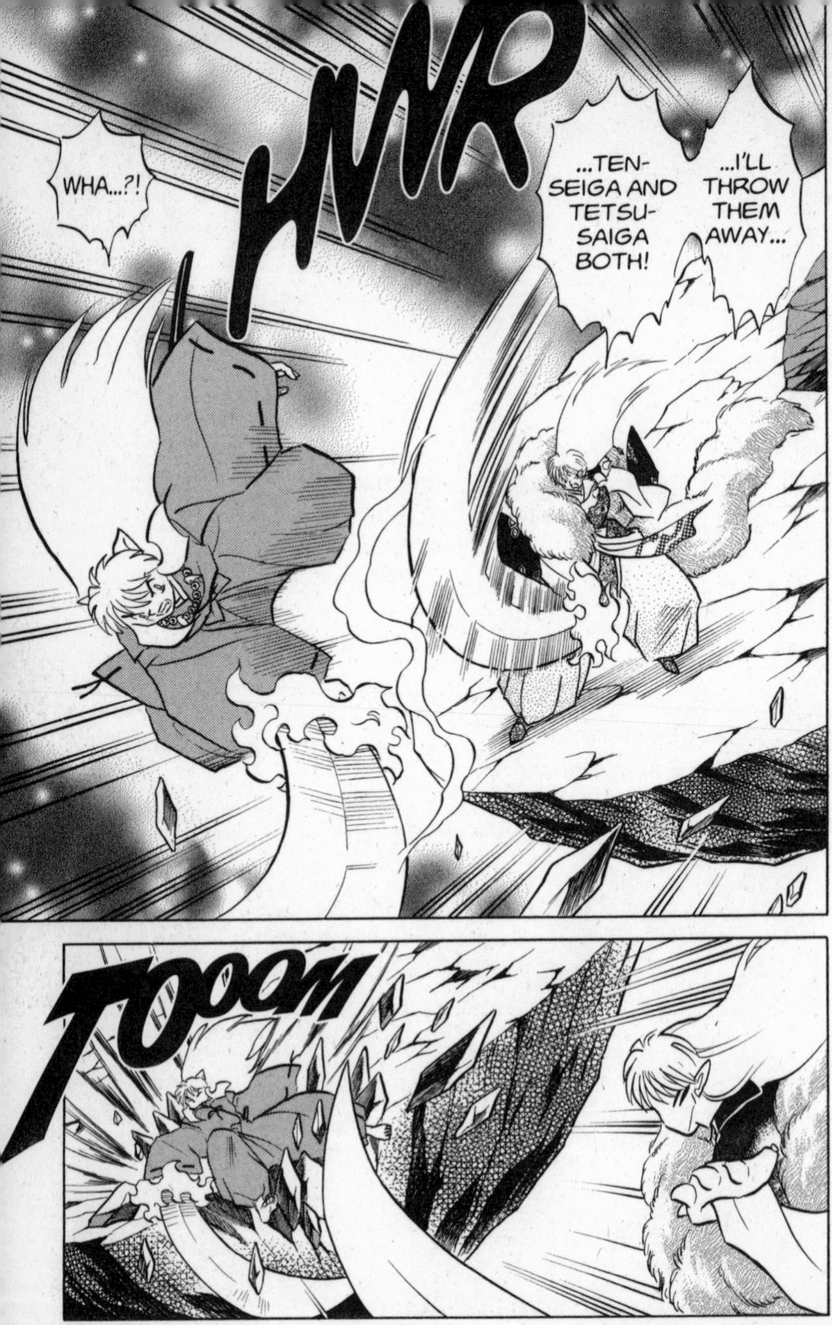
...I'LL THROW THEM AWAY...
...TEN-SEIGA AND TETSU-SAIGA BOTH!
WHA...?!
ZOOM

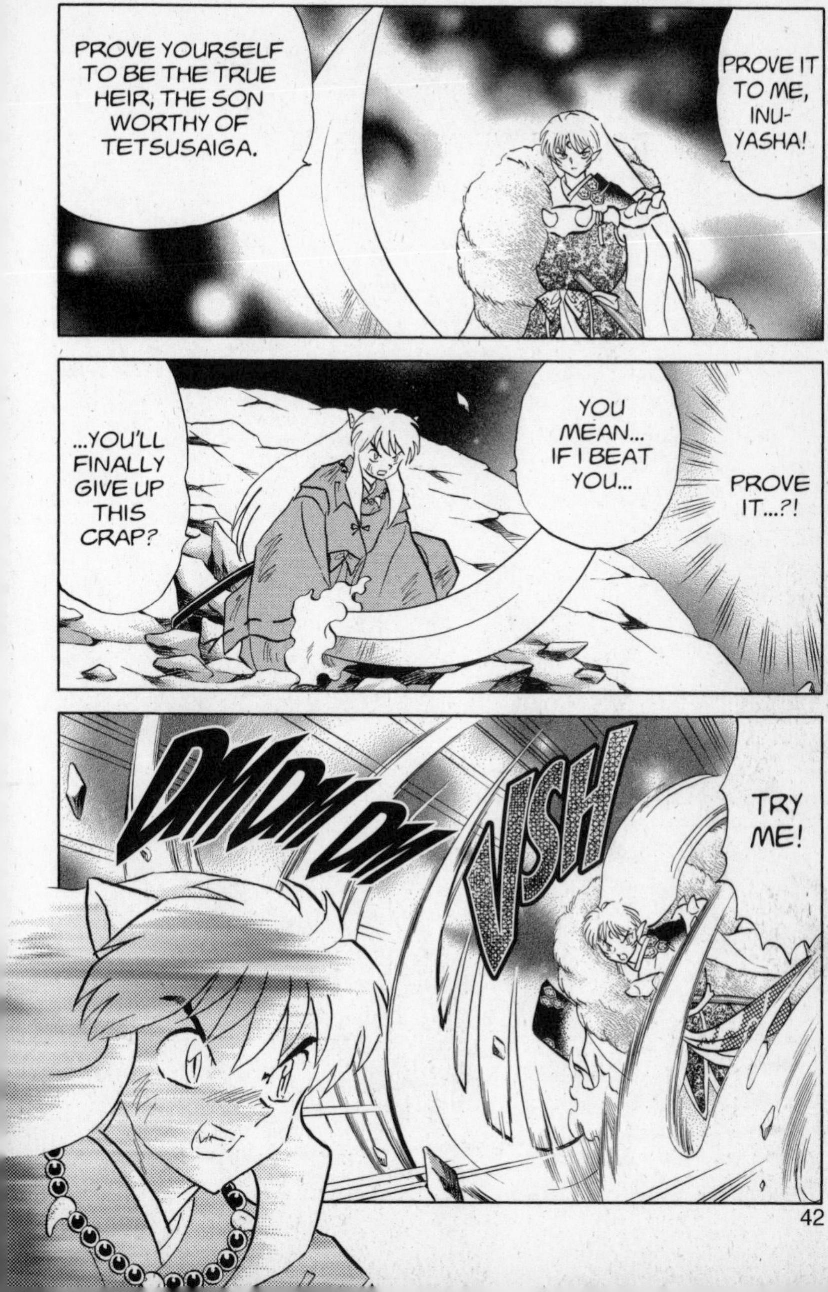
PROVE IT TO ME, INU-YASHA!
PROVE YOURSELF TO BE THE TRUE HEIR, THE SON WORTHY OF TETSUSAIGA.
PROVE IT...?!
YOU MEAN... IF I BEAT YOU...
...YOU'LL FINALLY GIVE UP THIS CRAP?
TRY ME!
VSH

SCROLL 3

REFLUX

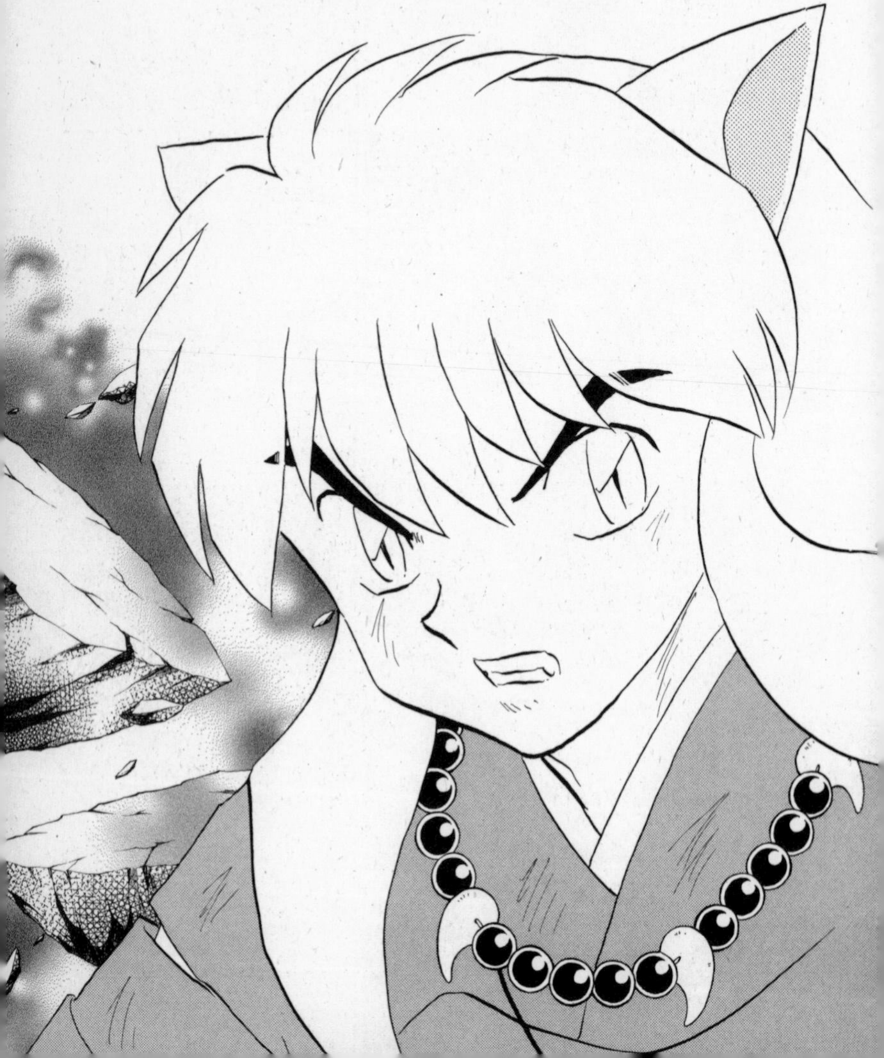

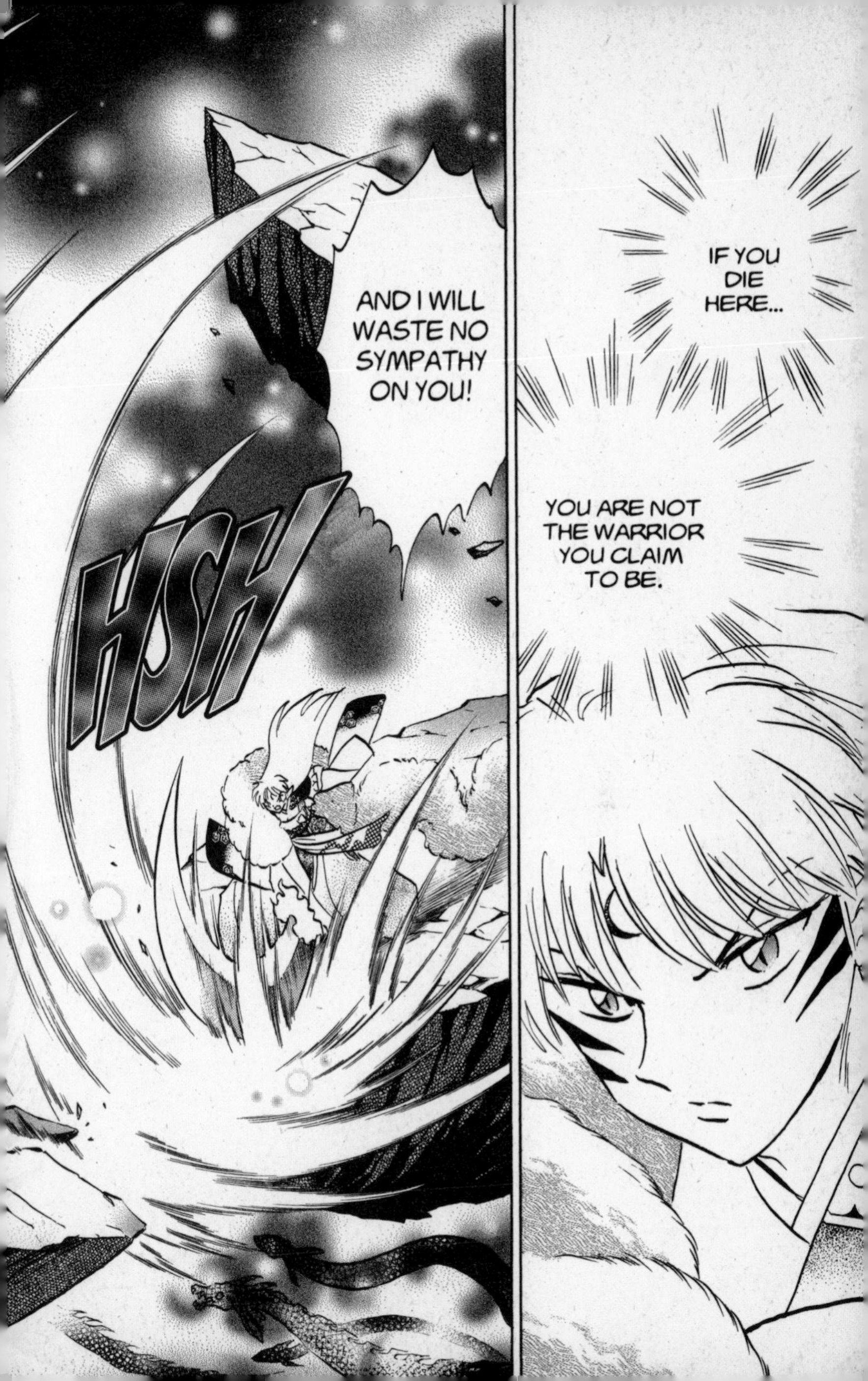
IF YOU DIE HERE...
YOU ARE NOT THE WARRIOR YOU CLAIM TO BE.
AND I WILL WASTE NO SYMPATHY ON YOU!
HSH

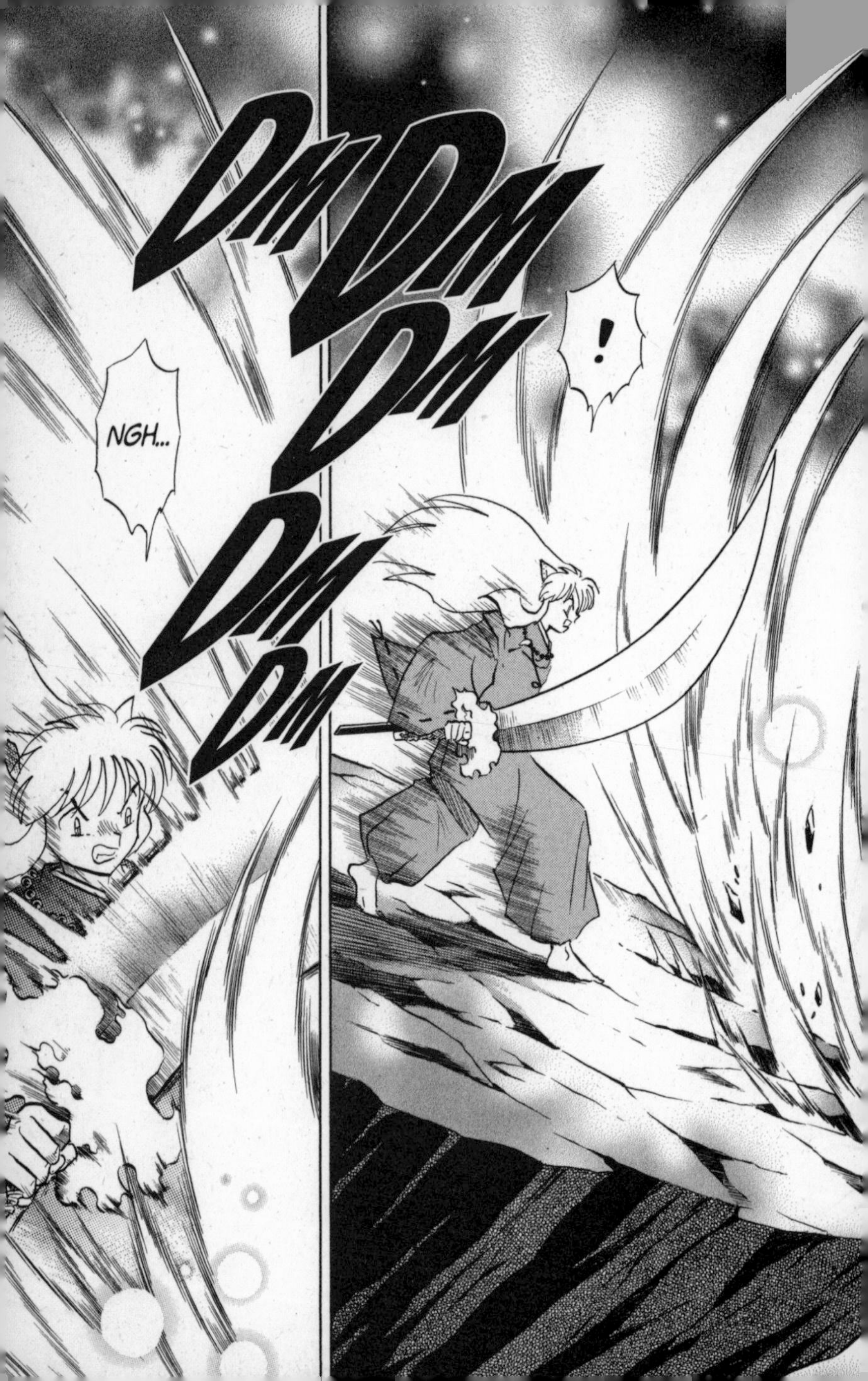
!
DMDM
DM
DM
DM
NGH...

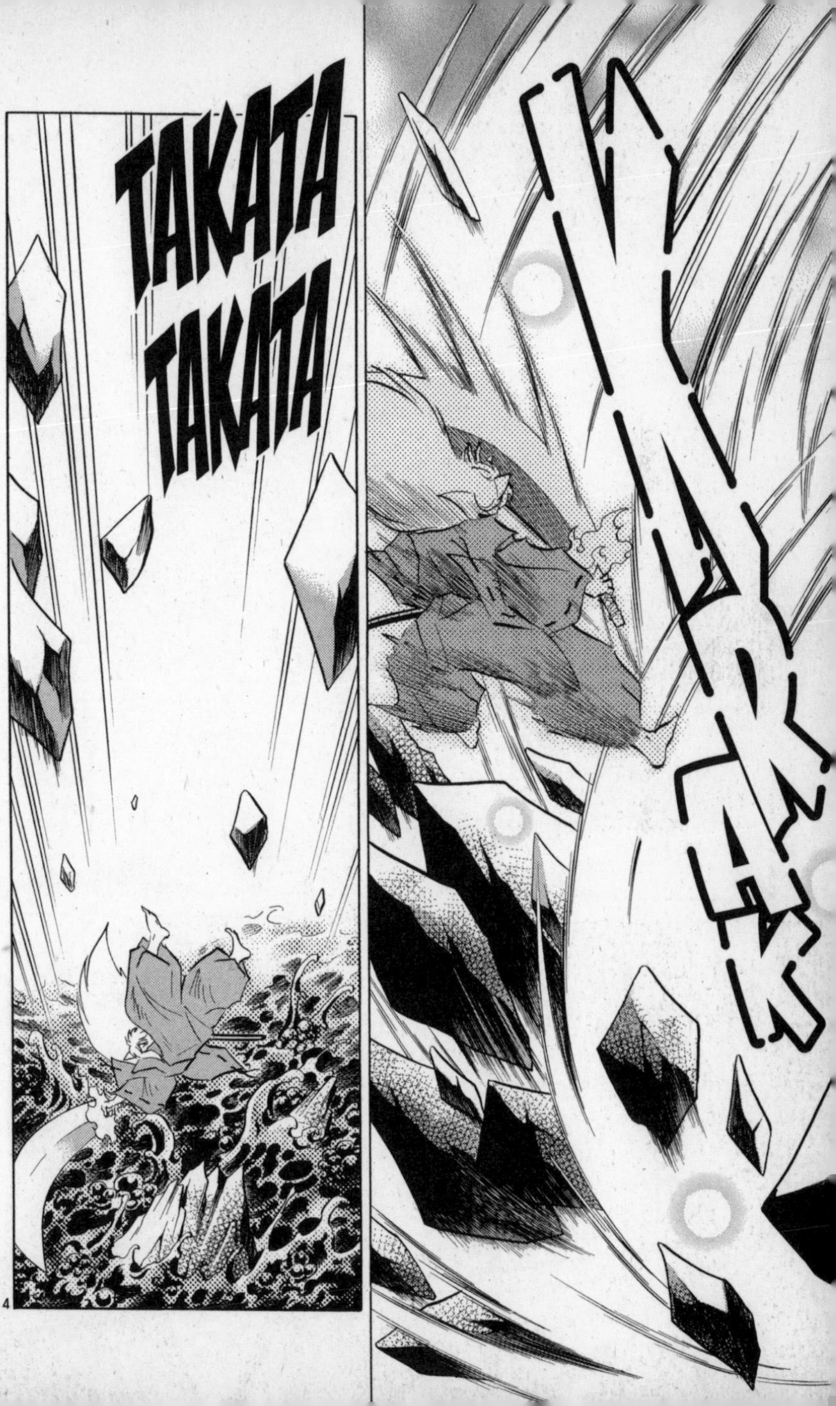
TAKATA
TAKATA

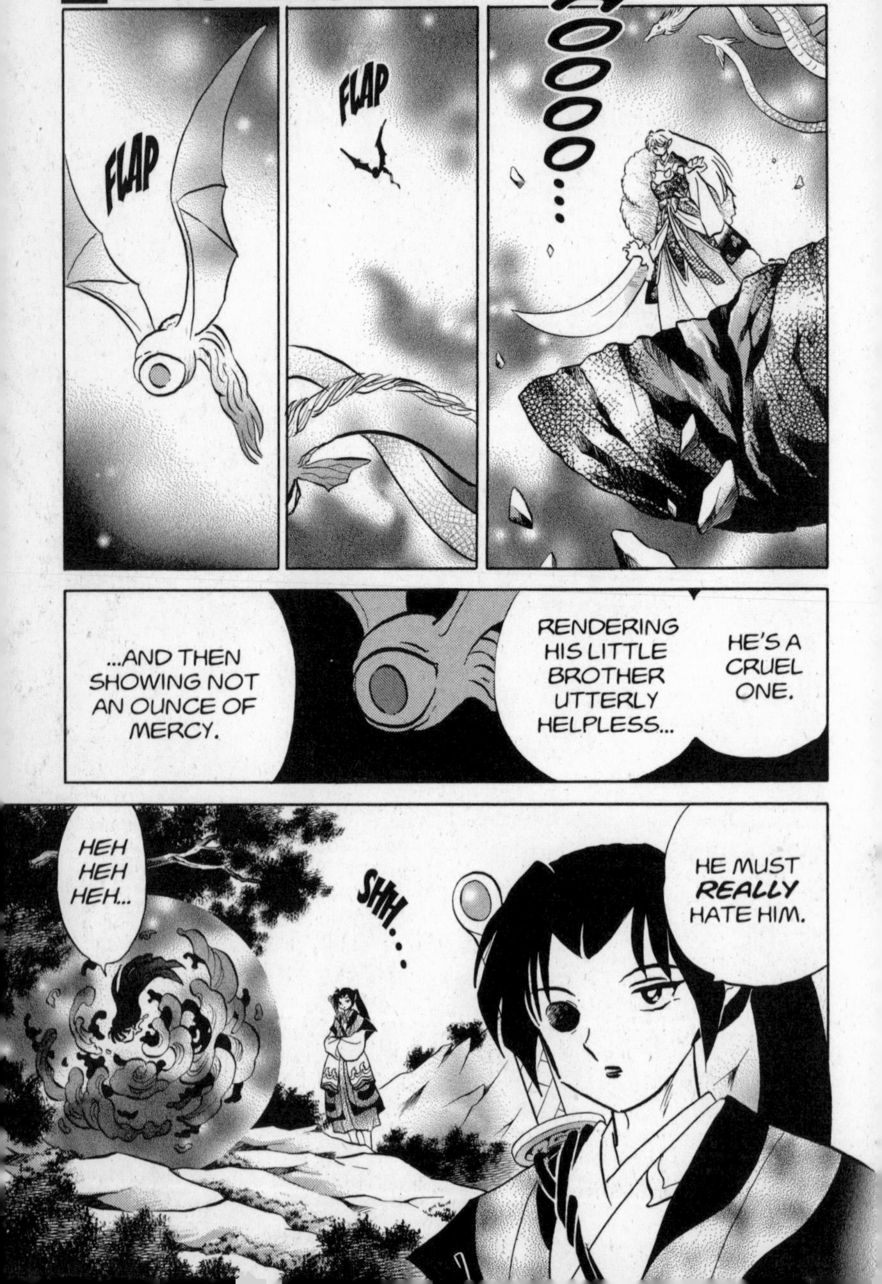
HOOOOO...
FLAP
FLAP
HE'S A CRUEL ONE.
RENDERING HIS LITTLE BROTHER UTTERLY HELPLESS...
...AND THEN SHOWING NOT AN OUNCE OF MERCY.
HE MUST REALLY HATE HIM.
SHH...
HEH HEH HEH...

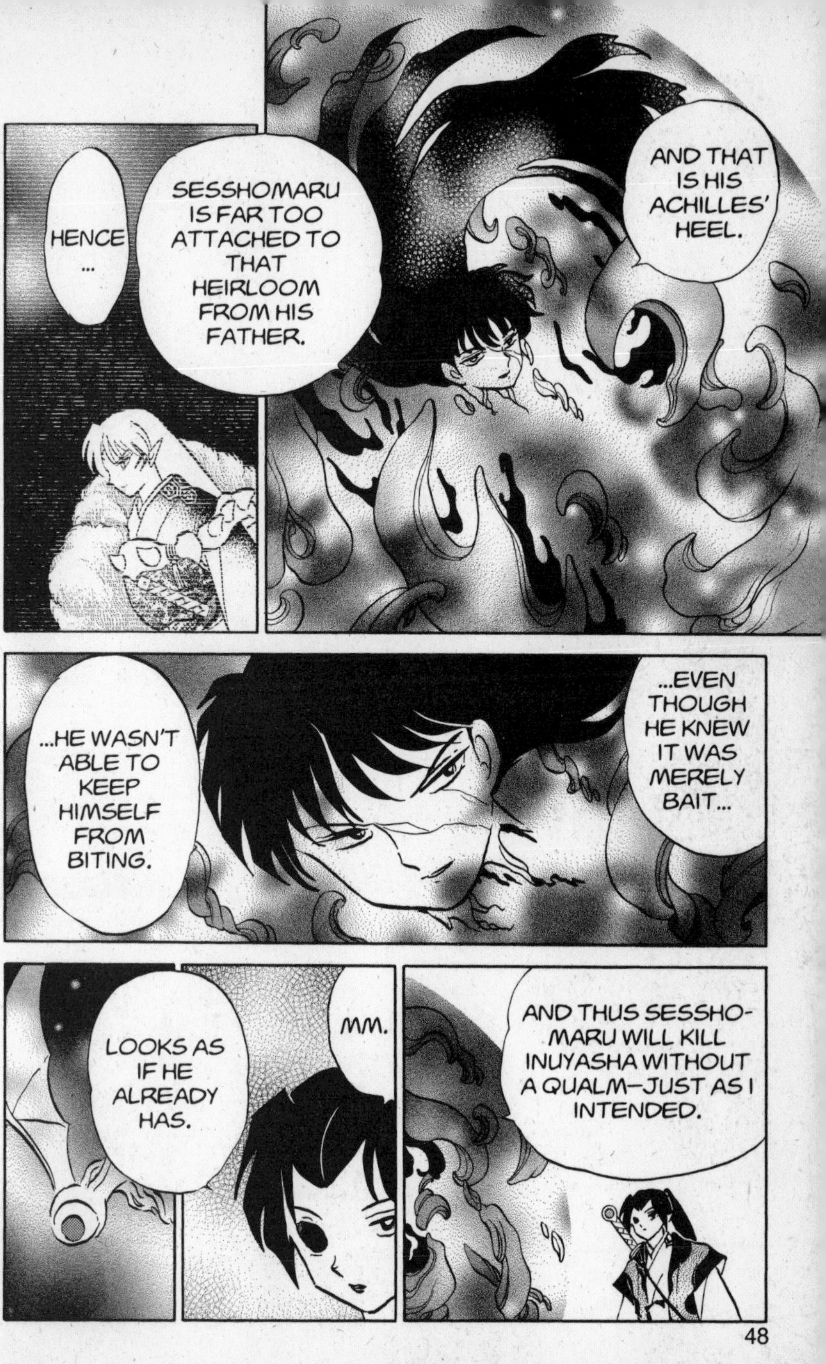
SESSHOMARU IS FAR TOO ATTACHED TO THAT HEIRLOOM FROM HIS FATHER.
AND THAT IS HIS ACHILLES' HEEL.
HENCE ...
...EVEN THOUGH HE KNEW IT WAS MERELY BAIT...
...HE WASN'T ABLE TO KEEP HIMSELF FROM BITING.
AND THUS SESSHO-MARU WILL KILL INUYASHA WITHOUT A QUALM—JUST AS I INTENDED.
MM.
LOOKS AS IF HE ALREADY HAS.

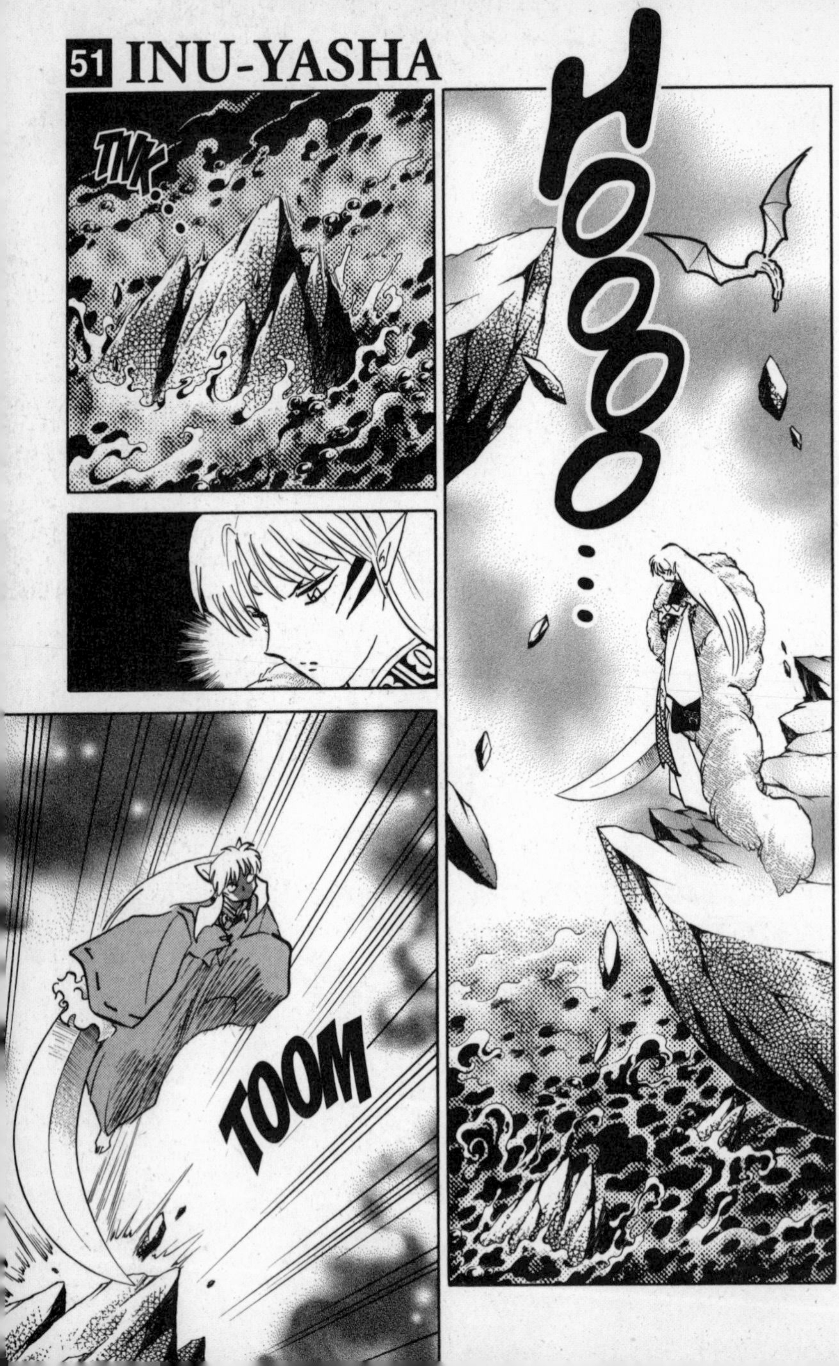
HOOOO...
TINK...
TOOM

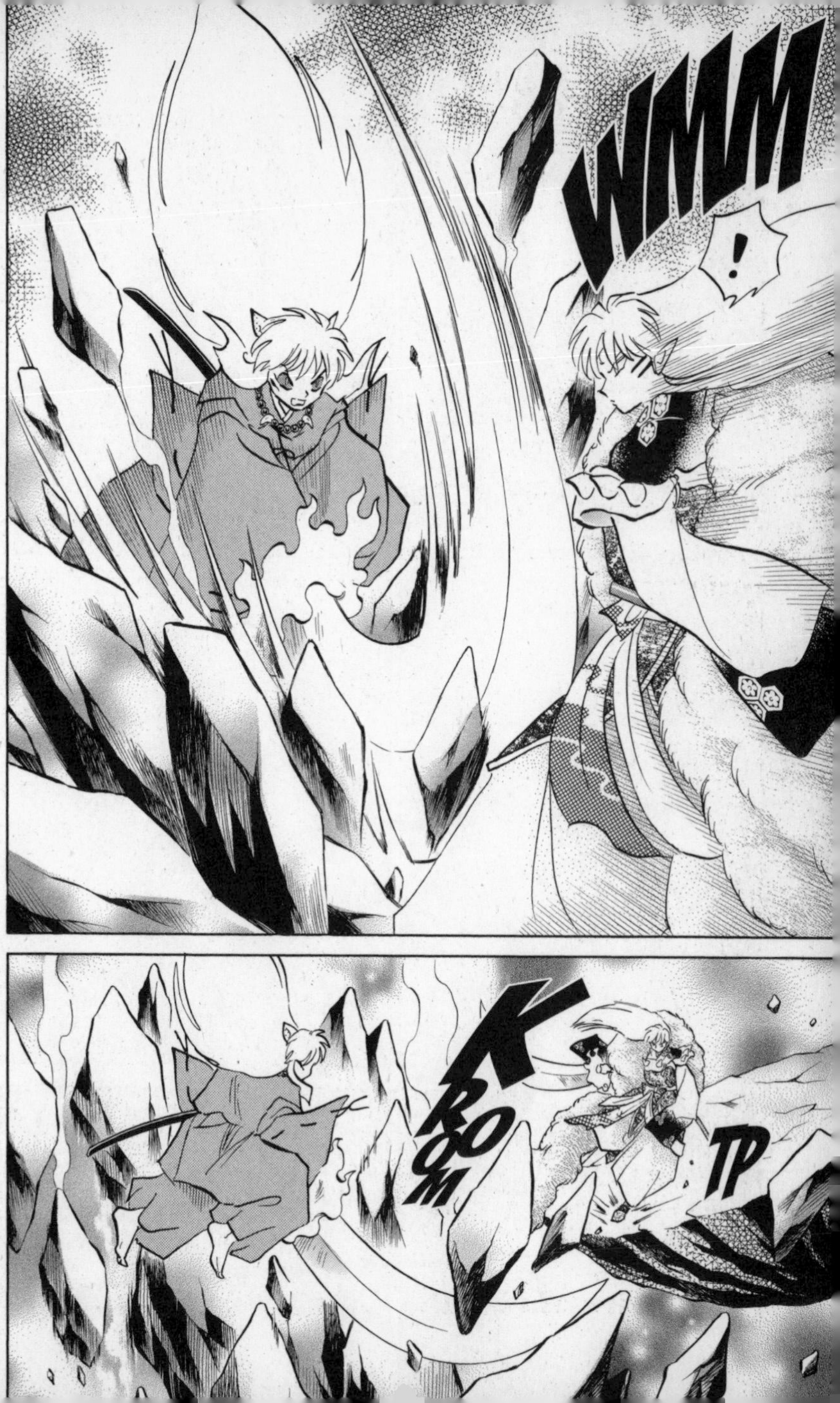
WMM
!
KROOM
TP

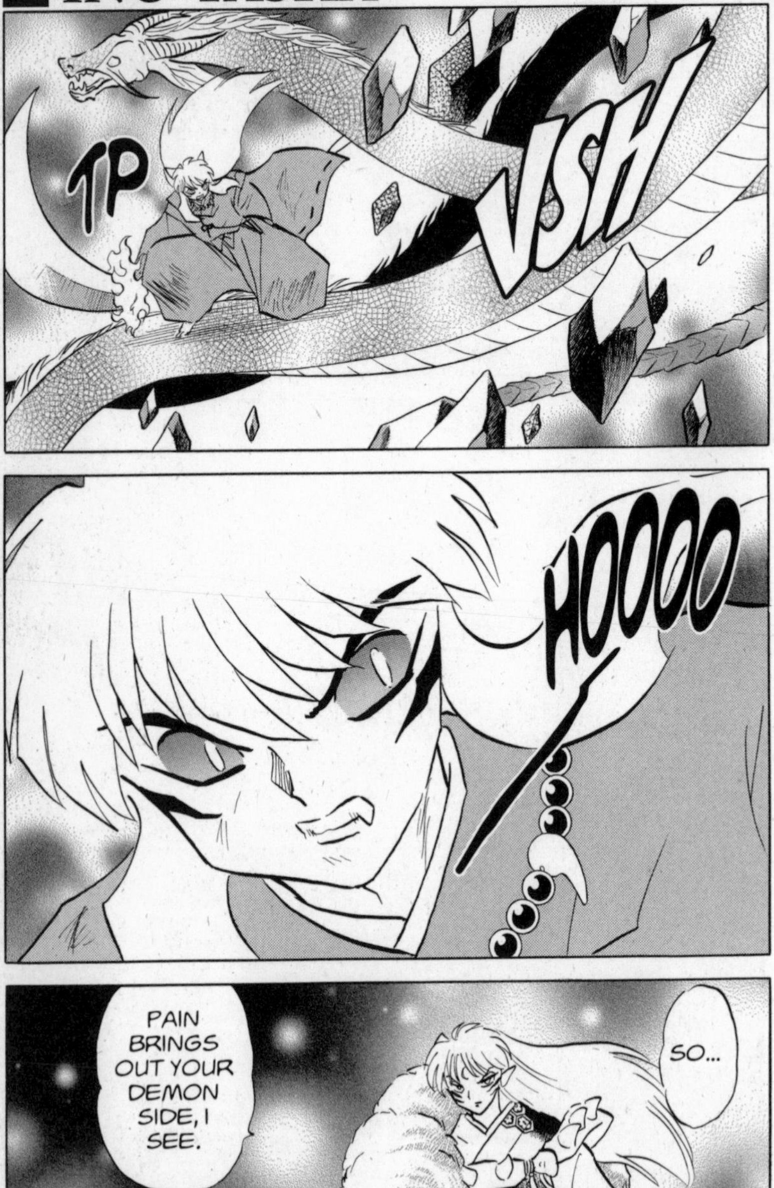
VSH
TP
HOOOO
SO...
PAIN BRINGS OUT YOUR DEMON SIDE, I SEE.

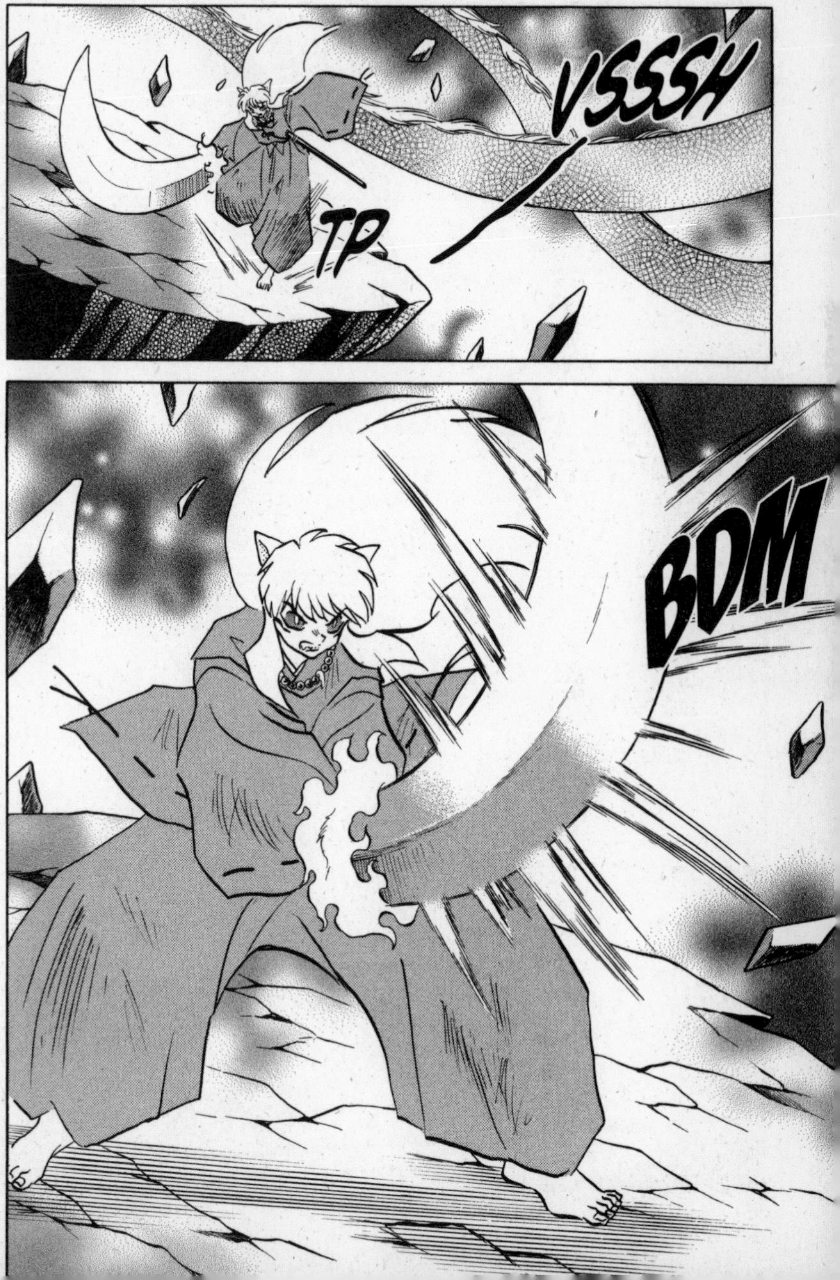
VSSSH
TP
BDM

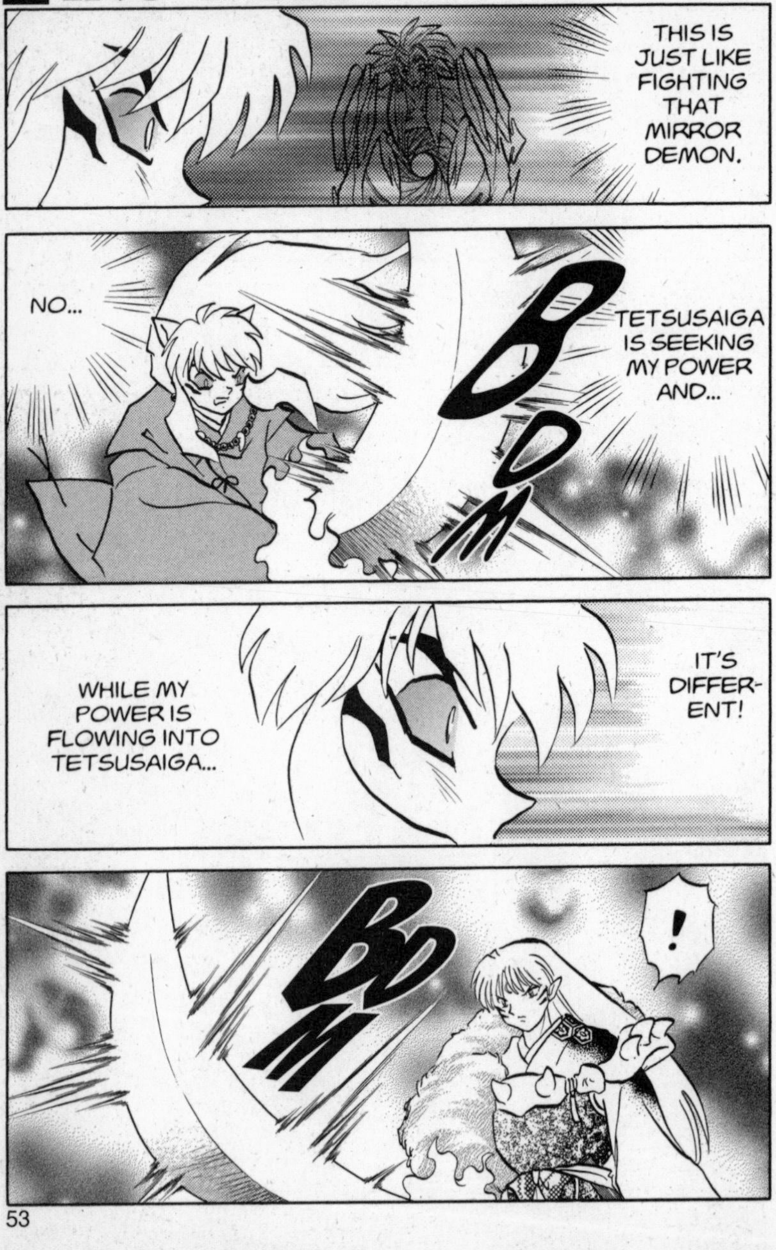
THIS IS JUST LIKE FIGHTING THAT MIRROR DEMON.
TETSUSAIGA IS SEEKING MY POWER AND...
BDOM
NO...
IT'S DIFFER-ENT!
WHILE MY POWER IS FLOWING INTO TETSUSAIGA...
!
BDOM

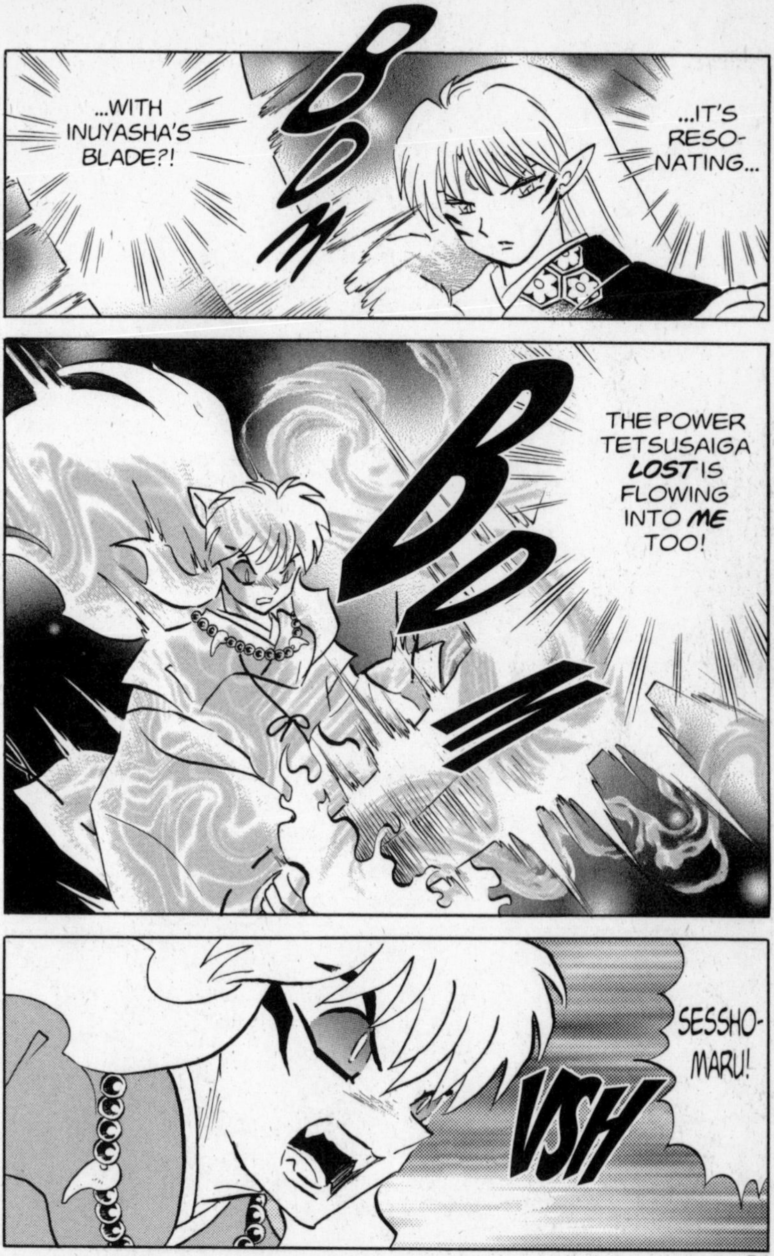

...IT'S RESO- NATING...
BOM
...WITH INUYASHA'S BLADE?!
THE POWER TETSUSAIGA LOST IS FLOWING INTO ME TOO!
BOOM
SESSHO- MARU!
VSH

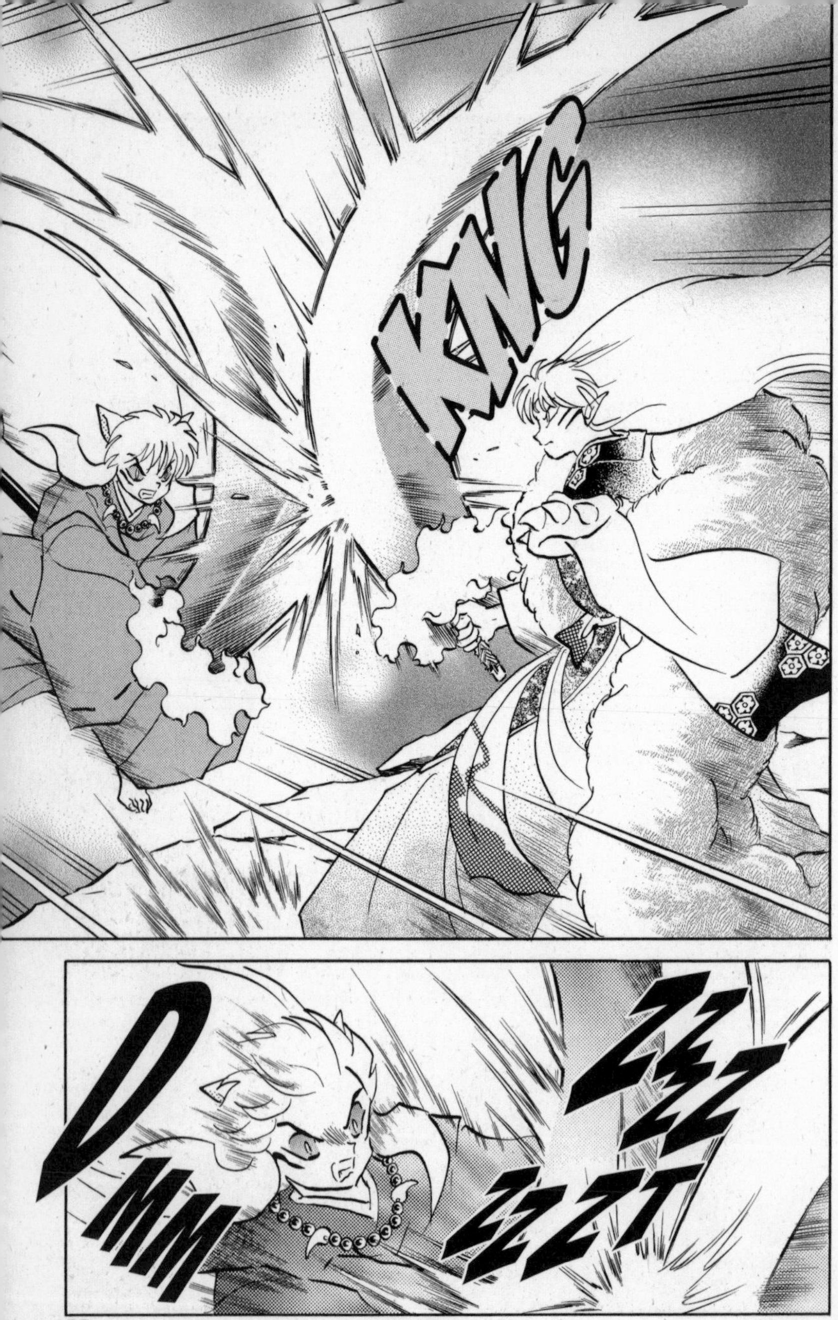
KANG
ZZZZZZT
DMMM

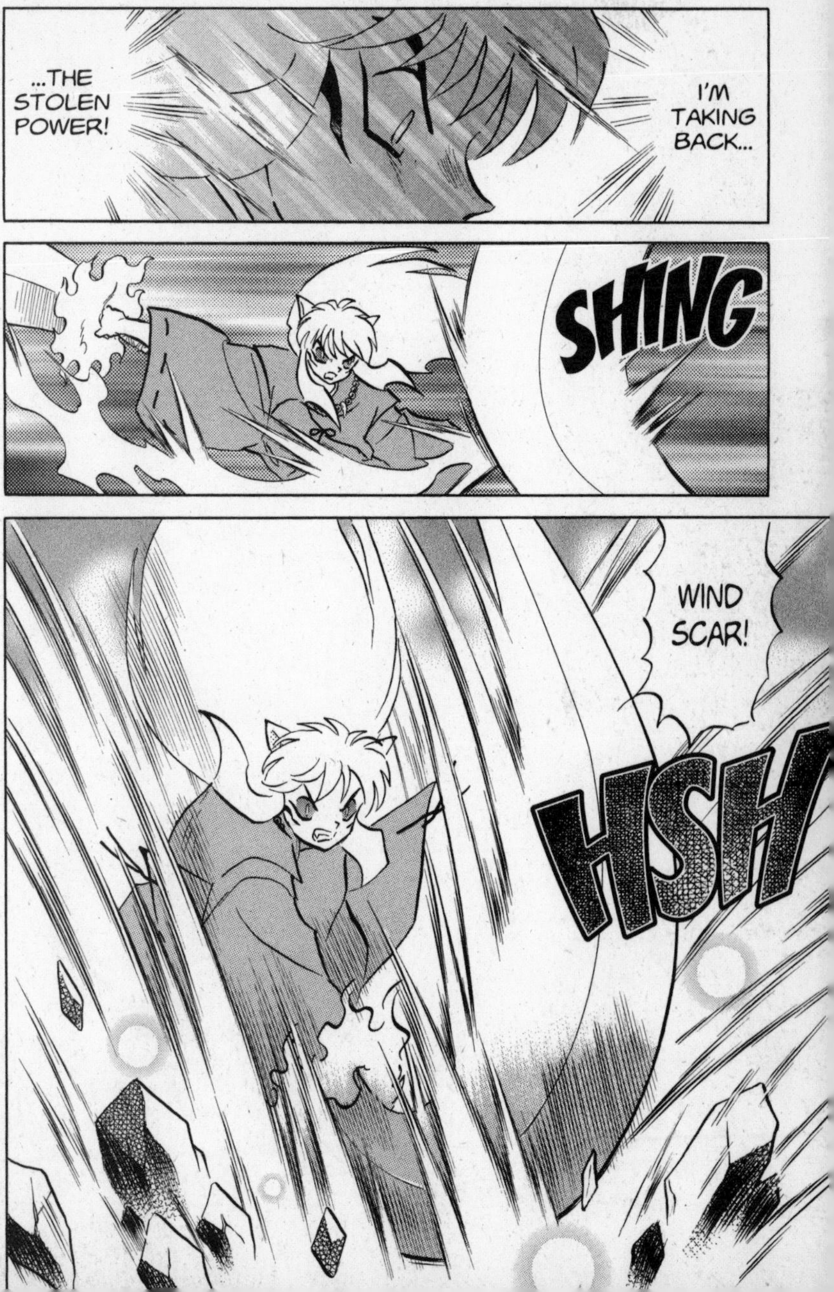
I'M TAKING BACK...
...THE STOLEN POWER!
SHING
WIND SCAR!
HSH

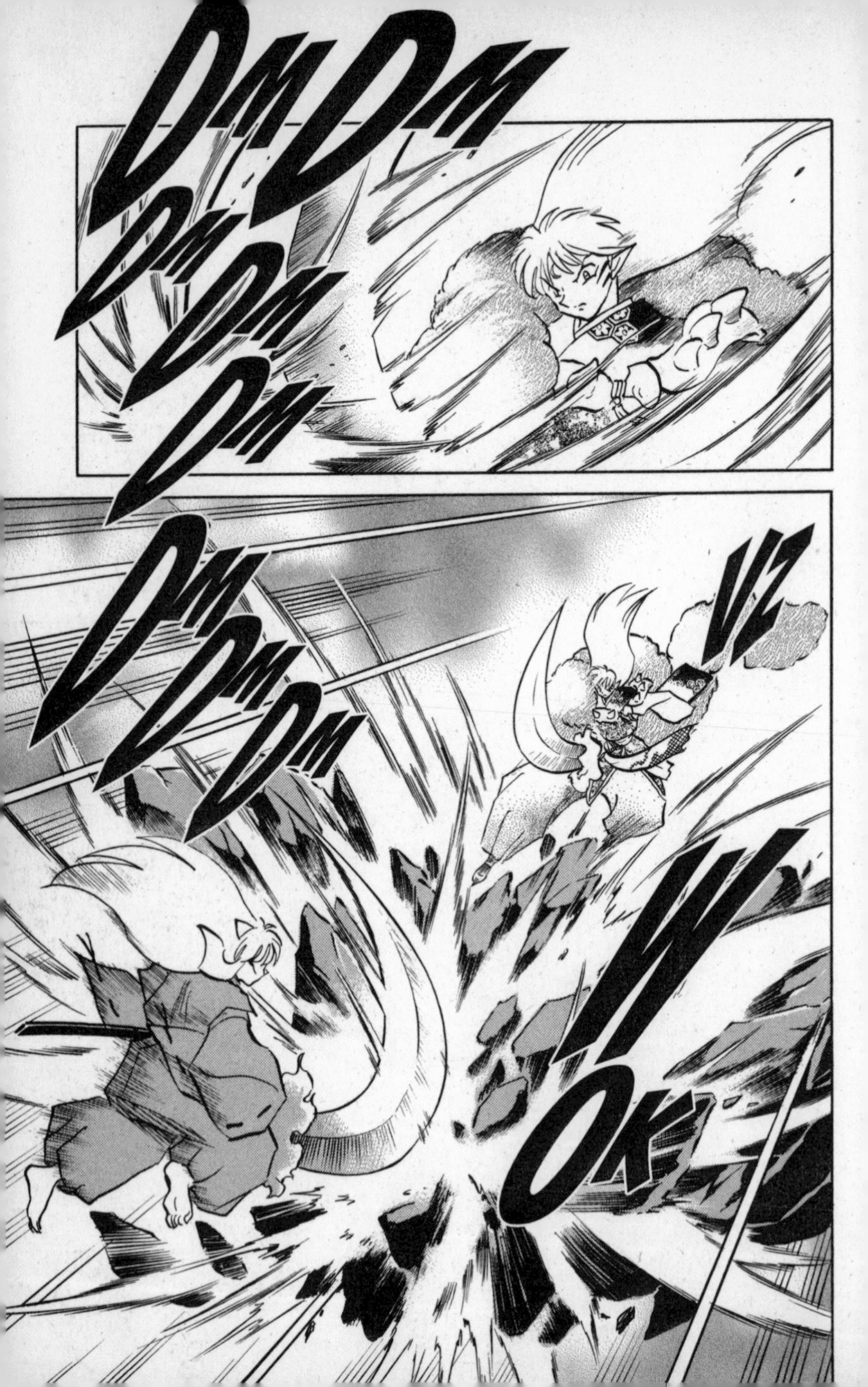
DMDM
DMDMDM
DMDMDM
VZWOK

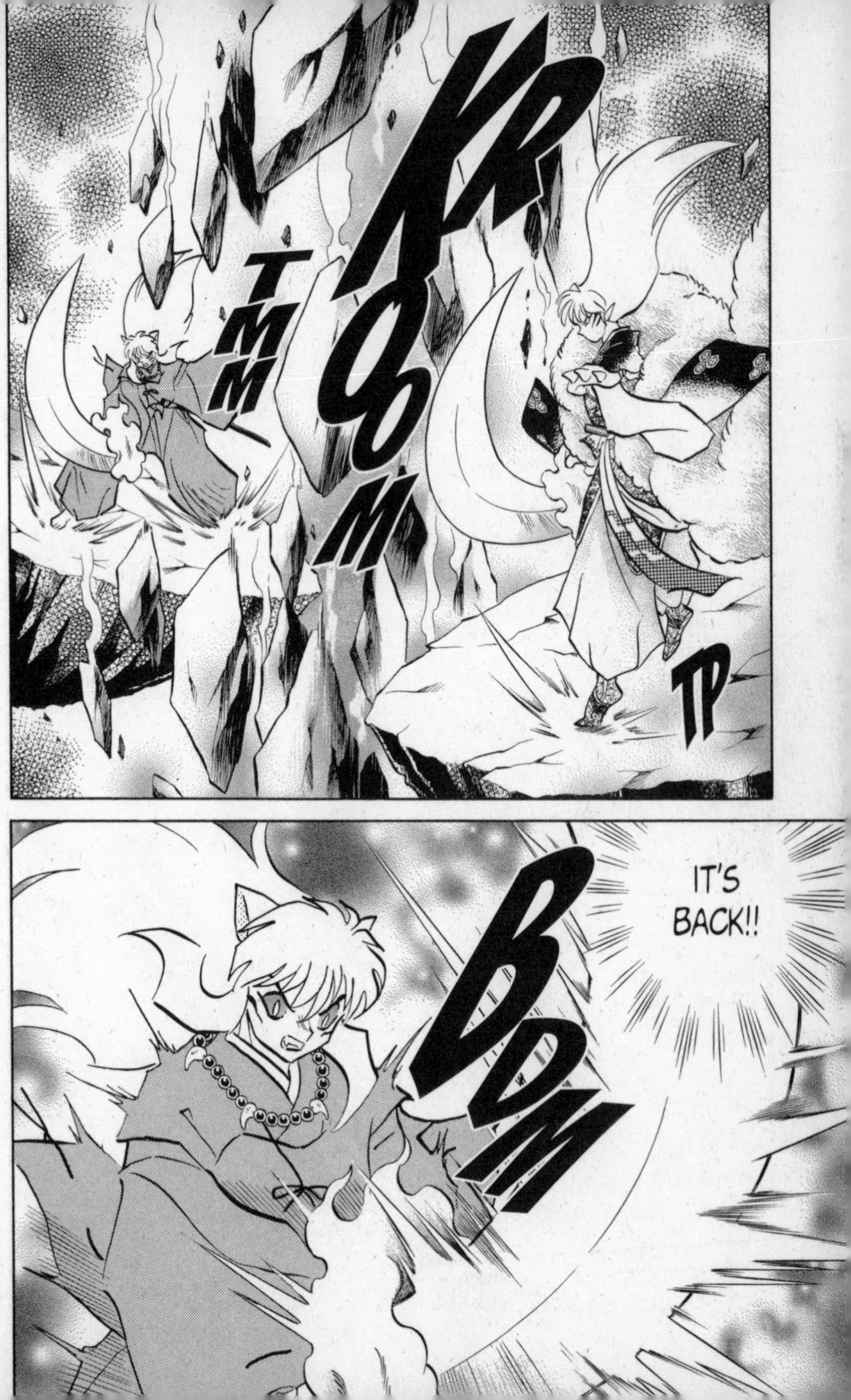
VROOM
TMM
TP
IT'S BACK!!
BDM

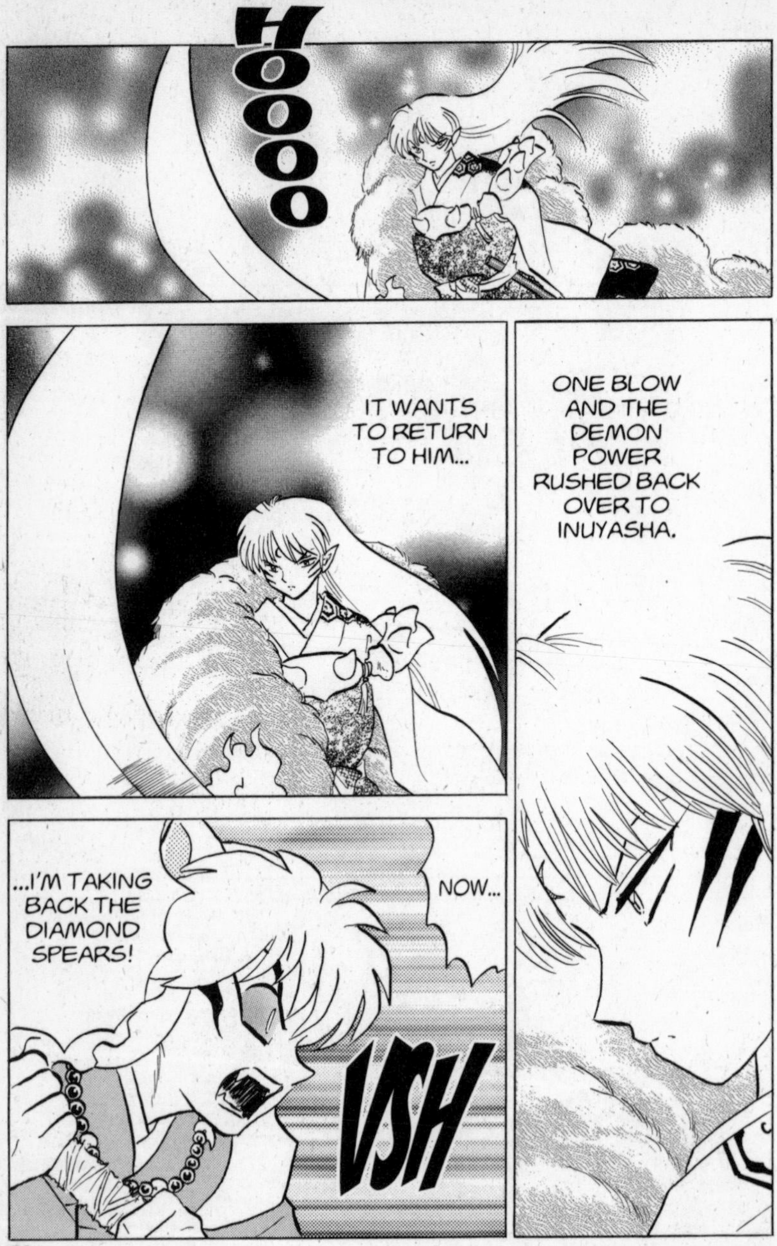
HOOOOO
ONE BLOW AND THE DEMON POWER RUSHED BACK OVER TO INUYASHA.
IT WANTS TO RETURN TO HIM...
NOW...
...I'M TAKING BACK THE DIAMOND SPEARS!
VSH

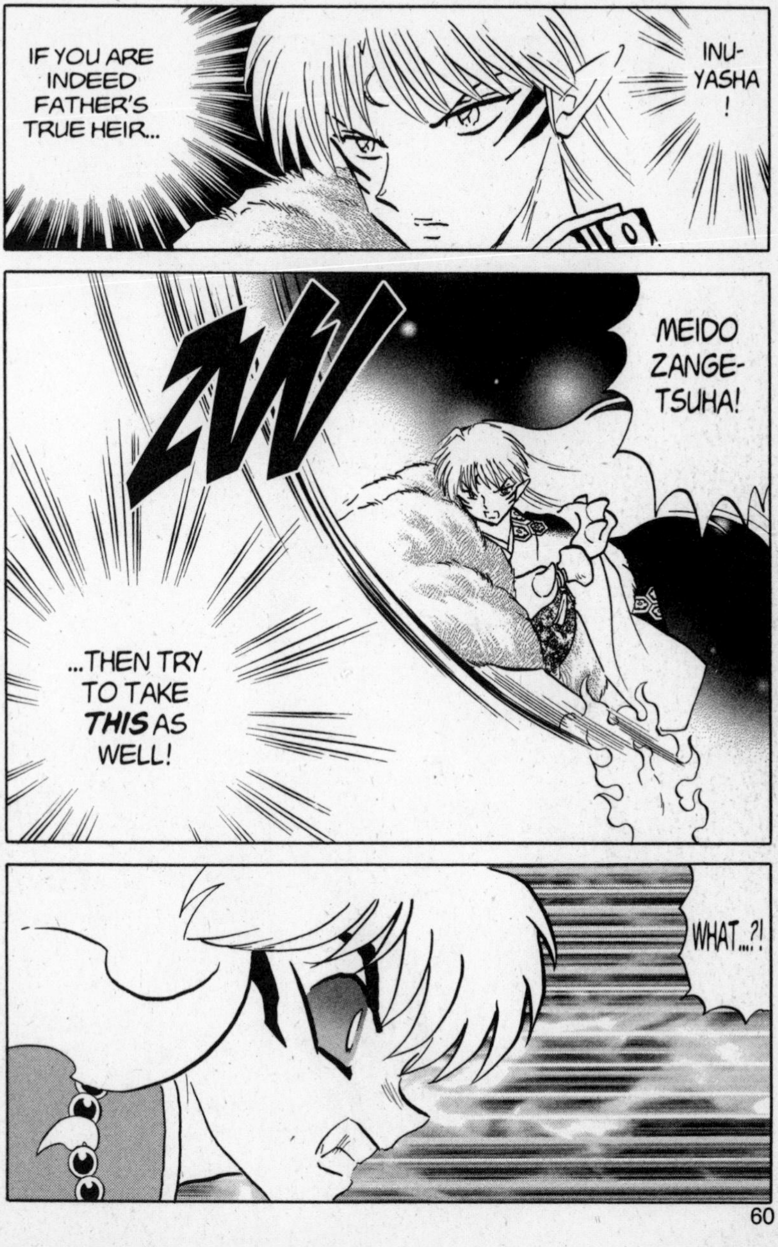
INU-YASHA!
IF YOU ARE INDEED FATHER'S TRUE HEIR...
MEIDO ZANGETSUHA!
ZW
...THEN TRY TO TAKE THIS AS WELL!
WHAT...?!

SCROLL 4
PROOF

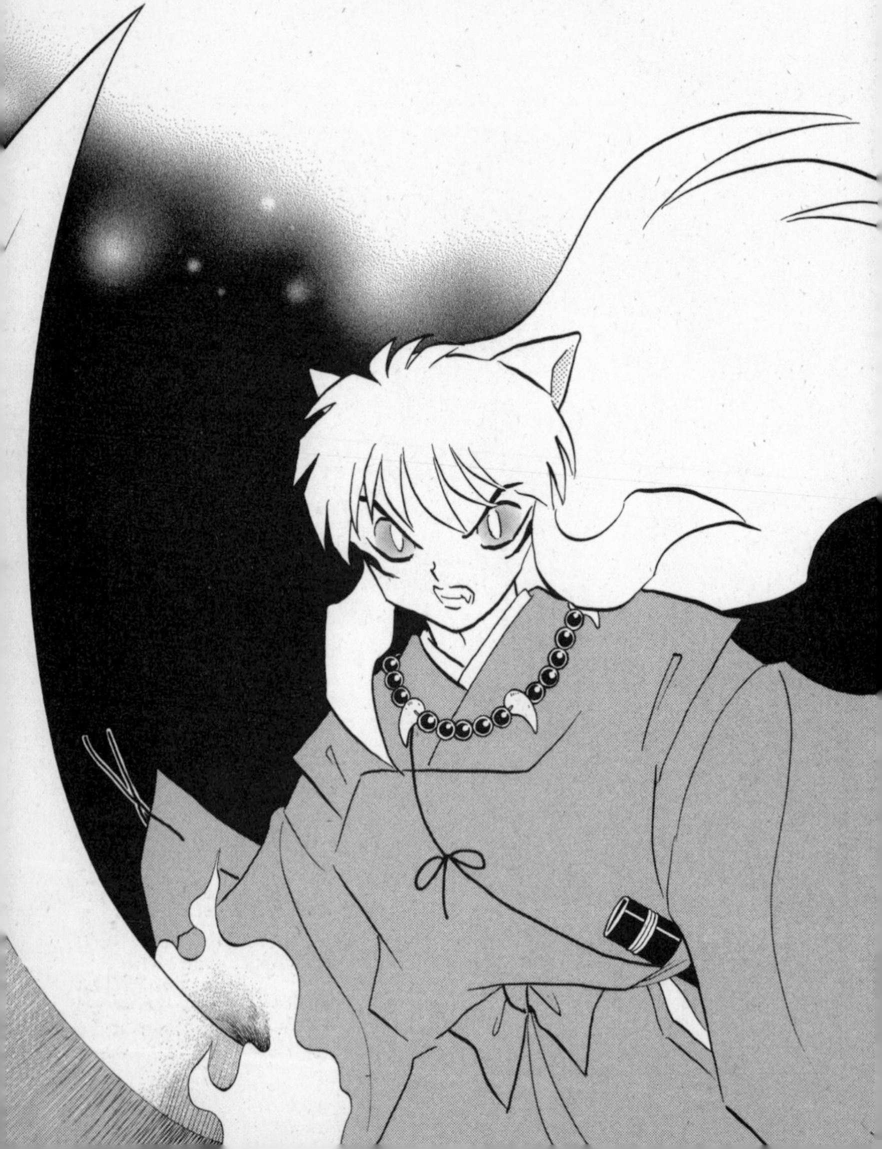

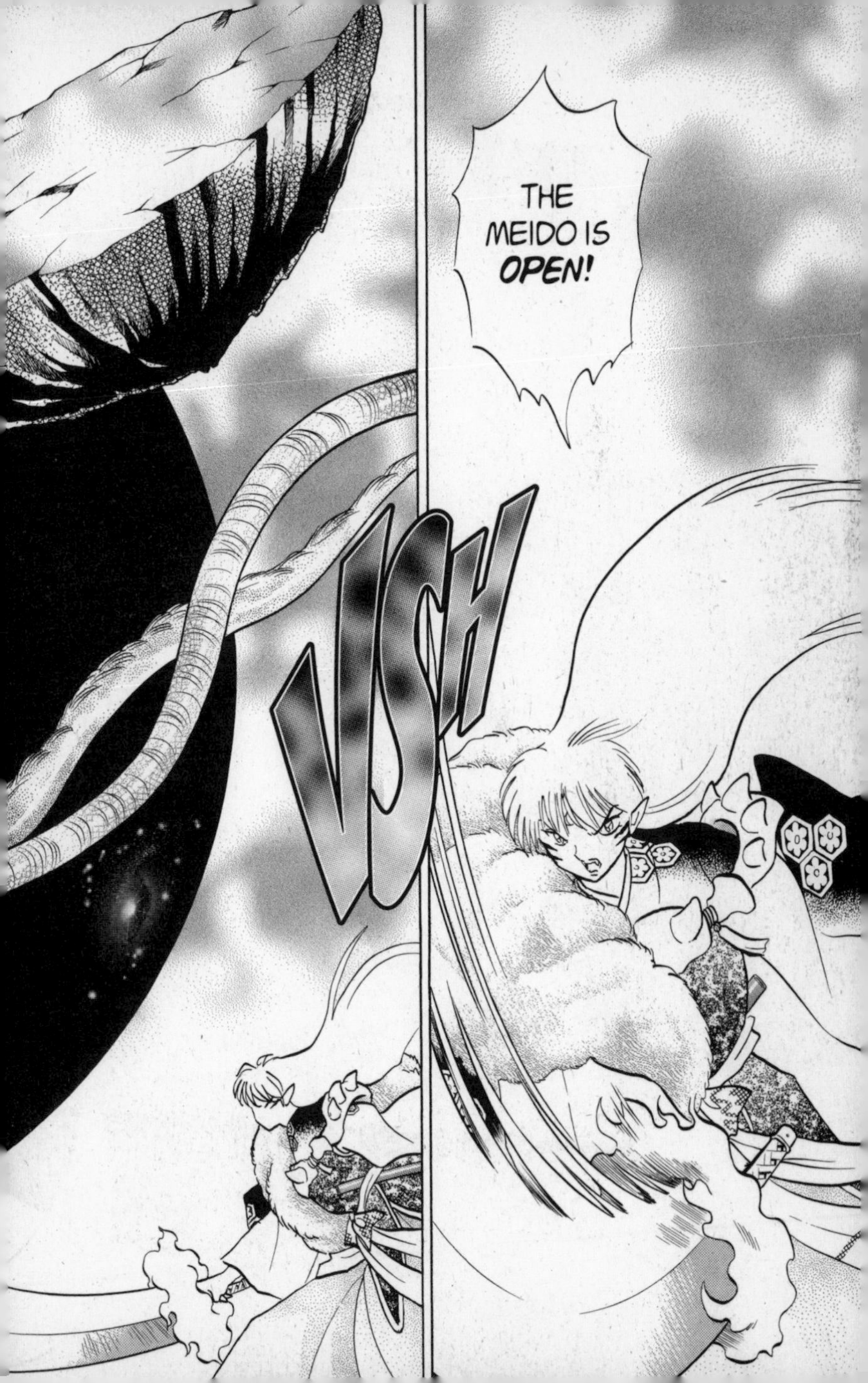
THE MEIDO IS OPEN!
VSH

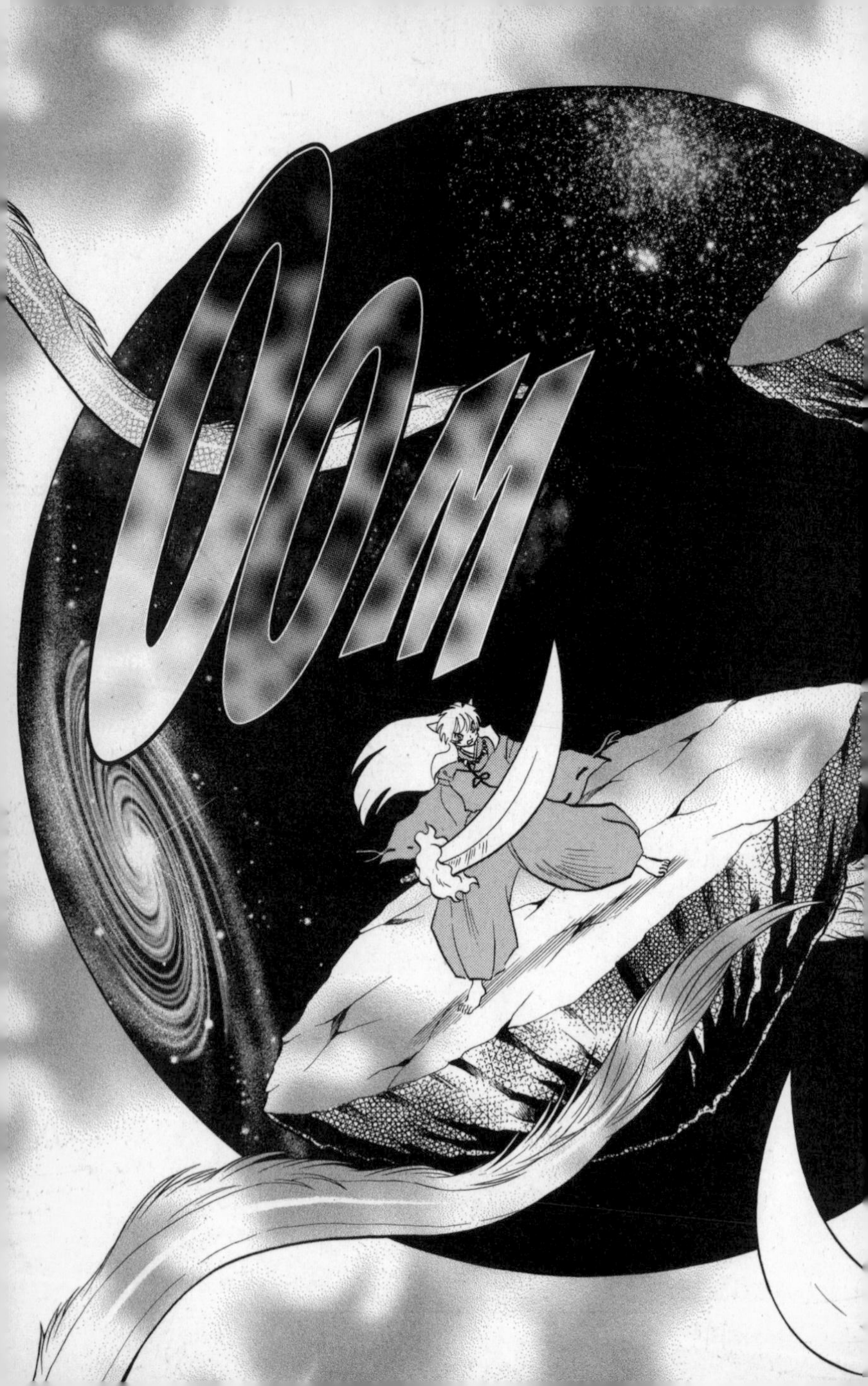
OOM

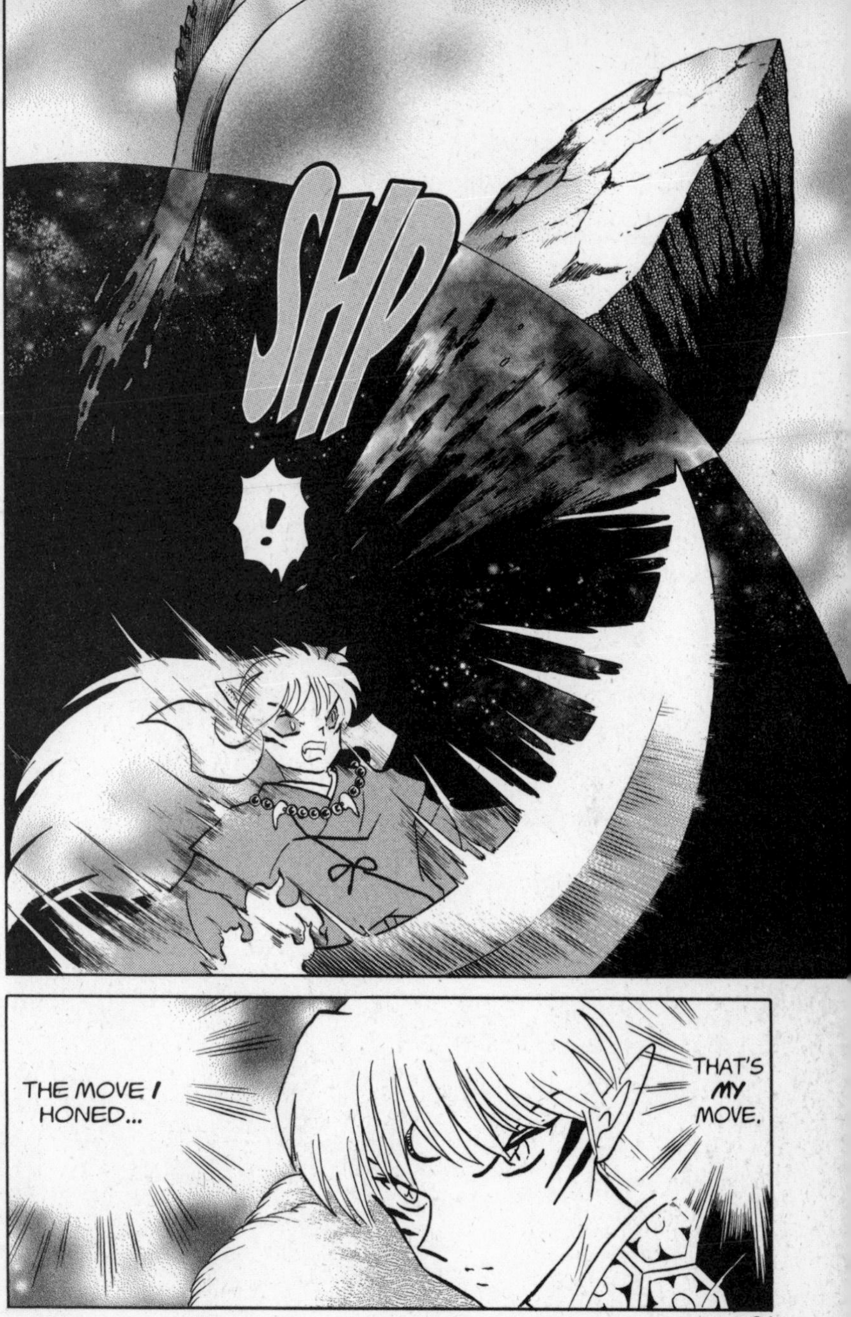
SHP
!
THAT'S MY MOVE.
THE MOVE I HONED...

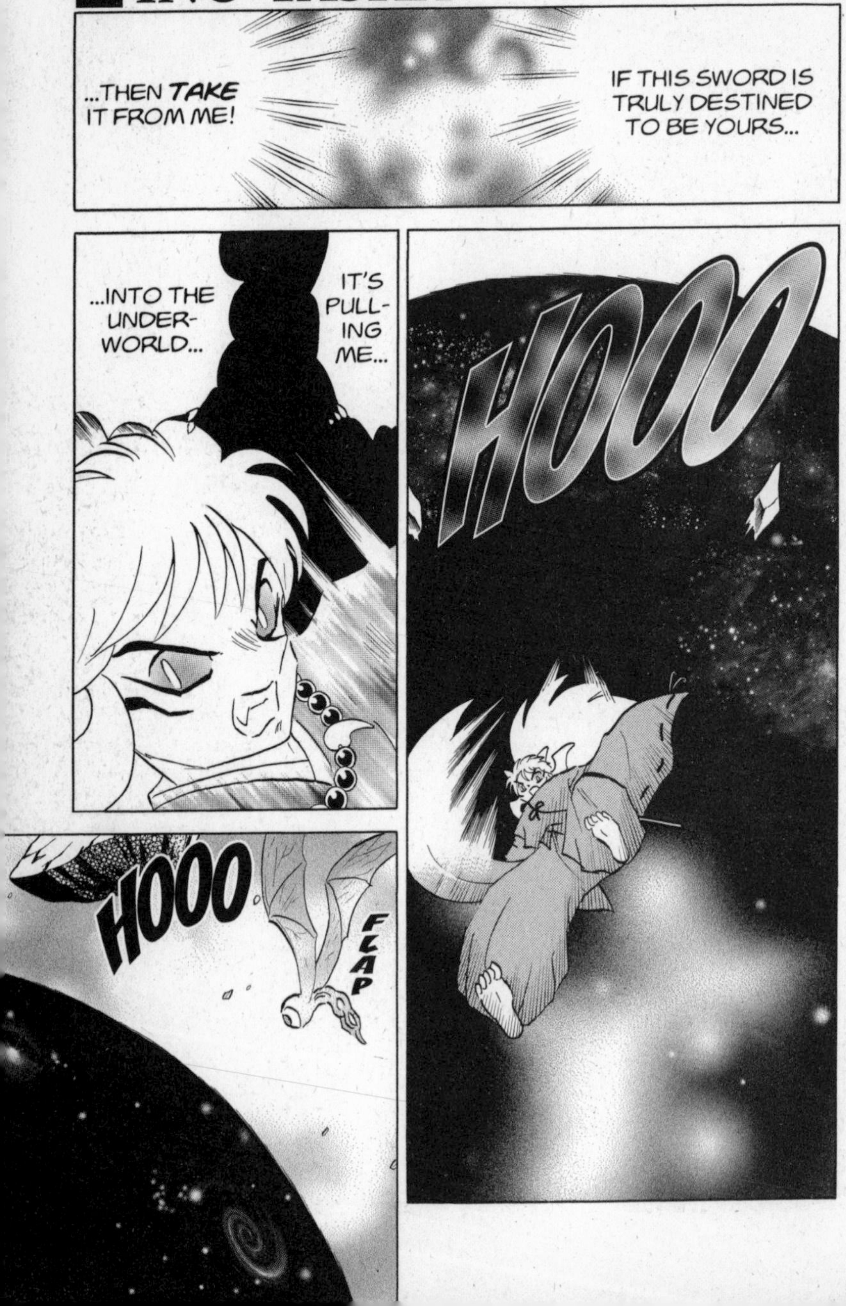
IF THIS SWORD IS TRULY DESTINED TO BE YOURS...
...THEN *TAKE* IT FROM ME!
HOOOO
IT'S PULL-ING ME...
...INTO THE UNDER-WORLD...
HOOO
FLAP

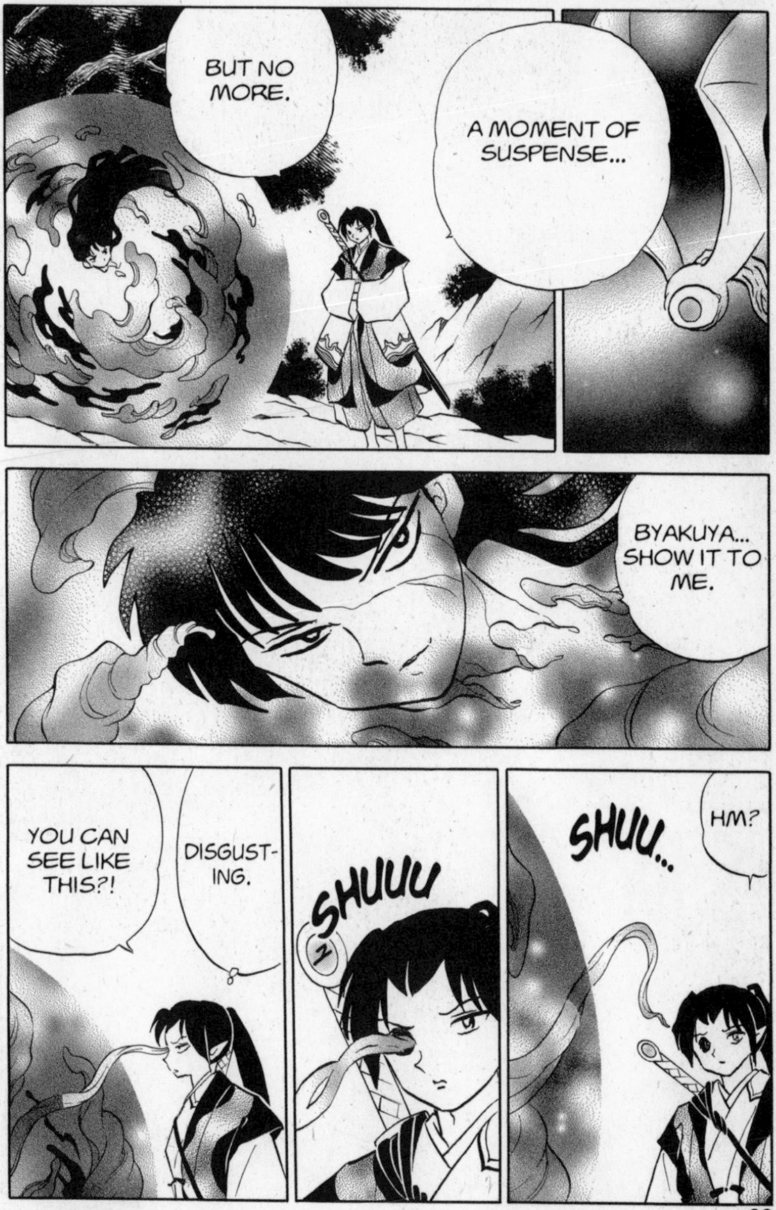
A MOMENT OF SUSPENSE...
BUT NO MORE.
BYAKUYA... SHOW IT TO ME.
HM?
SHUU...
SHUUU
DISGUST-ING.
YOU CAN SEE LIKE THIS?!

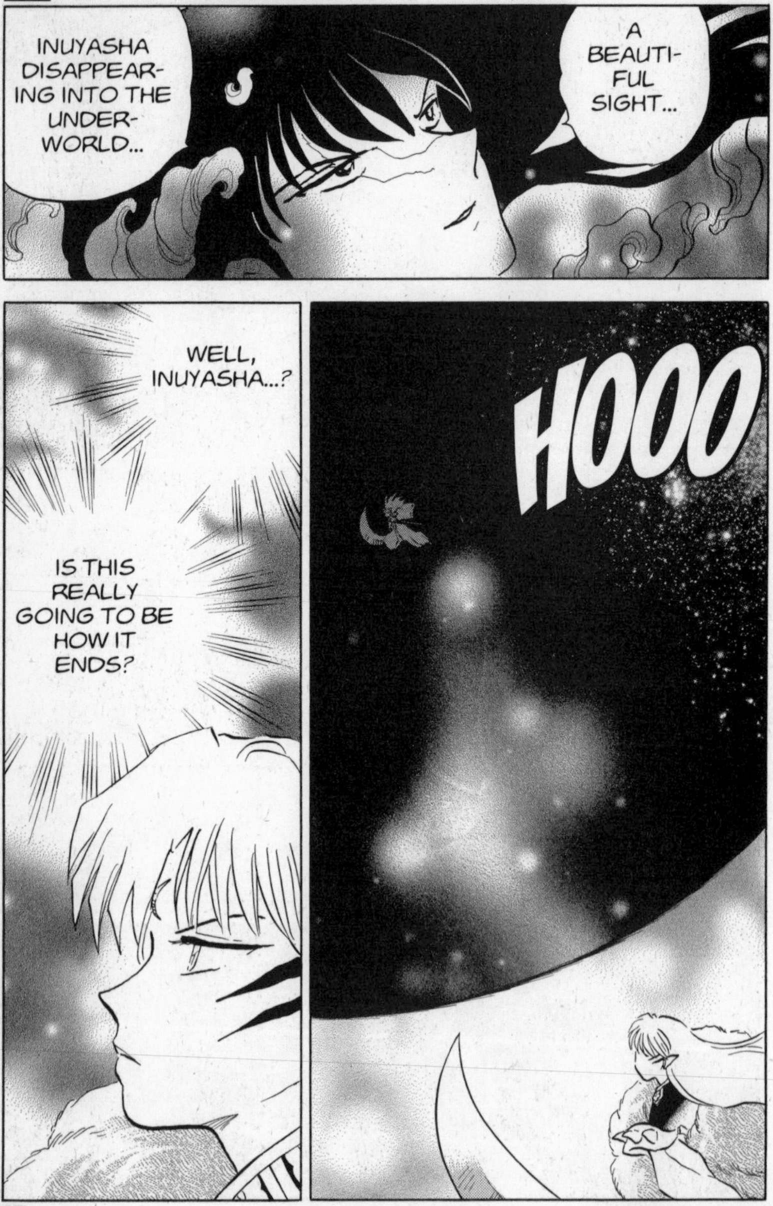
A BEAUTIFUL SIGHT...
INUYASHA DISAPPEARING INTO THE UNDERWORLD...
HOOO
WELL, INUYASHA...?
IS THIS REALLY GOING TO BE HOW IT ENDS?

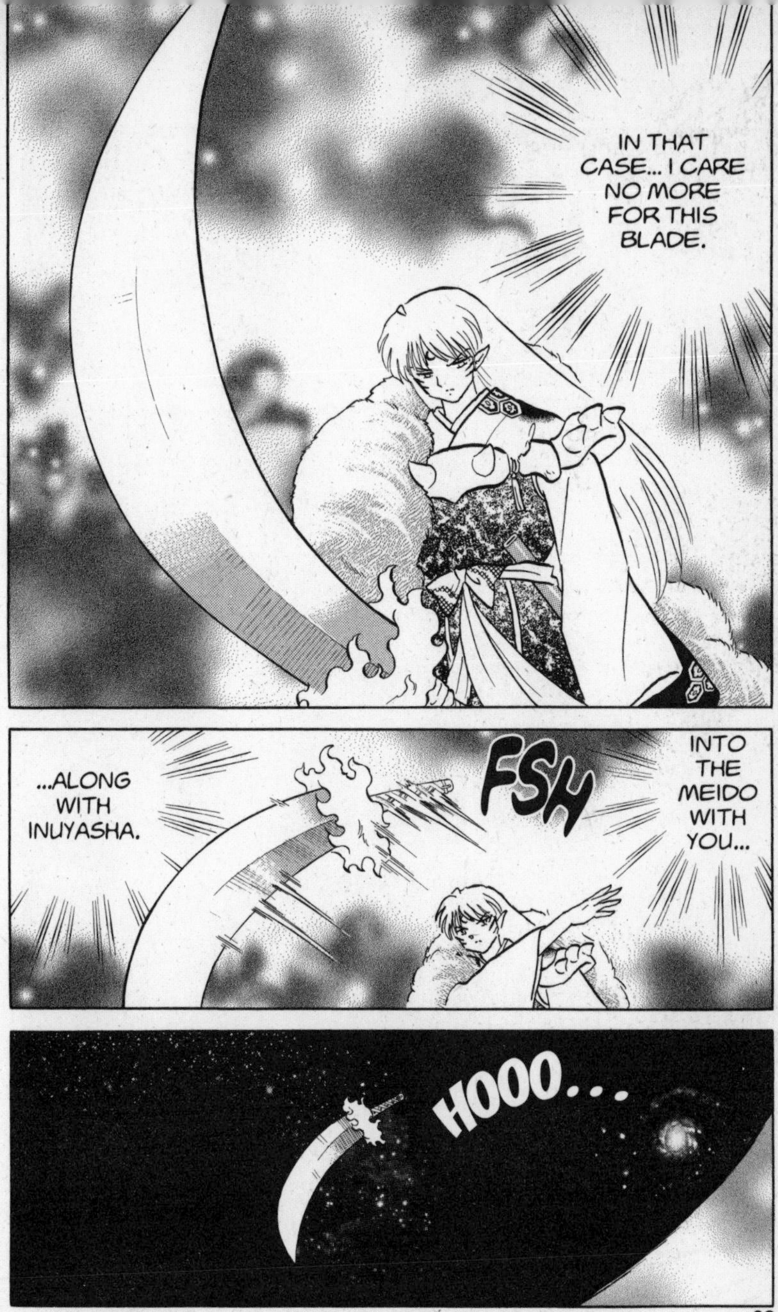
IN THAT CASE... I CARE NO MORE FOR THIS BLADE.
INTO THE MEIDO WITH YOU...
FSH
...ALONG WITH INUYASHA.
HOOO...

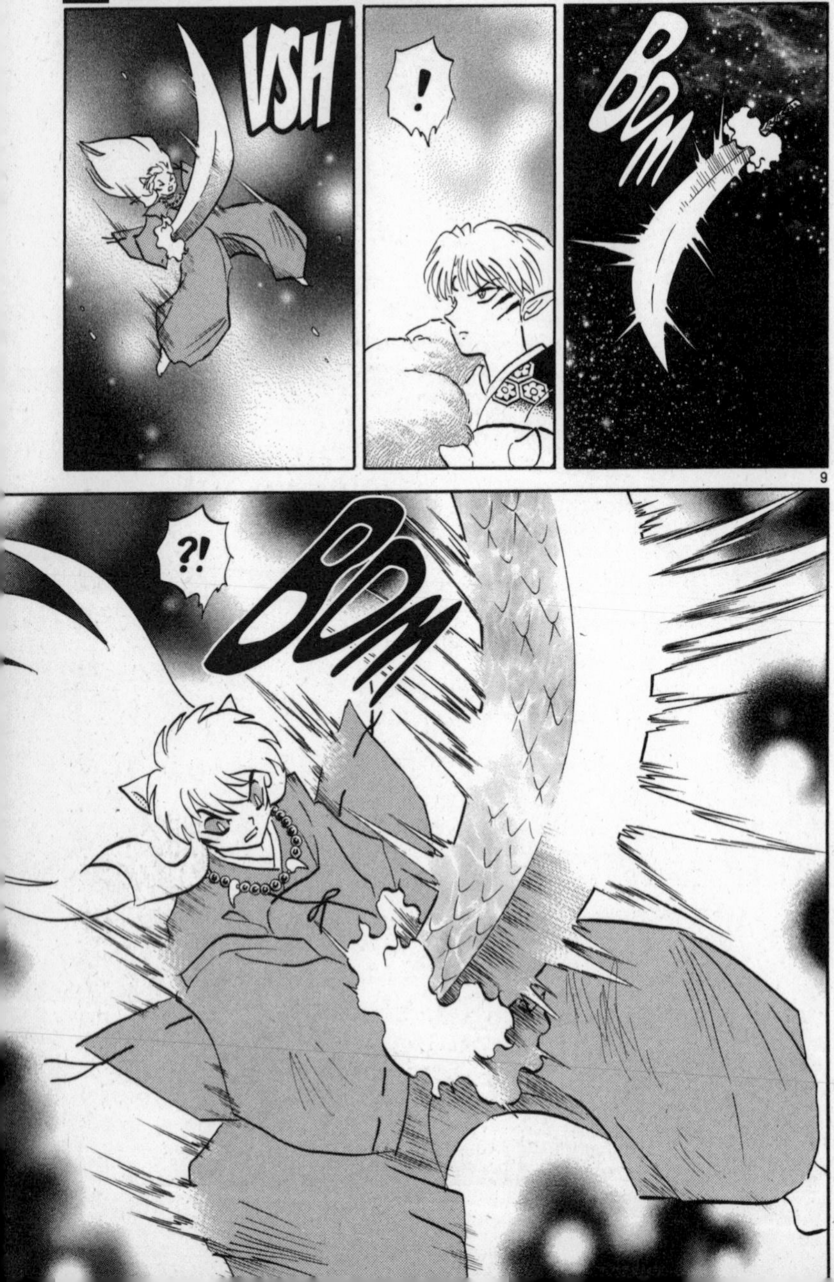
BOOM
!
VSH
?!
BOOM

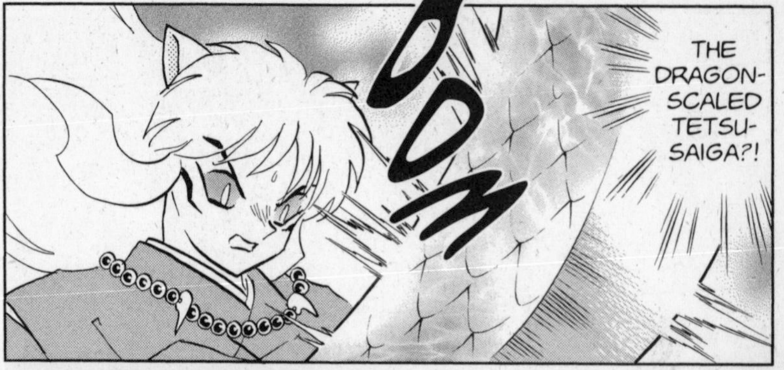
BDM
THE DRAGON-SCALED TETSU-SAIGA?!
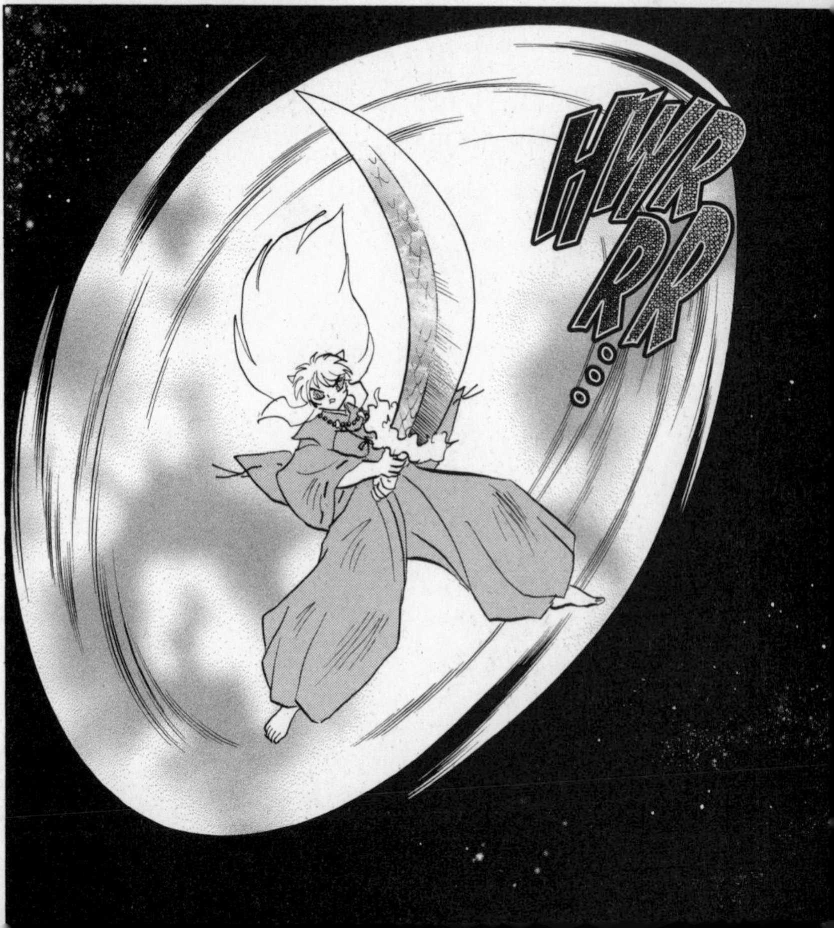
HWRRR...

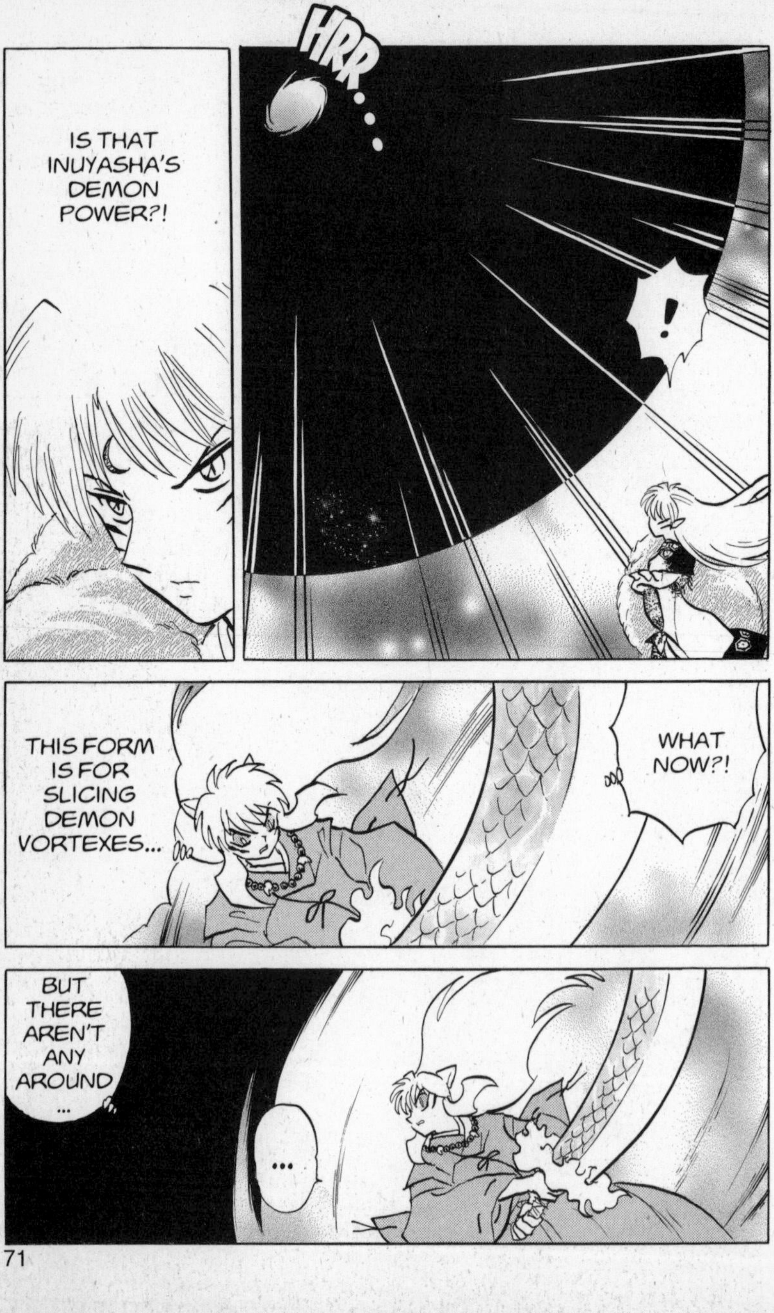
HRR
!
IS THAT INUYASHA'S DEMON POWER?!
WHAT NOW?!
THIS FORM IS FOR SLICING DEMON VORTEXES...
BUT THERE AREN'T ANY AROUND...
...

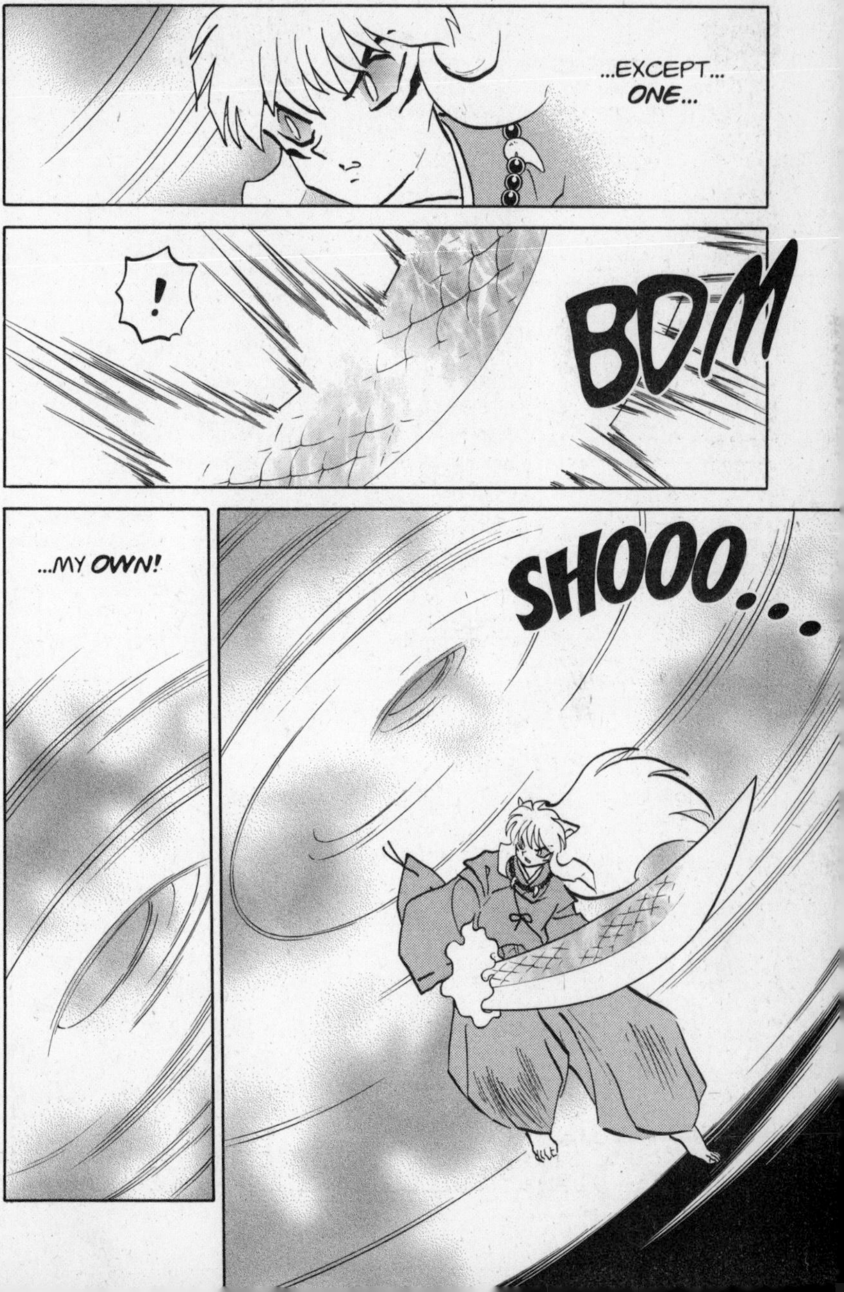
...EXCEPT... ONE...
!
BDM
SHOOO...
...MY OWN!

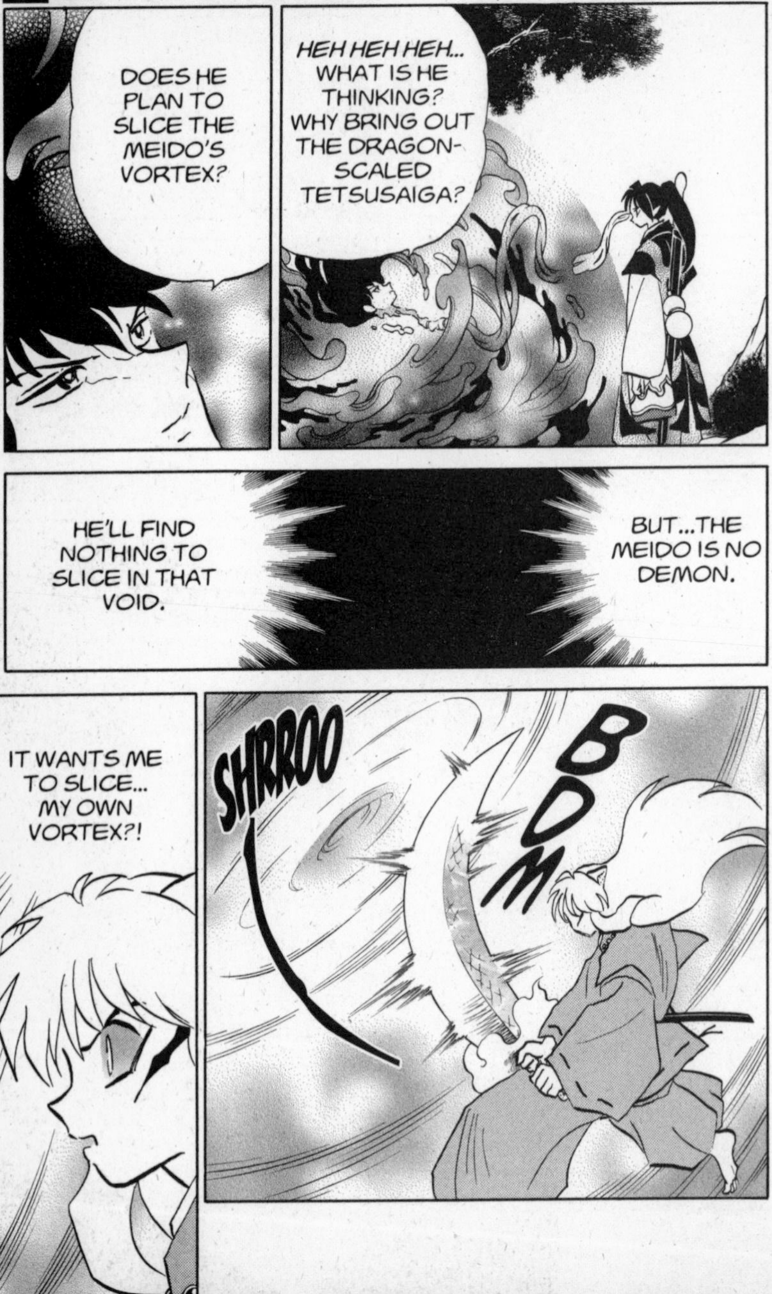
HEH HEH HEH... WHAT IS HE THINKING? WHY BRING OUT THE DRAGON-SCALED TETSUSAIGA?
DOES HE PLAN TO SLICE THE MEIDO'S VORTEX?
BUT...THE MEIDO IS NO DEMON.
HE'LL FIND NOTHING TO SLICE IN THAT VOID.
BDM
SHRROO
IT WANTS ME TO SLICE... MY OWN VORTEX?!

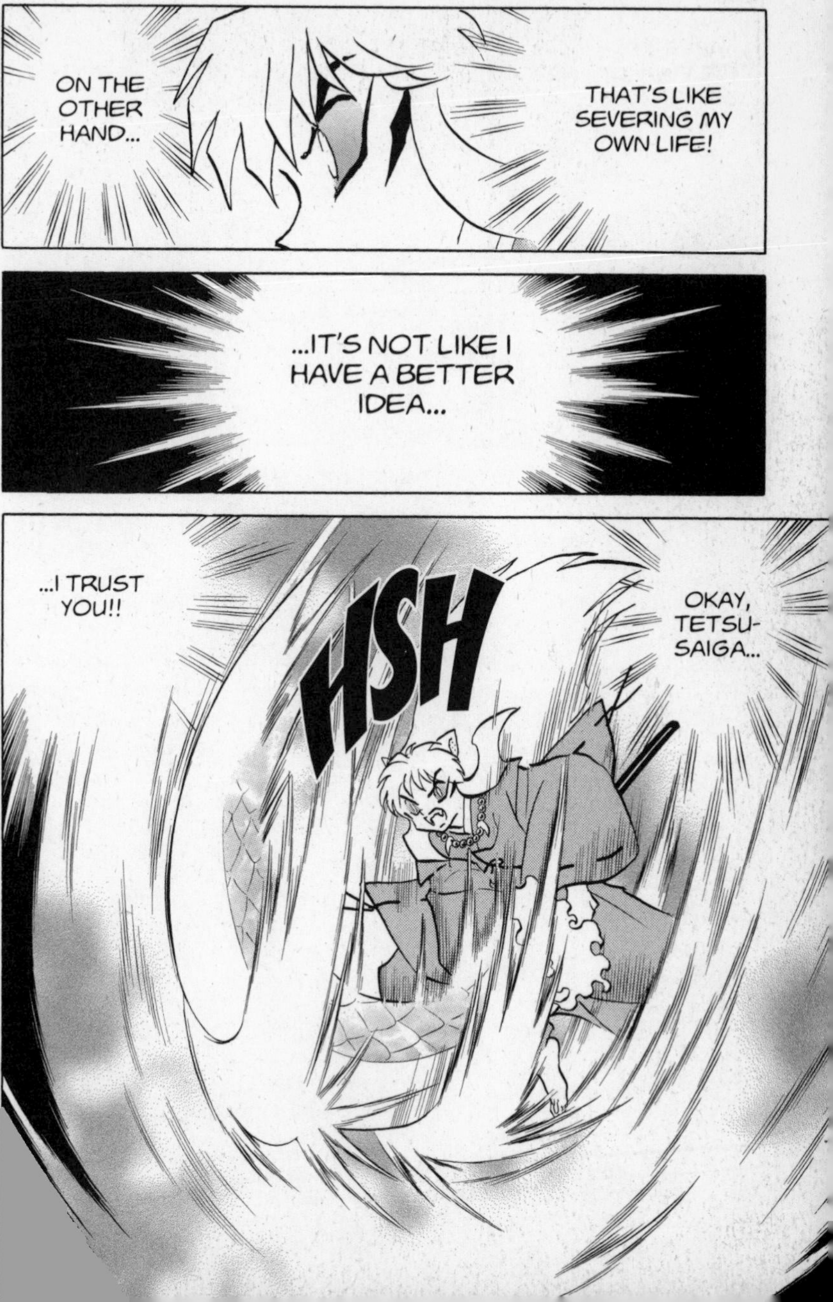
THAT'S LIKE SEVERING MY OWN LIFE!
ON THE OTHER HAND...
...IT'S NOT LIKE I HAVE A BETTER IDEA...
OKAY, TETSU-SAIGA...
HSH
...I TRUST YOU!!

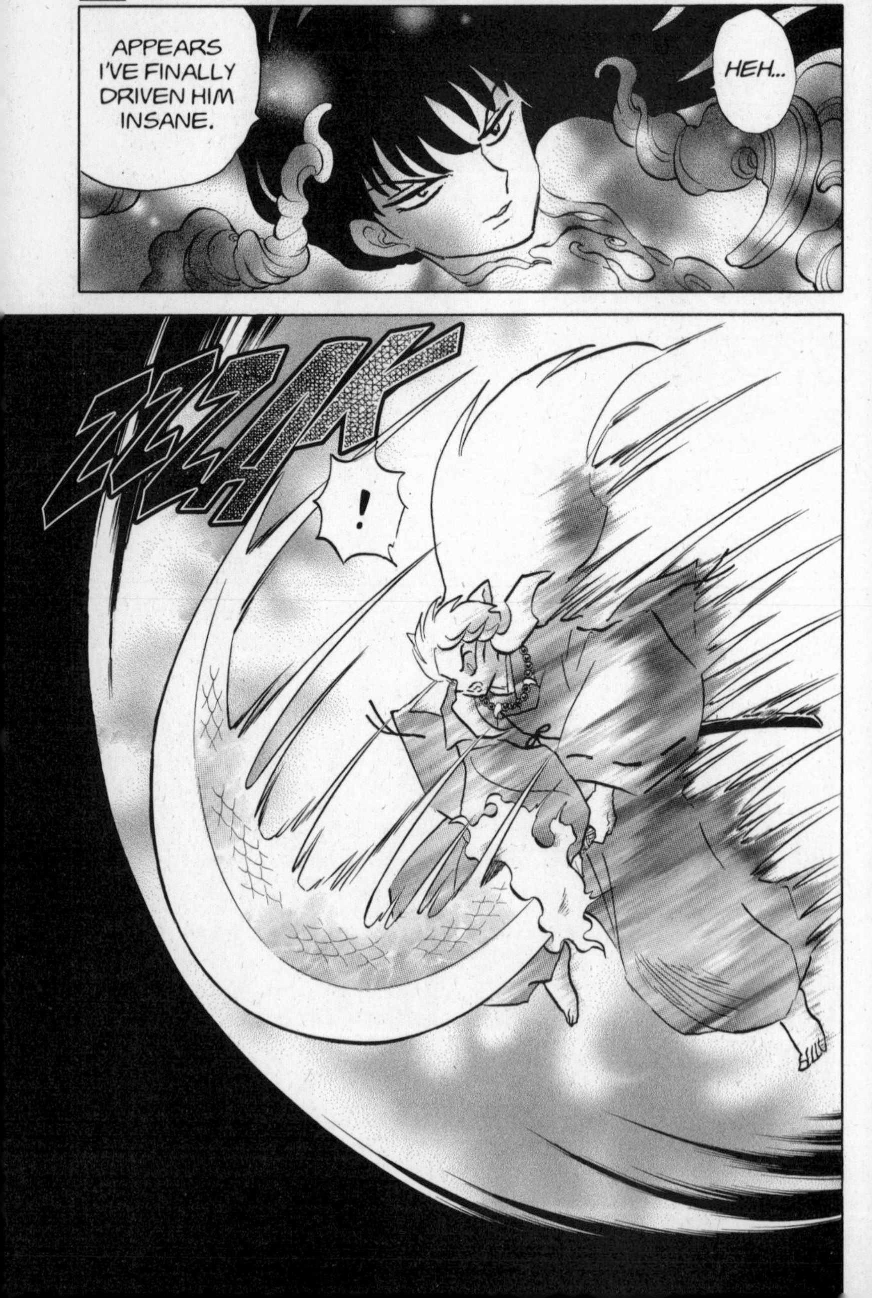
HEH...
APPEARS I'VE FINALLY DRIVEN HIM INSANE.
!

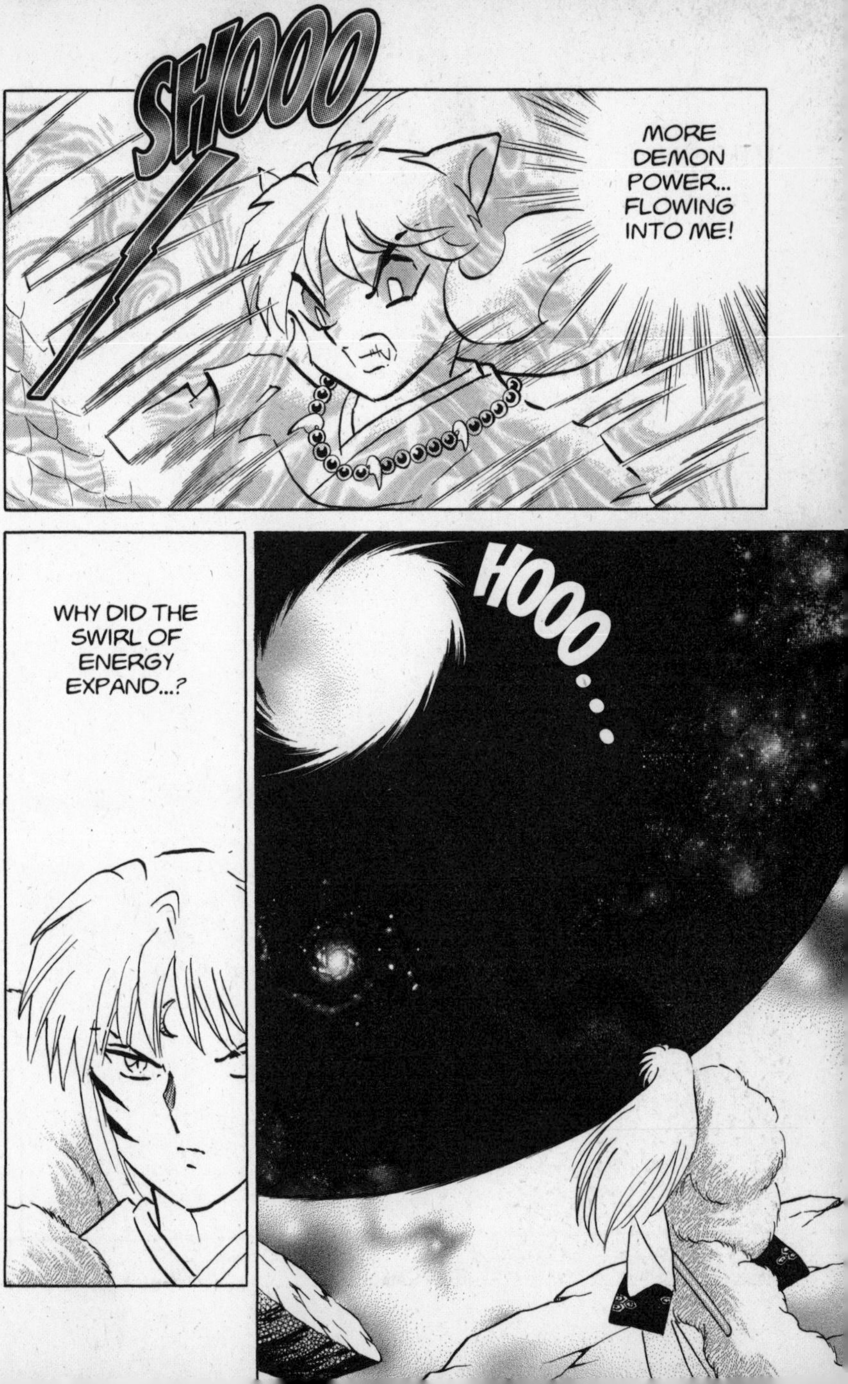
SHOOO
MORE DEMON POWER... FLOWING INTO ME!
HOOO...
WHY DID THE SWIRL OF ENERGY EXPAND...?

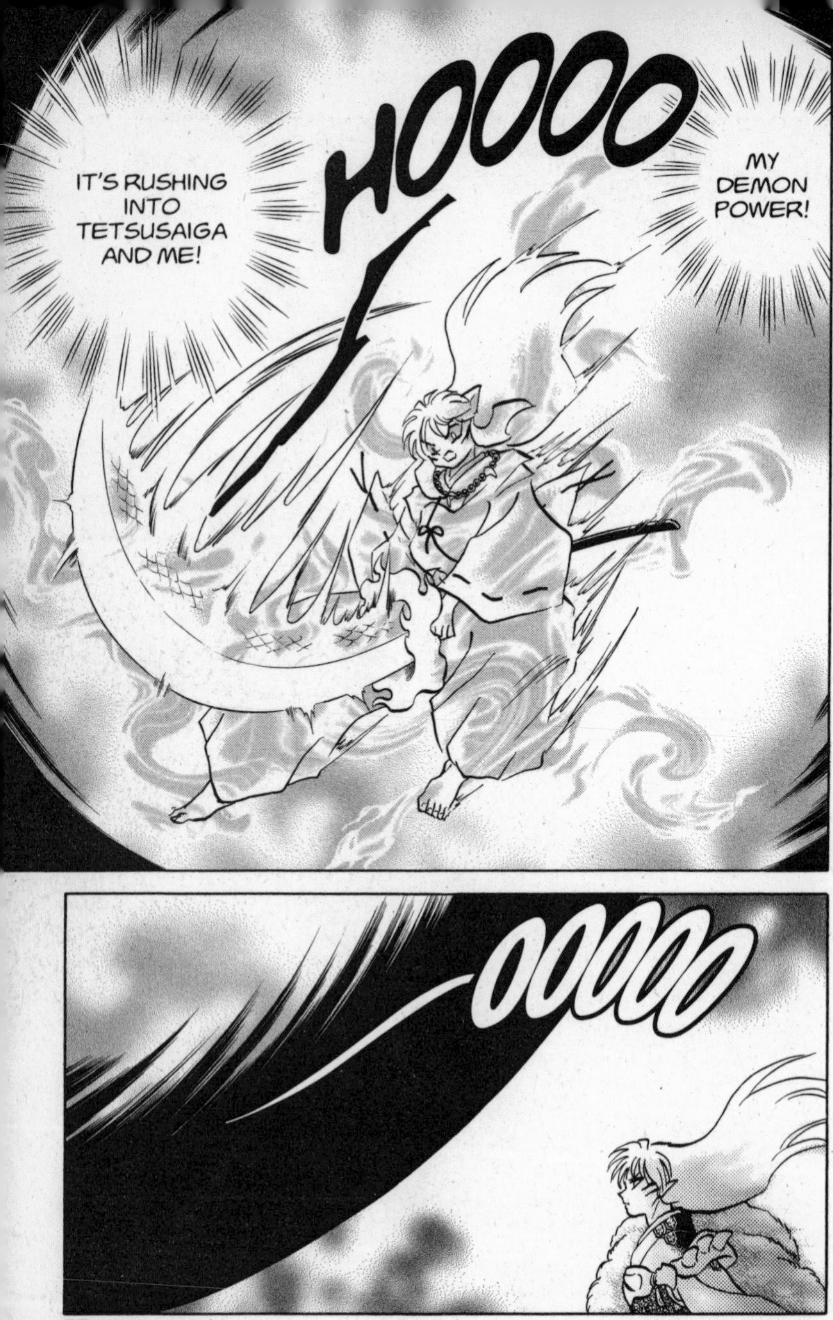
MY DEMON POWER!
HOOOO
IT'S RUSHING INTO TETSUSAIGA AND ME!
OOOOO

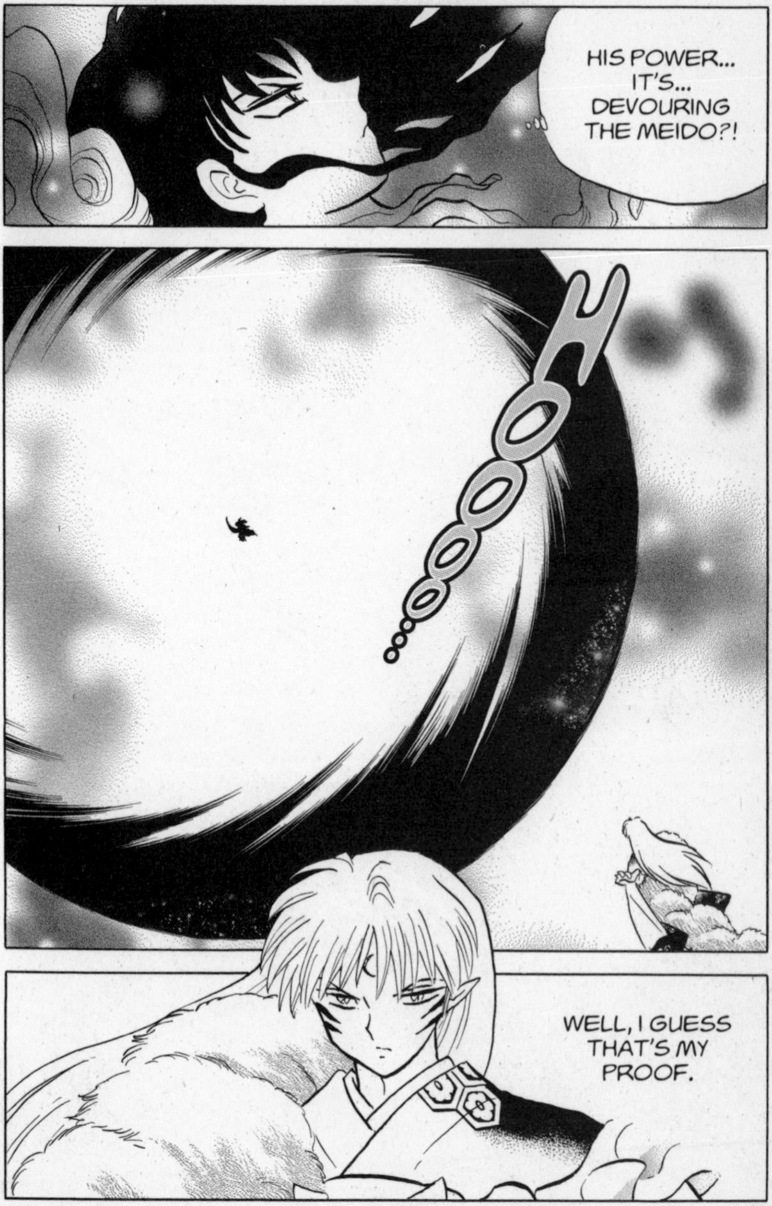
HIS POWER... IT'S... DEVOURING THE MEIDO?!
HOOOOOO...
WELL, I GUESS THAT'S MY PROOF.

SCROLL 5
THE BLACK BLADE

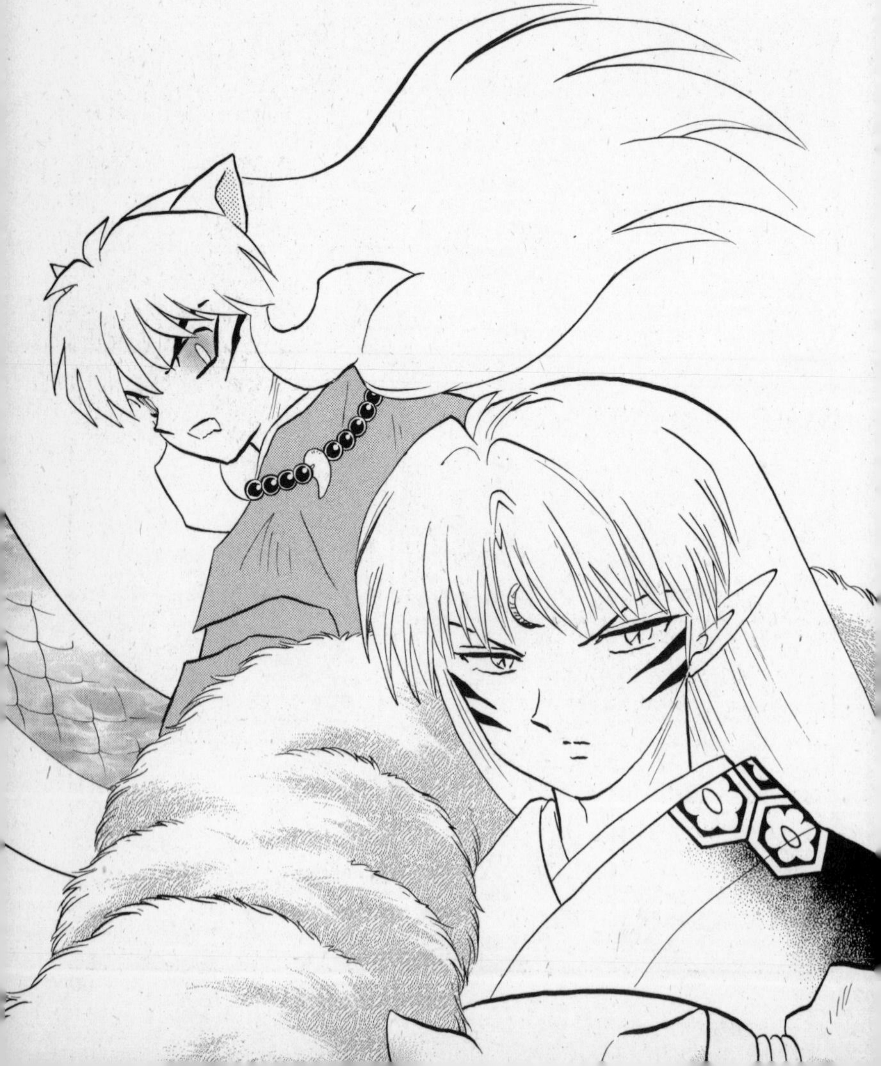

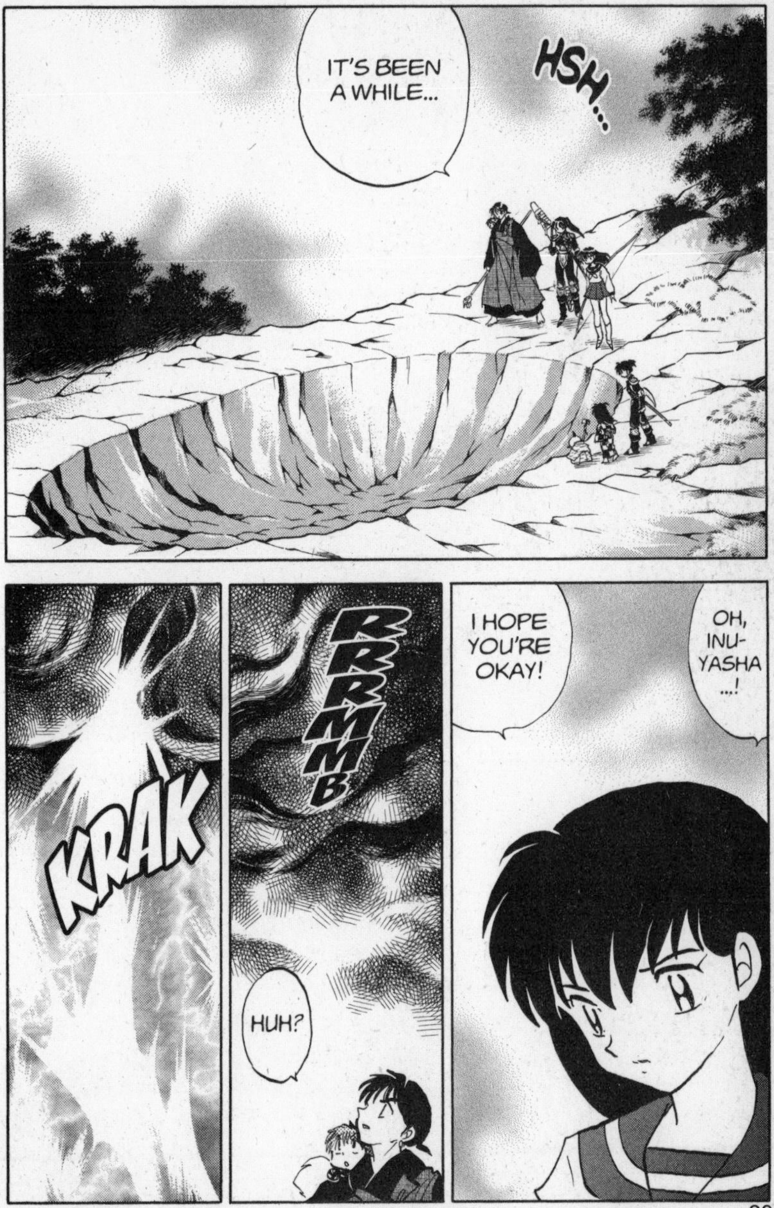
IT'S BEEN A WHILE...
HSH...
OH, INU-YASHA ...!
I HOPE YOU'RE OKAY!
RRRMMB
HUH?
KRAK

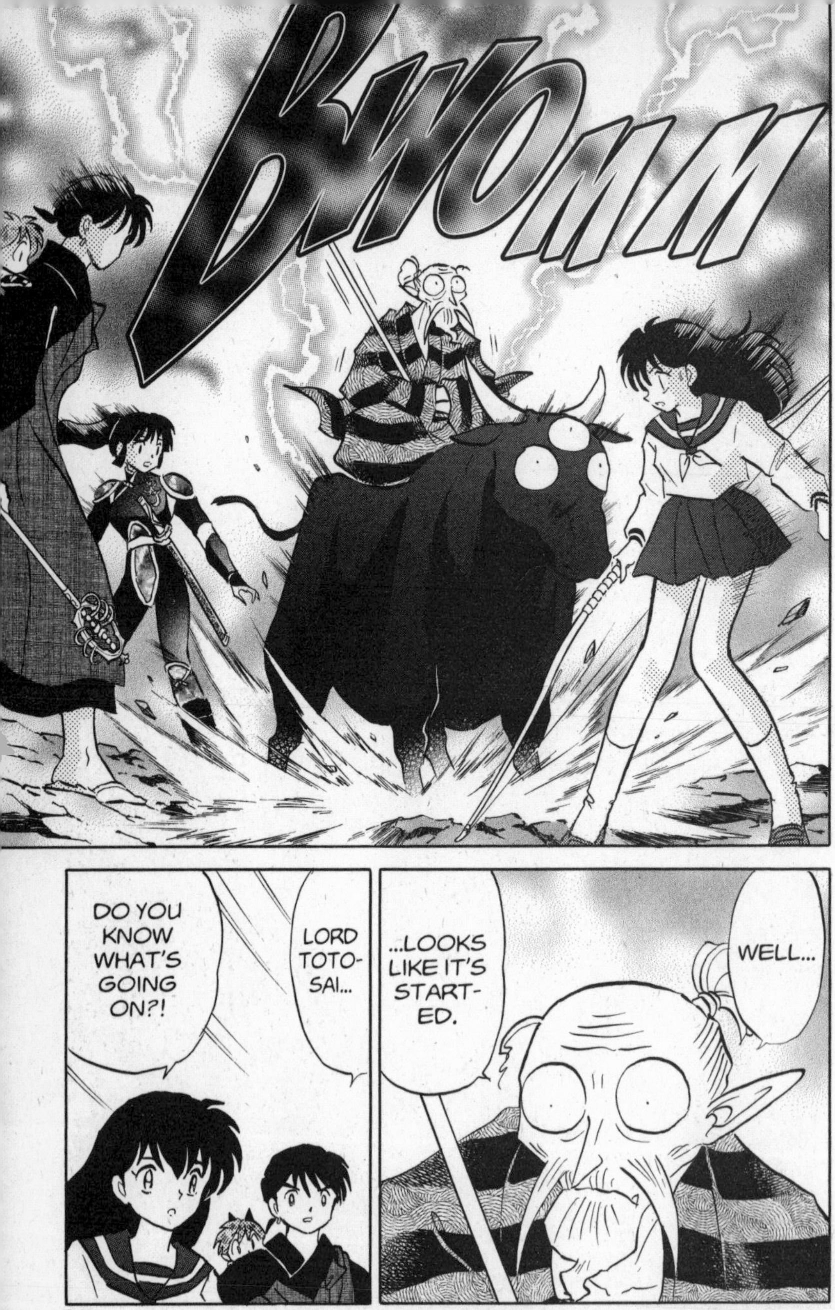
BWOMM
WELL...
...LOOKS LIKE IT'S START-ED.
LORD TOTO-SAI...
DO YOU KNOW WHAT'S GOING ON?!

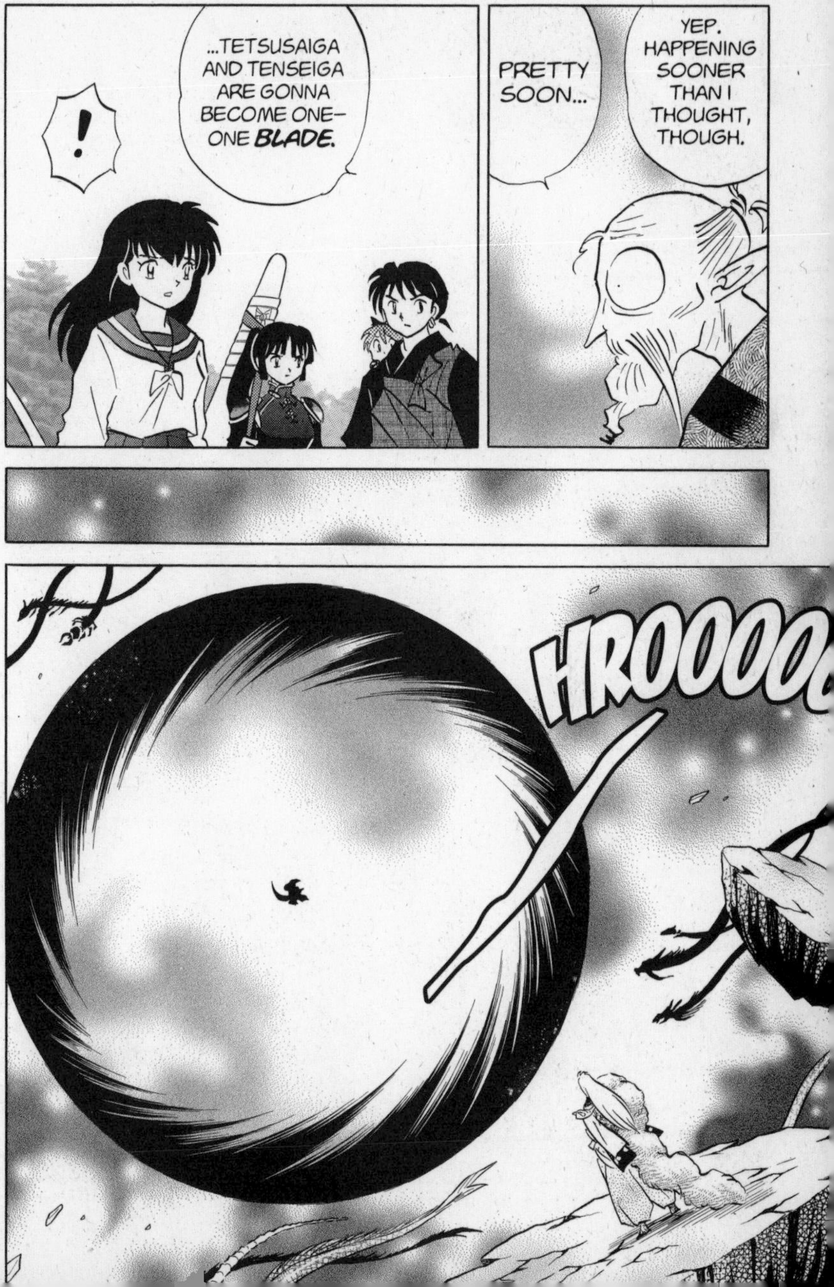
YEP. HAPPENING SOONER THAN I THOUGHT, THOUGH.
PRETTY SOON...
...TETSUSAIGA AND TENSEIGA ARE GONNA BECOME ONE– ONE **BLADE.**
!
HROOOO

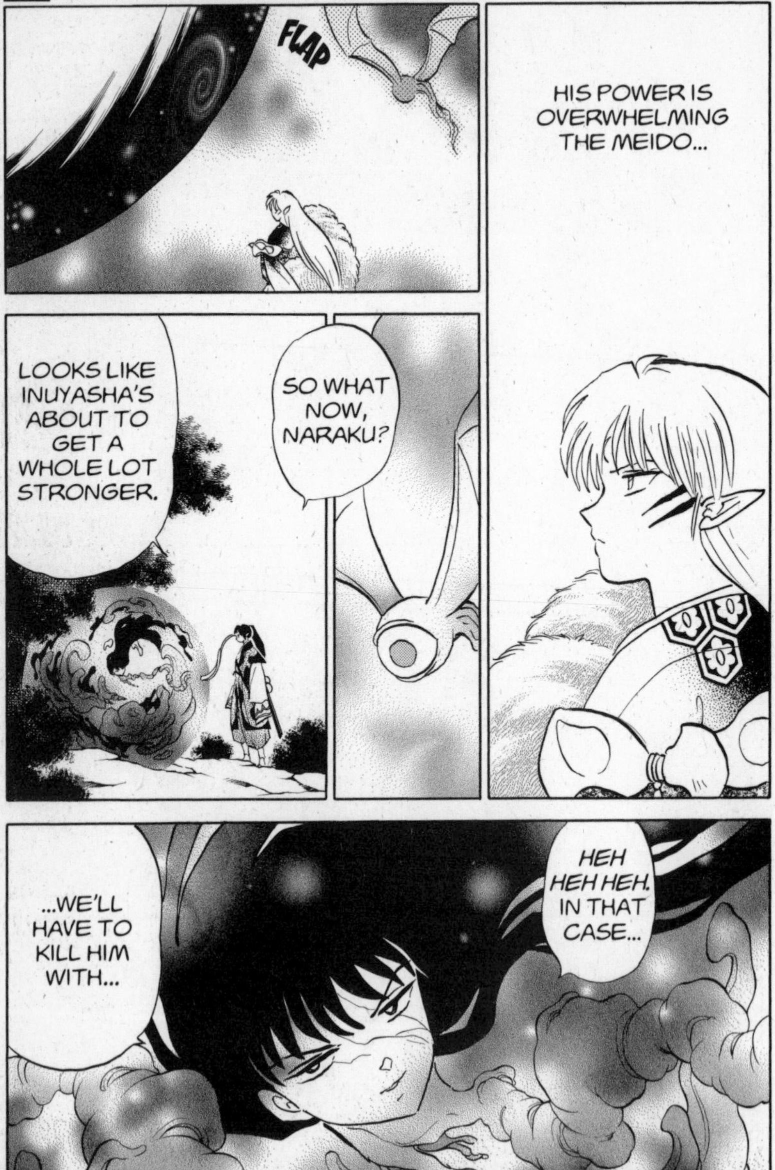
HIS POWER IS OVERWHELMING THE MEIDO...
FLAP
SO WHAT NOW, NARAKU?
LOOKS LIKE INUYASHA'S ABOUT TO GET A WHOLE LOT STRONGER.
HEH HEH HEH. IN THAT CASE...
...WE'LL HAVE TO KILL HIM WITH...

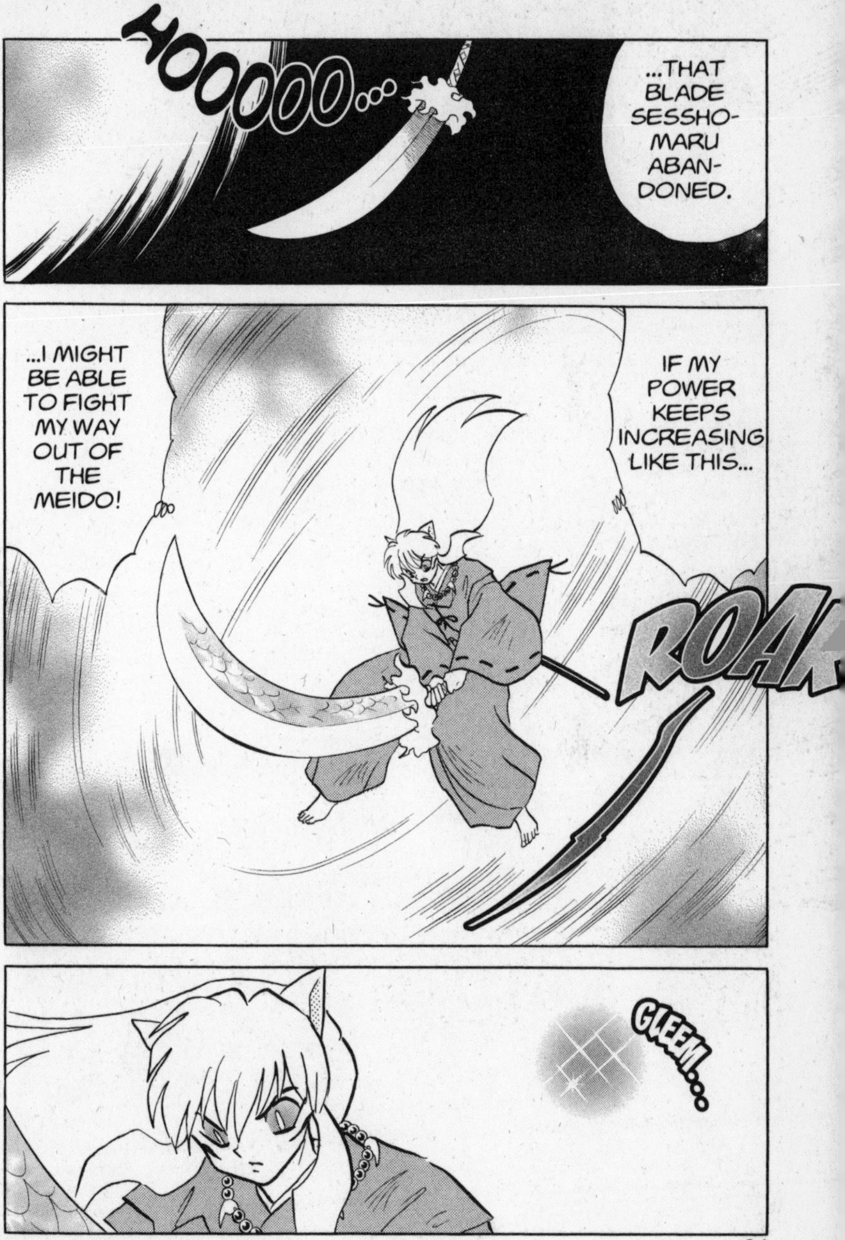
...THAT BLADE SESSHOMARU ABANDONED.
HOOOOO...
IF MY POWER KEEPS INCREASING LIKE THIS...
ROAR
...I MIGHT BE ABLE TO FIGHT MY WAY OUT OF THE MEIDO!
GLEEM...

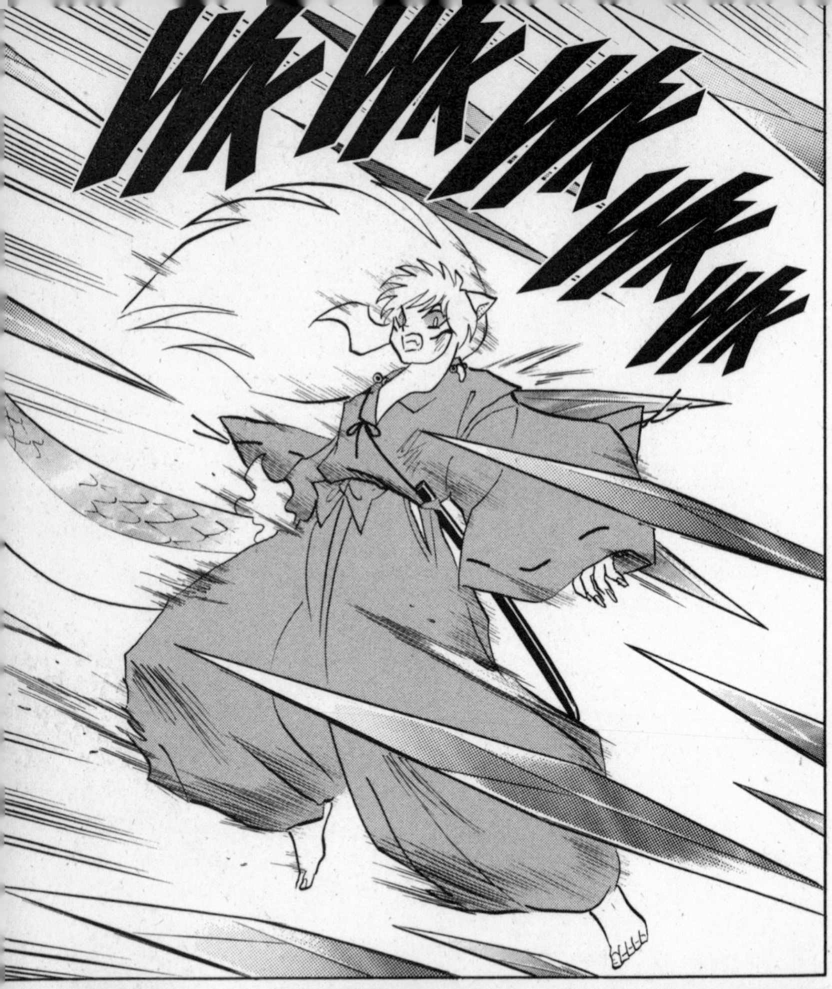
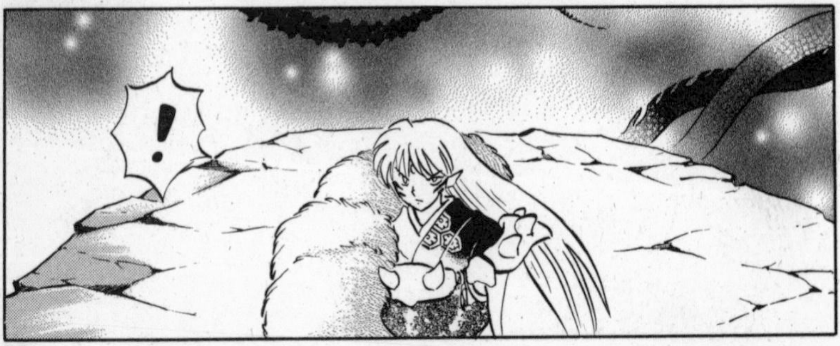
!

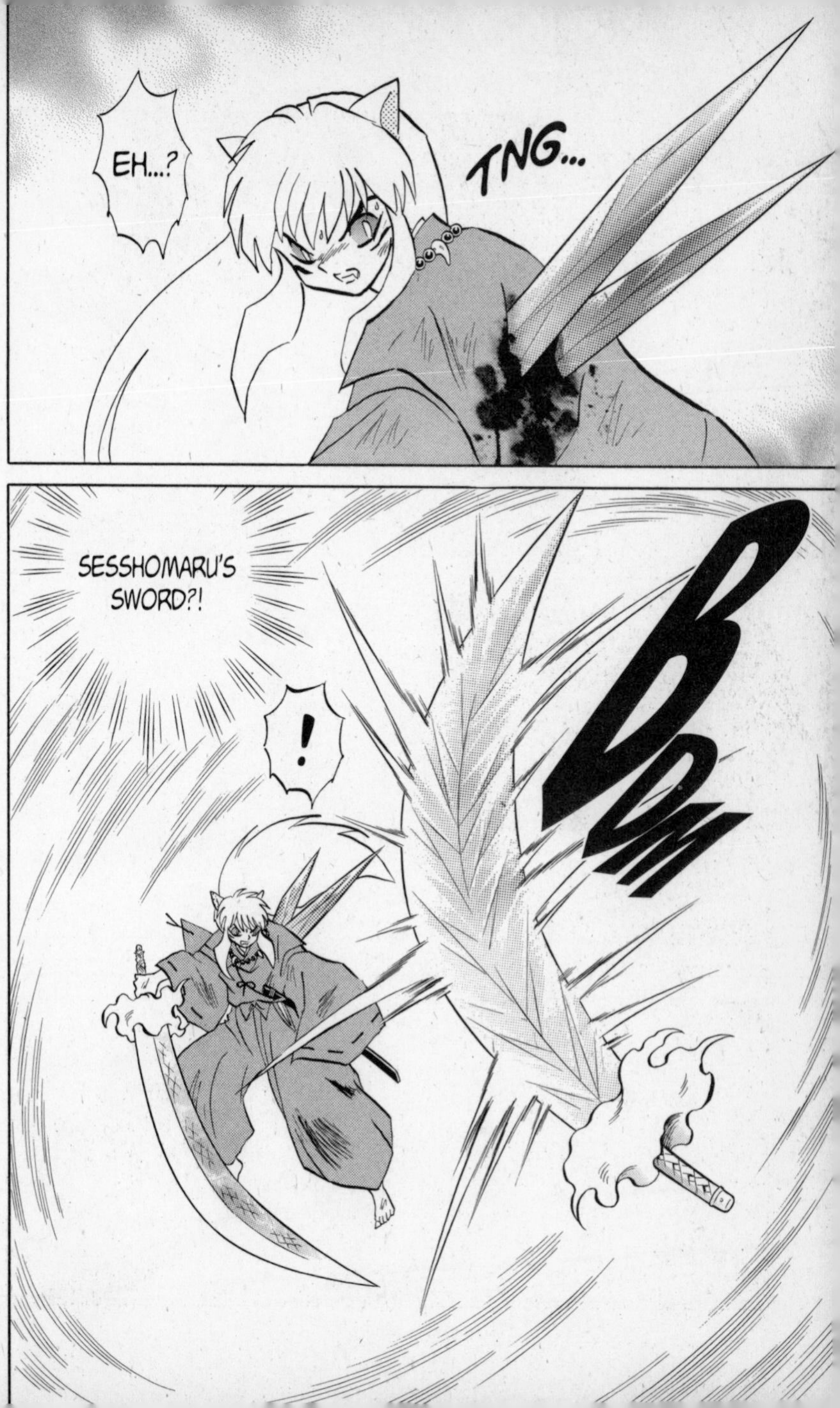
TNG...
EH...?
SESSHOMARU'S SWORD?!
!
BOOM

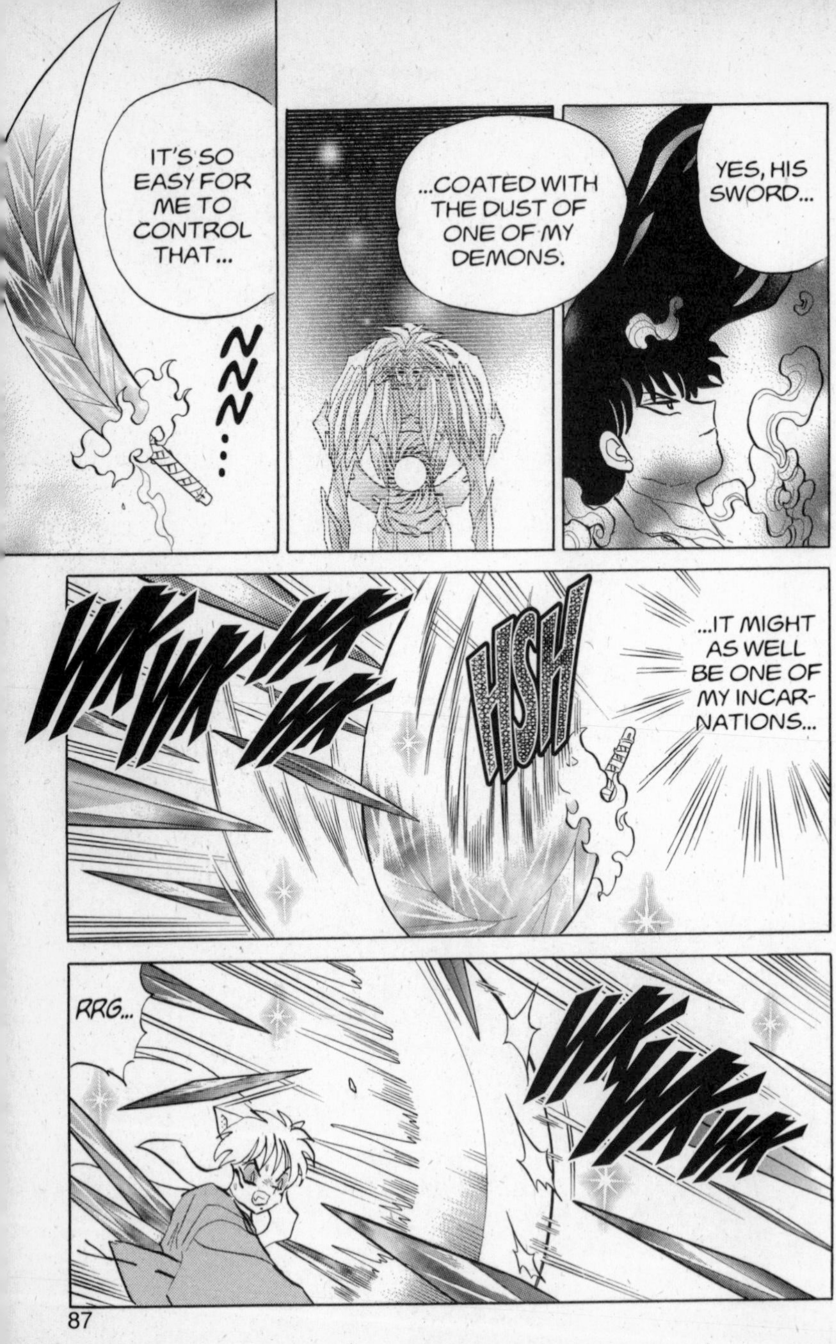
YES, HIS SWORD...
...COATED WITH THE DUST OF ONE OF MY DEMONS.
IT'S SO EASY FOR ME TO CONTROL THAT...
NNN...
...IT MIGHT AS WELL BE ONE OF MY INCARNATIONS...
HSH
WKWKWK
WKWK
WKWKWK
RRG...

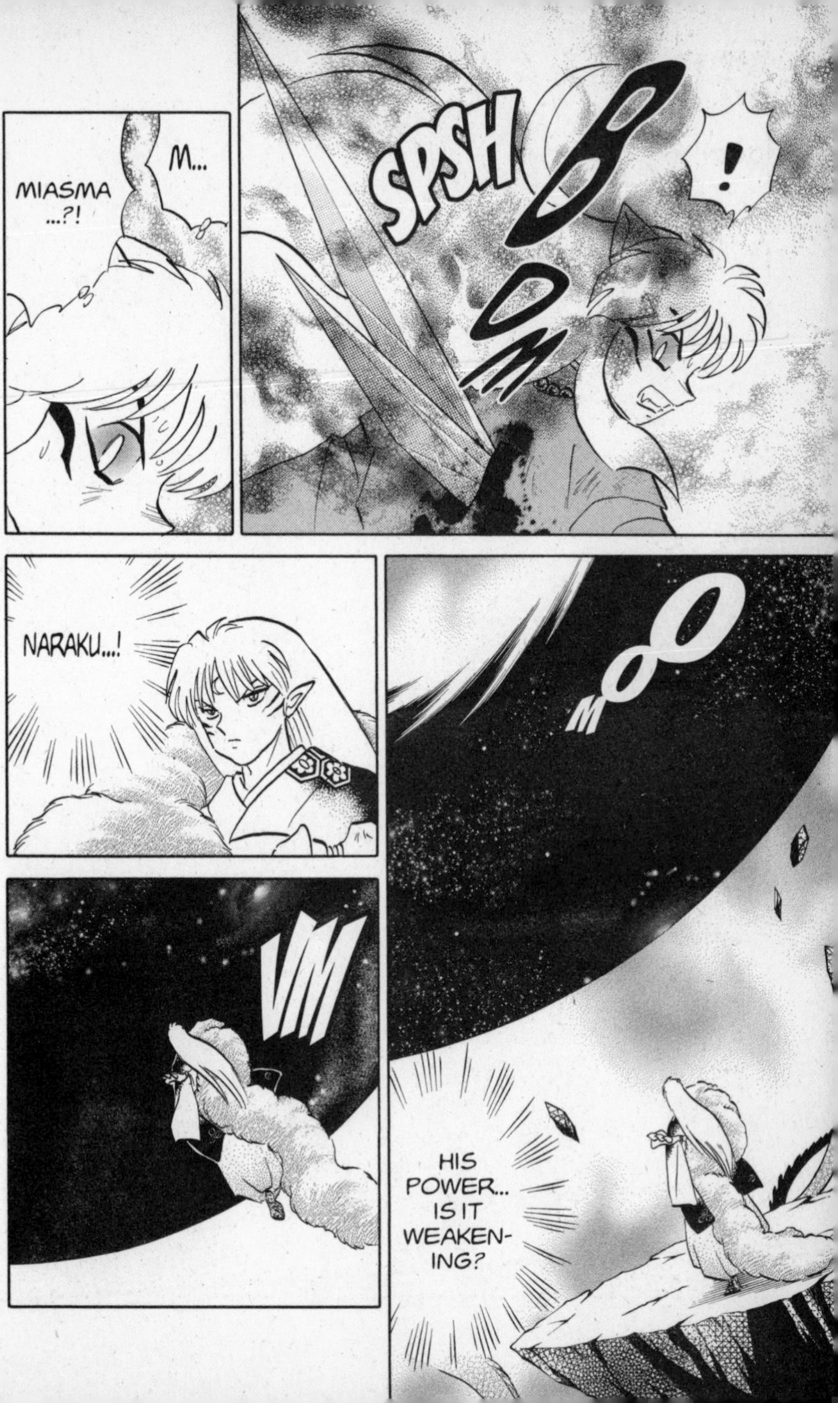
SPSH
BOM
!
M...
MIASMA ...?!
MOO
HIS POWER... IS IT WEAKENING?
NARAKU...!
VM

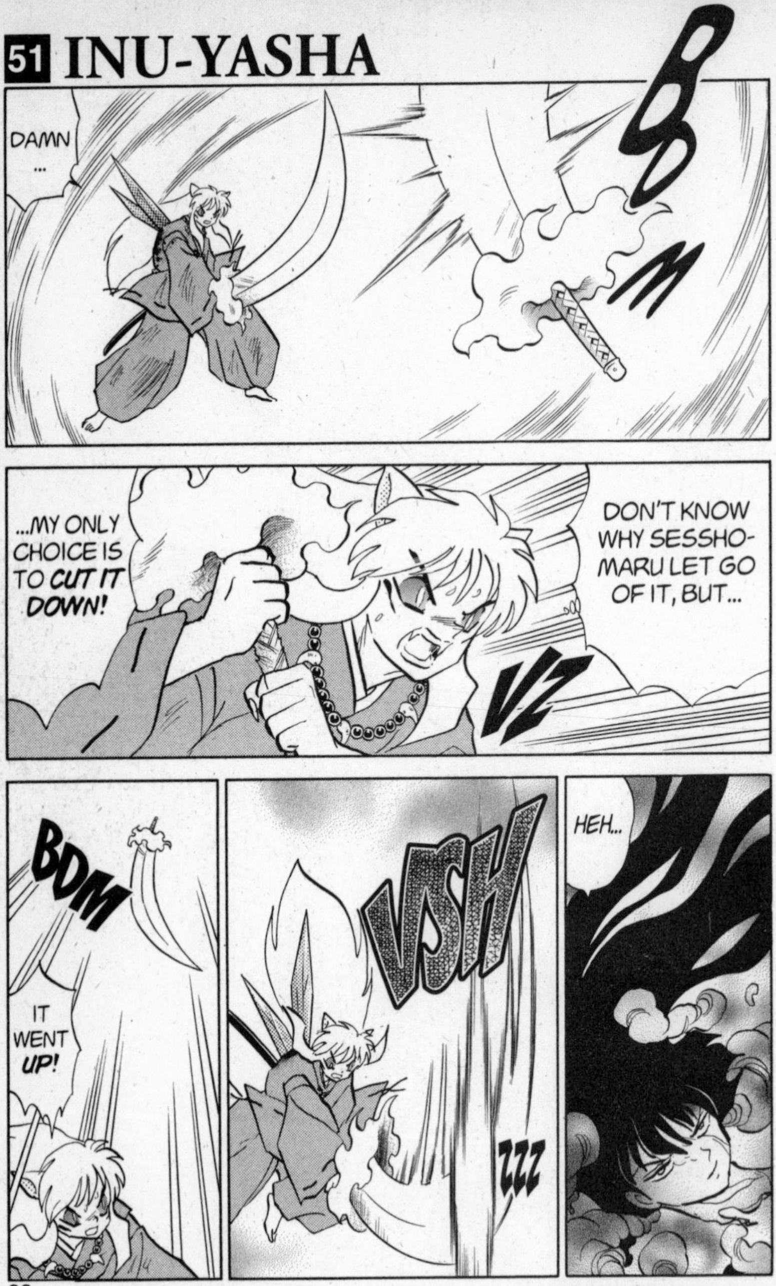
BOOM
DAMN ...
DON'T KNOW WHY SESSHO-MARU LET GO OF IT, BUT...
...MY ONLY CHOICE IS TO **CUT IT DOWN!**
VZ
HEH...
VSH
ZZZ
BDM
IT WENT **UP!**

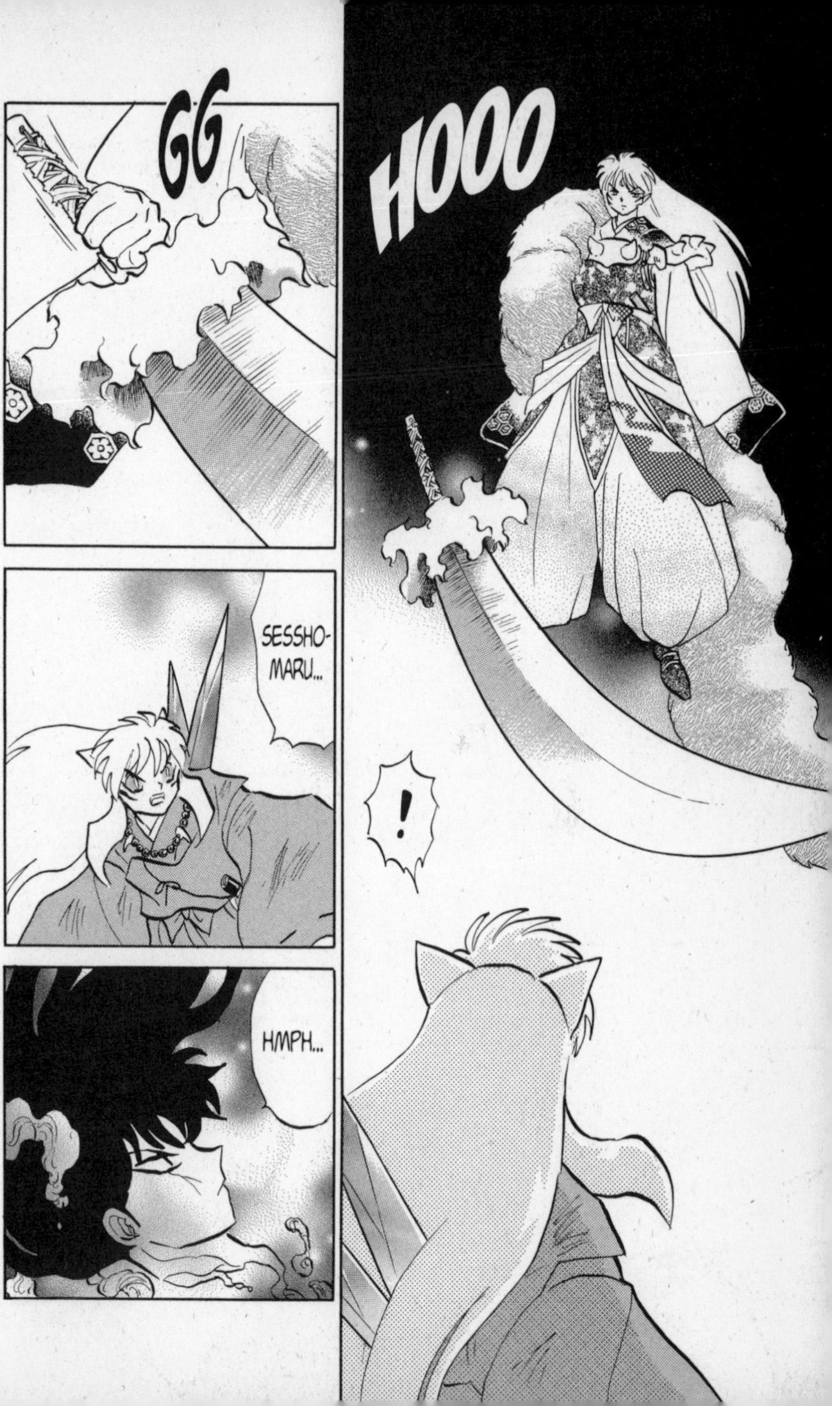
HOOO
!
GG
SESSHO-MARU...
HMPH...

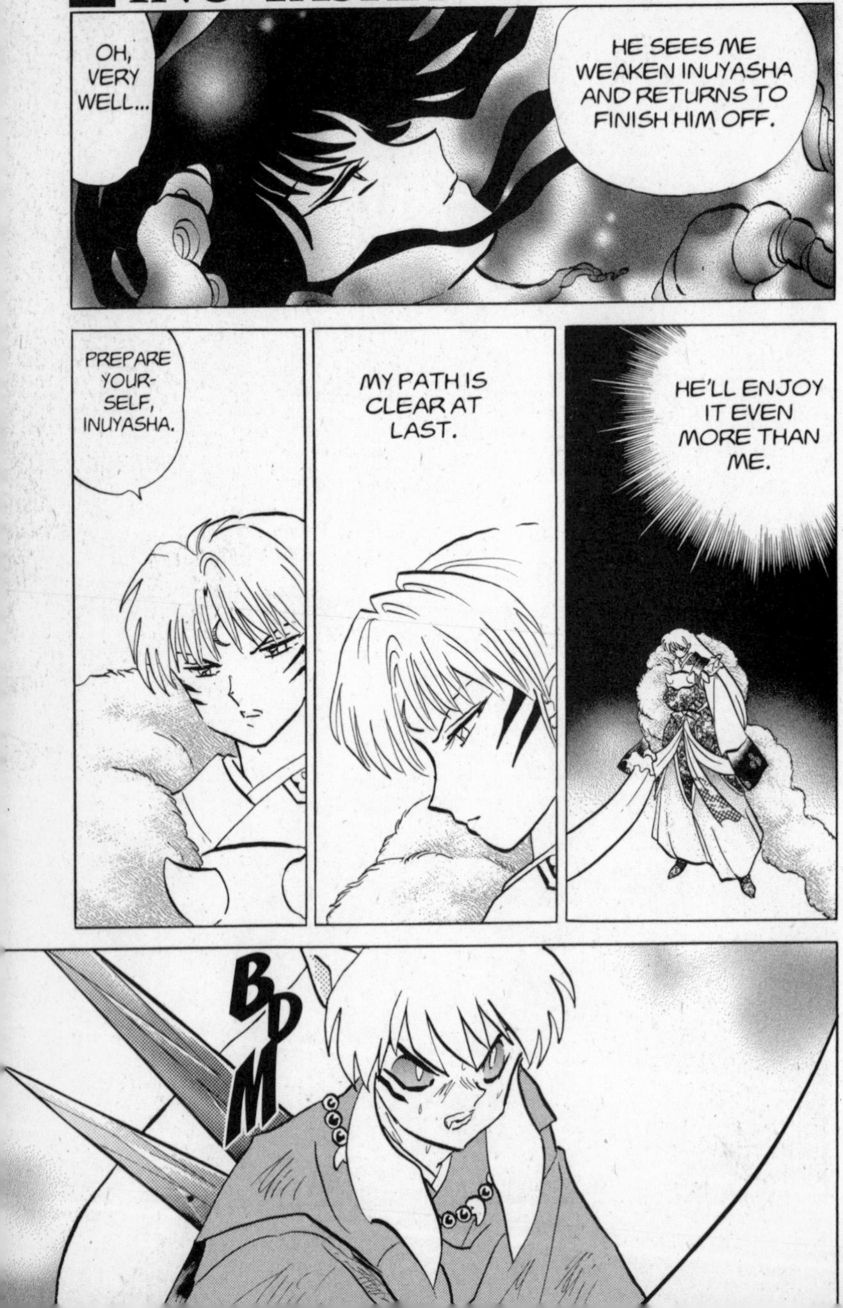
HE SEES ME WEAKEN INUYASHA AND RETURNS TO FINISH HIM OFF.
OH, VERY WELL...
HE'LL ENJOY IT EVEN MORE THAN ME.
MY PATH IS CLEAR AT LAST.
PREPARE YOUR-SELF, INUYASHA.
BDM

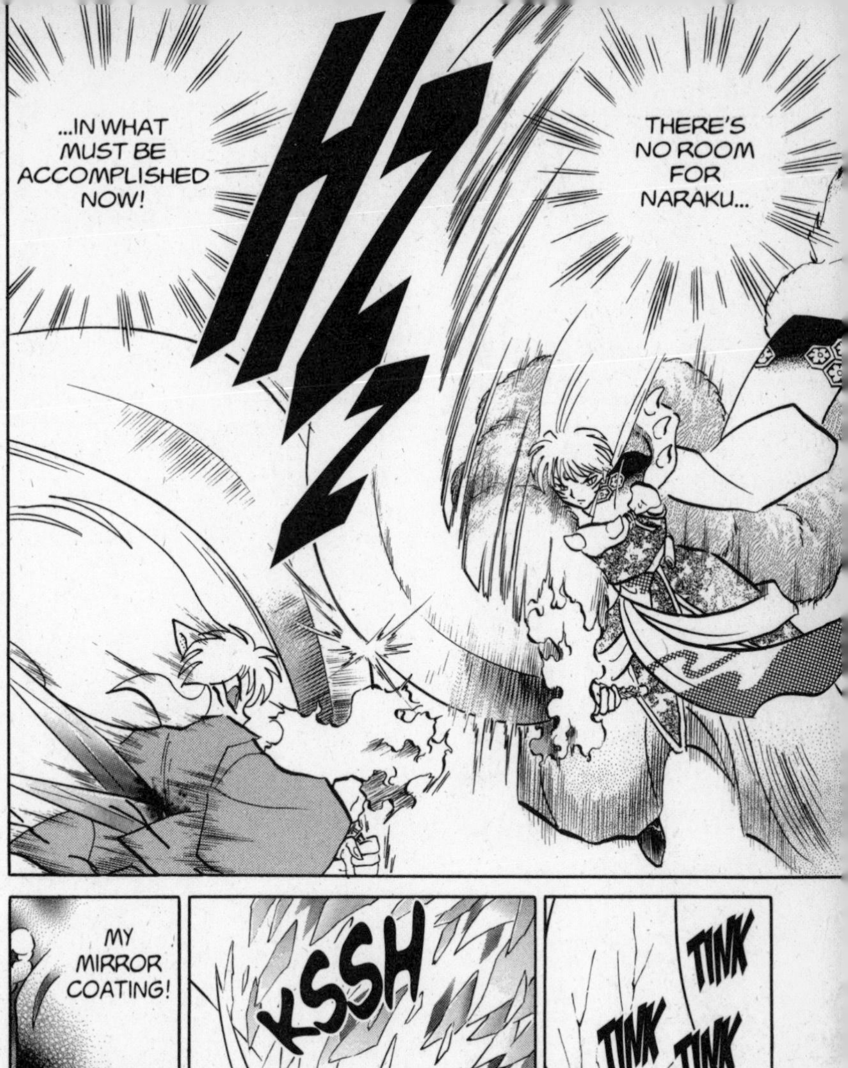
THERE'S NO ROOM FOR NARAKU...
...IN WHAT MUST BE ACCOMPLISHED NOW!
TINK
TINK
TINK
TINK
KSSH
MY MIRROR COATING!

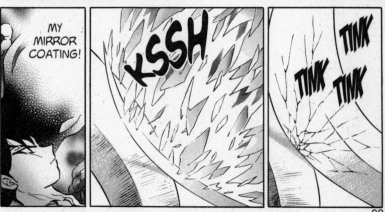

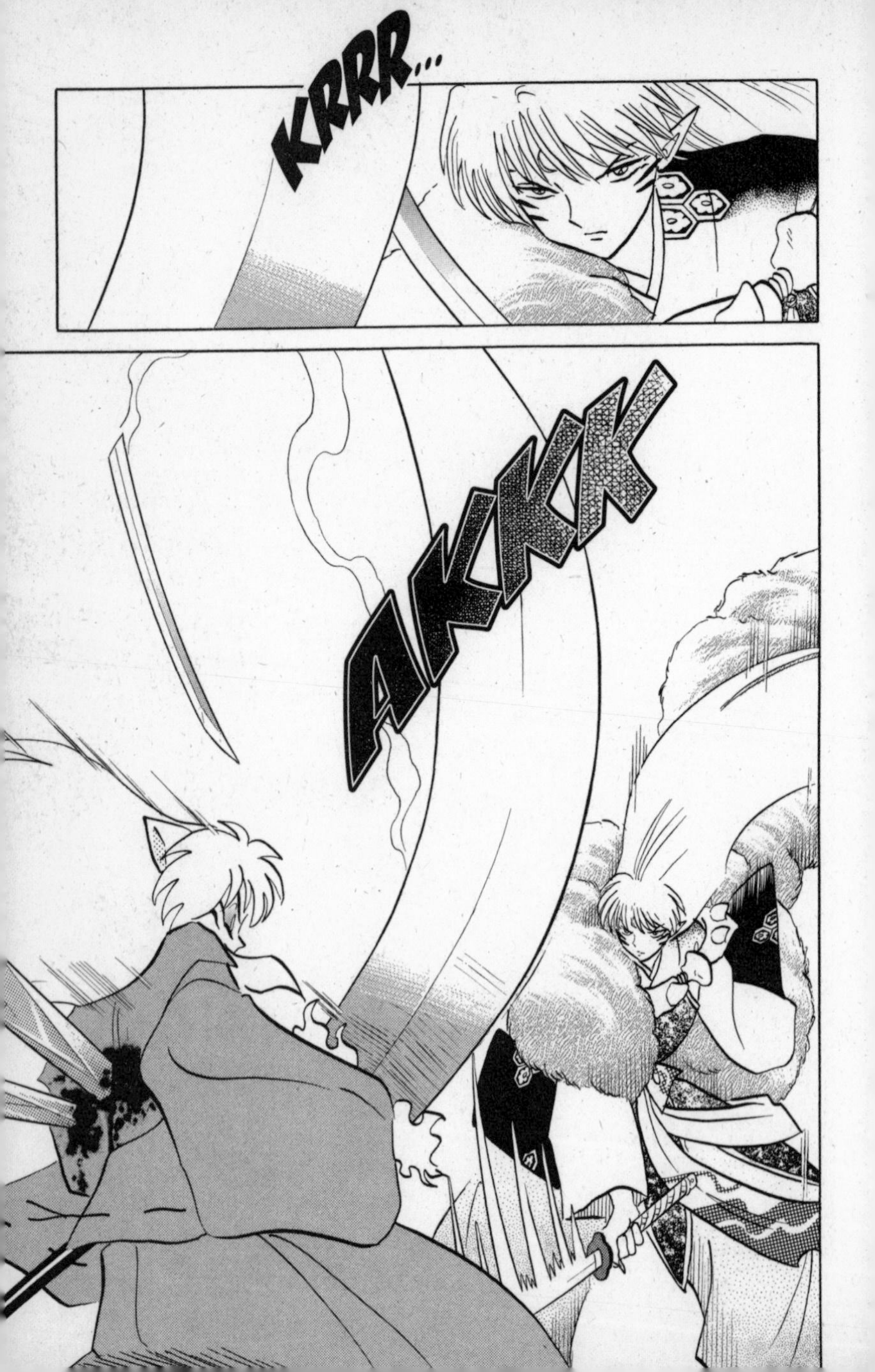
KRRR...
AKKK

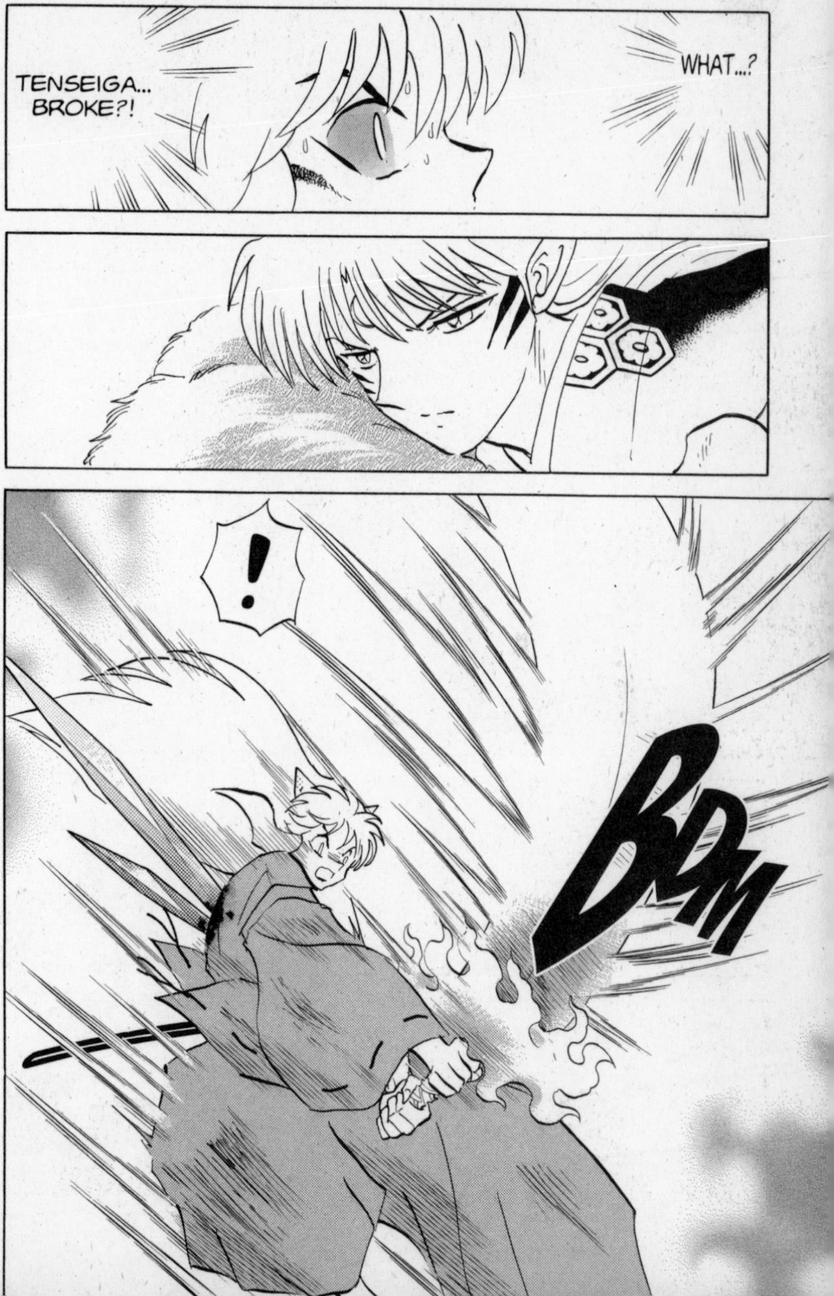
WHAT...?
TENSEIGA... BROKE?!
!
BDM

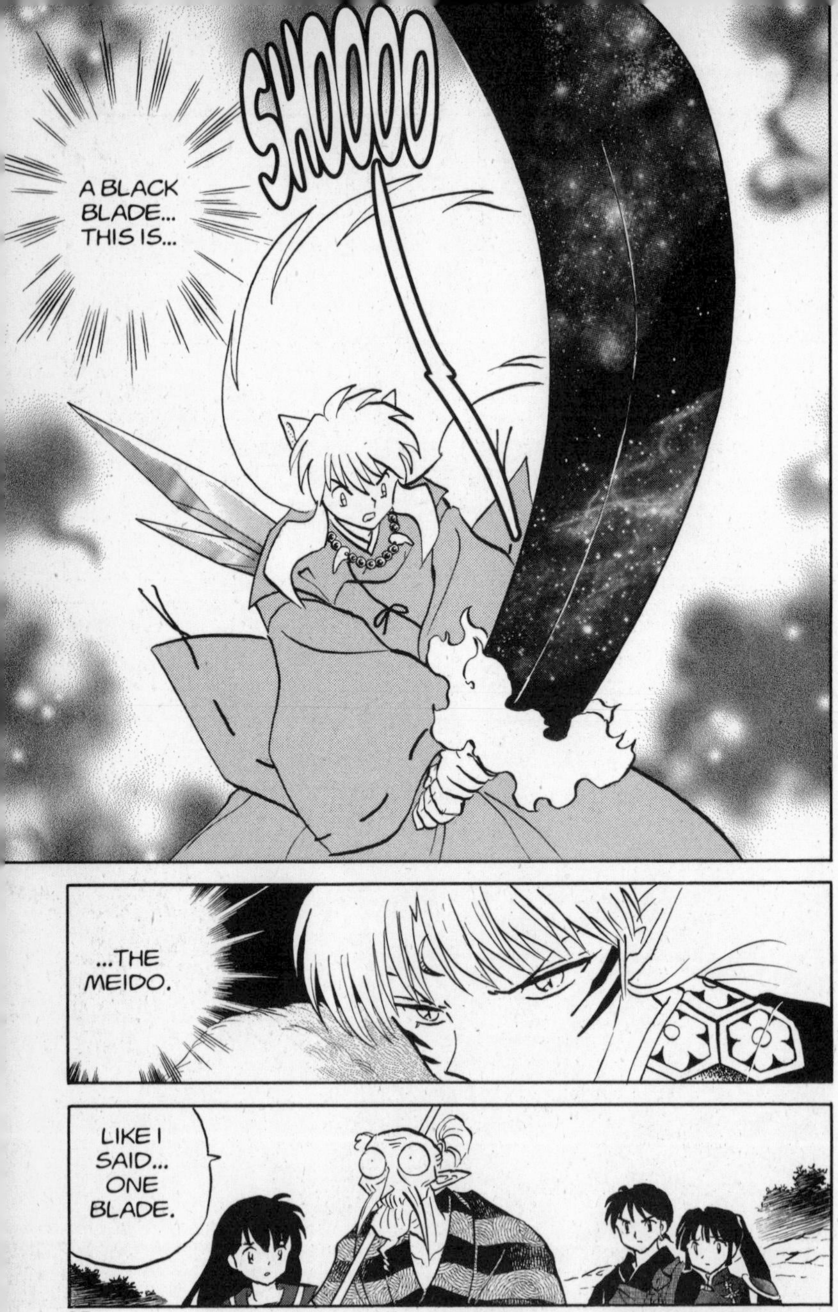
SHOOOO
A BLACK BLADE... THIS IS...
...THE MEIDO.
LIKE I SAID... ONE BLADE.

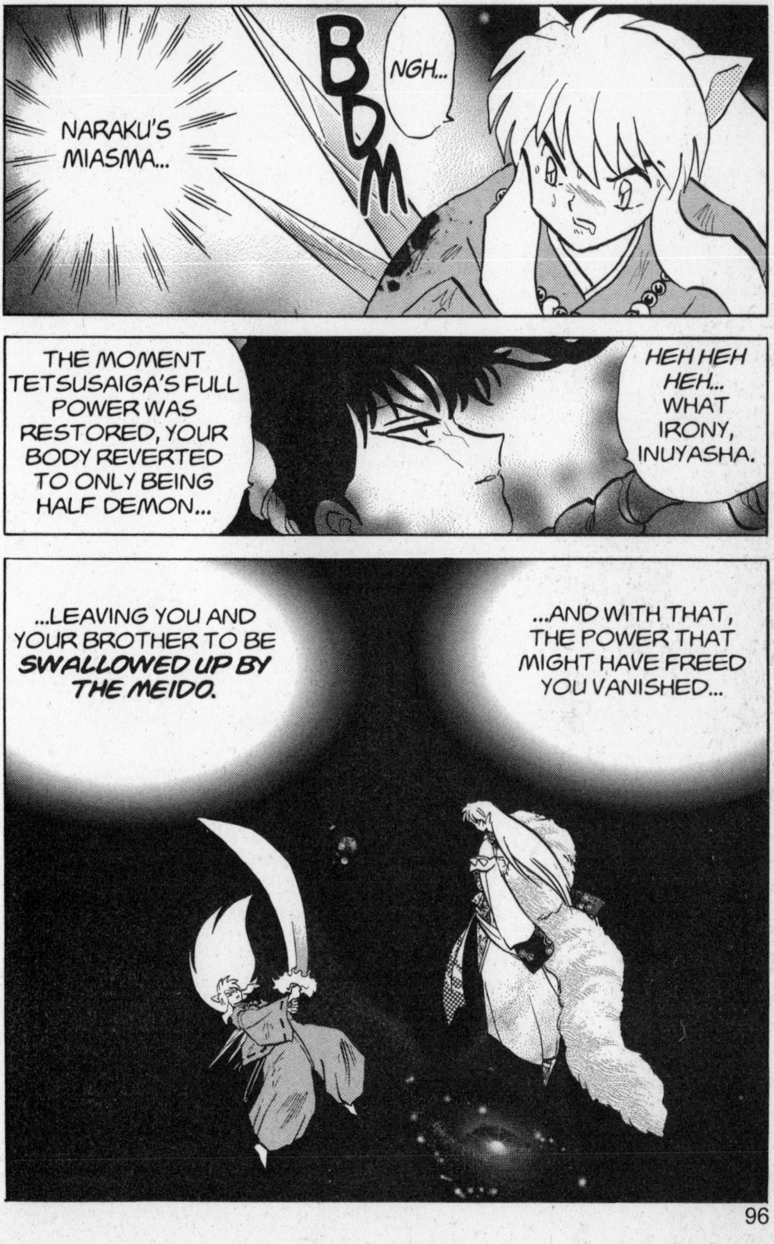
NGH...
BDM
NARAKU'S MIASMA...
HEH HEH HEH... WHAT IRONY, INUYASHA.
THE MOMENT TETSUSAIGA'S FULL POWER WAS RESTORED, YOUR BODY REVERTED TO ONLY BEING HALF DEMON...
...AND WITH THAT, THE POWER THAT MIGHT HAVE FREED YOU VANISHED...
...LEAVING YOU AND YOUR BROTHER TO BE ***SWALLOWED UP BY THE MEIDO.***

SCROLL 6

THE MEIDO'S LIGHT

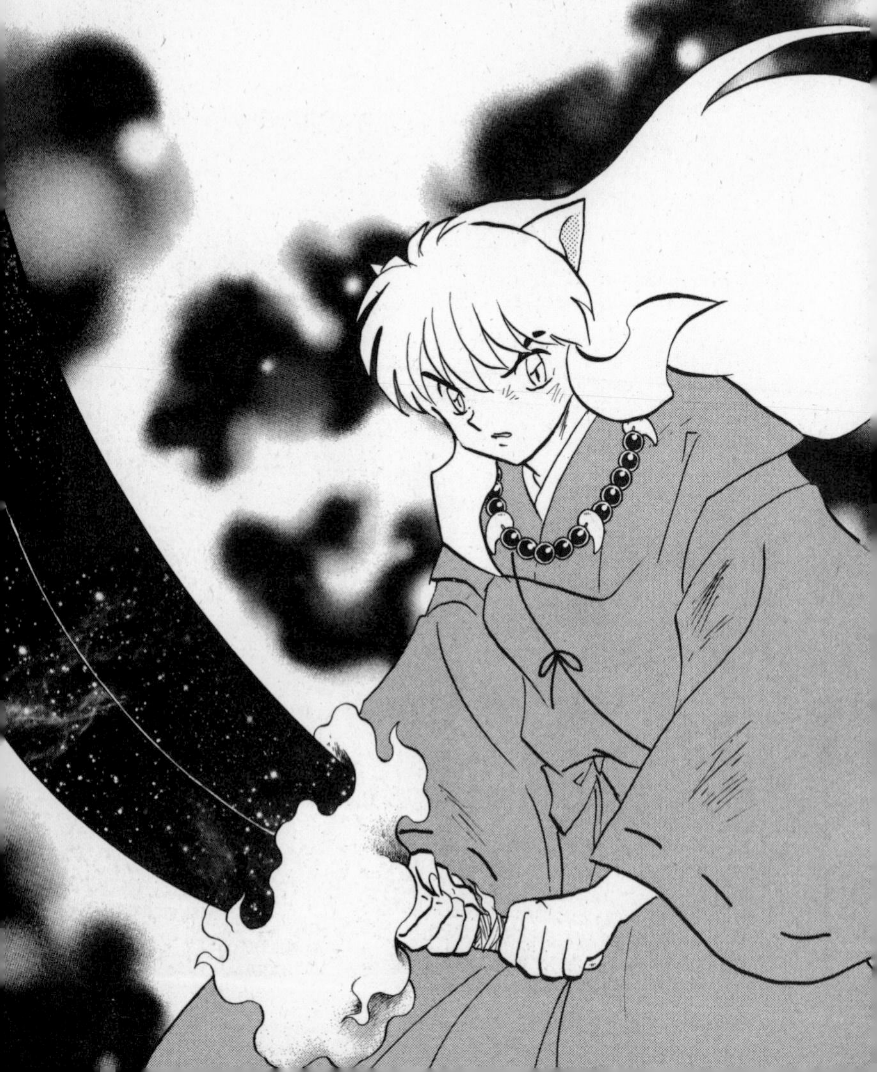

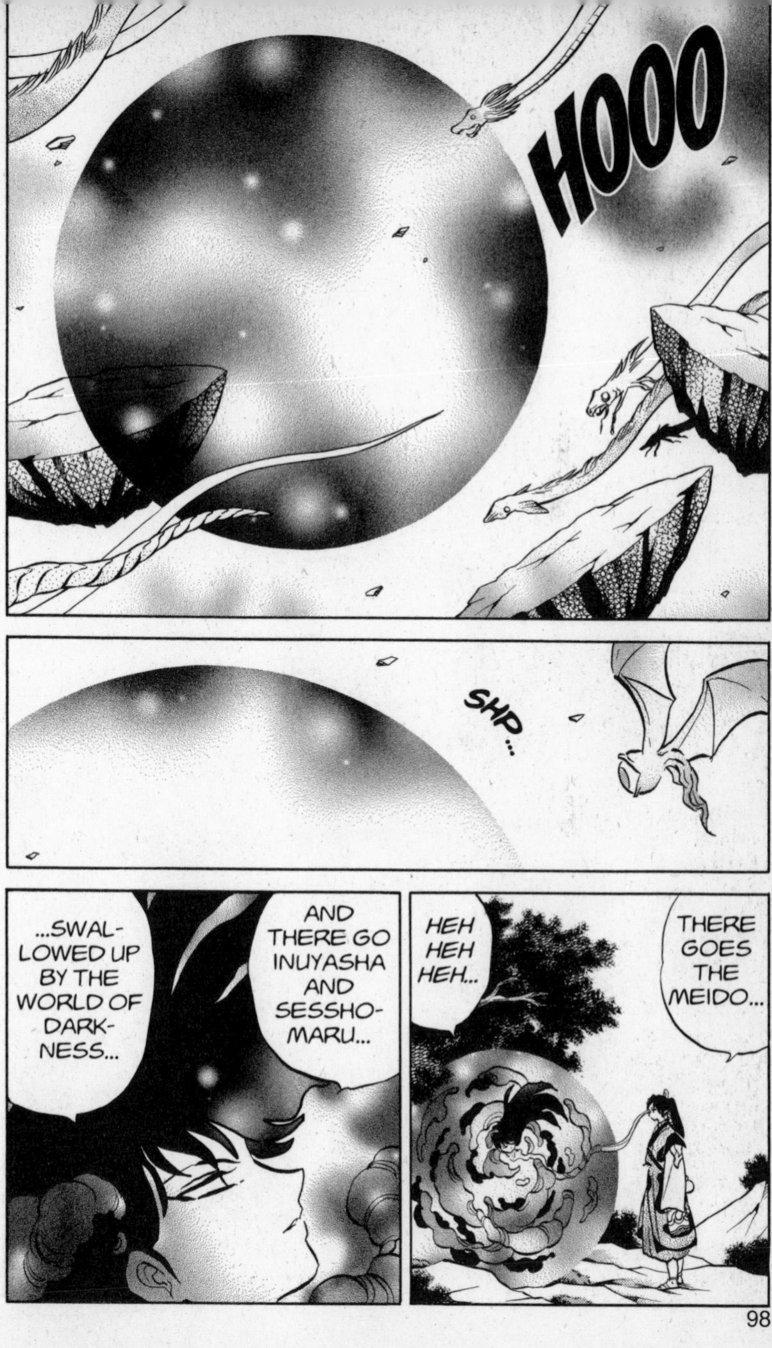
HOOO
SHP...
THERE GOES THE MEIDO...
HEH HEH HEH...
AND THERE GO INUYASHA AND SESSHO- MARU...
...SWAL- LOWED UP BY THE WORLD OF DARK- NESS...

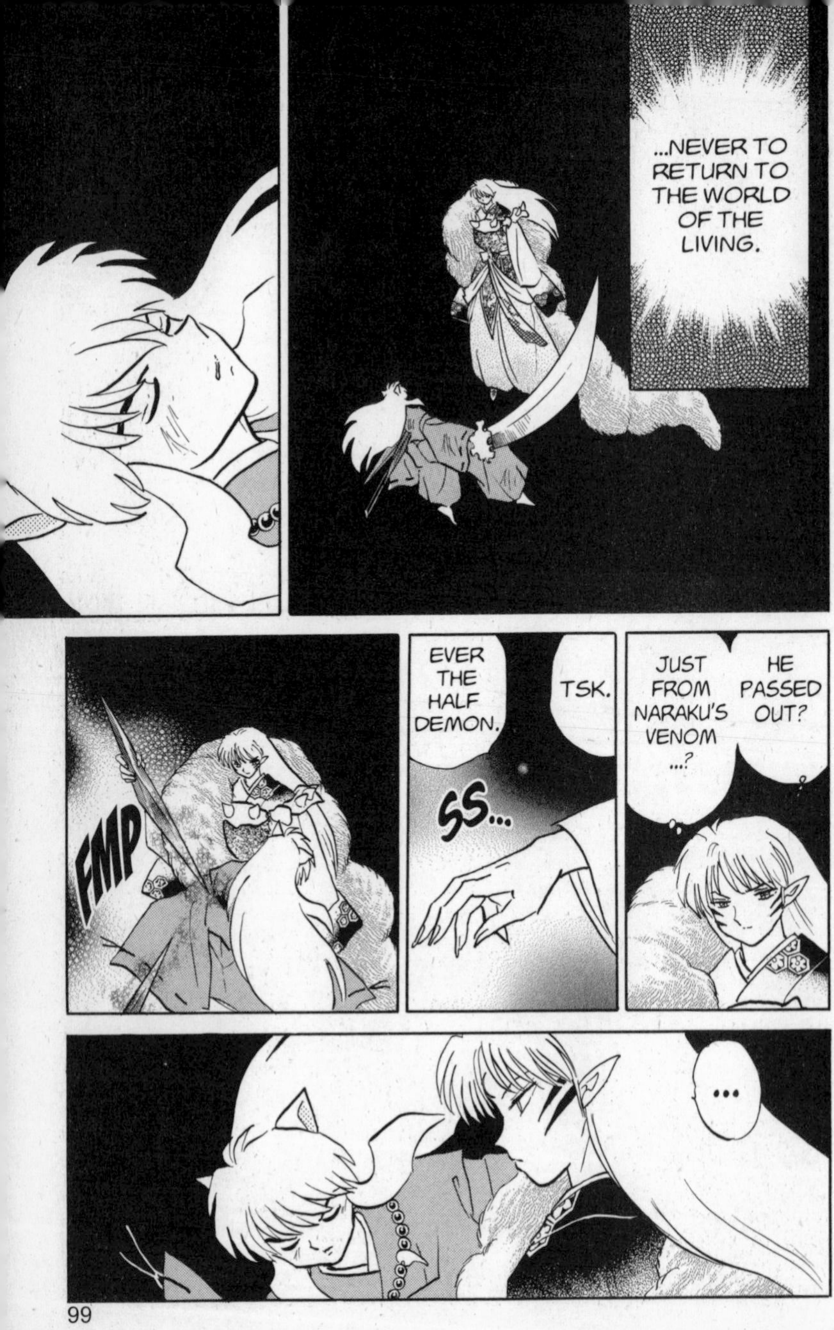
...NEVER TO RETURN TO THE WORLD OF THE LIVING.
HE PASSED OUT?
JUST FROM NARAKU'S VENOM ...?
TSK.
EVER THE HALF DEMON.
SS...
FMP
...

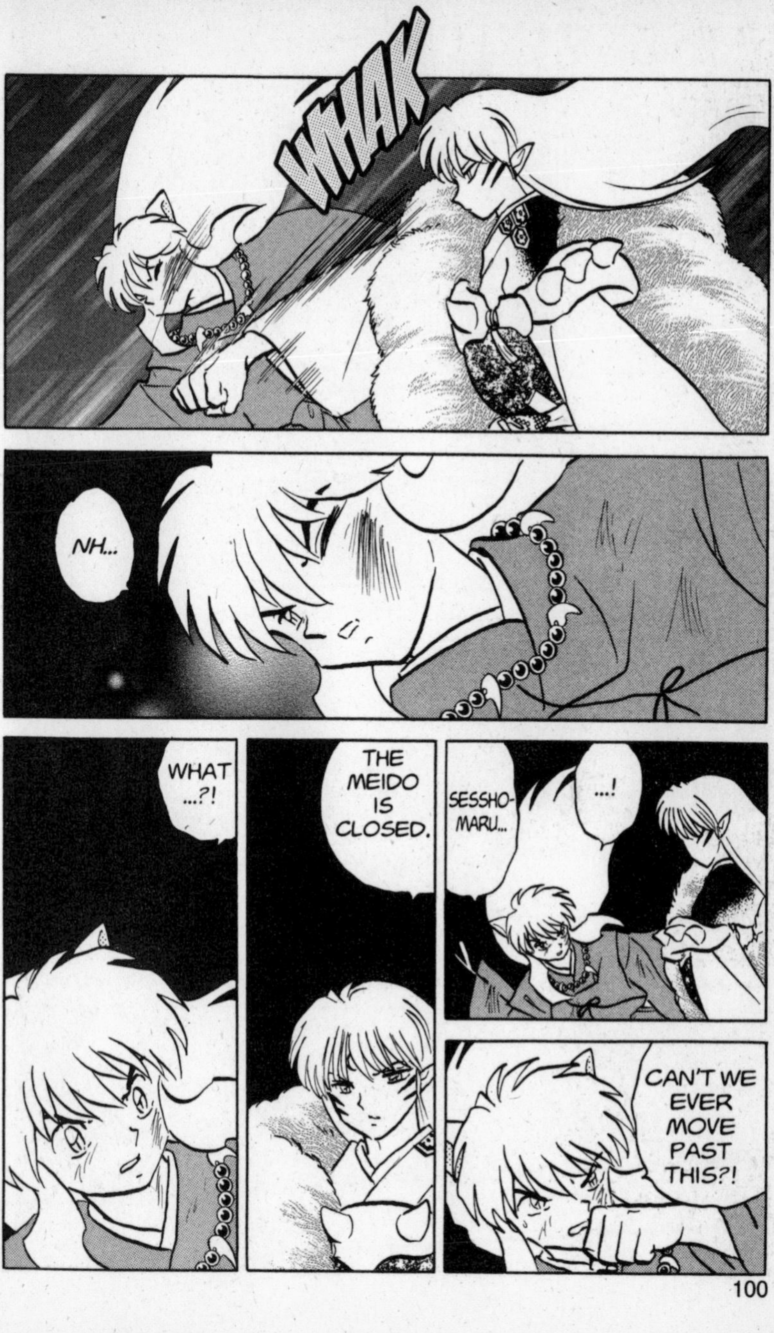
WHAK
NH...
...!
SESSHOMARU...
CAN'T WE EVER MOVE PAST THIS?!
THE MEIDO IS CLOSED.
WHAT ...?!

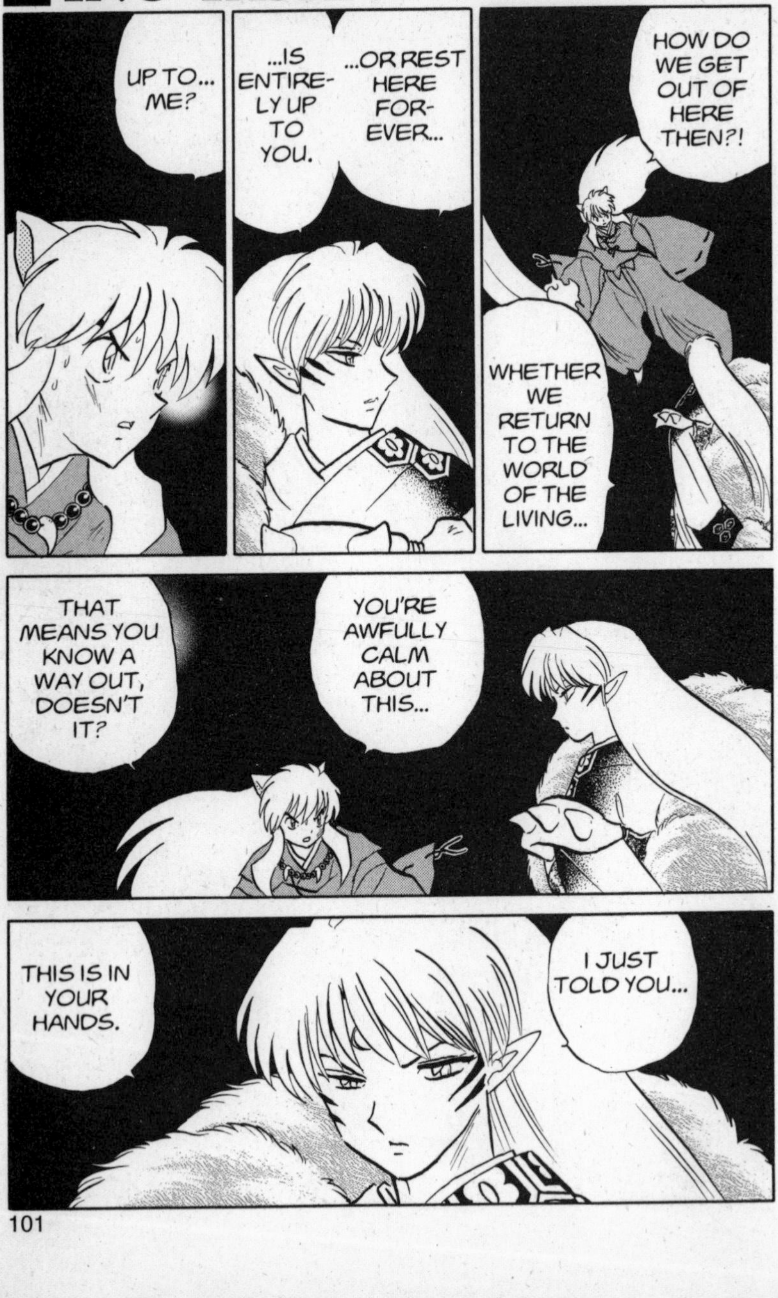
HOW DO WE GET OUT OF HERE THEN?!
WHETHER WE RETURN TO THE WORLD OF THE LIVING...
...OR REST HERE FOREVER...
...IS ENTIRELY UP TO YOU.
UP TO... ME?
YOU'RE AWFULLY CALM ABOUT THIS...
THAT MEANS YOU KNOW A WAY OUT, DOESN'T IT?
I JUST TOLD YOU...
THIS IS IN YOUR HANDS.

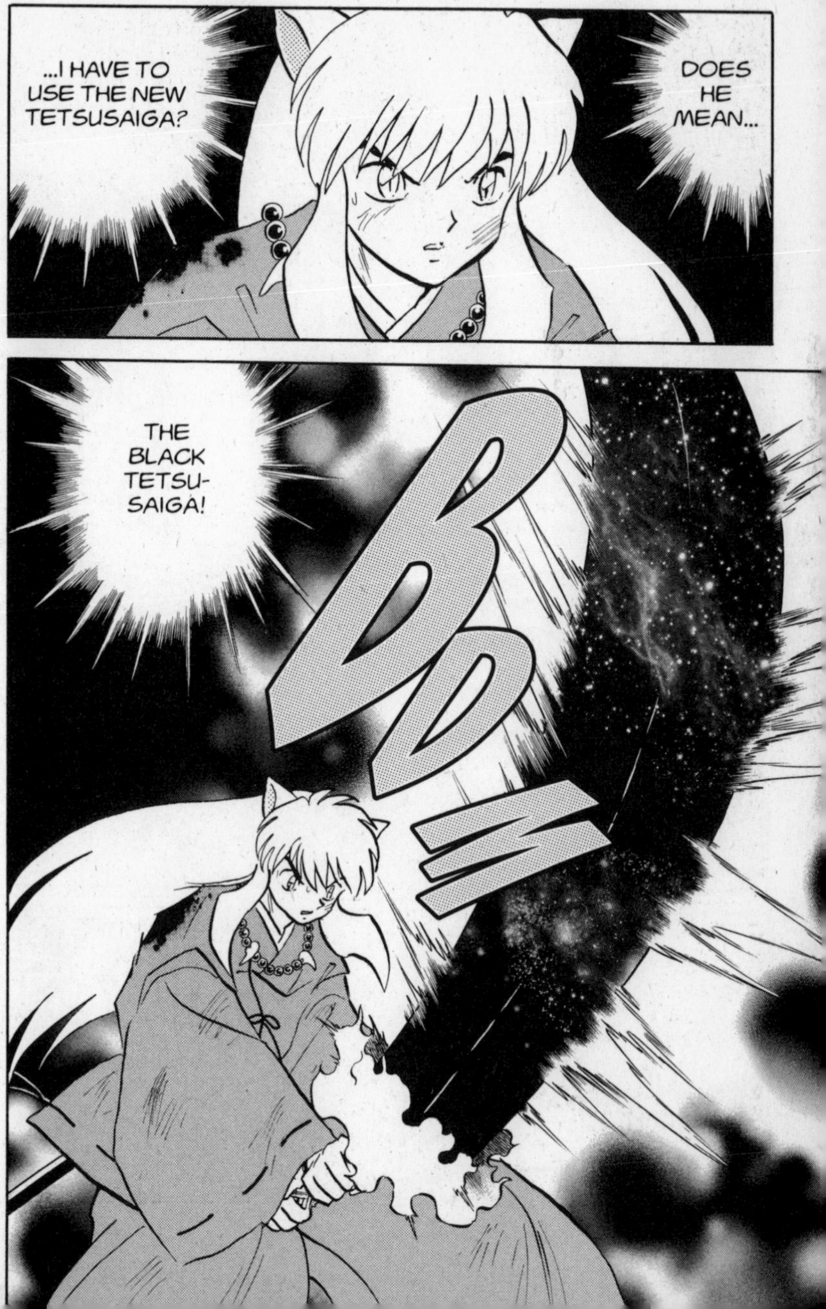
DOES HE MEAN...
...I HAVE TO USE THE NEW TETSUSAIGA?
THE BLACK TETSU-SAIGA!

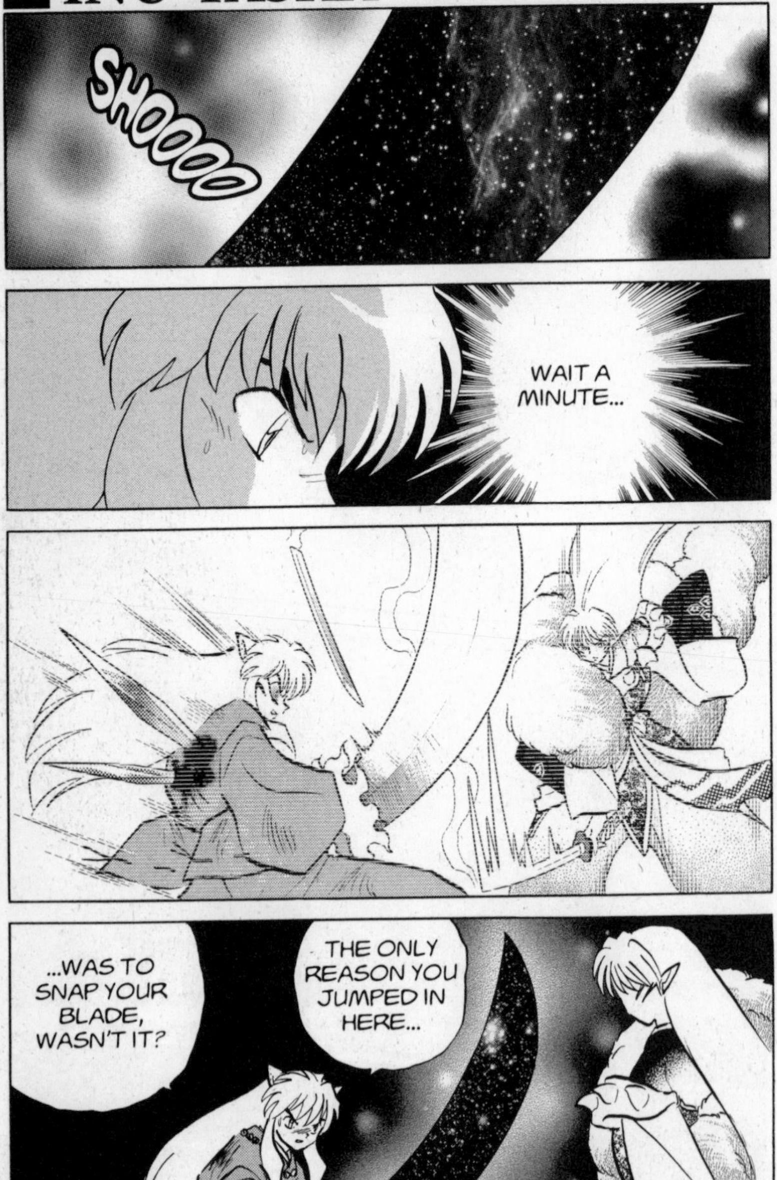
SHOOOO
WAIT A MINUTE...
THE ONLY REASON YOU JUMPED IN HERE...
...WAS TO SNAP YOUR BLADE, WASN'T IT?

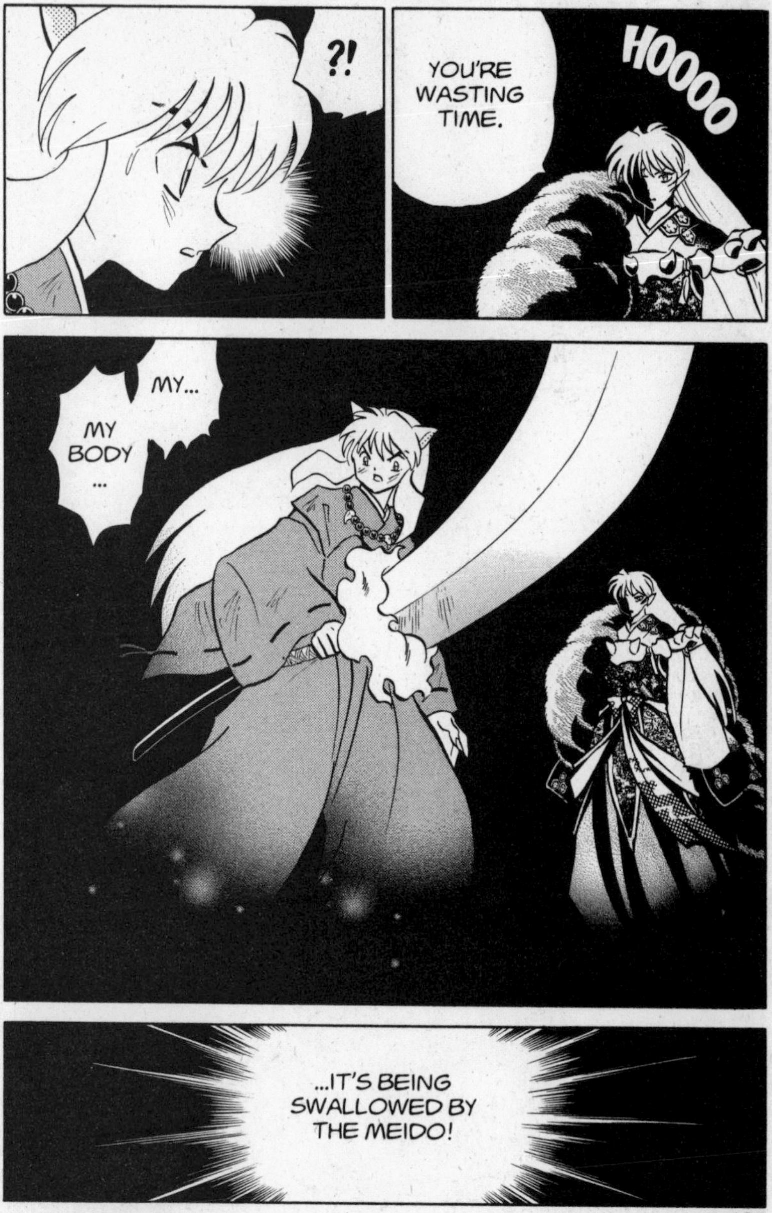
HOOOO
YOU'RE WASTING TIME.
?!
MY...
MY BODY ...
...IT'S BEING SWALLOWED BY THE MEIDO!

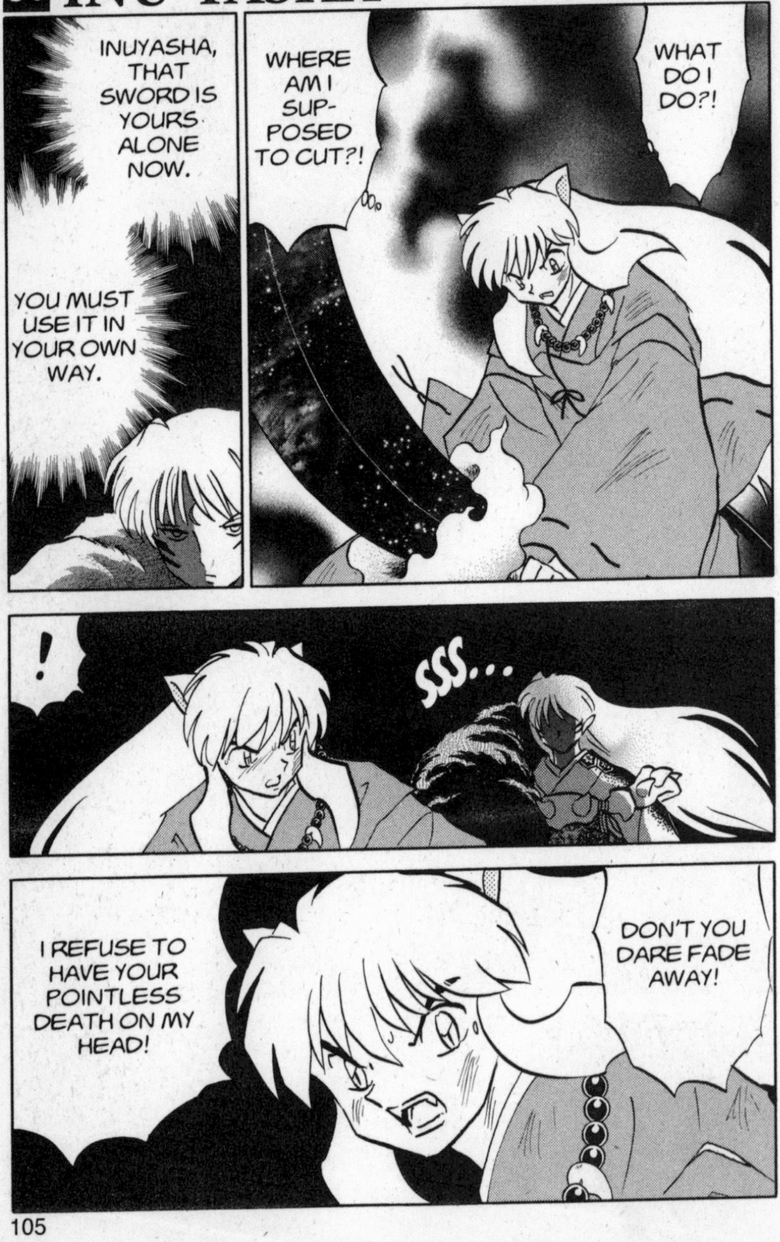
WHAT DO I DO?!
WHERE AM I SUP-POSED TO CUT?!
INUYASHA, THAT SWORD IS YOURS ALONE NOW.
YOU MUST USE IT IN YOUR OWN WAY.
SSS...
!
DON'T YOU DARE FADE AWAY!
I REFUSE TO HAVE YOUR POINTLESS DEATH ON MY HEAD!

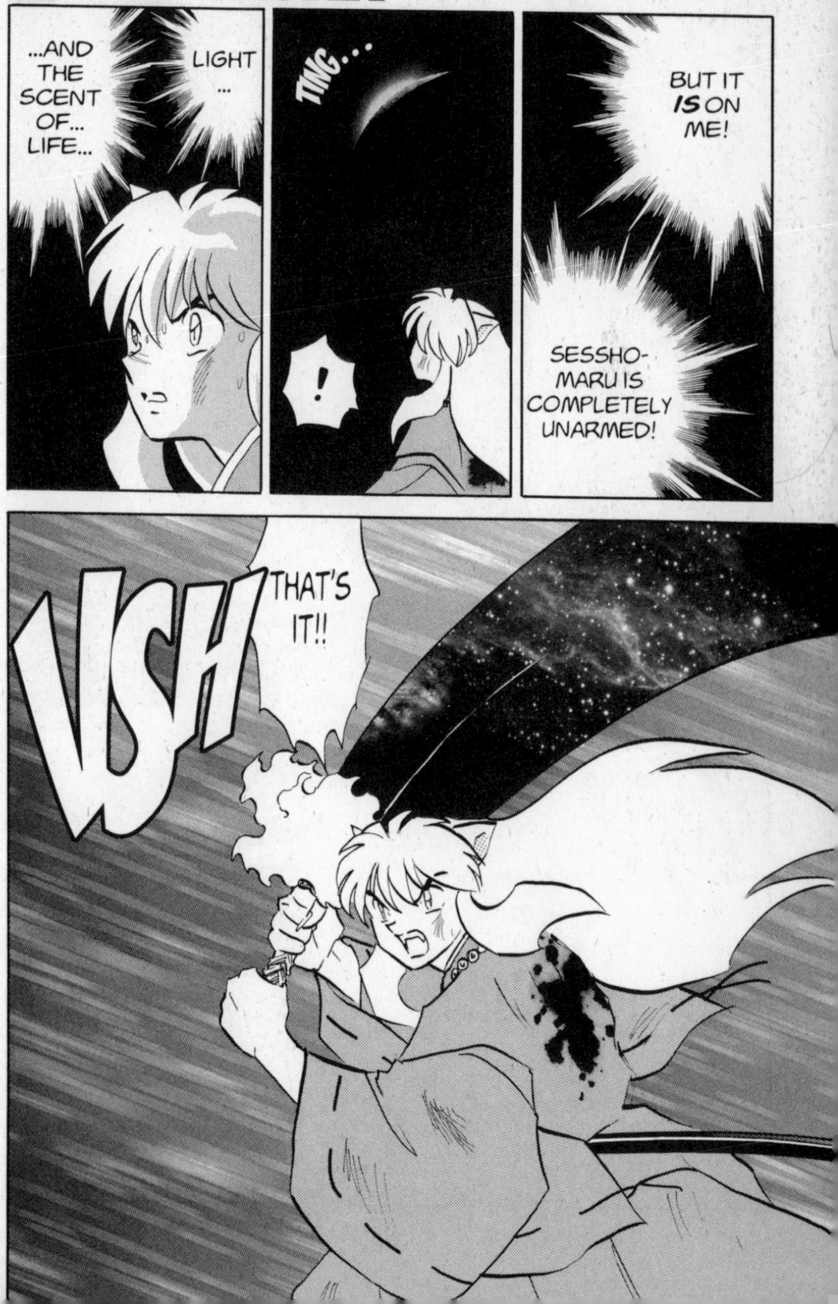
BUT IT *IS* ON ME!
SESSHO-MARU IS COMPLETELY UNARMED!
TING....
!
LIGHT ...
...AND THE SCENT OF... LIFE...
THAT'S IT!!
VSH

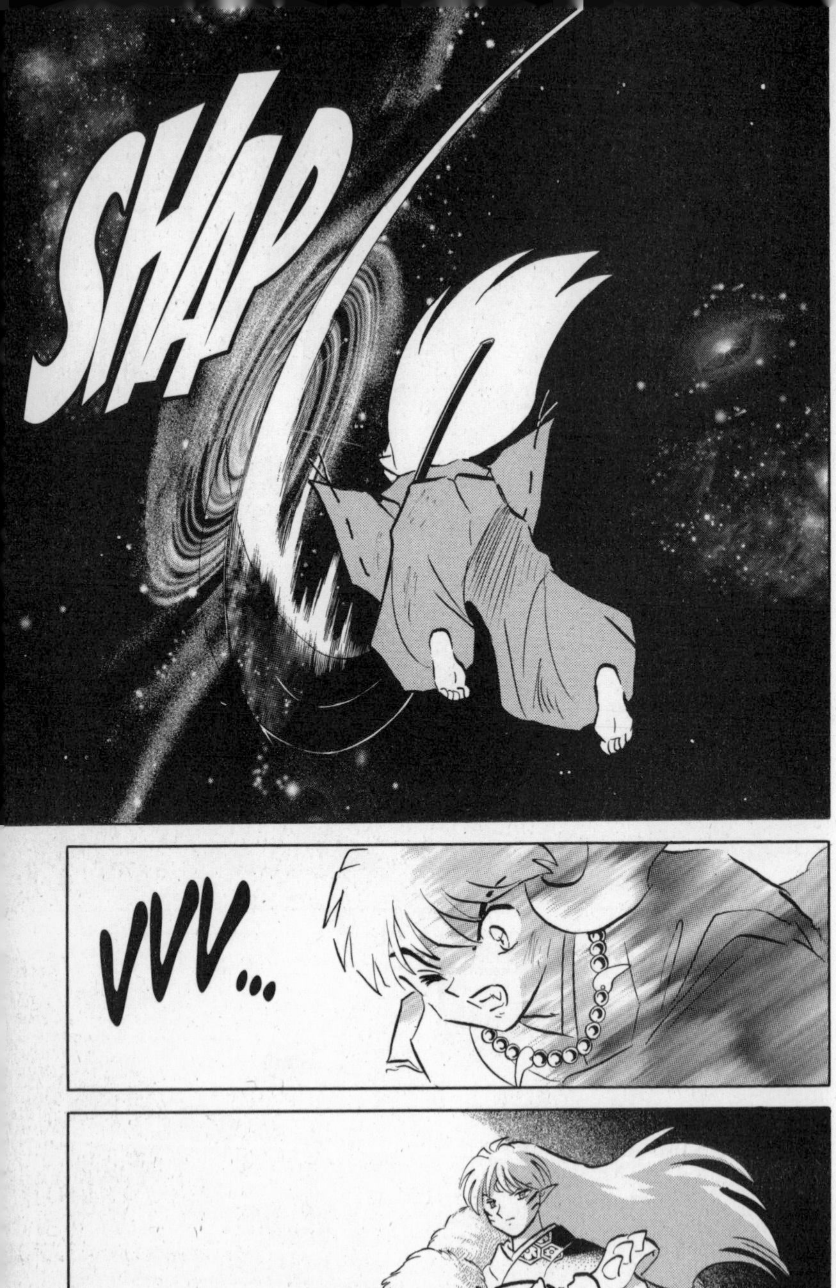
SHAP
VVV...

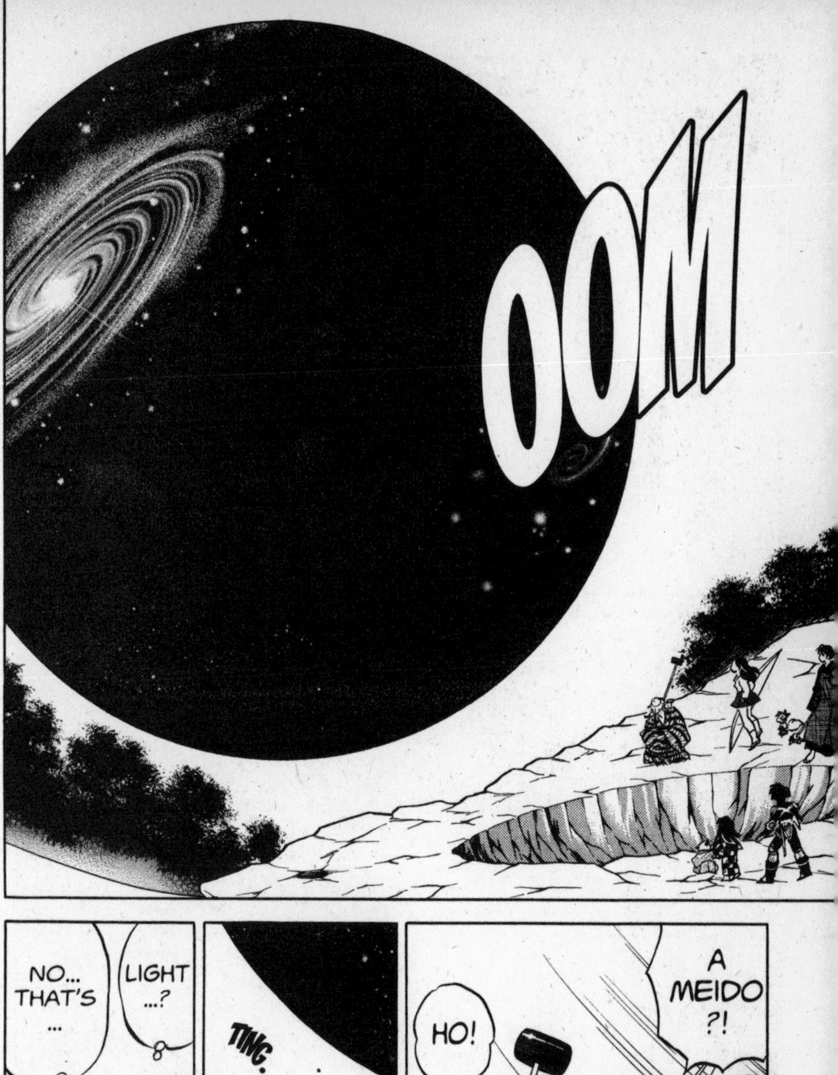
OOM
A MEIDO ?!
HO!
TING...
LIGHT ...?
NO... THAT'S ...

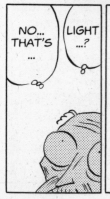

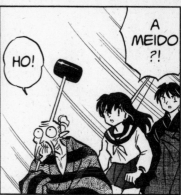

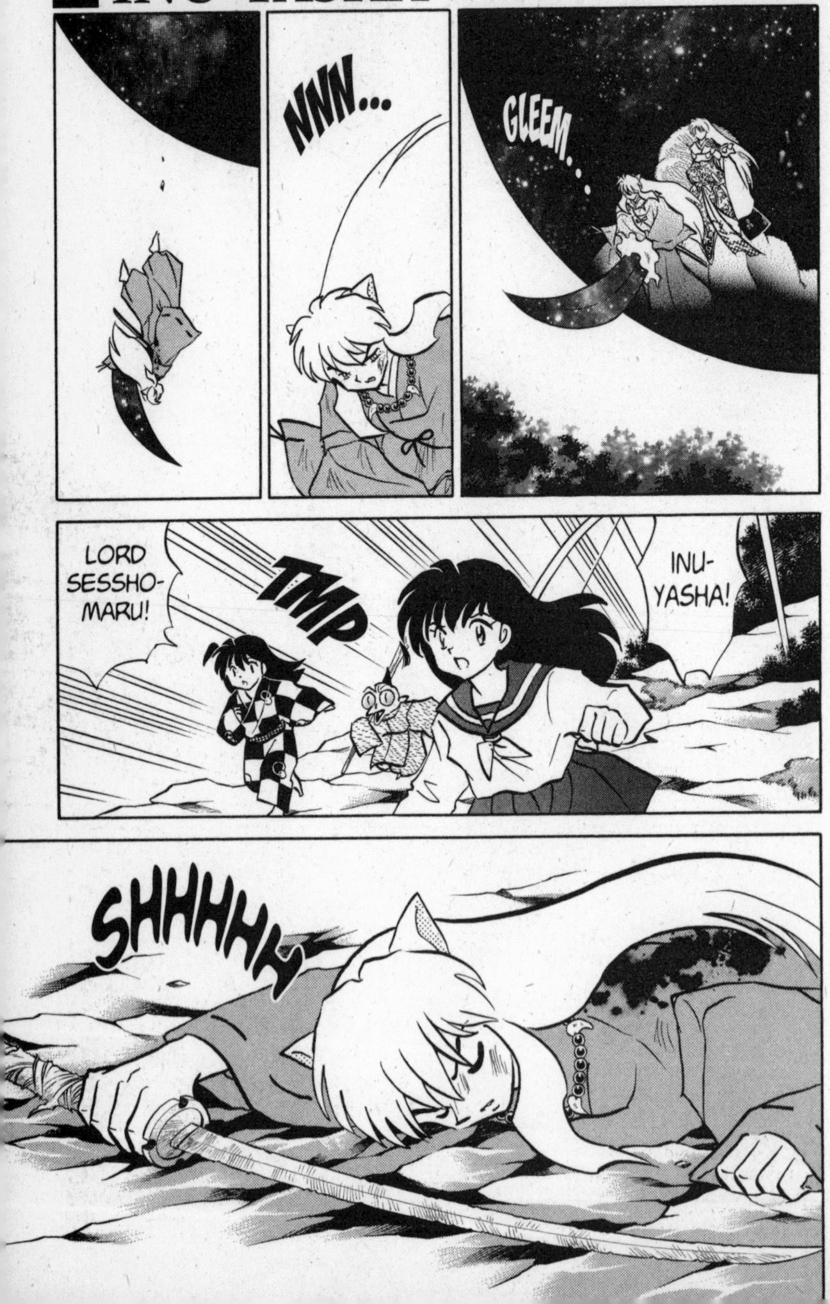
GLEEM...
NNN...
INU-YASHA!
TMP
LORD SESSHOMARU!
SHHHHH

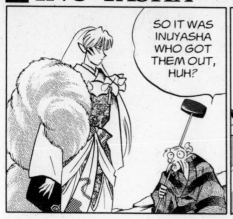

HE'S HURT...
SO IT WAS INUYASHA WHO GOT THEM OUT, HUH?
THEN ...
YOU'VE COME TO AN UNDERSTANDING?
LORD SESSHO-MARU!
HE'S NOT ARMED WITH HIS BLADE?
GASP
TH-THEN IT'S TRUE...?
TENSEIGA HAS BEEN ABSORBED INTO TETSU-SAIGA?!
BMP
BMP
BMP
IT CAN'T BE...
I NO LONGER HAVE ANY INTEREST IN THAT SWORD.

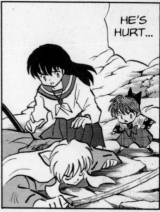

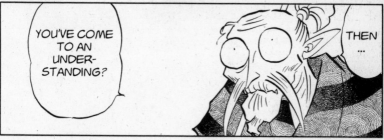

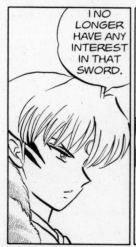

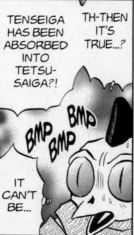

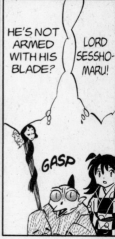

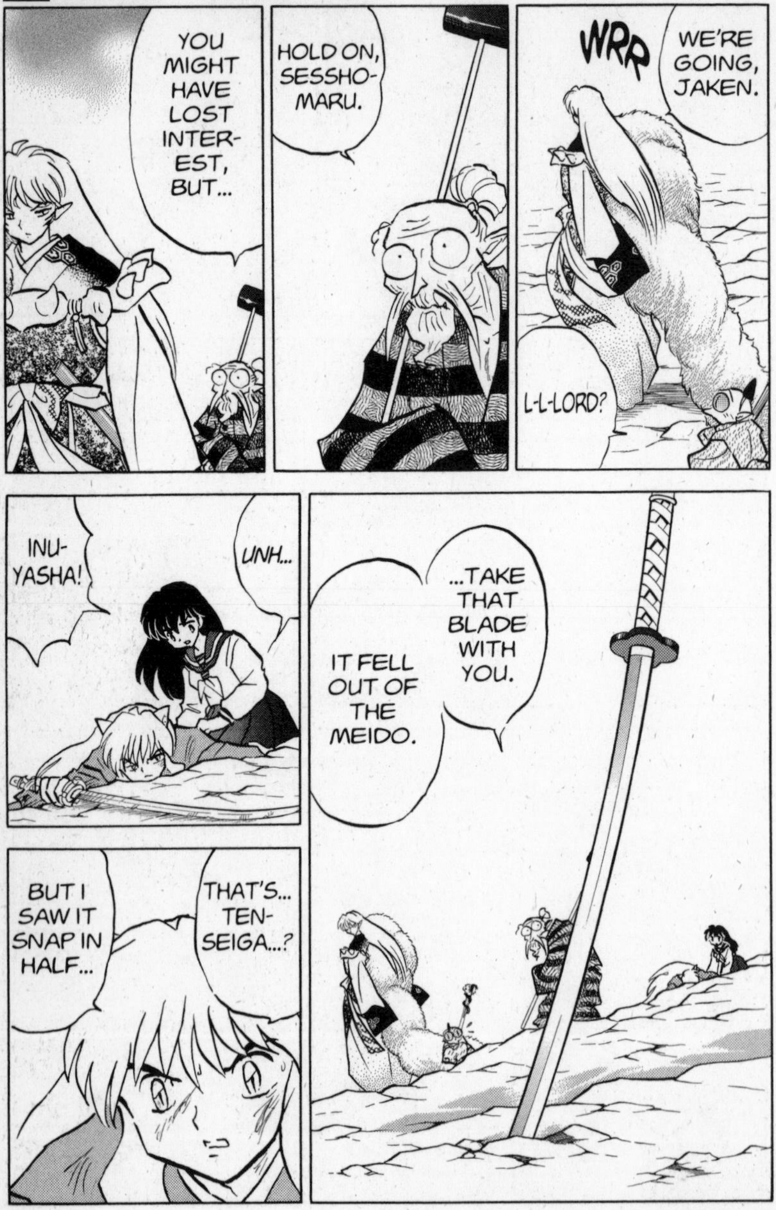
WE'RE GOING, JAKEN.
WRR
L-L-LORD?
HOLD ON, SESSHOMARU.
YOU MIGHT HAVE LOST INTEREST, BUT...
...TAKE THAT BLADE WITH YOU.
IT FELL OUT OF THE MEIDO.
UNH...
INU-YASHA!
THAT'S... TENSEIGA...?
BUT I SAW IT SNAP IN HALF...

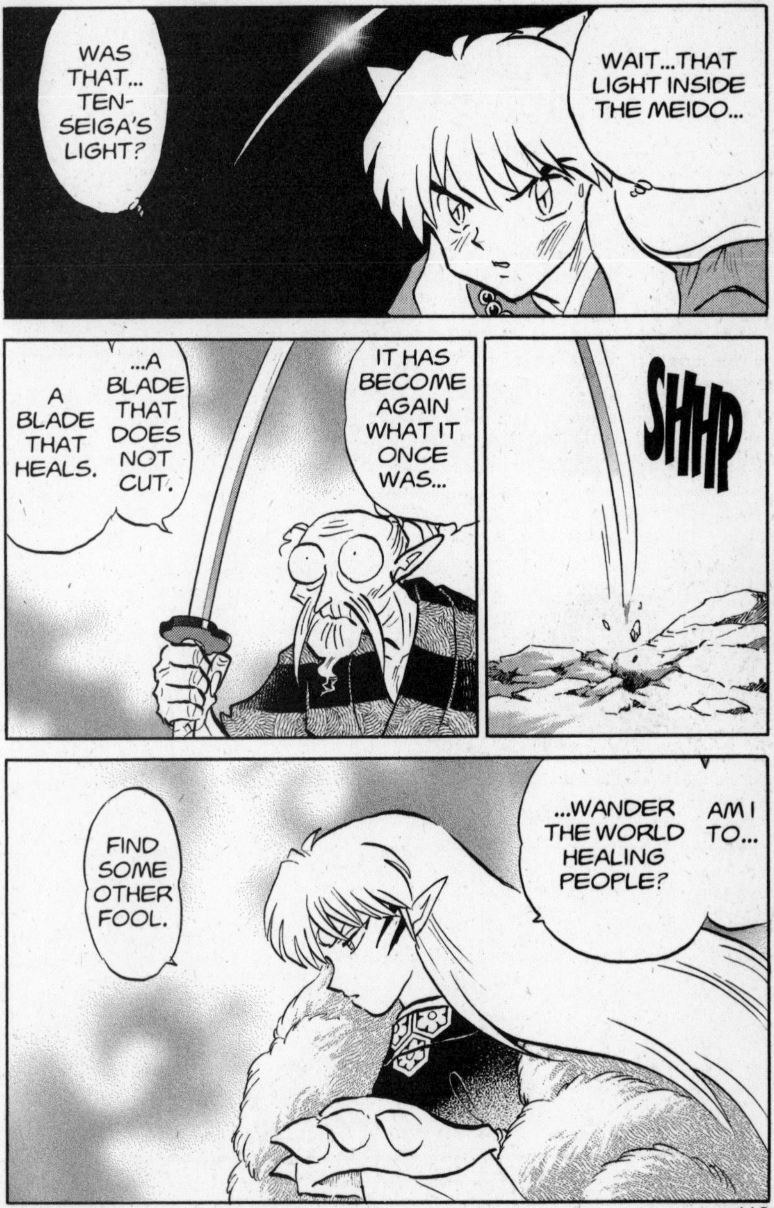
WAIT...THAT LIGHT INSIDE THE MEIDO...
WAS THAT... TEN-SEIGA'S LIGHT?
SHHP
IT HAS BECOME AGAIN WHAT IT ONCE WAS...
...A BLADE THAT DOES NOT CUT.
A BLADE THAT HEALS.
AM I TO...
...WANDER THE WORLD HEALING PEOPLE?
FIND SOME OTHER FOOL.

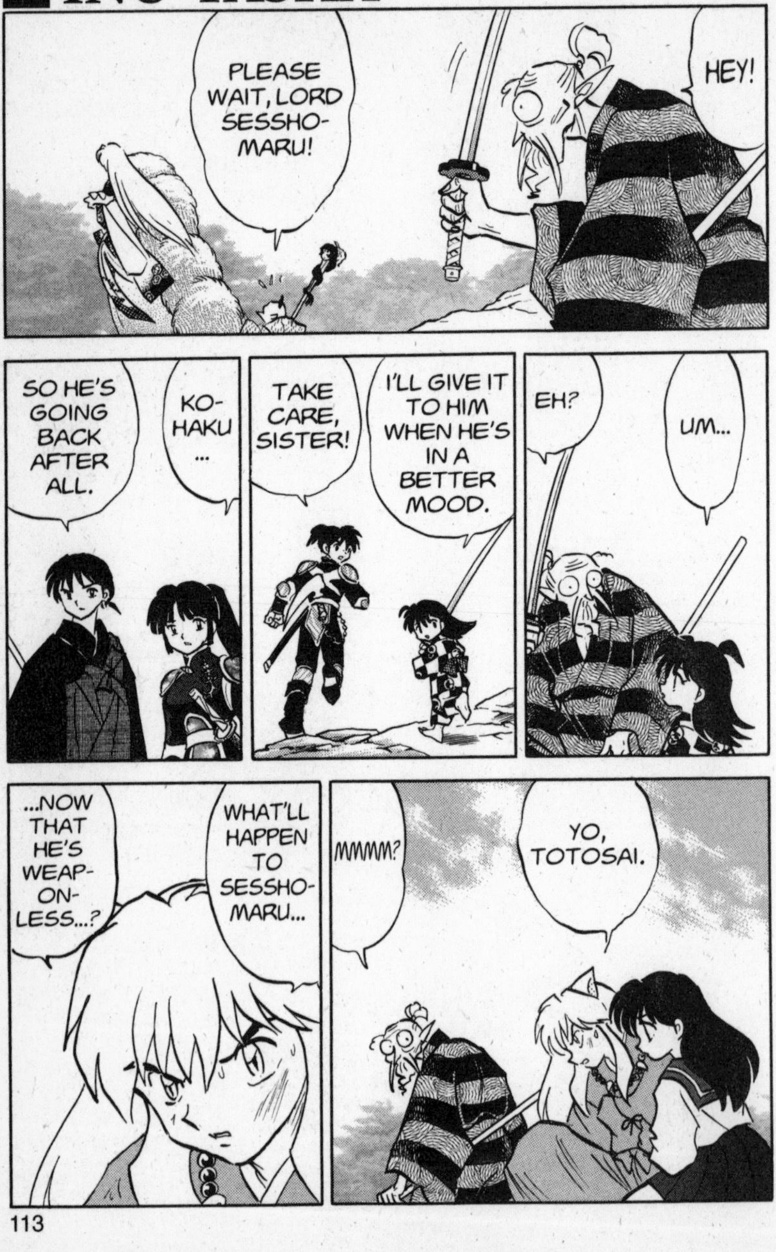
HEY!
PLEASE WAIT, LORD SESSHOMARU!
UM...
EH?
I'LL GIVE IT TO HIM WHEN HE'S IN A BETTER MOOD.
TAKE CARE, SISTER!
KOHAKU...
SO HE'S GOING BACK AFTER ALL.
YO, TOTOSAI.
MMMM?
WHAT'LL HAPPEN TO SESSHOMARU...
...NOW THAT HE'S WEAPONLESS...?

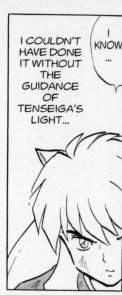

NOT YOUR CON-CERN.
FOCUS ON MASTERING YOUR NEW TETSUSAIGA AS FAST AS YOU CAN.
YOU REALIZE YOU DIDN'T ESCAPE THE MEIDO ALL ON YOUR OWN, DON'T YOU?
I KNOW...
I COULDN'T HAVE DONE IT WITHOUT THE GUIDANCE OF TENSEIGA'S LIGHT...
SESSHOMARU DOESN'T REALIZE IT, BUT...
...HE'S SO CLOSE TO EARNING HIS VERY OWN WEAPON...
...ONE THAT *ISN'T* HANDED DOWN FROM HIS FATHER.

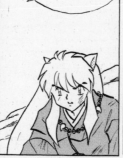

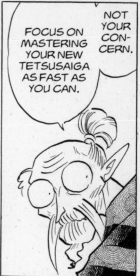

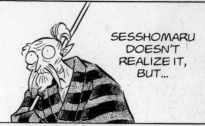

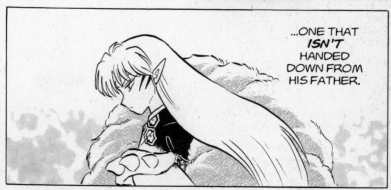

SCROLL 7

THE FOX INN

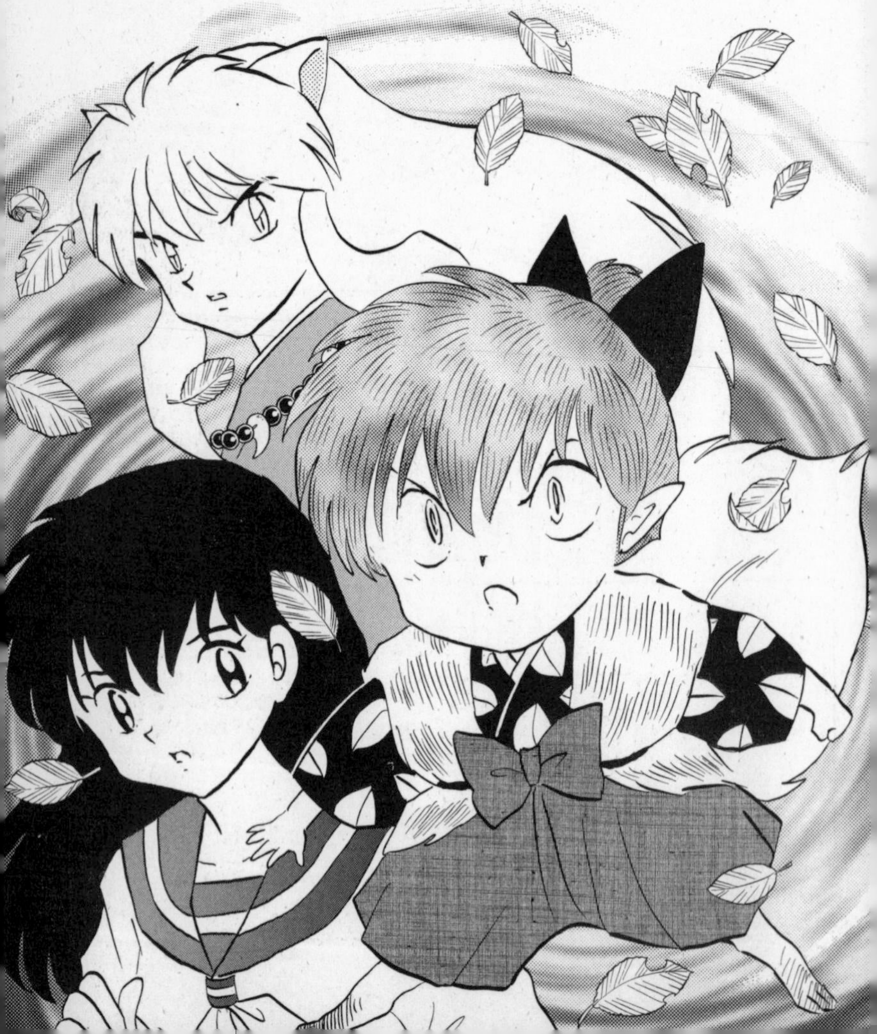

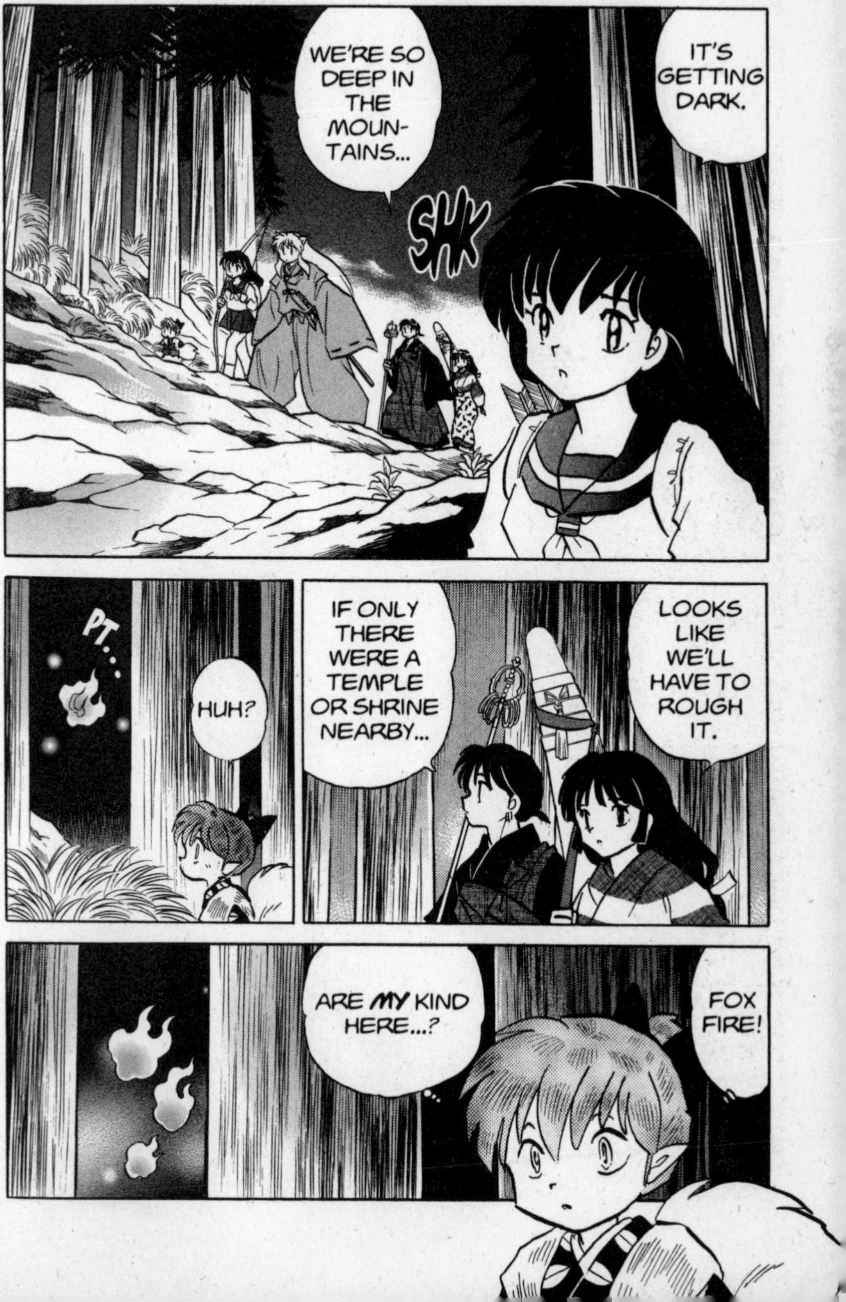
IT'S GETTING DARK.
WE'RE SO DEEP IN THE MOUN-TAINS...
SHK
LOOKS LIKE WE'LL HAVE TO ROUGH IT.
IF ONLY THERE WERE A TEMPLE OR SHRINE NEARBY...
HUH?
PT...
FOX FIRE!
ARE *MY* KIND HERE...?

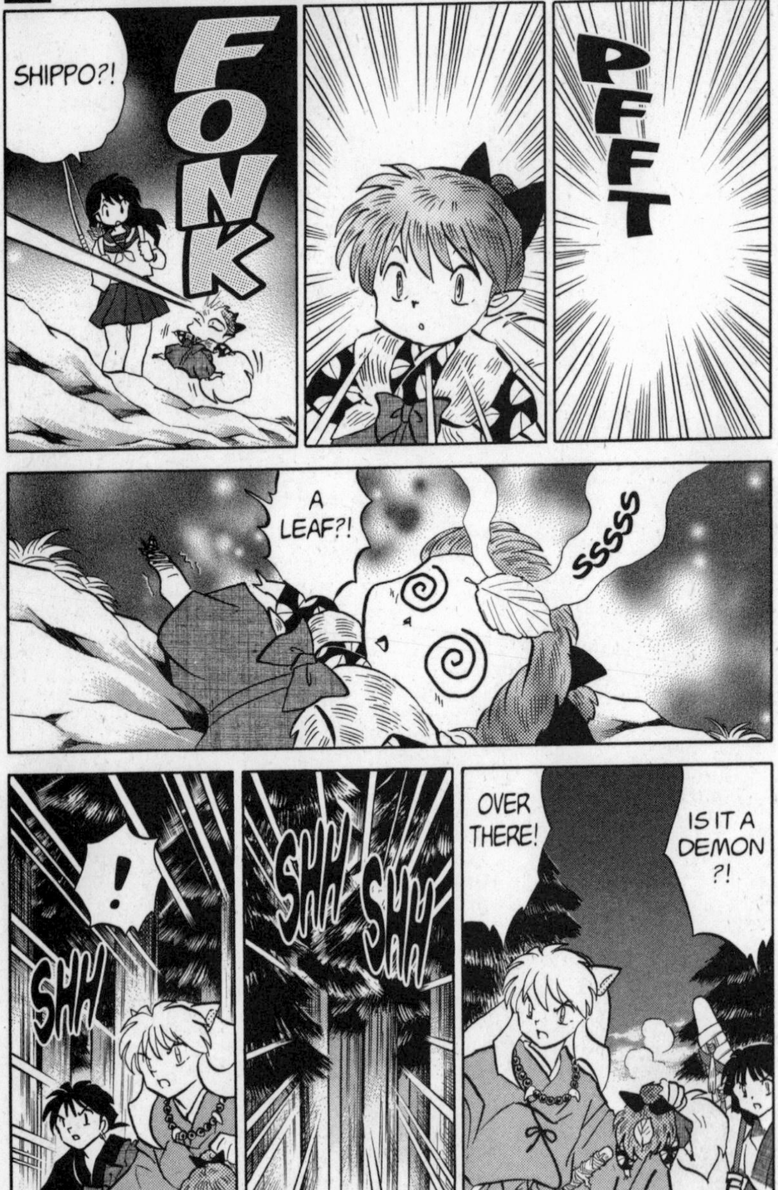
PFFT
FONK
SHIPPO?!
SSSSS
A LEAF?!
OVER THERE!
IS IT A DEMON ?!
SHH SHH
!
SHH

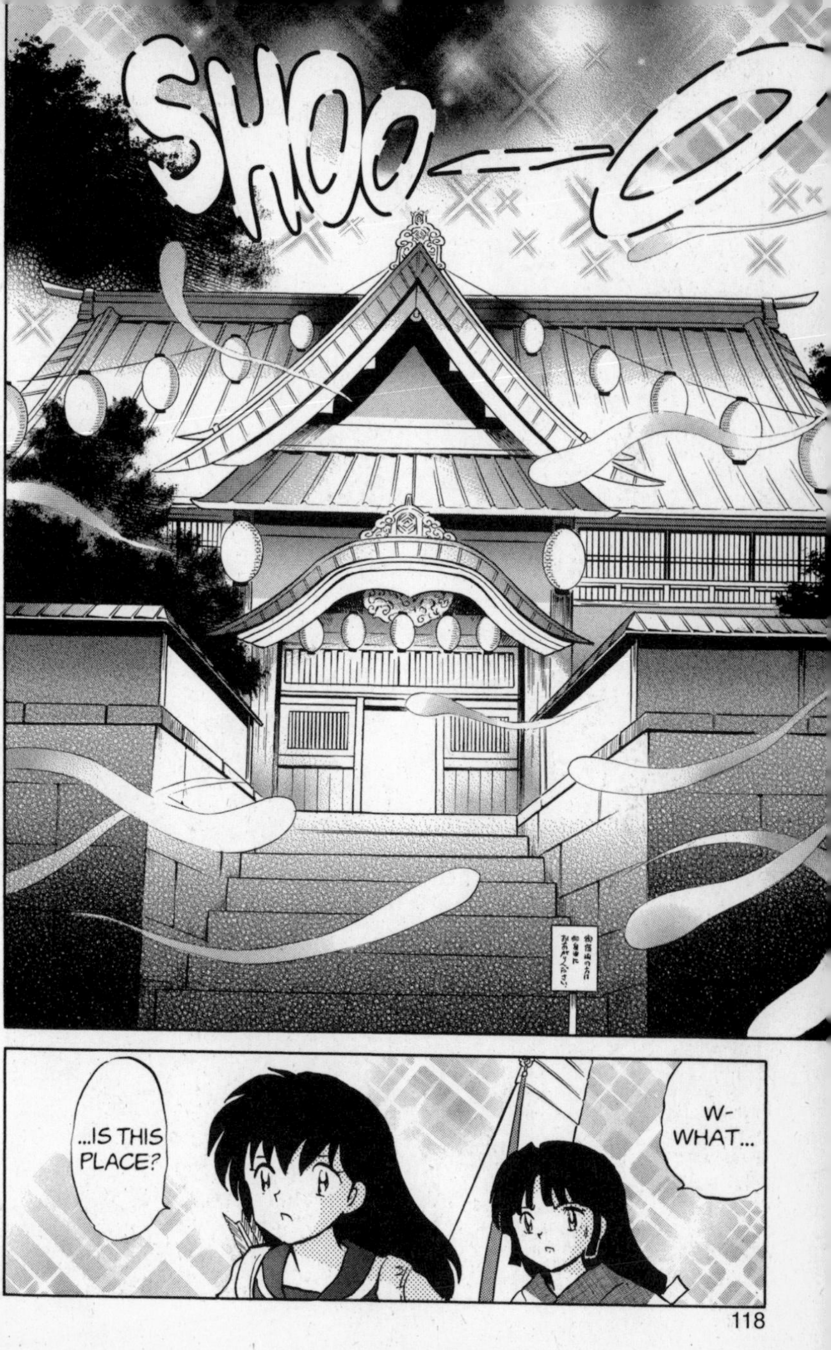
SHOO---O
W-WHAT...
...IS THIS PLACE?

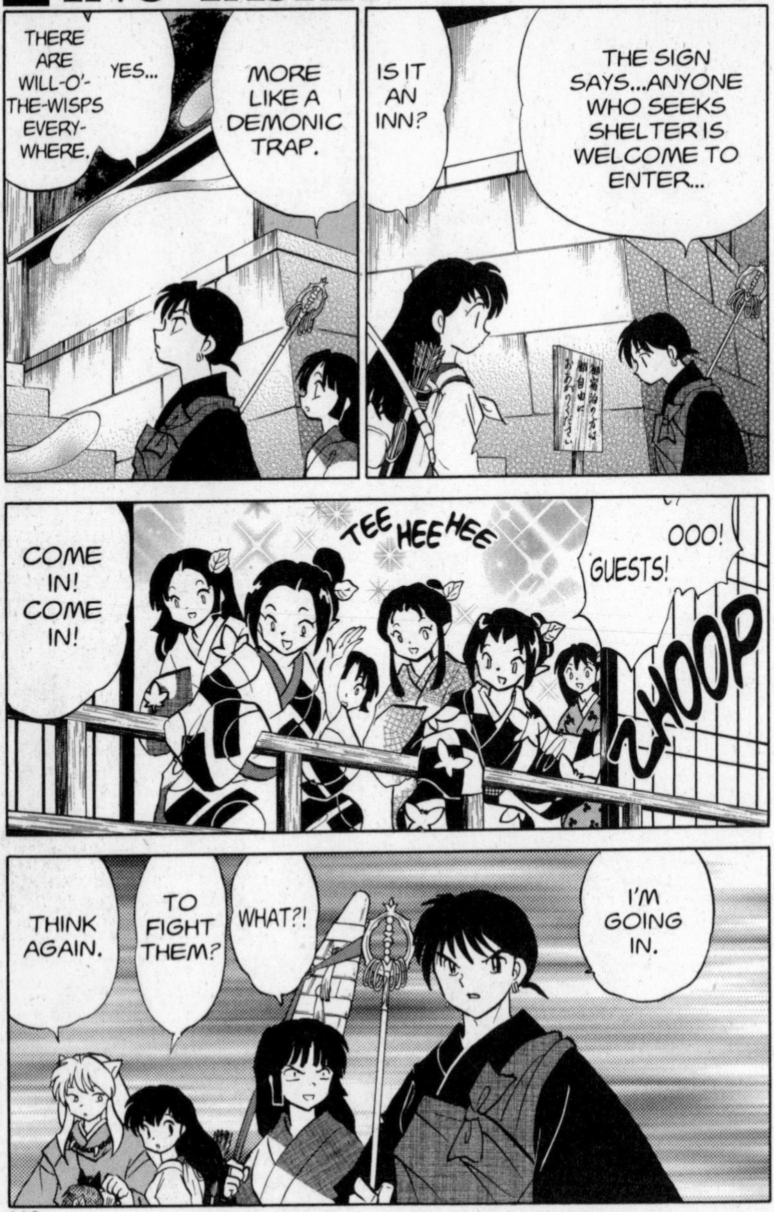
THE SIGN SAYS...ANYONE WHO SEEKS SHELTER IS WELCOME TO ENTER...
IS IT AN INN?
MORE LIKE A DEMONIC TRAP.
THERE ARE WILL-O'-THE-WISPS EVERY-WHERE.
YES...
OOO! GUESTS!
WHOOP
TEE HEE HEE
COME IN! COME IN!
I'M GOING IN.
WHAT?!
TO FIGHT THEM?
THINK AGAIN.

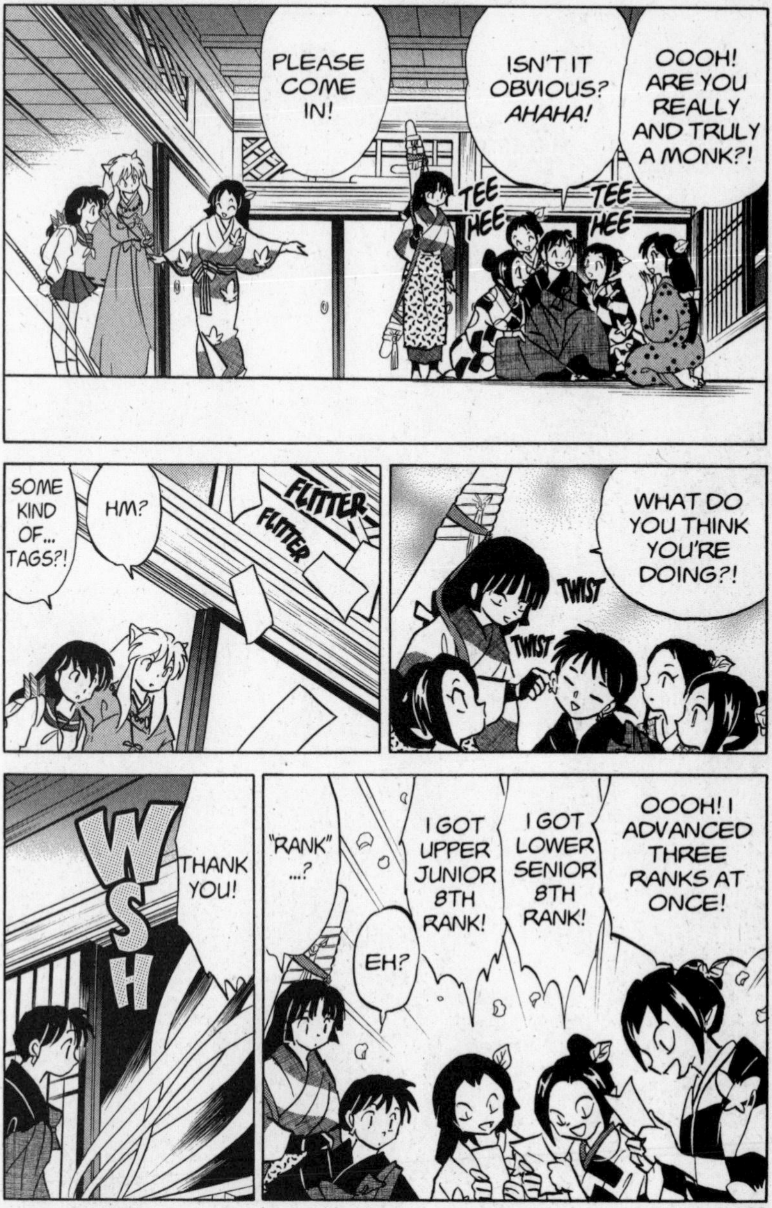
OOOH! ARE YOU REALLY AND TRULY A MONK?!
TEE HEE
ISN'T IT OBVIOUS? AHAHA!
TEE HEE
PLEASE COME IN!
WHAT DO YOU THINK YOU'RE DOING?!
TWIST
TWIST
FLITTER
FLITTER
HM?
SOME KIND OF... TAGS?!
OOOH! I ADVANCED THREE RANKS AT ONCE!
I GOT LOWER SENIOR 8TH RANK!
I GOT UPPER JUNIOR 8TH RANK!
"RANK" ...?
EH?
THANK YOU!
WSH

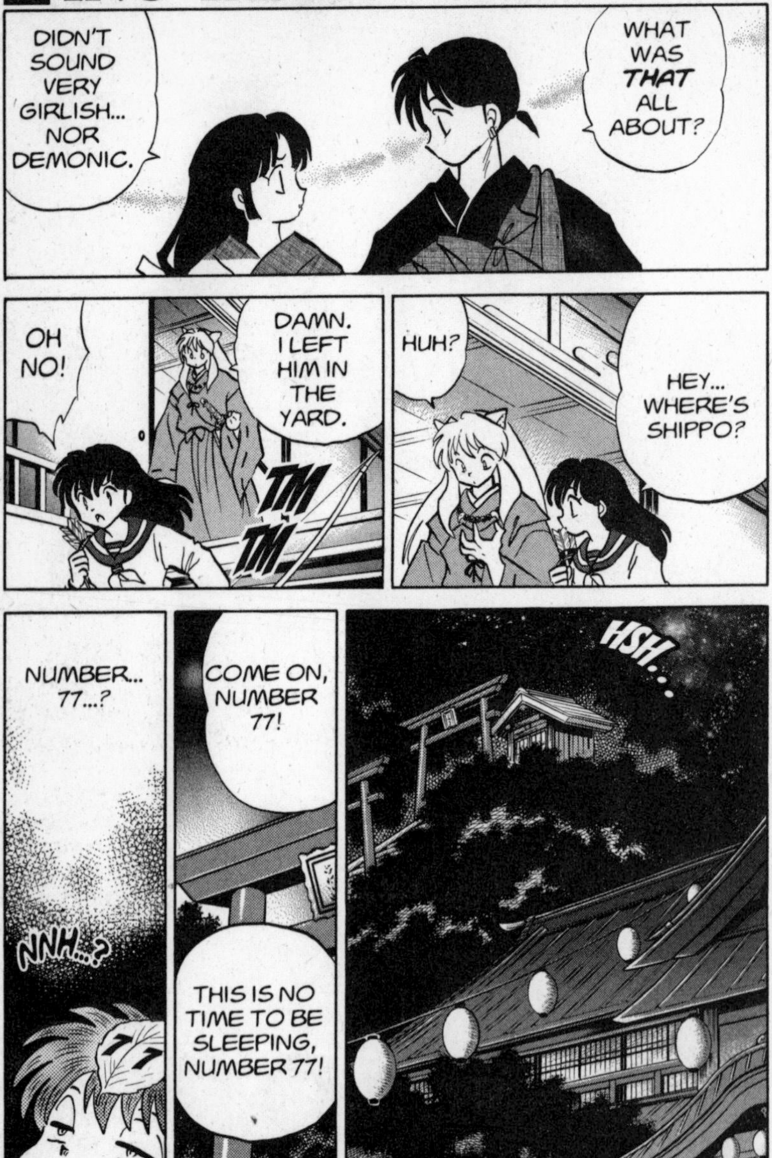
WHAT WAS THAT ALL ABOUT?
DIDN'T SOUND VERY GIRLISH... NOR DEMONIC.
HEY... WHERE'S SHIPPO?
HUH?
DAMN. I LEFT HIM IN THE YARD.
TM TM
OH NO!
HSH...
COME ON, NUMBER 77!
THIS IS NO TIME TO BE SLEEPING, NUMBER 77!
NUMBER... 77...?
NNH...?
77

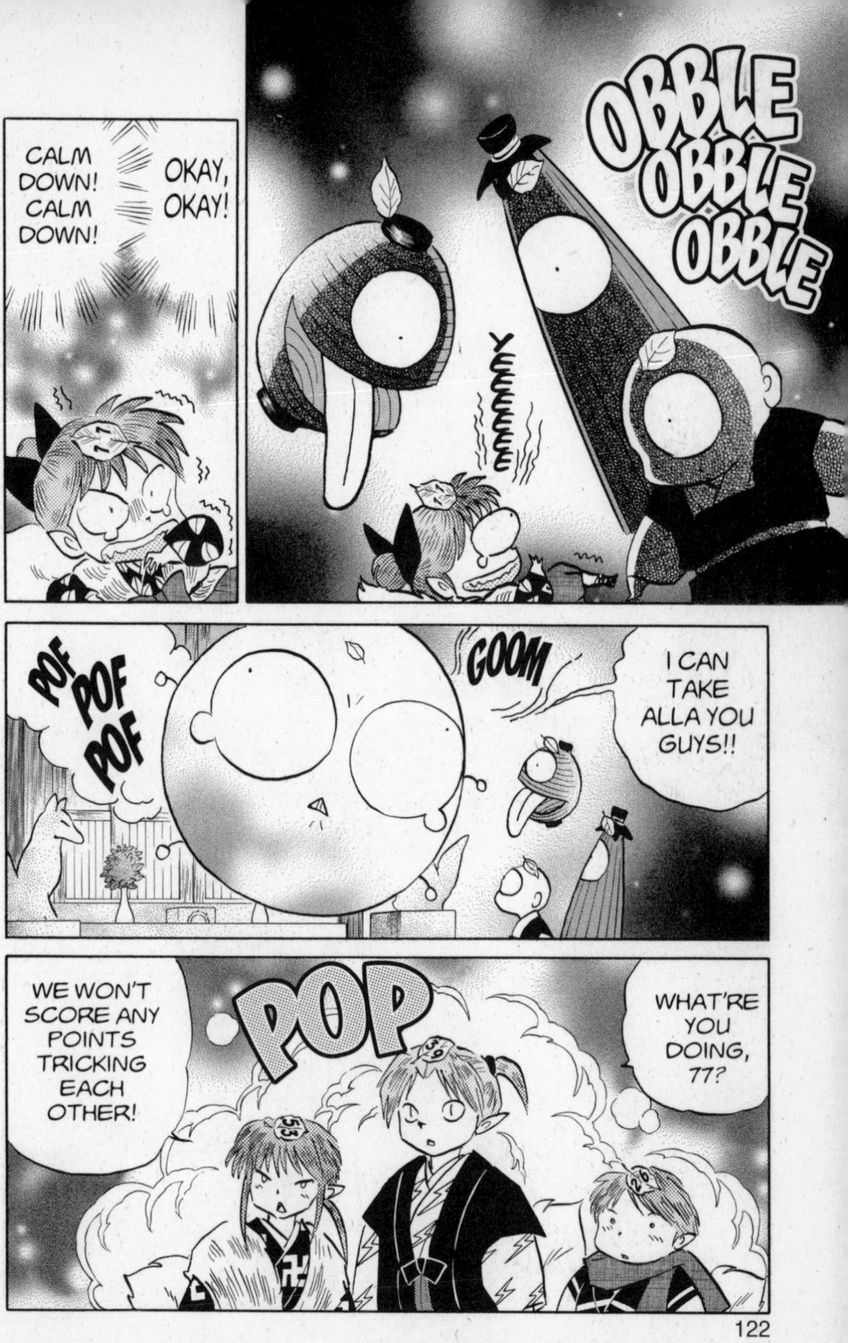
OBBLE OBBLE OBBLE
YEEEEEE
OKAY, OKAY!
CALM DOWN! CALM DOWN!
I CAN TAKE ALLA YOU GUYS!!
GOOM
POF POF POF
WHAT'RE YOU DOING, 77?
POP
WE WON'T SCORE ANY POINTS TRICKING EACH OTHER!

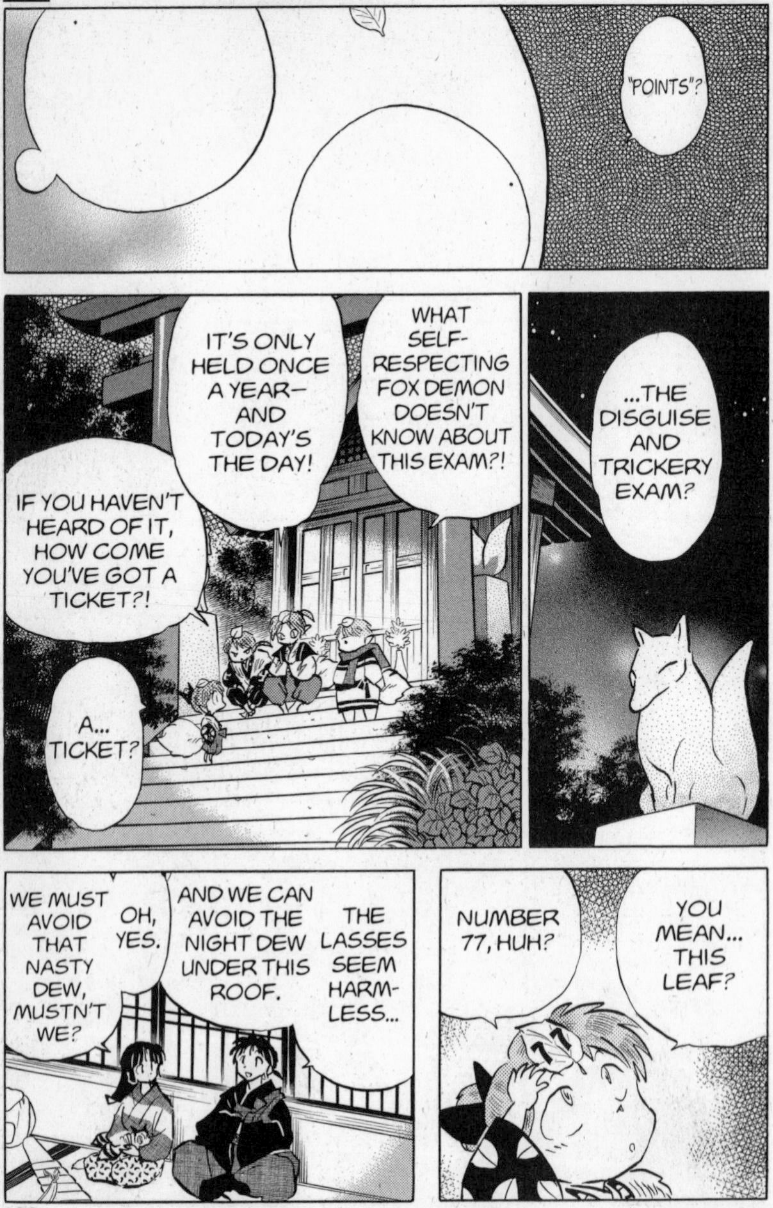
"POINTS"?
...THE DISGUISE AND TRICKERY EXAM?
WHAT SELF-RESPECTING FOX DEMON DOESN'T KNOW ABOUT THIS EXAM?!
IT'S ONLY HELD ONCE A YEAR—AND TODAY'S THE DAY!
IF YOU HAVEN'T HEARD OF IT, HOW COME YOU'VE GOT A TICKET?!
A... TICKET?
YOU MEAN... THIS LEAF?
NUMBER 77, HUH?
THE LASSES SEEM HARMLESS...
AND WE CAN AVOID THE NIGHT DEW UNDER THIS ROOF.
OH, YES.
WE MUST AVOID THAT NASTY DEW, MUSTN'T WE?

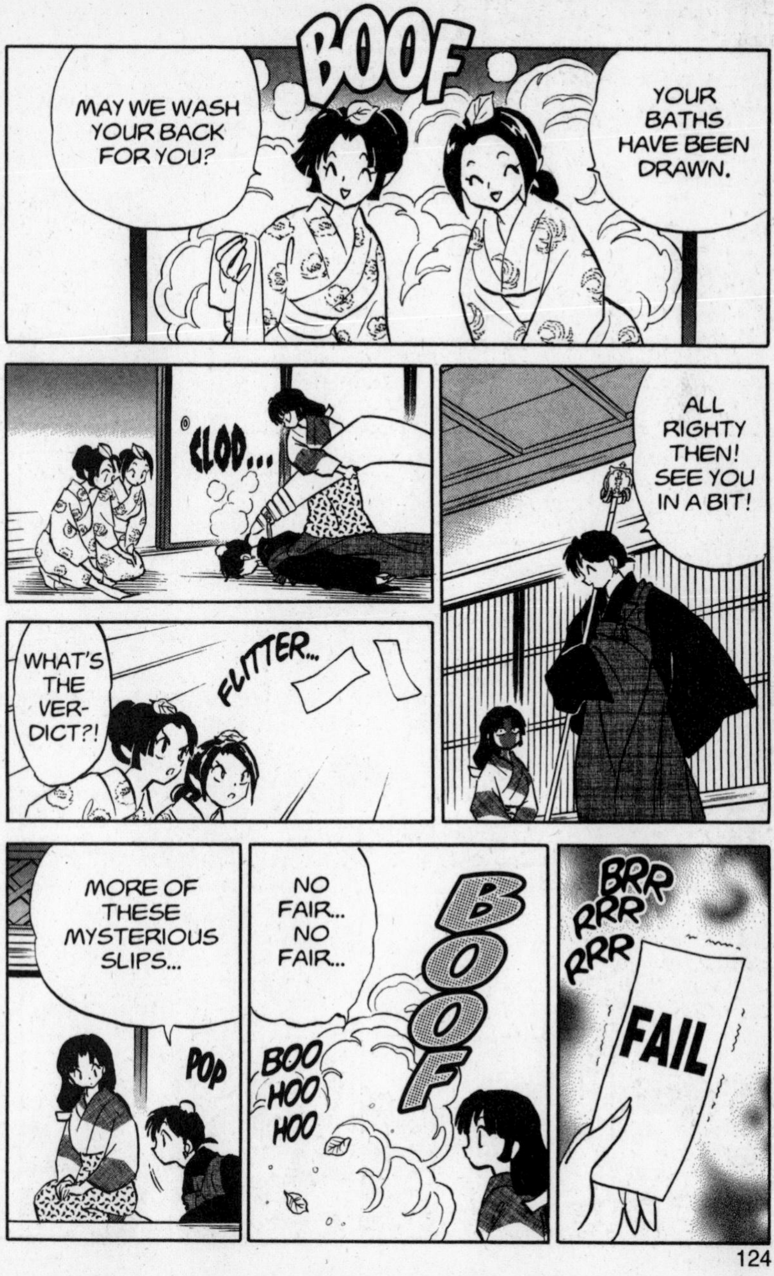
BOOF
YOUR BATHS HAVE BEEN DRAWN.
MAY WE WASH YOUR BACK FOR YOU?
ALL RIGHTY THEN! SEE YOU IN A BIT!
CLOD...
FLITTER...
WHAT'S THE VER-DICT?!
BRR RRR RRR
FAIL
NO FAIR... NO FAIR...
BOOOF
BOO HOO HOO
MORE OF THESE MYSTERIOUS SLIPS...
POP

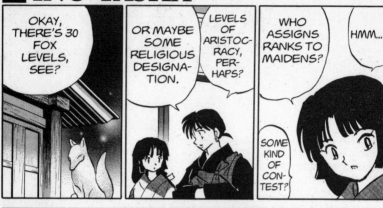

OKAY, THERE'S 30 FOX LEVELS, SEE?

OR MAYBE SOME RELIGIOUS DESIGNATION.

LEVELS OF ARISTOCRACY, PERHAPS?

WHO ASSIGNS RANKS TO MAIDENS?

HMM...

SOME KIND OF CONTEST?

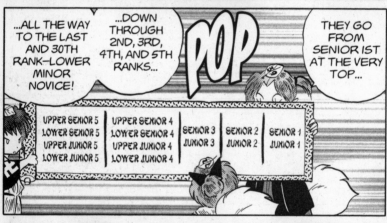

...ALL THE WAY TO THE LAST AND 30TH RANK—LOWER MINOR NOVICE!

...DOWN THROUGH 2ND, 3RD, 4TH, AND 5TH RANKS...

POP

THEY GO FROM SENIOR 1ST AT THE VERY TOP...

UPPER SENIOR 5	UPPER SENIOR 4	SENIOR 3	SENIOR 2	SENIOR 1
LOWER SENIOR 5	LOWER SENIOR 4	JUNIOR 3	JUNIOR 2	JUNIOR 1
UPPER JUNIOR 5	UPPER JUNIOR 4			
LOWER JUNIOR 5	LOWER JUNIOR 4			

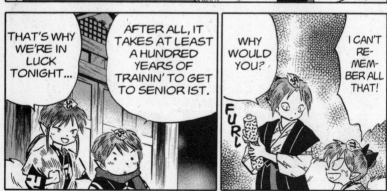

THAT'S WHY WE'RE IN LUCK TONIGHT...

AFTER ALL, IT TAKES AT LEAST A HUNDRED YEARS OF TRAININ' TO GET TO SENIOR 1ST.

WHY WOULD YOU?

I CAN'T REMEMBER ALL THAT!

FURL

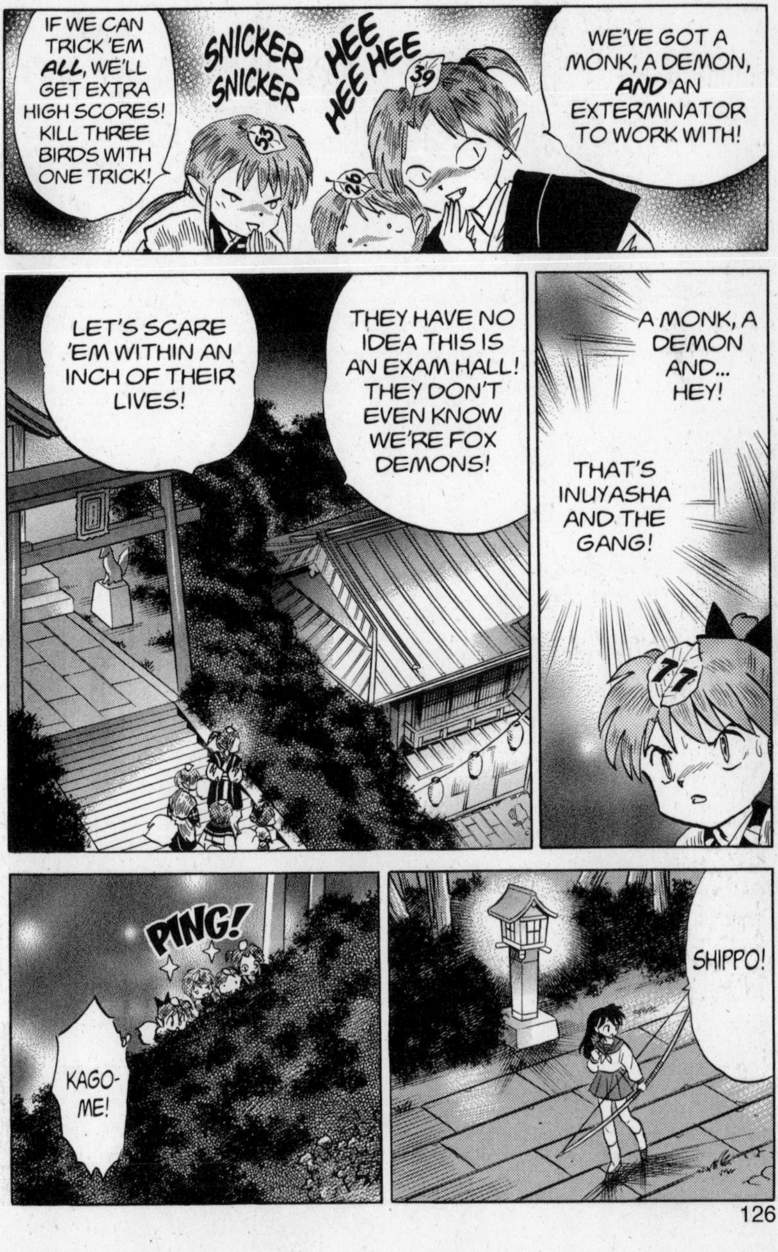
WE'VE GOT A MONK, A DEMON, **AND** AN EXTERMINATOR TO WORK WITH!
HEE HEE HEE
SNICKER SNICKER
IF WE CAN TRICK 'EM **ALL**, WE'LL GET EXTRA HIGH SCORES! KILL THREE BIRDS WITH ONE TRICK!
A MONK, A DEMON AND... HEY!
THAT'S INUYASHA AND THE GANG!
THEY HAVE NO IDEA THIS IS AN EXAM HALL! THEY DON'T EVEN KNOW WE'RE FOX DEMONS!
LET'S SCARE 'EM WITHIN AN INCH OF THEIR LIVES!
SHIPPO!
PING!
KAGO-ME!

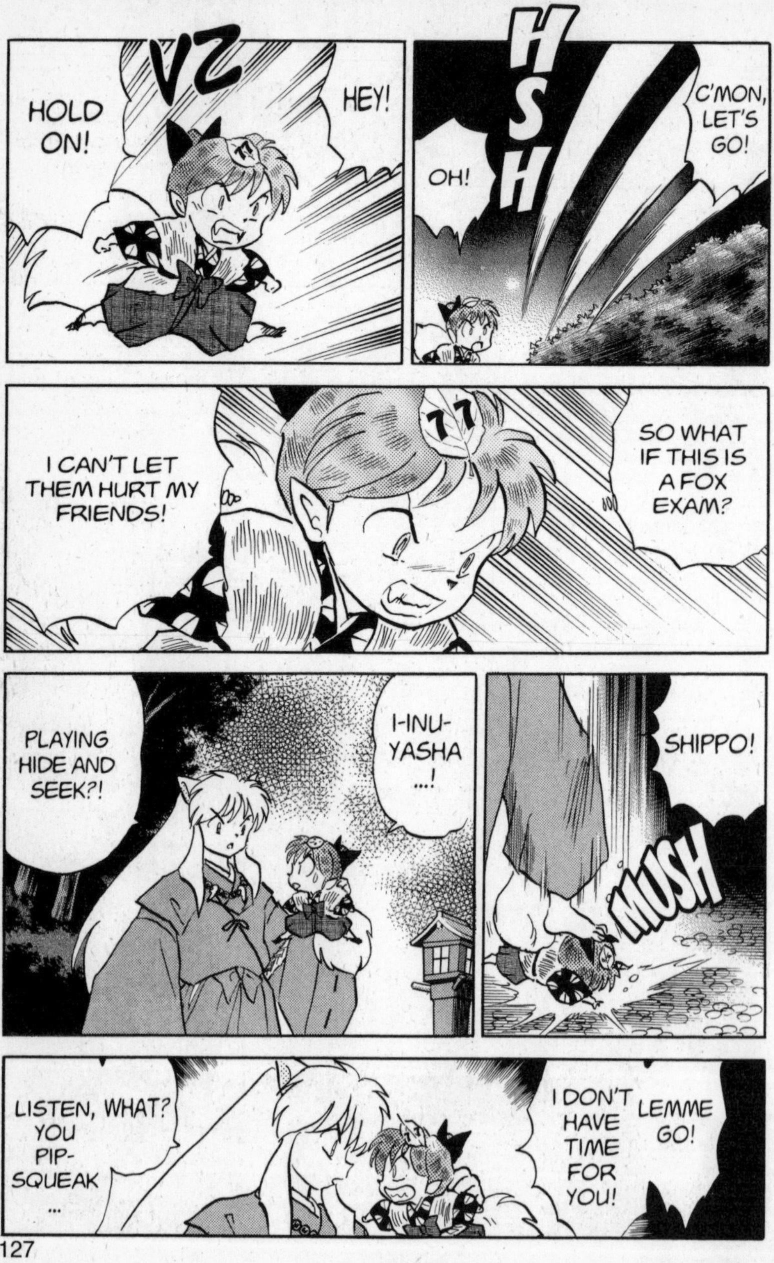
C'MON, LET'S GO!
HSH
OH!
HEY!
VZ
HOLD ON!
SO WHAT IF THIS IS A FOX EXAM?
I CAN'T LET THEM HURT MY FRIENDS!
SHIPPO!
MUSH
I-INU-YASHA ...!
PLAYING HIDE AND SEEK?!
LEMME GO!
I DON'T HAVE TIME FOR YOU!
LISTEN, WHAT? YOU PIP-SQUEAK ...

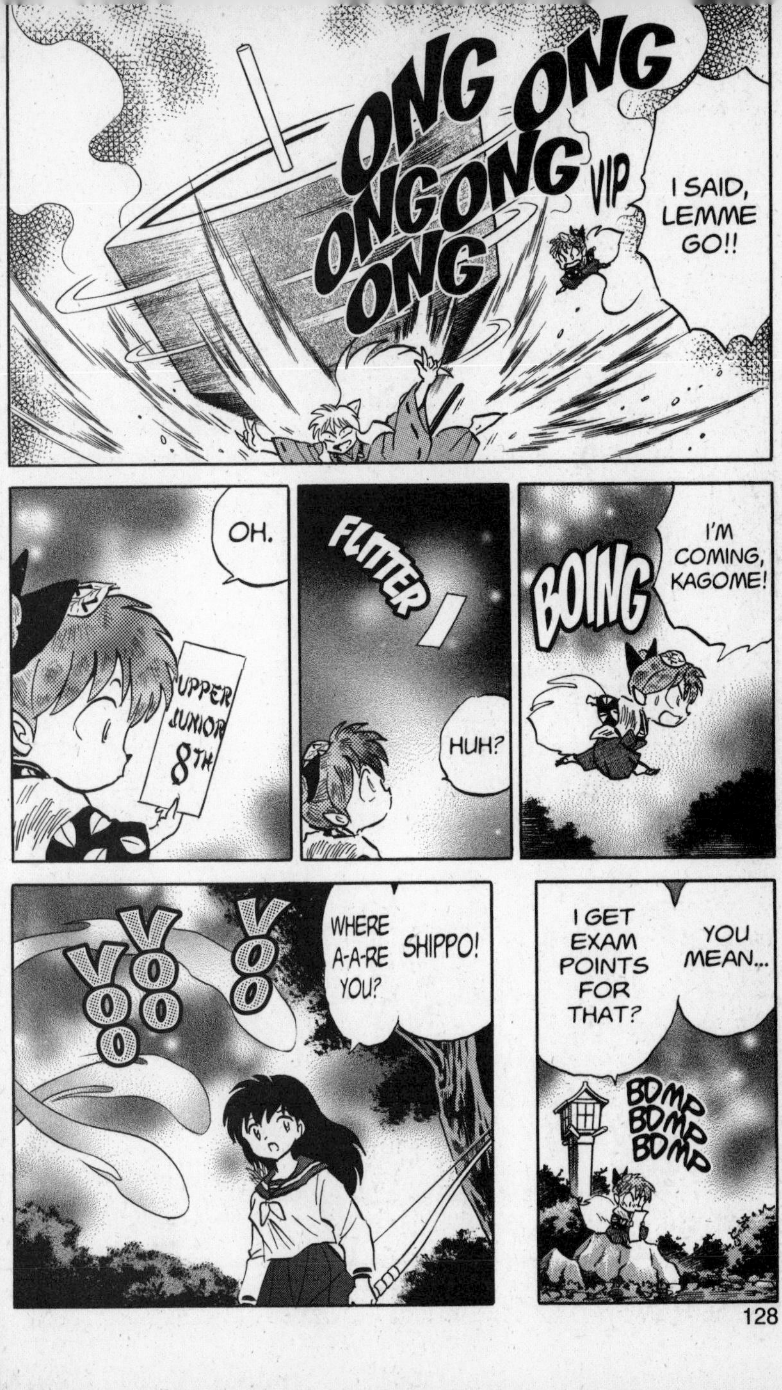
ONG ONG
ONG ONG
ONG
VIP
I SAID, LEMME GO!!
I'M COMING, KAGOME!
BOING
FLITTER
HUH?
OH.
UPPER JUNIOR 8TH
YOU MEAN...
I GET EXAM POINTS FOR THAT?
BDMP BDMP BDMP
SHIPPO!
WHERE A-A-RE YOU?
VOO VOO VOO

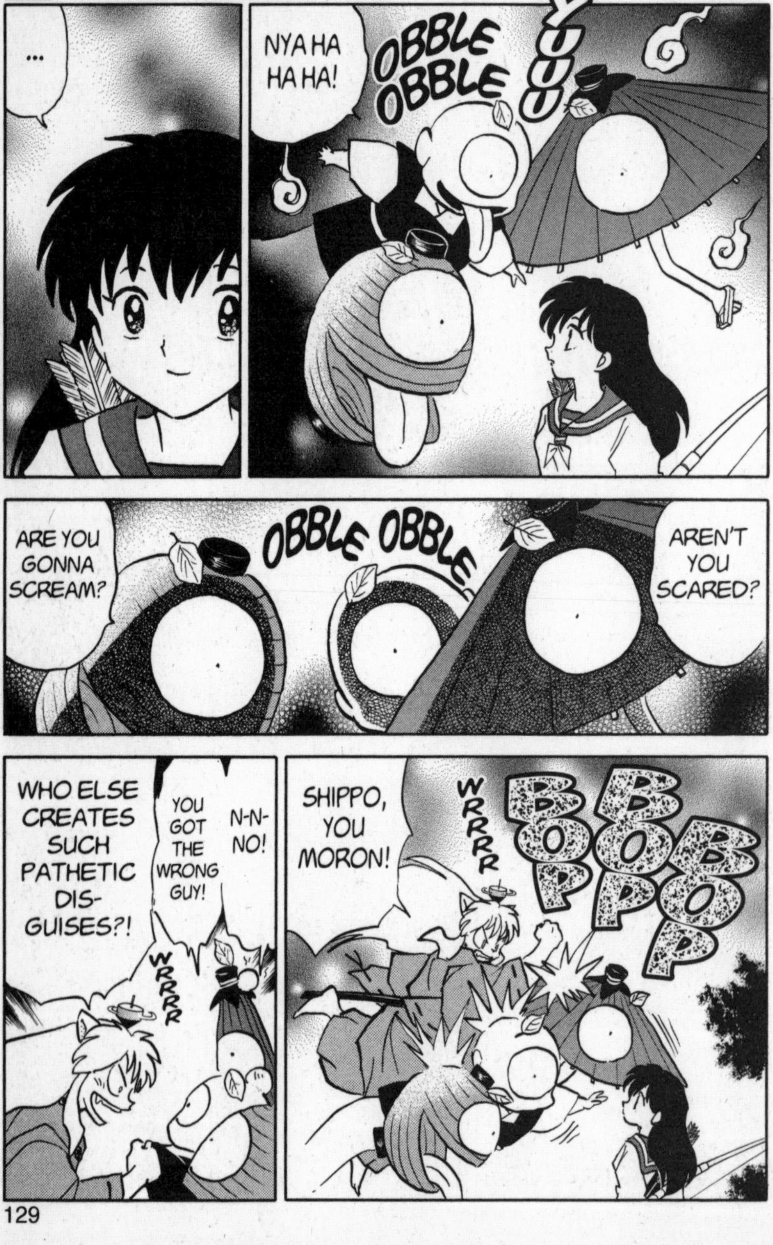
HYUUU
OBBLE OBBLE
NYA HA HA HA!
...
AREN'T YOU SCARED?
OBBLE OBBLE
ARE YOU GONNA SCREAM?
BOOP BOOP BOOP
WRRRR
SHIPPO, YOU MORON!
N-N-NO!
YOU GOT THE WRONG GUY!
WHO ELSE CREATES SUCH PATHETIC DIS-GUISES?!
WRRRR

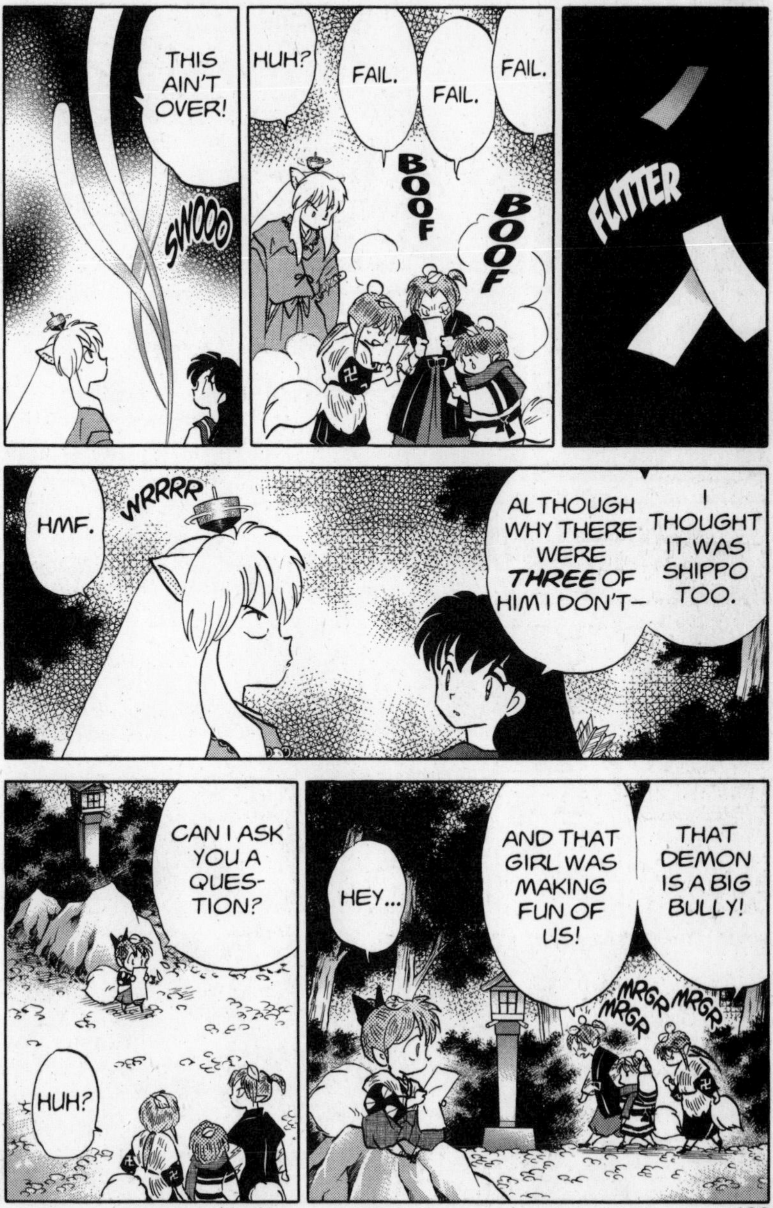
FLITTER
FAIL.
FAIL.
FAIL.
BOOF
BOOF
HUH?
THIS AIN'T OVER!
SWOOO
I THOUGHT IT WAS SHIPPO TOO.
ALTHOUGH WHY THERE WERE THREE OF HIM I DON'T—
WRRRR
HMF.
THAT DEMON IS A BIG BULLY!
AND THAT GIRL WAS MAKING FUN OF US!
MRGR MRGR
MRGR
HEY...
CAN I ASK YOU A QUES-TION?
HUH?

51 INU-YASHA

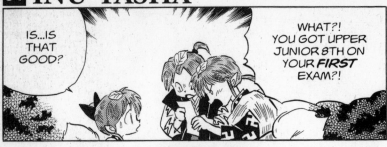

IS...IS THAT GOOD?

WHAT?! YOU GOT UPPER JUNIOR 8TH ON YOUR *FIRST* EXAM?!

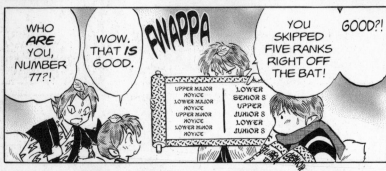

WHO *ARE* YOU, NUMBER 77?!

WOW. THAT *IS* GOOD.

FWAPPA

UPPER MAJOR NOVICE	LOWER SENIOR 8
LOWER MAJOR NOVICE	UPPER JUNIOR 8
UPPER MINOR NOVICE	LOWER JUNIOR 8
LOWER MINOR NOVICE	

YOU SKIPPED FIVE RANKS RIGHT OFF THE BAT!

GOOD?!

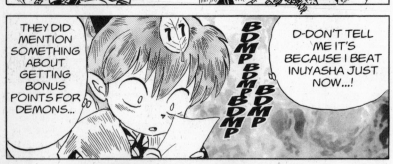

THEY DID MENTION SOMETHING ABOUT GETTING BONUS POINTS FOR DEMONS...

BDMP BDMP BDMP BDMP

D-DON'T TELL ME IT'S BECAUSE I BEAT INUYASHA JUST NOW...!

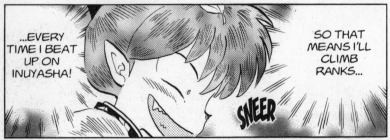

...EVERY TIME I BEAT UP ON INUYASHA!

SO THAT MEANS I'LL CLIMB RANKS...

SNEER

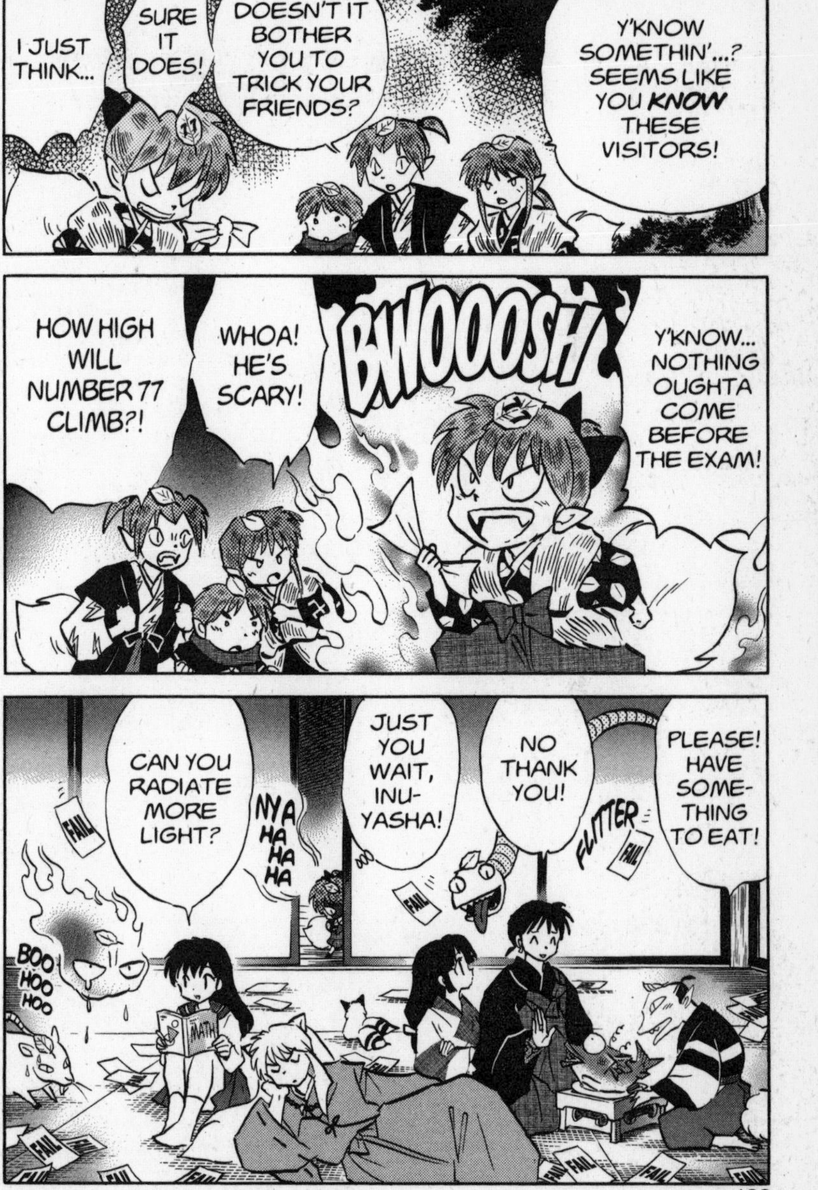
Y'KNOW SOMETHIN'...? SEEMS LIKE YOU **KNOW** THESE VISITORS!
DOESN'T IT BOTHER YOU TO TRICK YOUR FRIENDS?
SURE IT DOES!
I JUST THINK...
Y'KNOW... NOTHING OUGHTA COME BEFORE THE EXAM!
BWOOOSH
WHOA! HE'S SCARY!
HOW HIGH WILL NUMBER 77 CLIMB?!
PLEASE! HAVE SOME-THING TO EAT!
NO THANK YOU!
FLITTER
FAIL
JUST YOU WAIT, INU-YASHA!
NYA HA HA HA HA
CAN YOU RADIATE MORE LIGHT?
FAIL
BOO HOO HOO
MATH

SCROLL 8
EXAM NUMBER 77

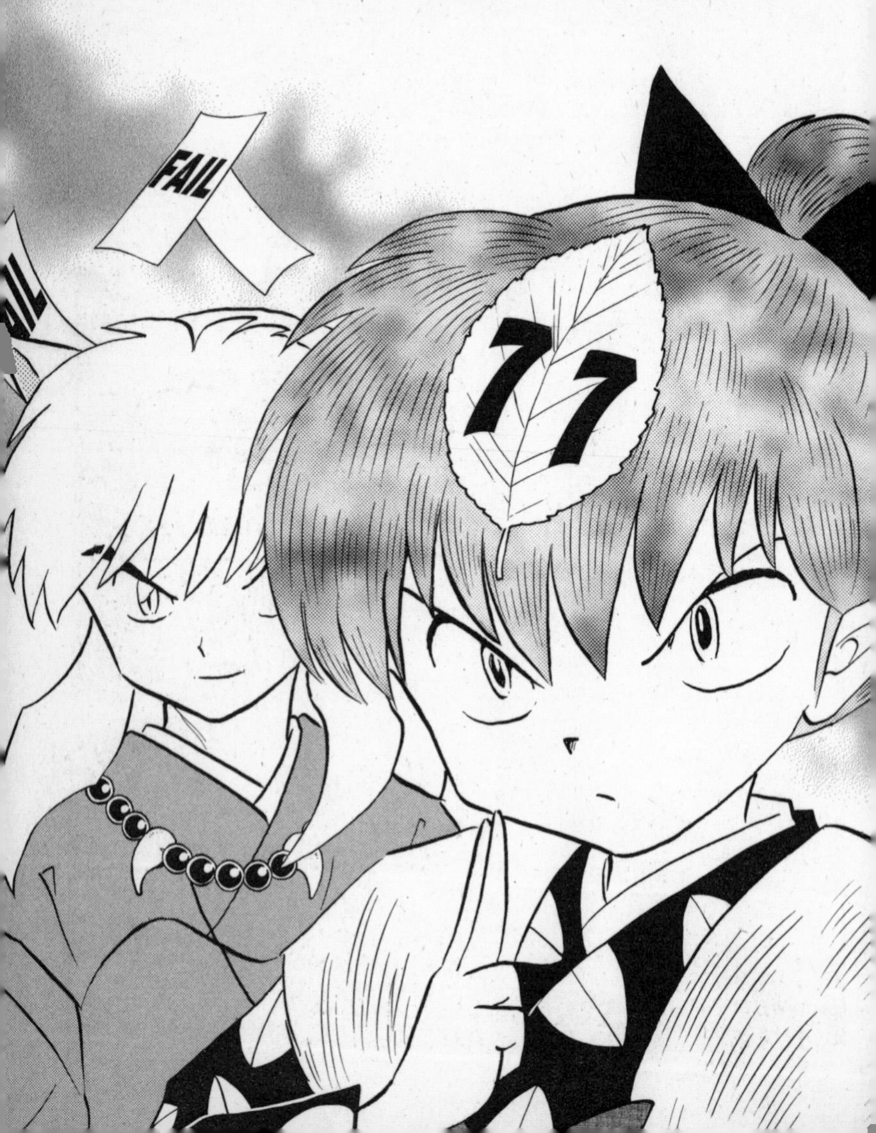
FAIL
FAIL
77

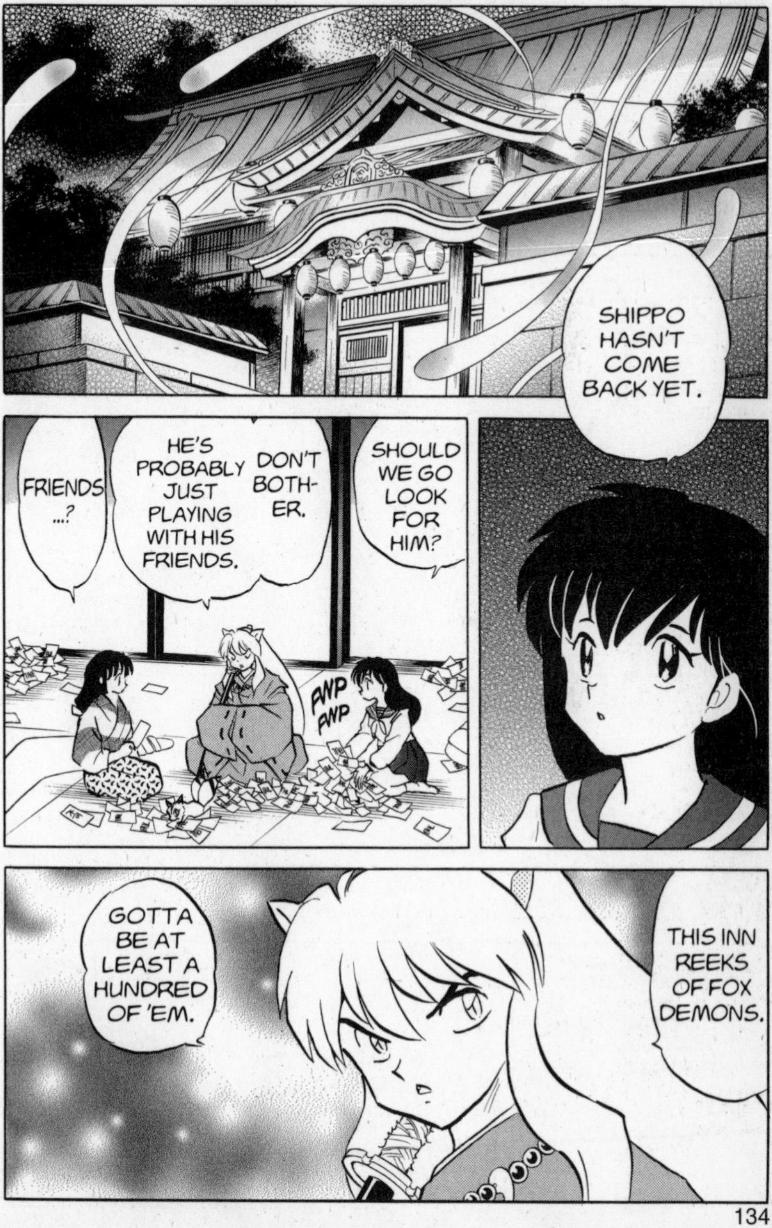
SHIPPO HASN'T COME BACK YET.
SHOULD WE GO LOOK FOR HIM?
DON'T BOTH-ER.
HE'S PROBABLY JUST PLAYING WITH HIS FRIENDS.
FRIENDS ...?
FWP FWP
THIS INN REEKS OF FOX DEMONS.
GOTTA BE AT LEAST A HUNDRED OF 'EM.

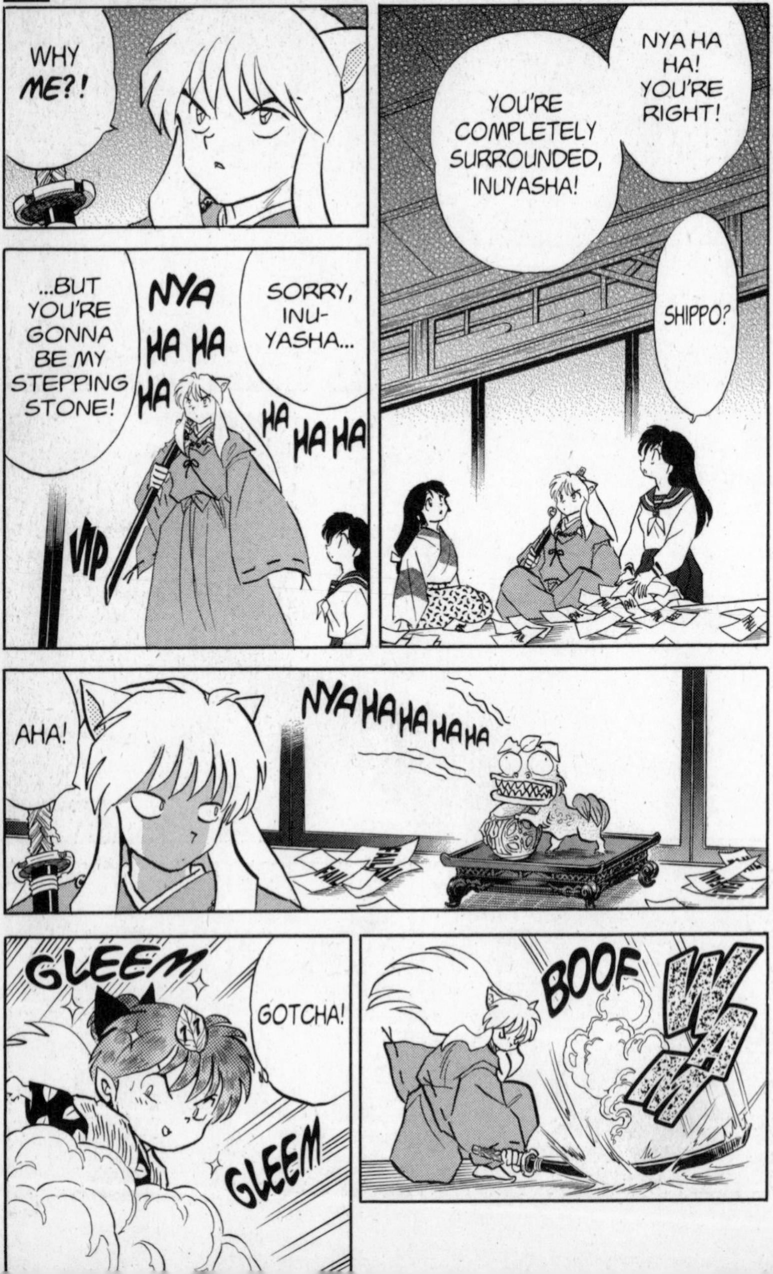
NYA HA HA! YOU'RE RIGHT!
YOU'RE COMPLETELY SURROUNDED, INUYASHA!
SHIPPO?
WHY ME?!
SORRY, INU-YASHA...
NYA HA HA HA
...BUT YOU'RE GONNA BE MY STEPPING STONE!
HA HA HA
VIP
NYA HA HA HA HA HA
AHA!
BOOF
WHA
GOTCHA!
GLEEM
GLEEM

GONG
WOO-HOO!
INU-YASHA!
FLITTER
HUH?!
UPPER JUNIOR 8TH AGAIN?!
UPPER JUNIOR 8
I BEAT INUYASHA UP!! I'M SUPPOSED TO ADVANCE!!
BOOF
BUT YOU DID ADVANCE, 77.
SEE HERE?
THAT TWO?
WHEN THAT GETS TO TEN YOU'LL MOVE UP ONE RANK.
BUT LAST TIME I JUMPED FIVE RANKS AT ONCE!
THE HIGHER THE RANK, THE HARDER IT IS TO ADVANCE.

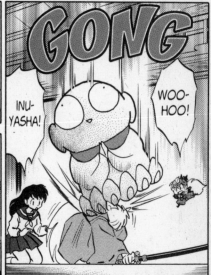

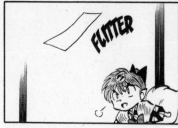

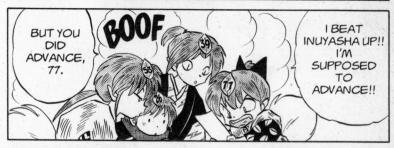

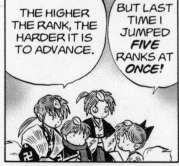

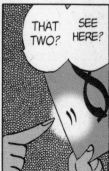

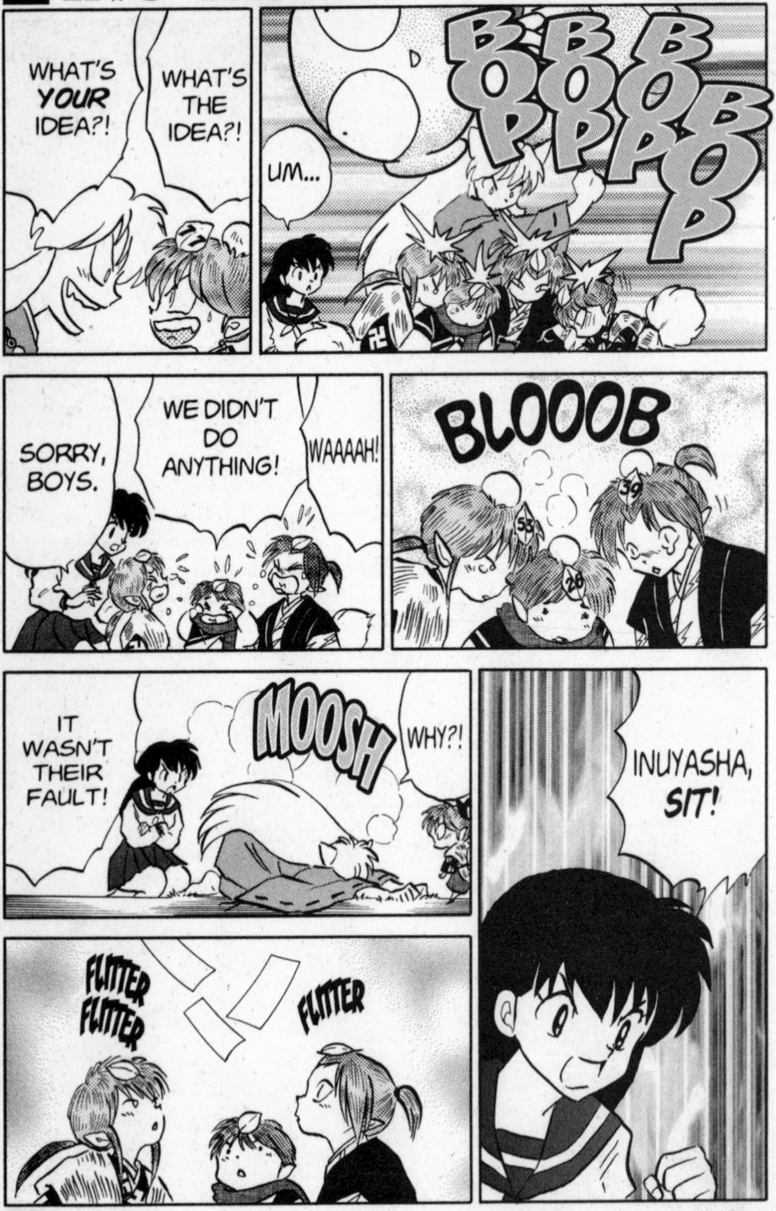
BOP BOP BOP BOP
UM...
WHAT'S THE IDEA?!
WHAT'S **YOUR** IDEA?!
BLOOOB
WAAAAH!
WE DIDN'T DO ANYTHING!
SORRY, BOYS.
INUYASHA, **SIT!**
WHY?!
MOOSH
IT WASN'T THEIR FAULT!
FLITTER
FLITTER FLITTER

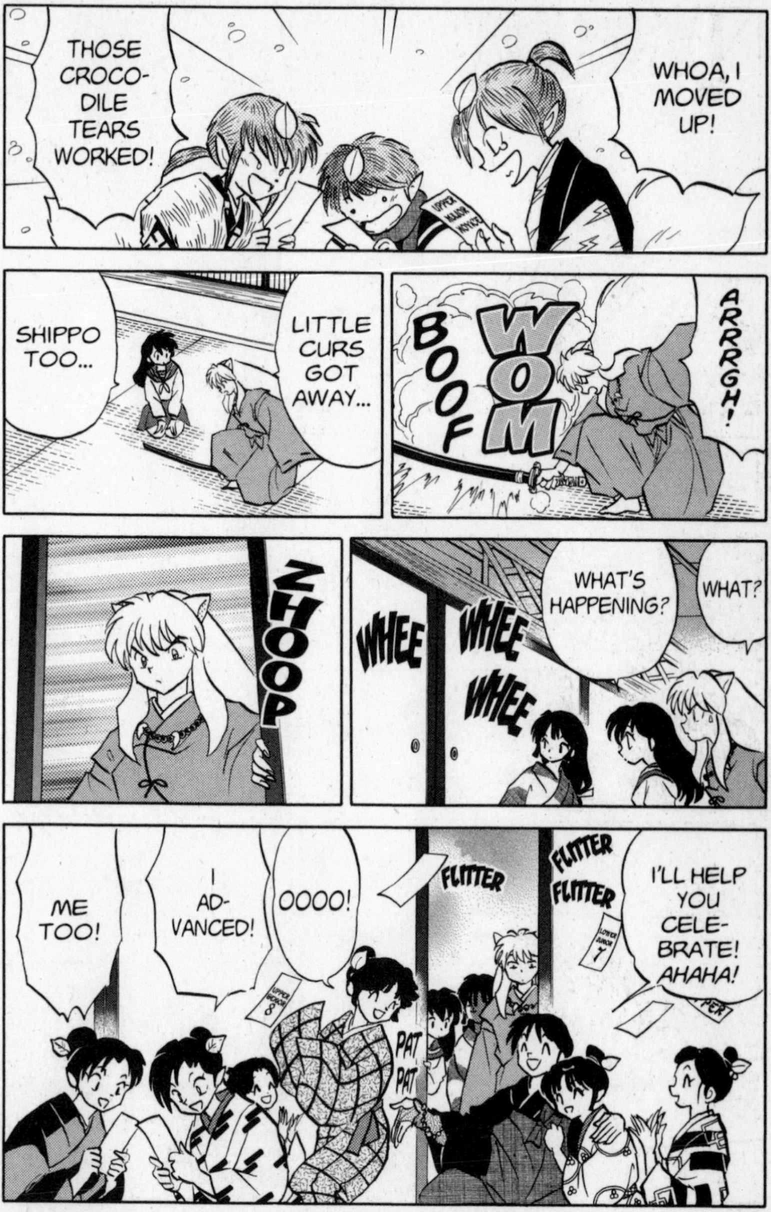
WHOA, I MOVED UP!
THOSE CROCODILE TEARS WORKED!
ARRRGH!
WOM
BOOF
LITTLE CURS GOT AWAY...
SHIPPO TOO...
WHAT?
WHAT'S HAPPENING?
WHEE
WHEE
WHEE
ZHOOP
I'LL HELP YOU CELEBRATE! AHAHA!
FLITTER
FLITTER
FLITTER
PAT
PAT
OOOO!
I ADVANCED!
ME TOO!

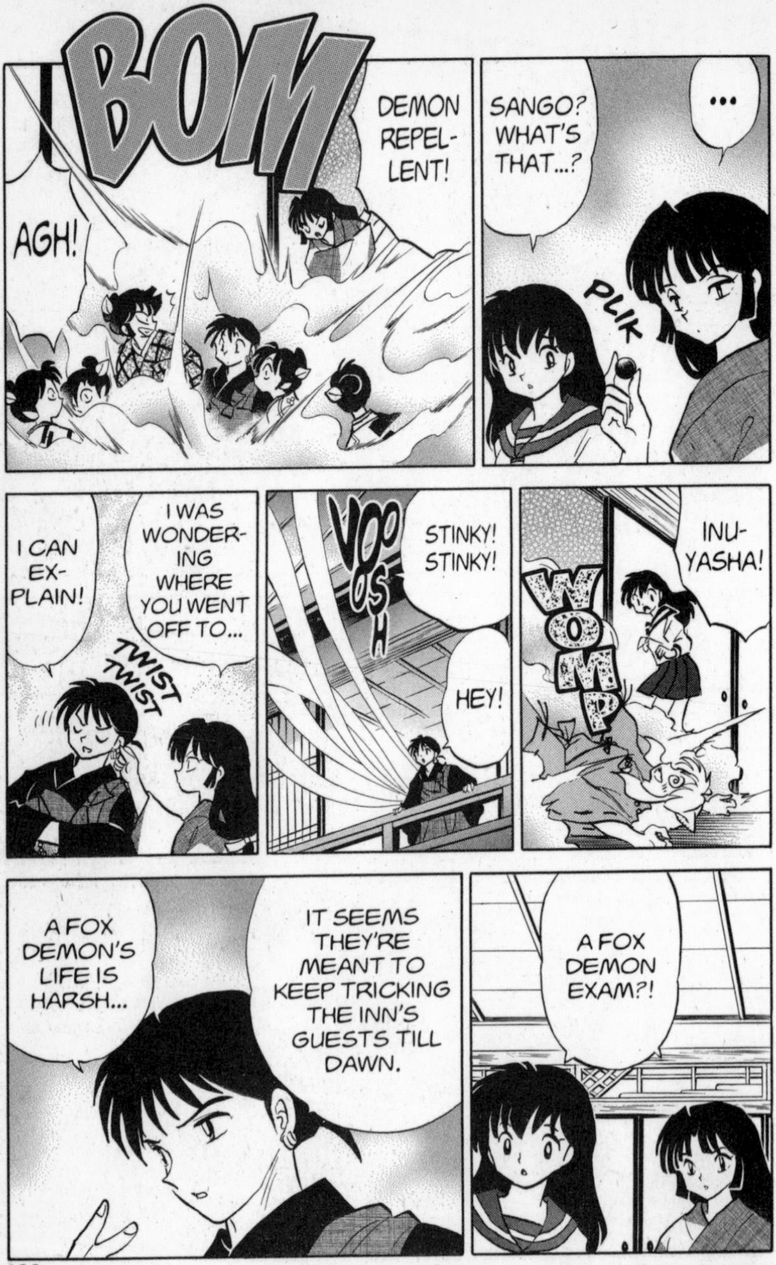

...
SANGO? WHAT'S THAT...?
PLIK
BOM
DEMON REPEL-LENT!
AGH!
INU-YASHA!
WOMP
STINKY! STINKY!
VOOOSH
HEY!
I WAS WONDER-ING WHERE YOU WENT OFF TO...
I CAN EX-PLAIN!
TWIST TWIST
A FOX DEMON EXAM?!
IT SEEMS THEY'RE MEANT TO KEEP TRICKING THE INN'S GUESTS TILL DAWN.
A FOX DEMON'S LIFE IS HARSH...

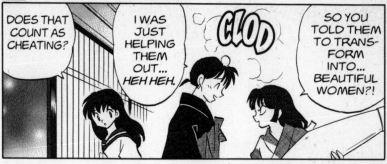

SO YOU TOLD THEM TO TRANS-FORM INTO... BEAUTIFUL WOMEN?!
CLOD
I WAS JUST HELPING THEM OUT... HEH HEH.
DOES THAT COUNT AS CHEATING?
FLIP FLIP
FLIP FLIP
NYA HA HA HA! INUYASHA PASSED OUT!
THIS IS OUR CHANCE!
STRIKE!
FOM
BOOP
THAT TEARS IT!
BONG

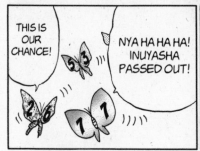

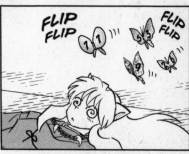

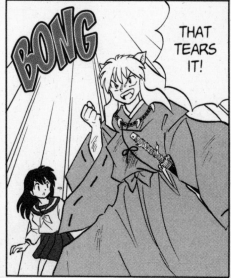

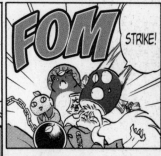

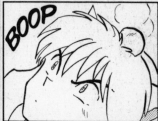

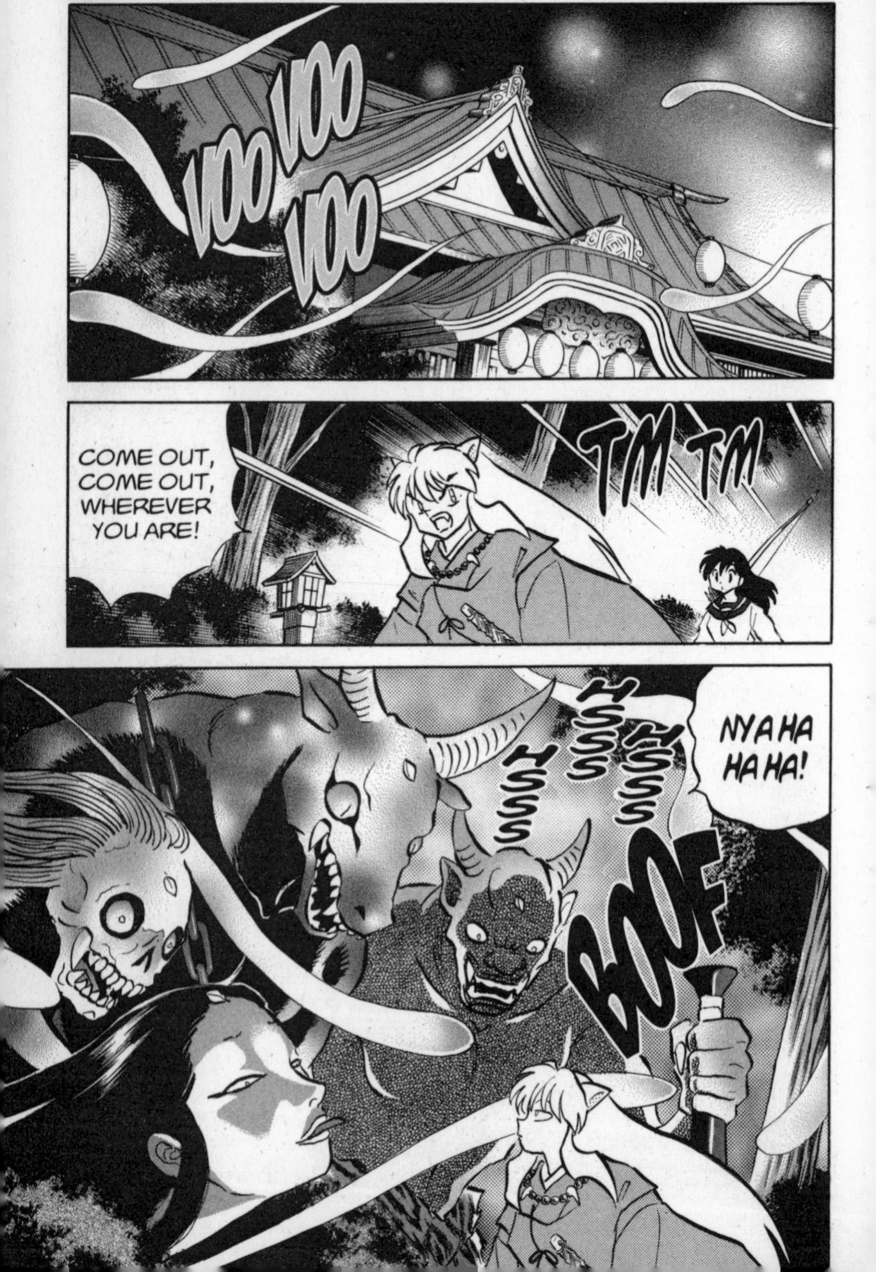
VOO VOO
VOO VOO
TM TM
COME OUT, COME OUT, WHEREVER YOU ARE!
NYA HA HA HA!
HSSS HSSS HSSS
BOOF

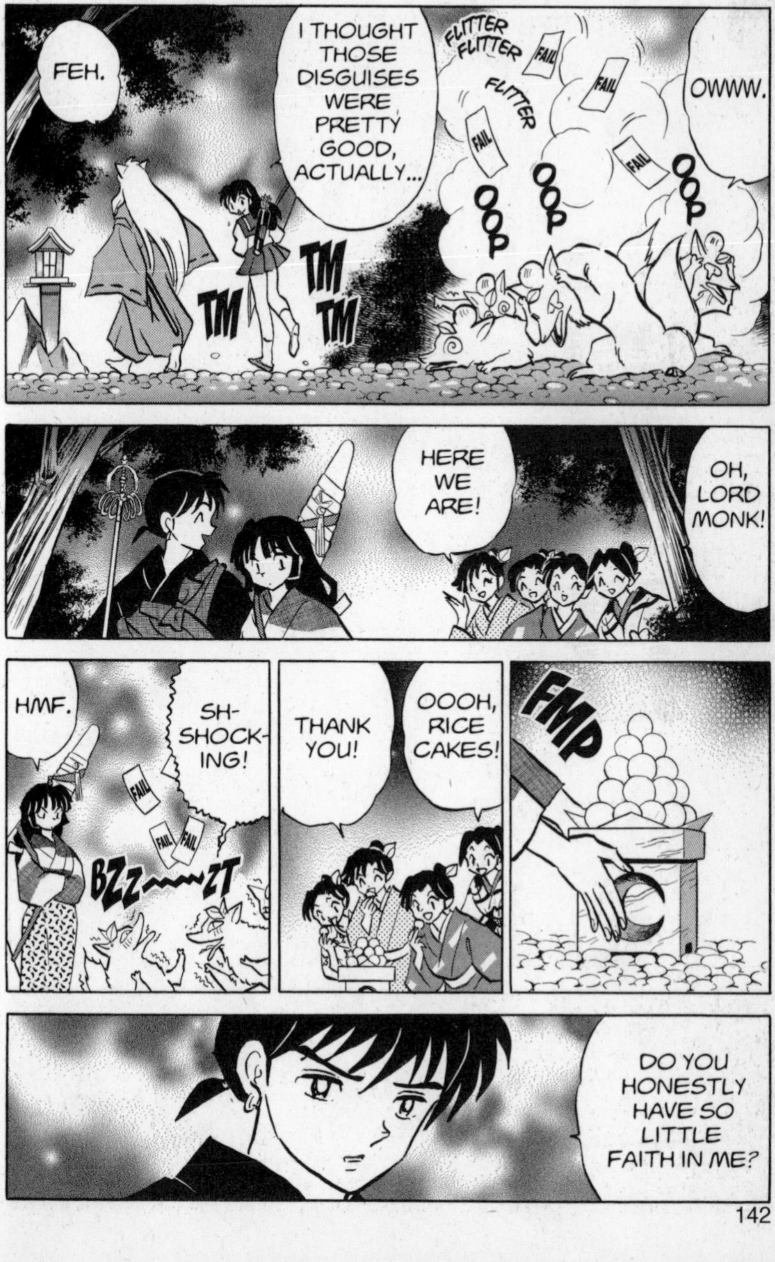
OWWW.
FLITTER FLITTER
FAIL
FAIL
FLITTER
FAIL
FAIL
OOP
OOP
OOP
I THOUGHT THOSE DISGUISES WERE PRETTY GOOD, ACTUALLY...
FEH.
TM TM
TM
TM
OH, LORD MONK!
HERE WE ARE!
FMP
OOOH, RICE CAKES!
THANK YOU!
SH-SHOCKING!
HMF.
FAIL
FAIL
FAIL
BZZ~~~ZT
DO YOU HONESTLY HAVE SO LITTLE FAITH IN ME?

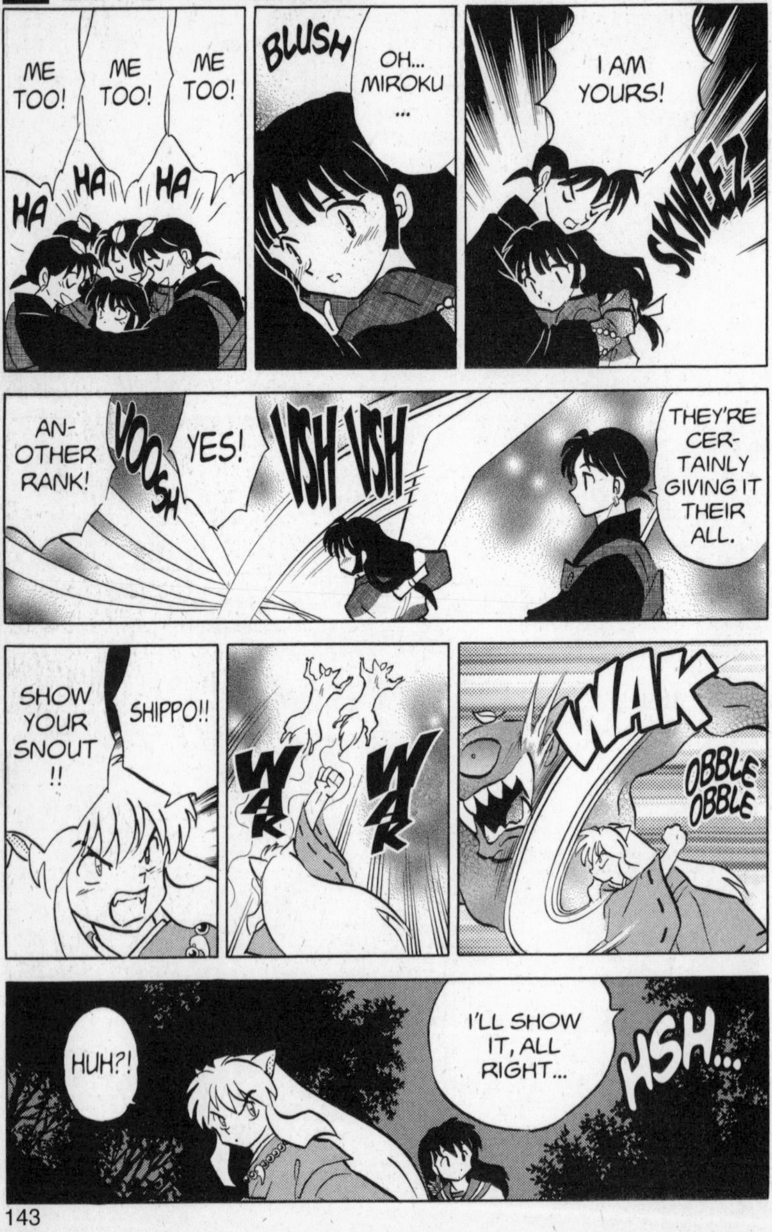
I AM YOURS!
SKWEEZ
BLUSH
OH... MIROKU ...
ME TOO!
ME TOO!
ME TOO!
HA
HA
HA
THEY'RE CER-TAINLY GIVING IT THEIR ALL.
VSH VSH
YES!
VOOSH
AN-OTHER RANK!
WAK
OBBLE OBBLE
WAK
WAK
SHIPPO!!
SHOW YOUR SNOUT !!
HSH...
I'LL SHOW IT, ALL RIGHT...
HUH?!

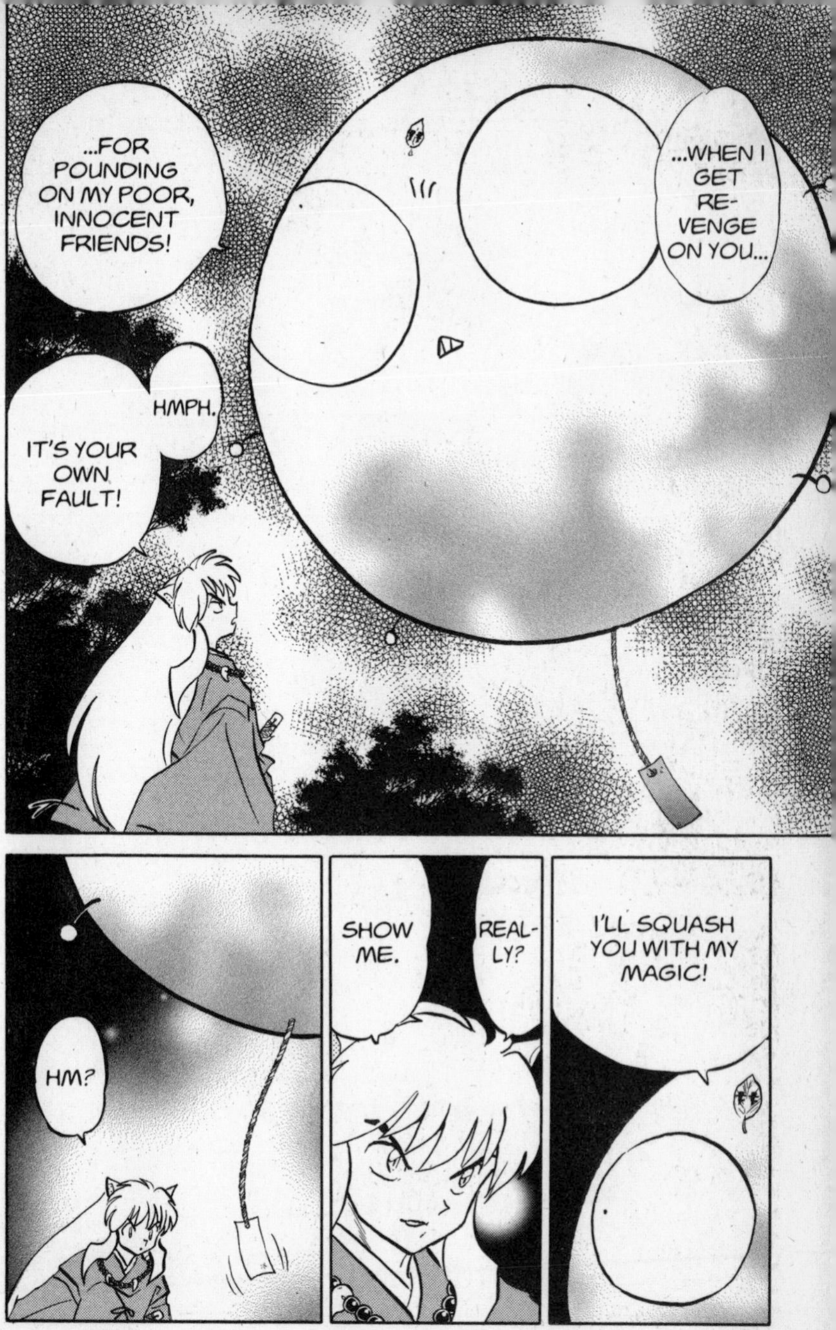
...WHEN I GET RE- VENGE ON YOU...
...FOR POUNDING ON MY POOR, INNOCENT FRIENDS!
HMPH.
IT'S YOUR OWN FAULT!
I'LL SQUASH YOU WITH MY MAGIC!
REAL- LY?
SHOW ME.
HM?

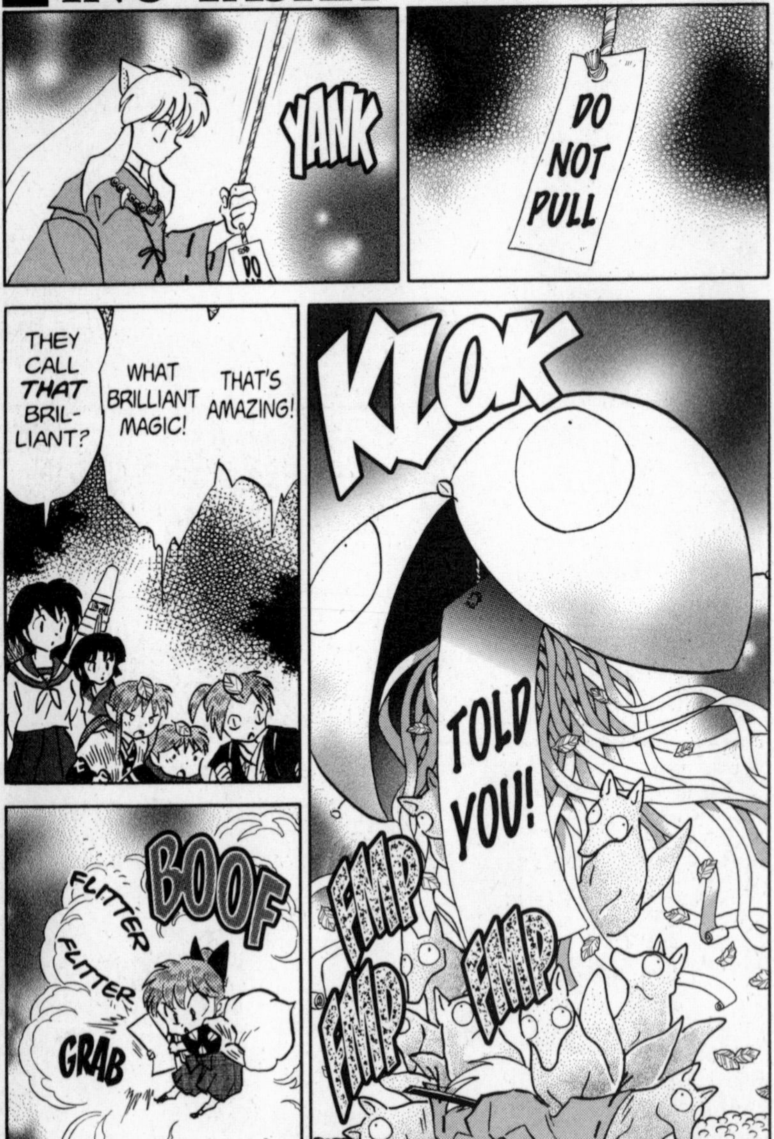
DO NOT PULL
YANK
DO
KLOK
TOLD YOU!
EMP
EMP
EMP
THAT'S AMAZING!
WHAT BRILLIANT MAGIC!
THEY CALL *THAT* BRIL-LIANT?
BOOF
FLUTTER
FLUTTER
GRAB

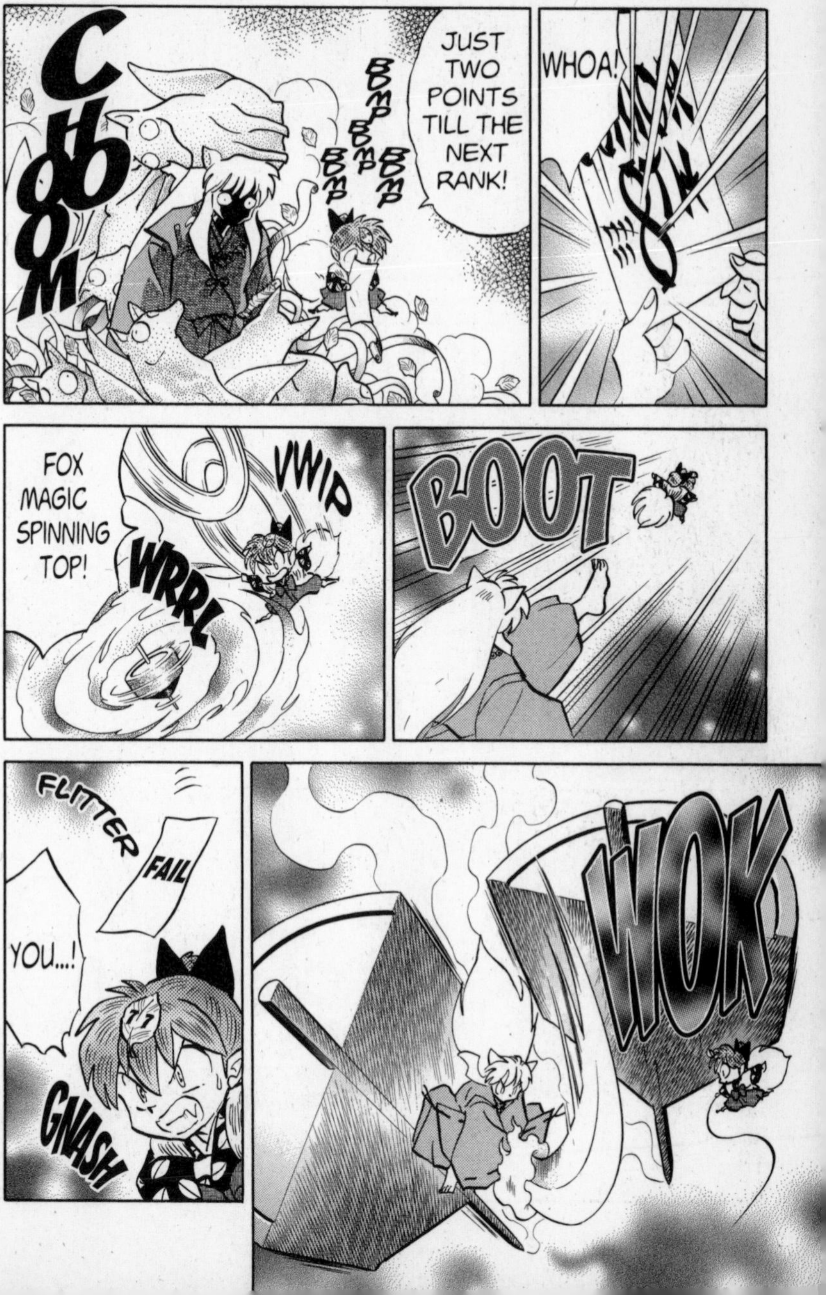
WHOA!
JUST TWO POINTS TILL THE NEXT RANK!
BOMP BOMP BOMP BOMP
CHOOOM
BOOT
VWIP
FOX MAGIC SPINNING TOP!
WRRL
WOK
FLUTTER
FAIL
YOU...!
GNASH

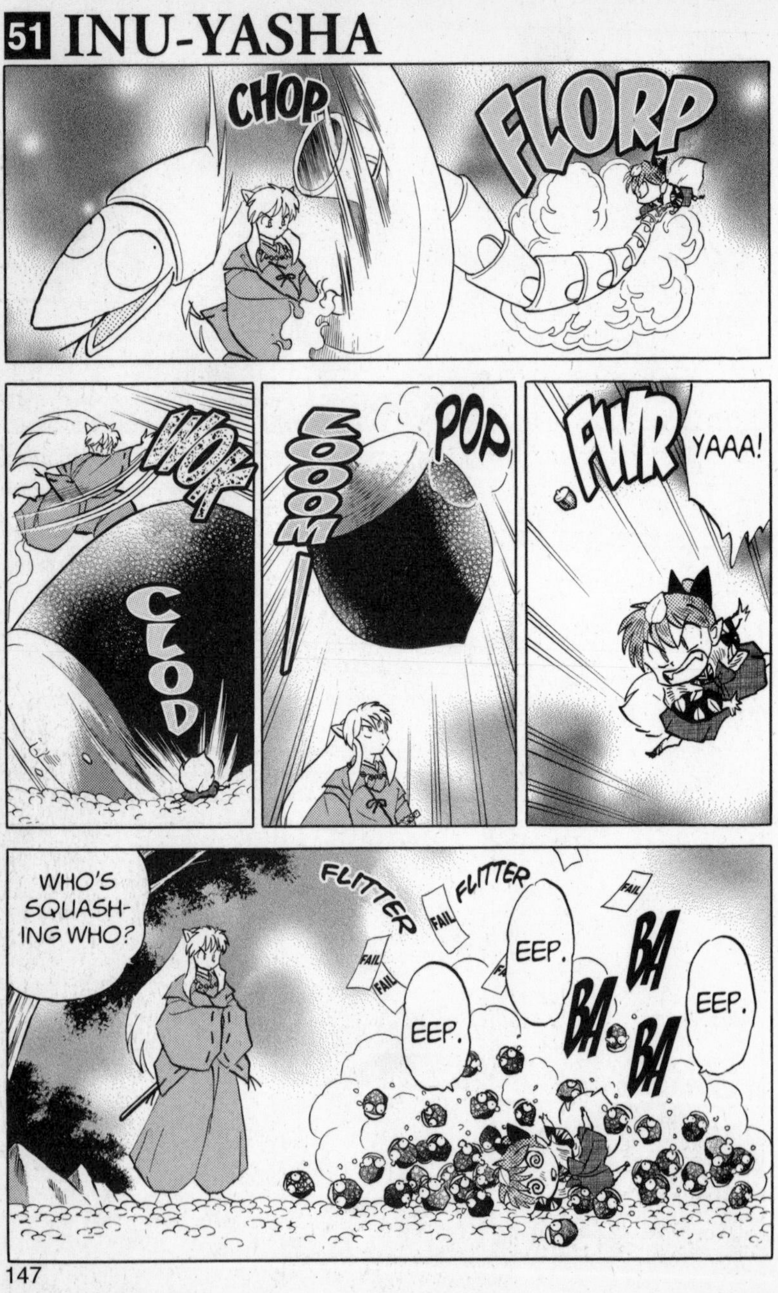
FLORP
CHOP
FWR
YAAA!
POP
VOOOOM
WOK
CLOD
EEP.
BA
BA
BA
BA
EEP.
EEP.
FLITTER
FAIL
FLITTER
FAIL
FAIL
FAIL
WHO'S SQUASHING WHO?

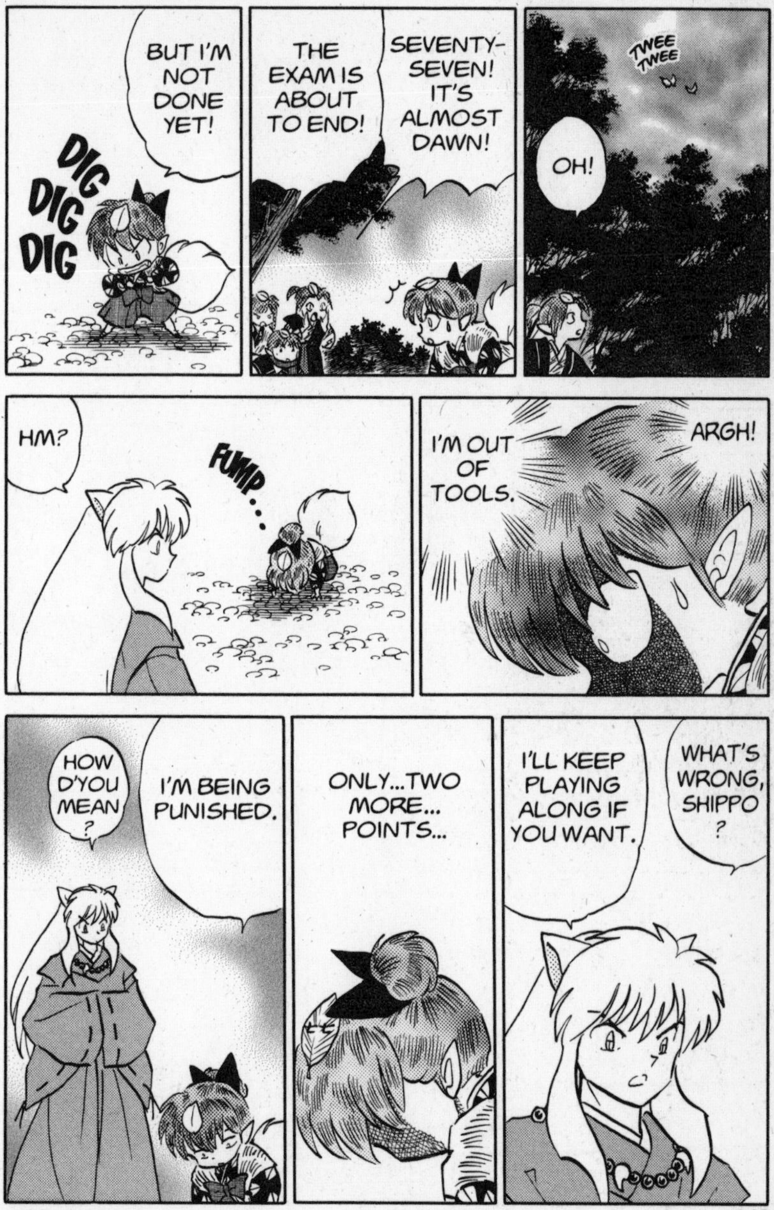
TWEE TWEE
OH!
SEVENTY-SEVEN! IT'S ALMOST DAWN!
THE EXAM IS ABOUT TO END!
BUT I'M NOT DONE YET!
DIG DIG DIG
ARGH!
I'M OUT OF TOOLS.
HM?
FUMP...
WHAT'S WRONG, SHIPPO?
I'LL KEEP PLAYING ALONG IF YOU WANT.
ONLY...TWO MORE... POINTS...
I'M BEING PUNISHED.
HOW D'YOU MEAN?

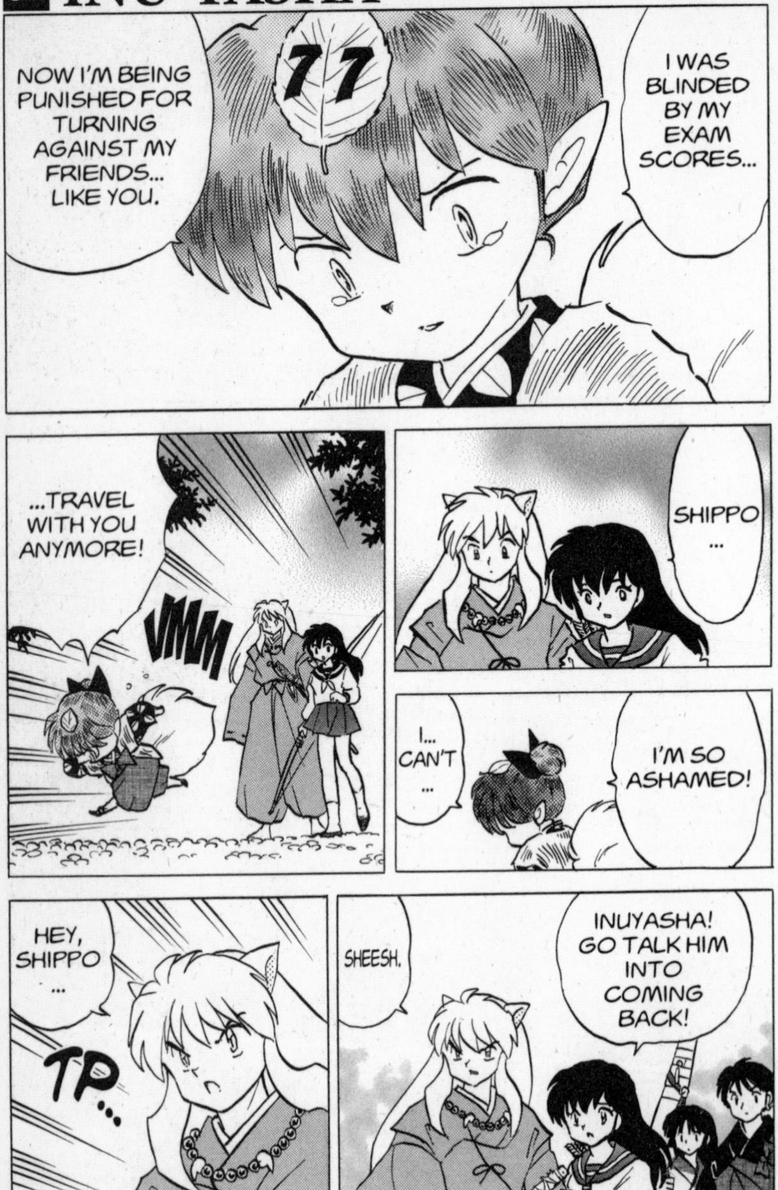
I WAS BLINDED BY MY EXAM SCORES...
NOW I'M BEING PUNISHED FOR TURNING AGAINST MY FRIENDS... LIKE YOU.
SHIPPO ...
I'M SO ASHAMED!
I... CAN'T ...
...TRAVEL WITH YOU ANYMORE!
VMM
INUYASHA! GO TALK HIM INTO COMING BACK!
SHEESH.
HEY, SHIPPO ...
TP...

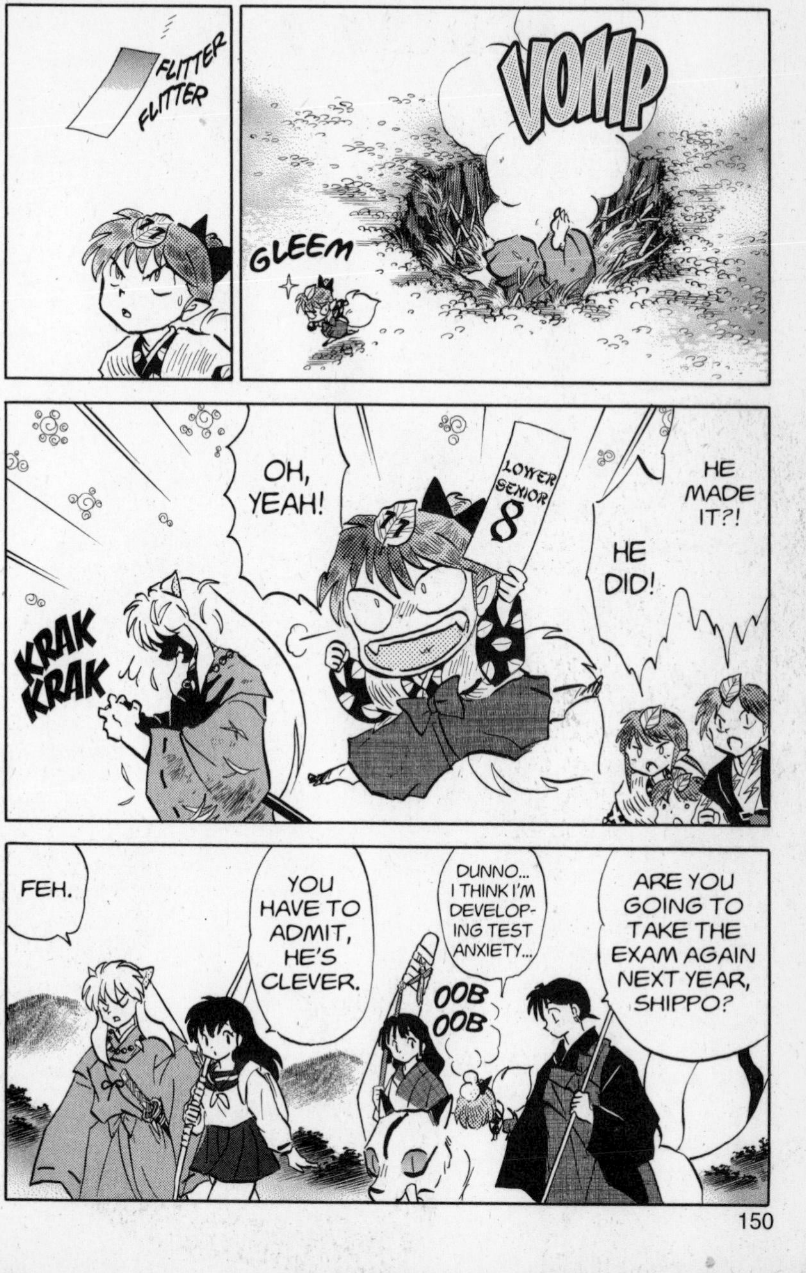
VOMP
GLEEM
FLITTER FLITTER
HE MADE IT?!
HE DID!
LOWER SENIOR 8
OH, YEAH!
KRAK KRAK
ARE YOU GOING TO TAKE THE EXAM AGAIN NEXT YEAR, SHIPPO?
DUNNO... I THINK I'M DEVELOP-ING TEST ANXIETY...
OOB OOB
YOU HAVE TO ADMIT, HE'S CLEVER.
FEH.

SCROLL 9
HITOMIKO

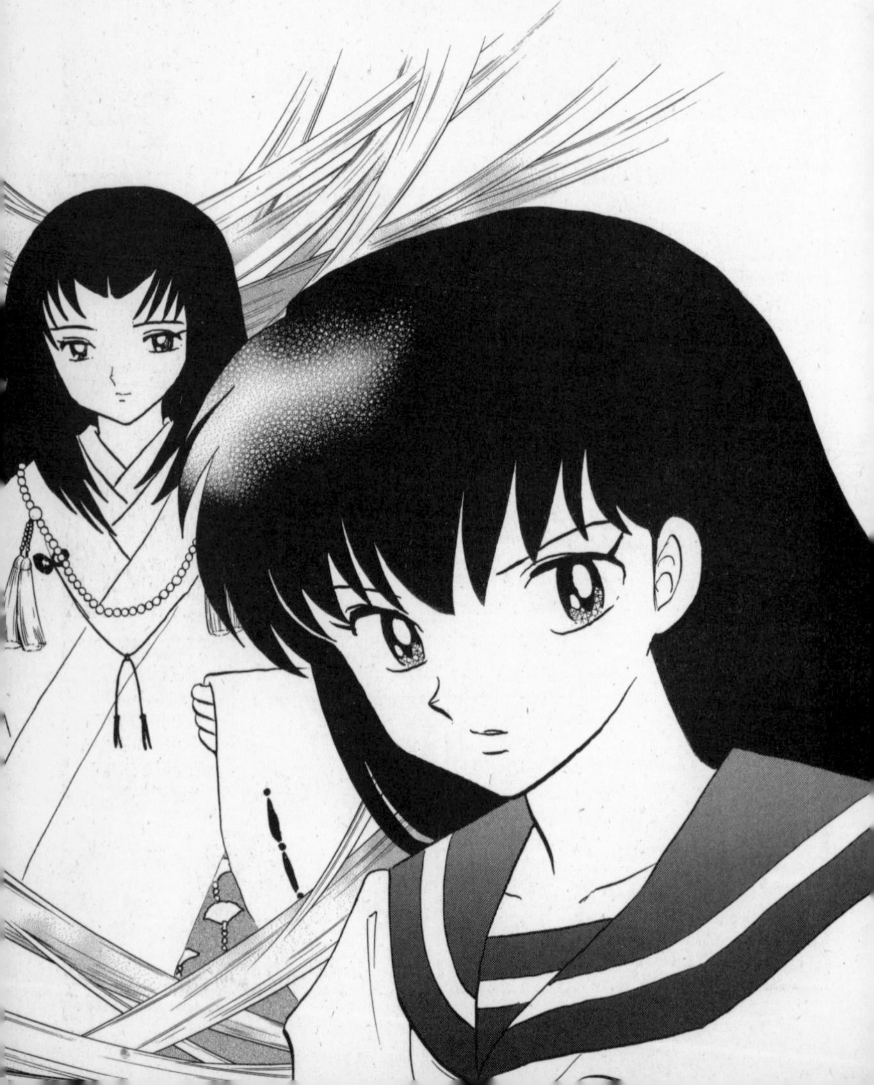

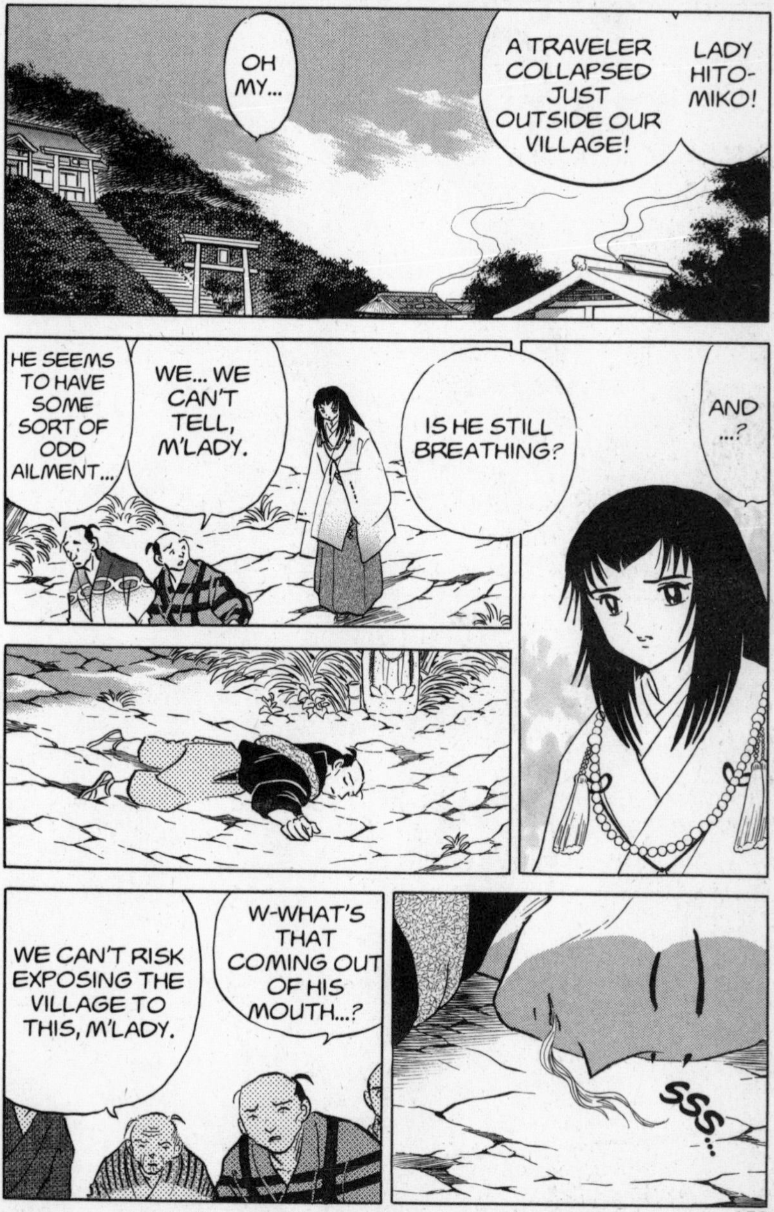
LADY HITO-MIKO!
A TRAVELER COLLAPSED JUST OUTSIDE OUR VILLAGE!
OH MY...
AND ...?
IS HE STILL BREATHING?
WE... WE CAN'T TELL, M'LADY.
HE SEEMS TO HAVE SOME SORT OF ODD AILMENT...
SSS...
W-WHAT'S THAT COMING OUT OF HIS MOUTH...?
WE CAN'T RISK EXPOSING THE VILLAGE TO THIS, M'LADY.

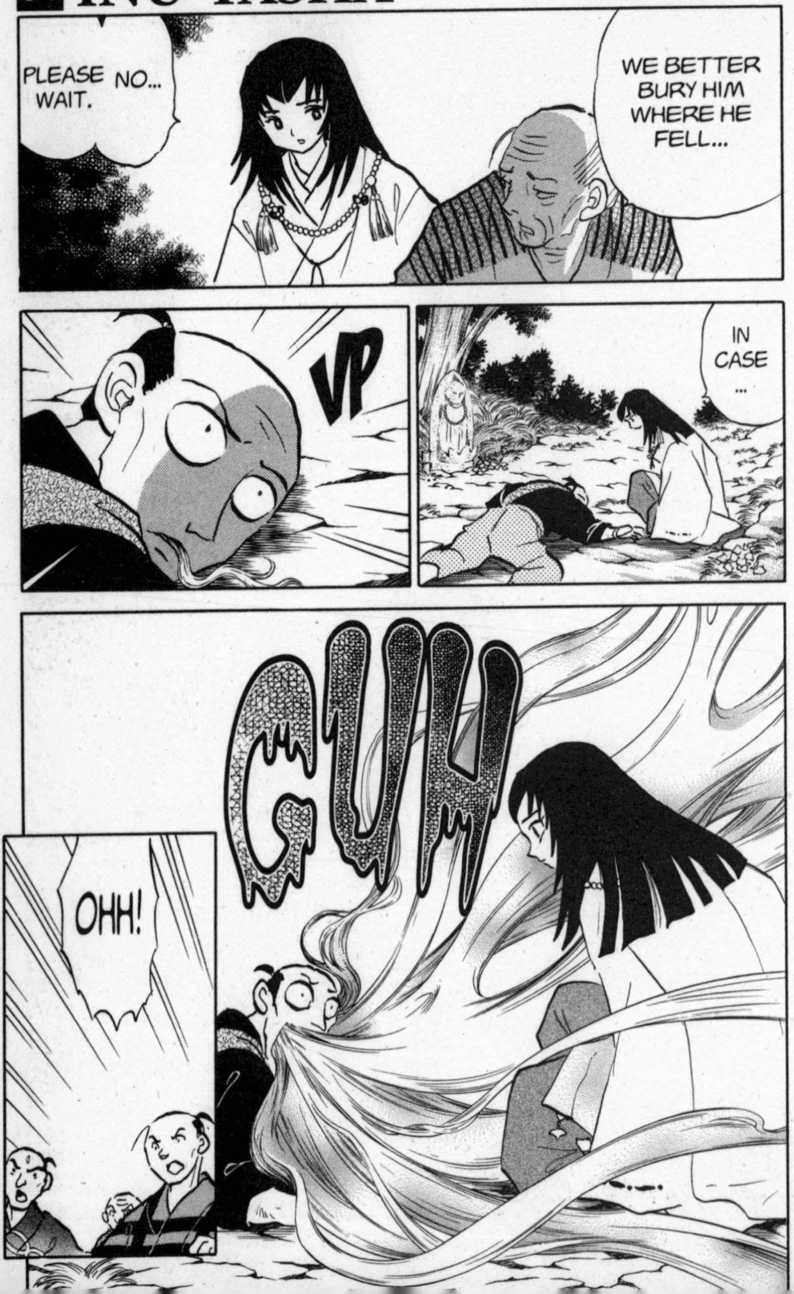
WE BETTER BURY HIM WHERE HE FELL...
NO...
PLEASE WAIT.
IN CASE ...
VP
GUH
OHH!

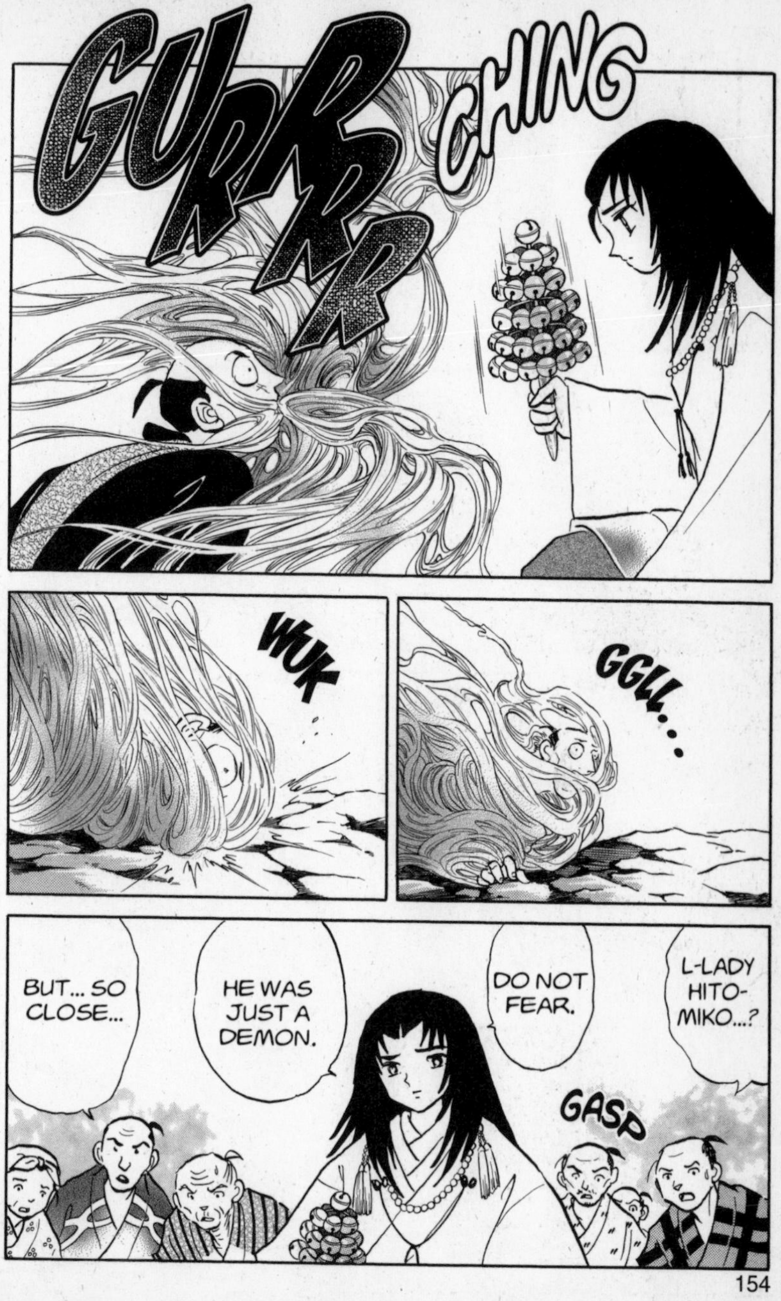
CHING
GURRRR
GGLL...
WUK
L-LADY HITO-MIKO...?
GASP
DO NOT FEAR.
HE WAS JUST A DEMON.
BUT... SO CLOSE...

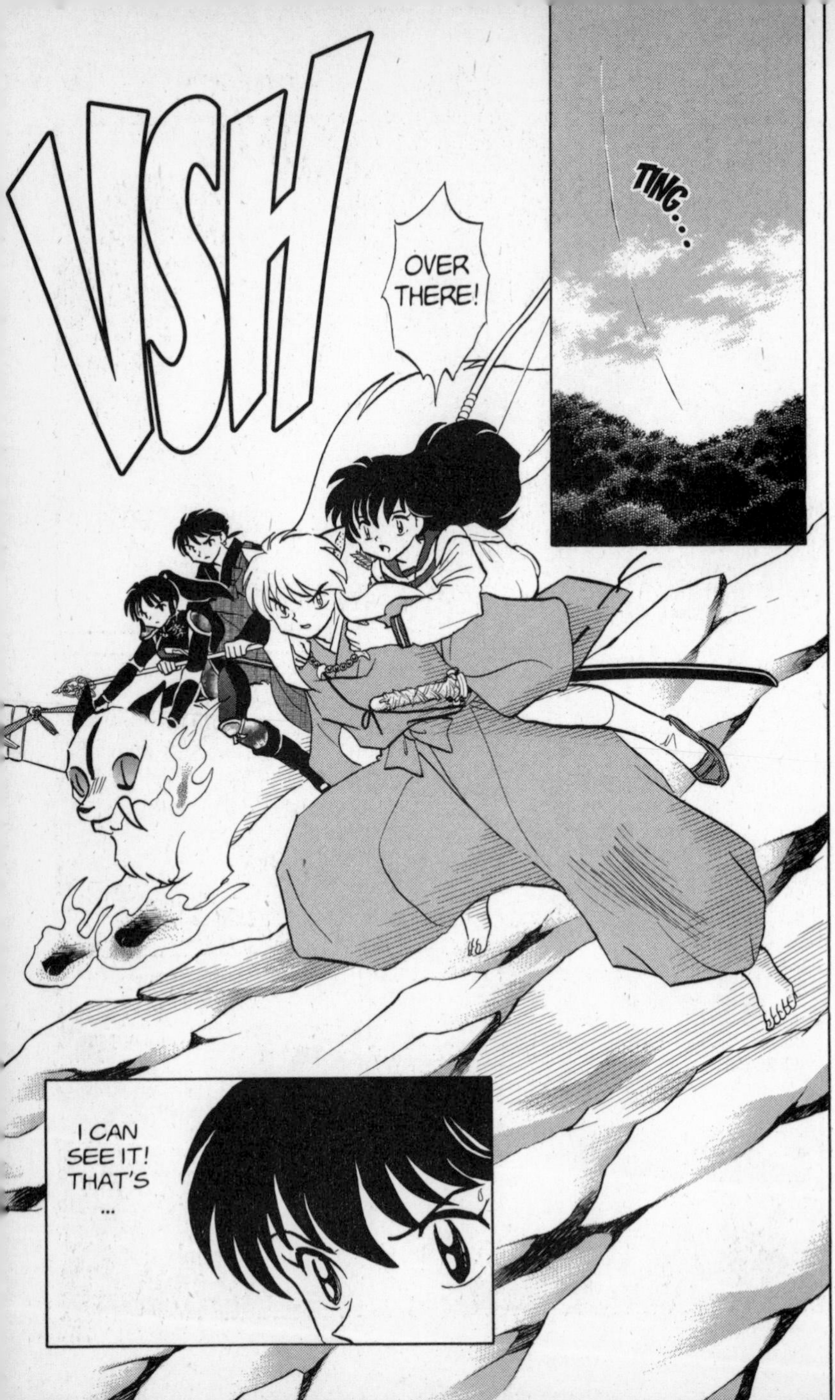
TING...
VSH
OVER THERE!
I CAN SEE IT! THAT'S ...

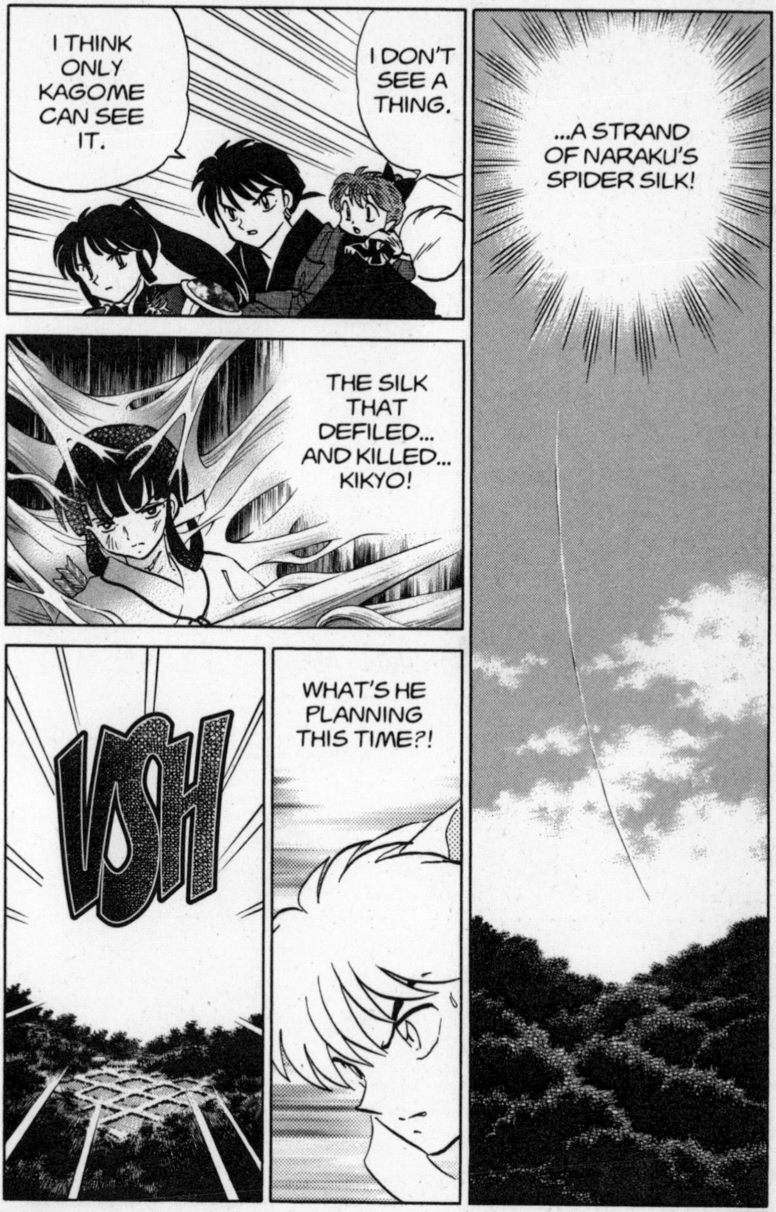
...A STRAND OF NARAKU'S SPIDER SILK!
I DON'T SEE A THING.
I THINK ONLY KAGOME CAN SEE IT.
THE SILK THAT DEFILED... AND KILLED... KIKYO!
WHAT'S HE PLANNING THIS TIME?!
VSH

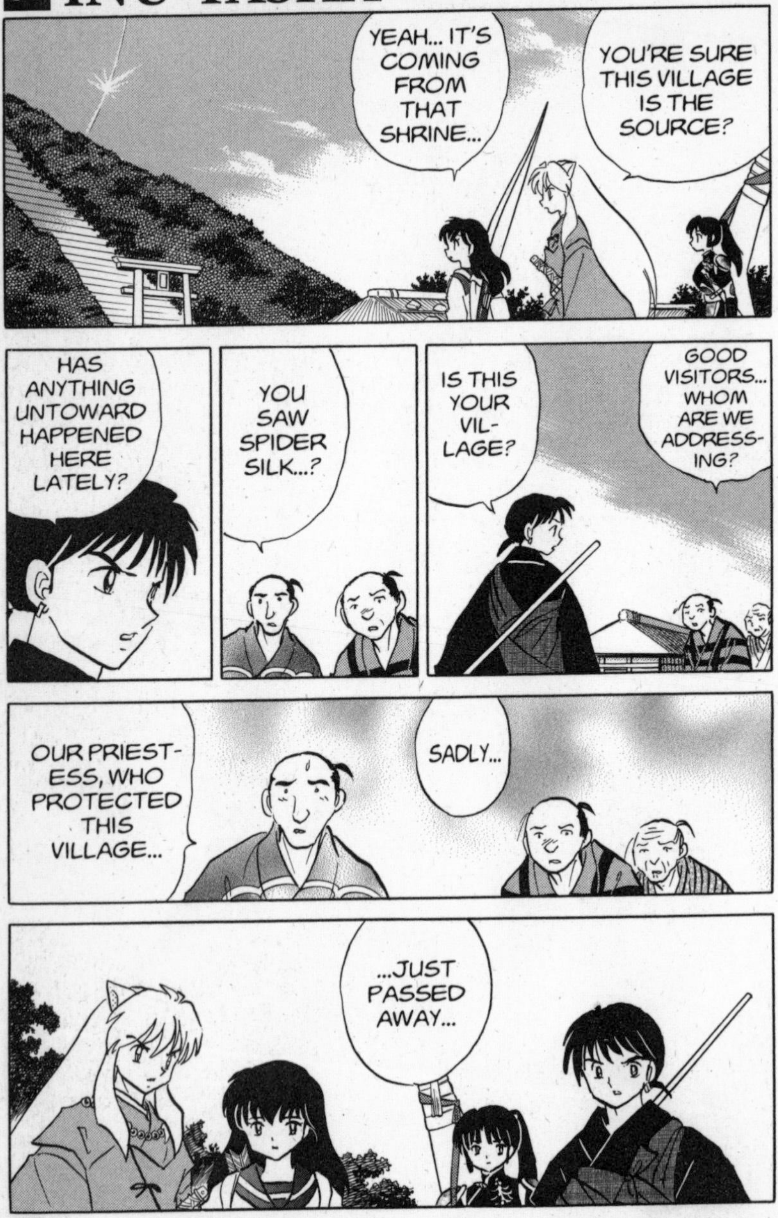
YOU'RE SURE THIS VILLAGE IS THE SOURCE?
YEAH... IT'S COMING FROM THAT SHRINE...
GOOD VISITORS... WHOM ARE WE ADDRESS-ING?
IS THIS YOUR VIL-LAGE?
YOU SAW SPIDER SILK...?
HAS ANYTHING UNTOWARD HAPPENED HERE LATELY?
SADLY...
OUR PRIEST-ESS, WHO PROTECTED THIS VILLAGE...
...JUST PASSED AWAY...

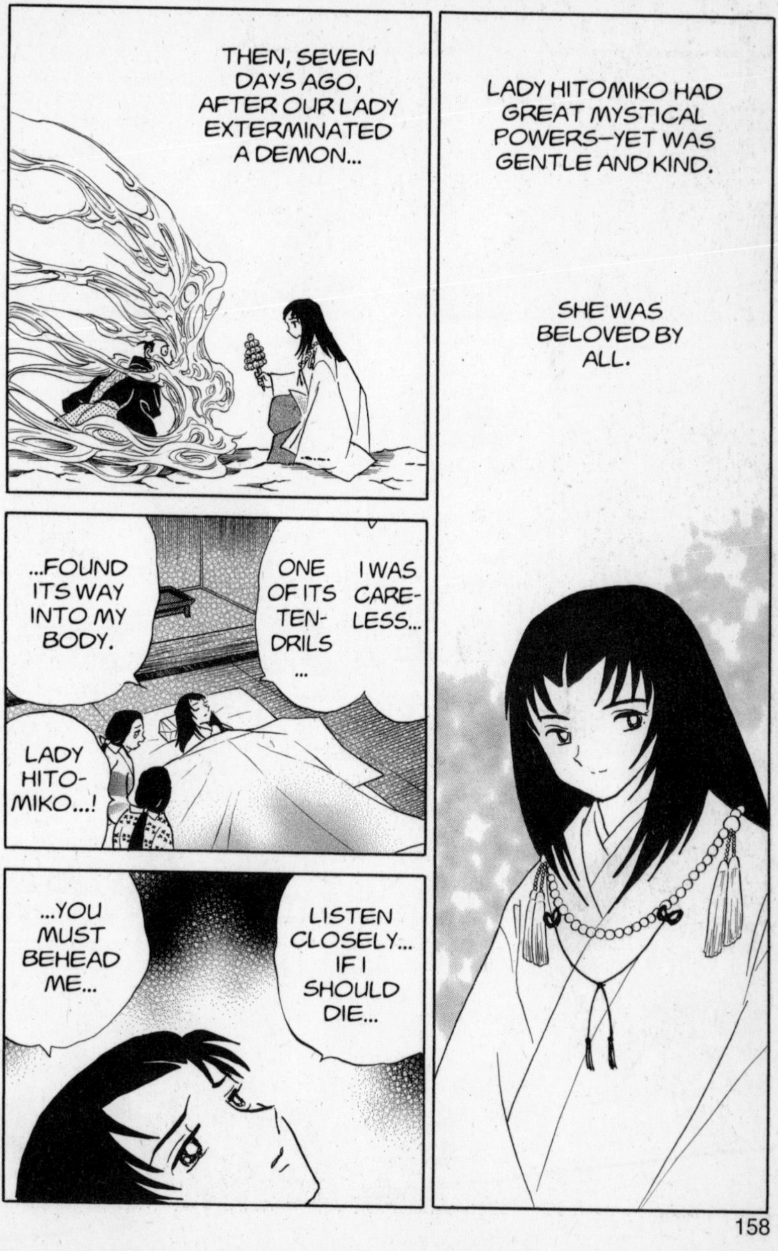
LADY HITOMIKO HAD GREAT MYSTICAL POWERS—YET WAS GENTLE AND KIND.
SHE WAS BELOVED BY ALL.
THEN, SEVEN DAYS AGO, AFTER OUR LADY EXTERMINATED A DEMON...
I WAS CARE-LESS...
ONE OF ITS TEN-DRILS ...
...FOUND ITS WAY INTO MY BODY.
LADY HITO-MIKO...!
LISTEN CLOSELY... IF I SHOULD DIE...
...YOU MUST BEHEAD ME...

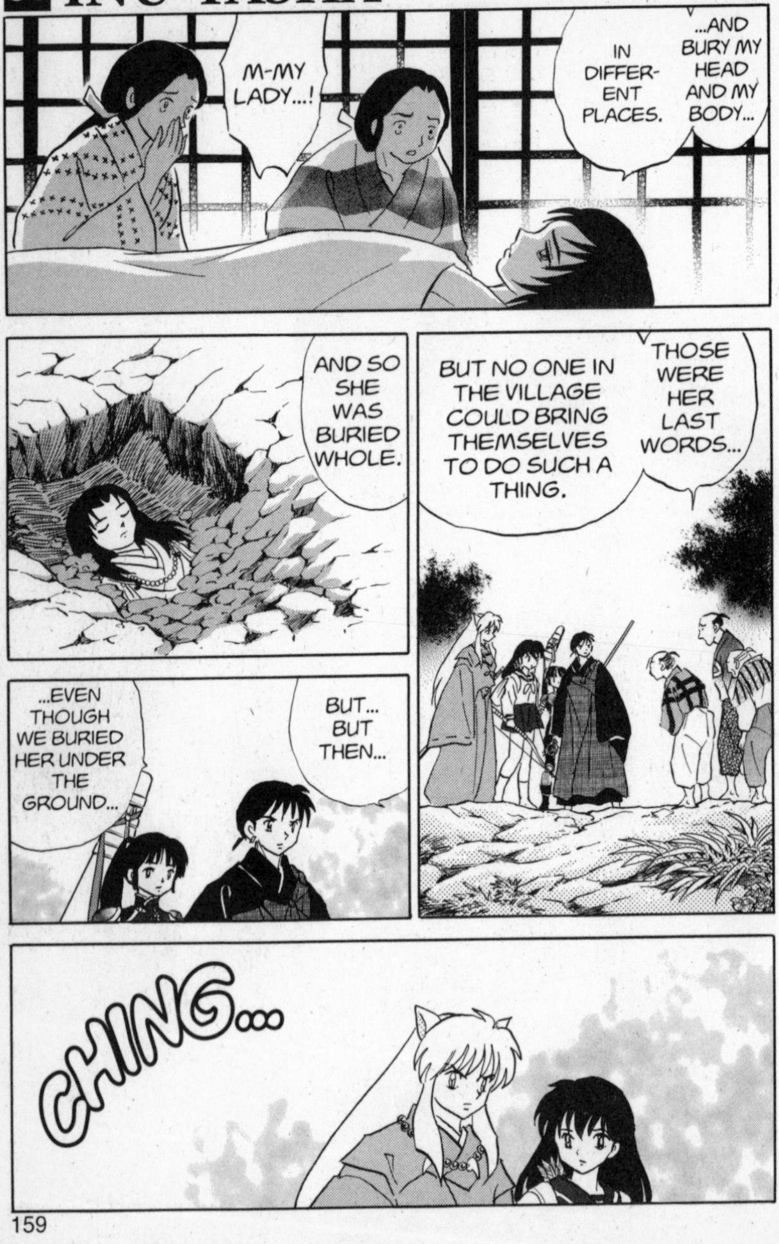
...AND BURY MY HEAD AND MY BODY...
IN DIFFER-ENT PLACES.
M-MY LADY...!
THOSE WERE HER LAST WORDS...
BUT NO ONE IN THE VILLAGE COULD BRING THEMSELVES TO DO SUCH A THING.
AND SO SHE WAS BURIED WHOLE.
BUT... BUT THEN...
...EVEN THOUGH WE BURIED HER UNDER THE GROUND...
CHING...

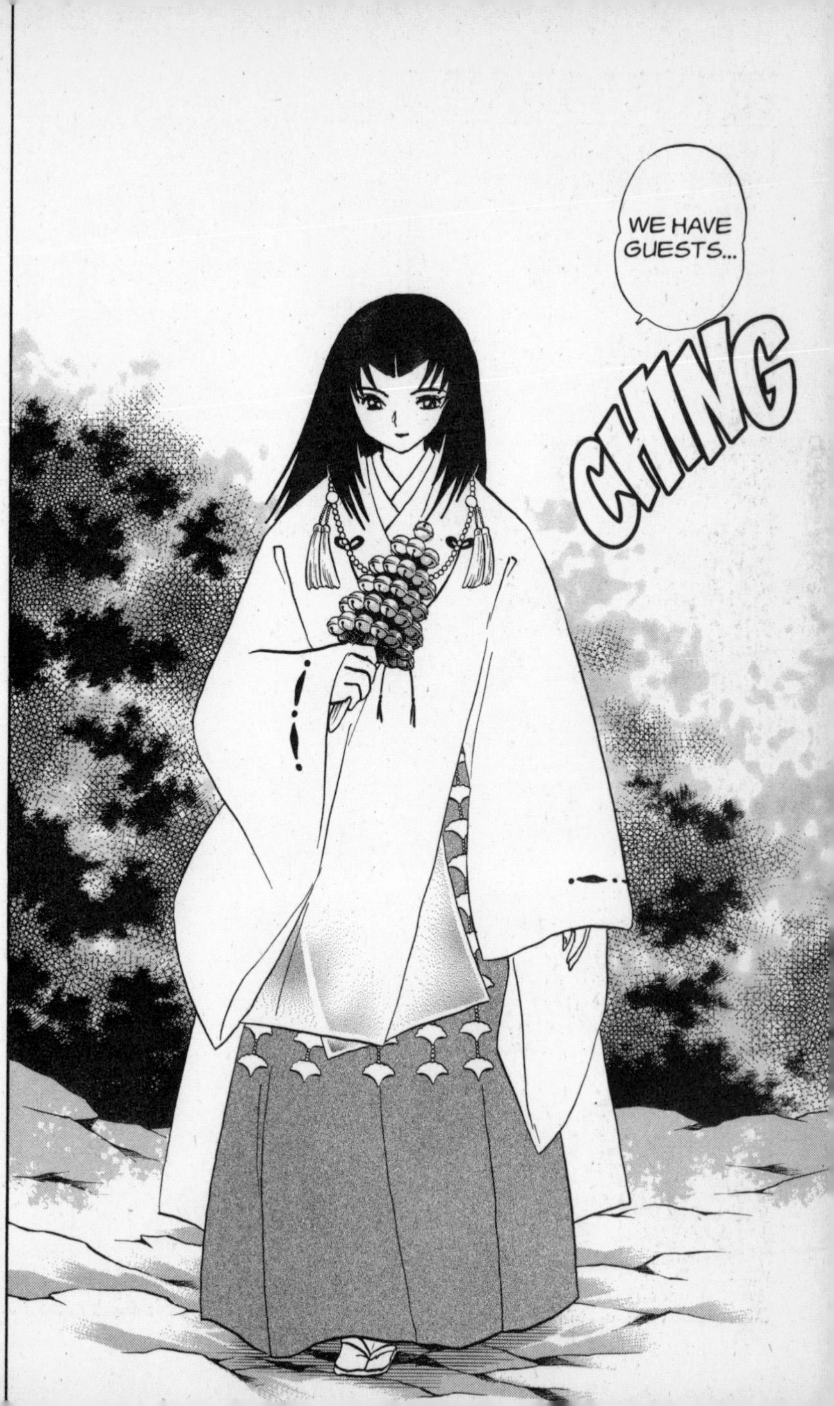
WE HAVE GUESTS...
CHING

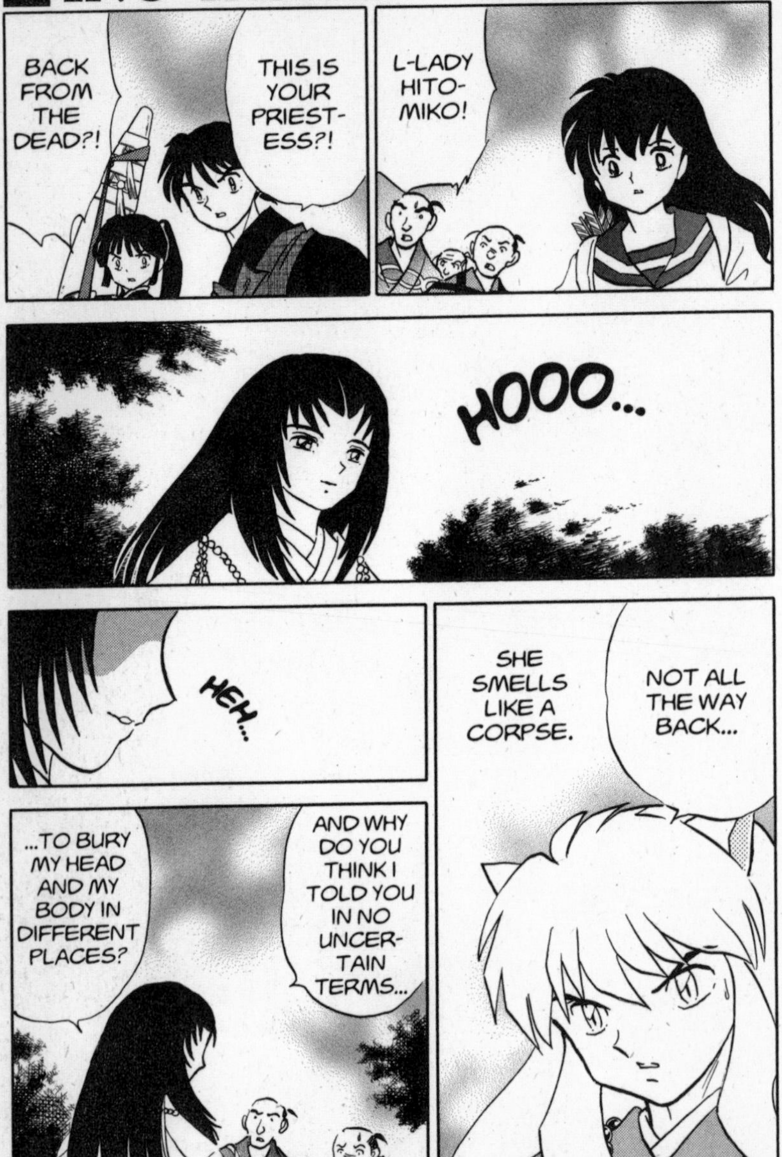
L-LADY HITO-MIKO!
THIS IS YOUR PRIEST-ESS?!
BACK FROM THE DEAD?!
HOOO...
NOT ALL THE WAY BACK...
SHE SMELLS LIKE A CORPSE.
HEH...
AND WHY DO YOU THINK I TOLD YOU IN NO UNCERTAIN TERMS...
...TO BURY MY HEAD AND MY BODY IN DIFFERENT PLACES?

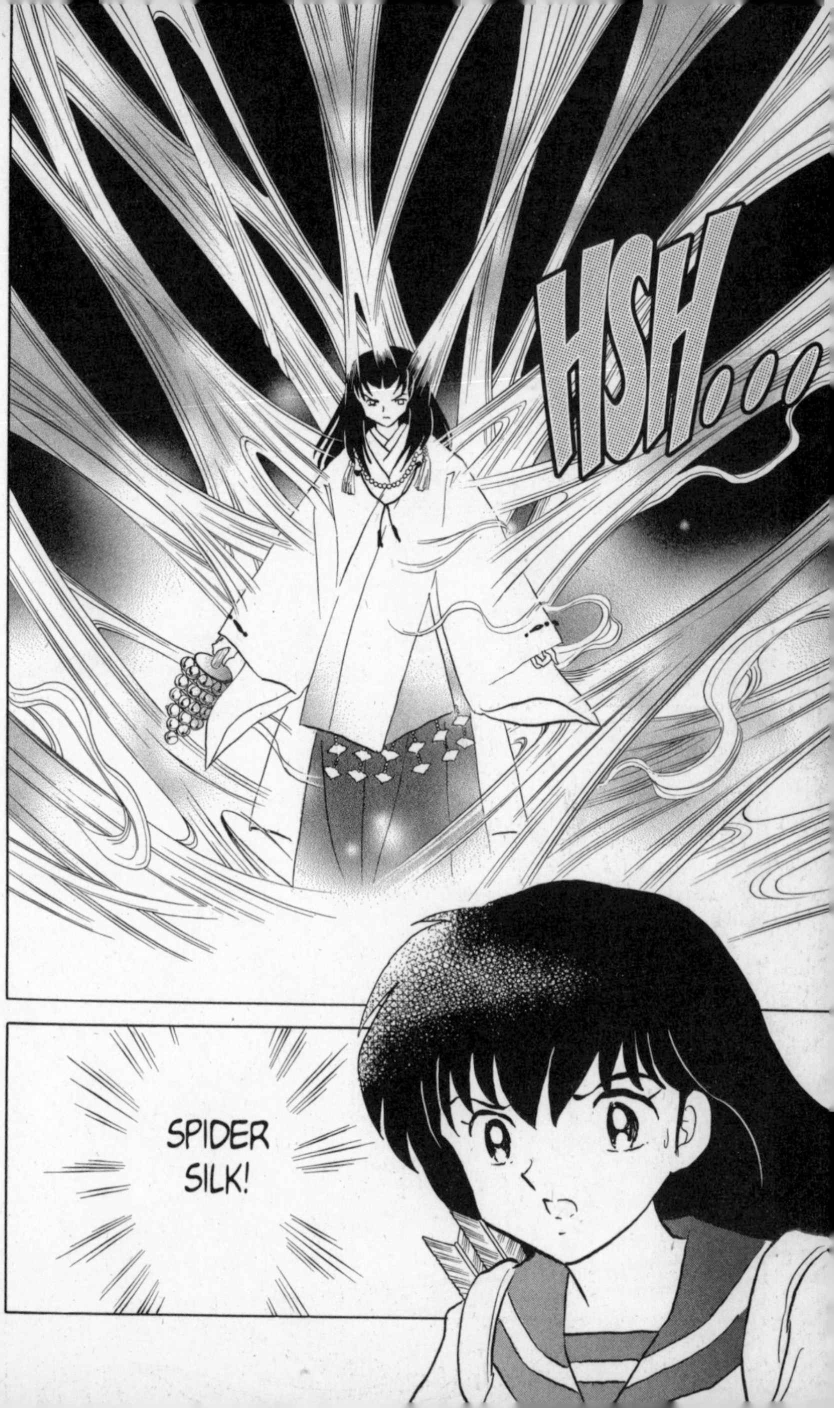
HSH...
SPIDER SILK!

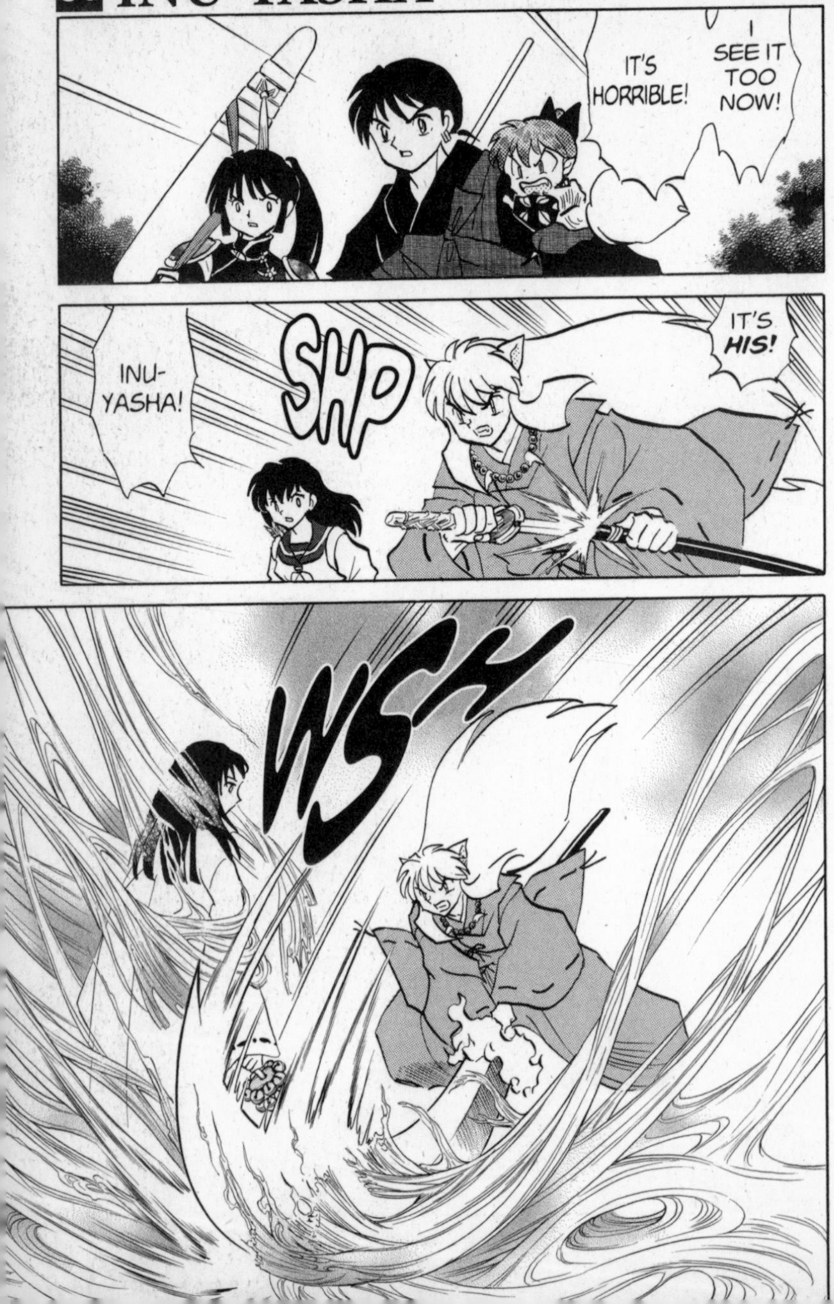
I SEE IT TOO NOW!
IT'S HORRIBLE!
IT'S **HIS!**
SHP
INU-YASHA!
WSH

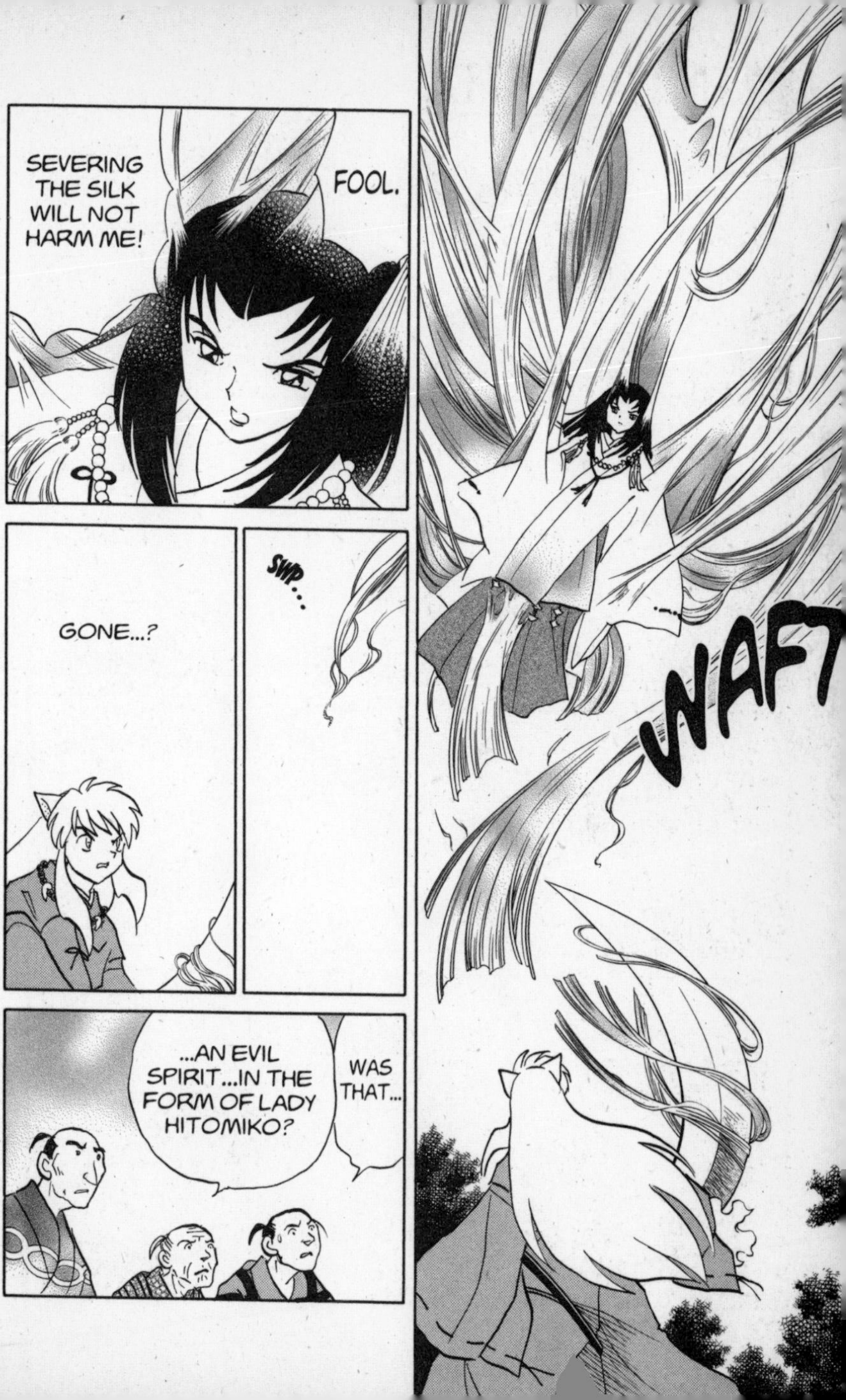
WAFT
FOOL.
SEVERING THE SILK WILL NOT HARM ME!
SWP...
GONE...?
WAS THAT...
...AN EVIL SPIRIT...IN THE FORM OF LADY HITOMIKO?

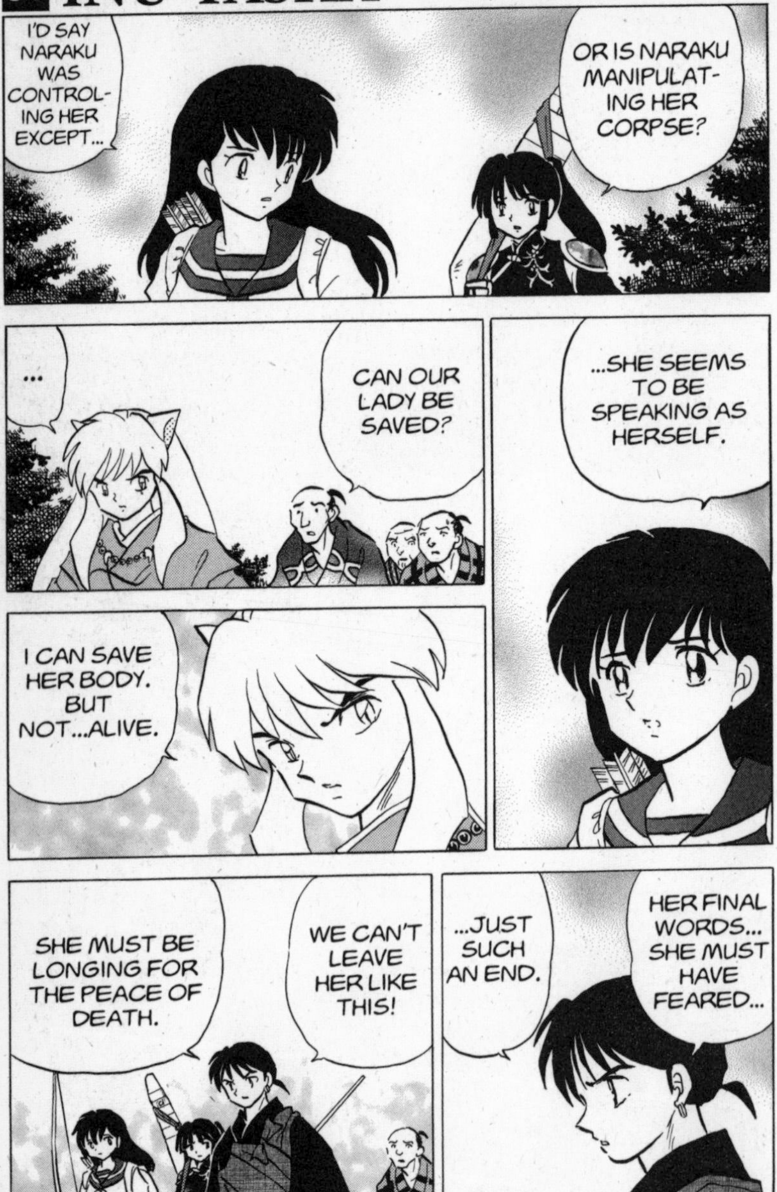
OR IS NARAKU MANIPULATING HER CORPSE?
I'D SAY NARAKU WAS CONTROLLING HER EXCEPT...
...SHE SEEMS TO BE SPEAKING AS HERSELF.
CAN OUR LADY BE SAVED?
...
I CAN SAVE HER BODY. BUT NOT...ALIVE.
HER FINAL WORDS... SHE MUST HAVE FEARED...
...JUST SUCH AN END.
WE CAN'T LEAVE HER LIKE THIS!
SHE MUST BE LONGING FOR THE PEACE OF DEATH.

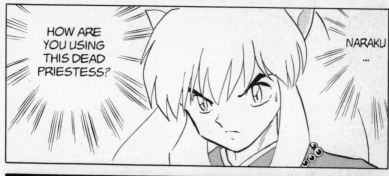

HOW ARE YOU USING THIS DEAD PRIESTESS?

NARAKU...

HSH...

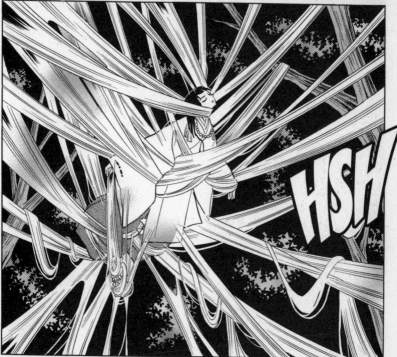

HSH!

166

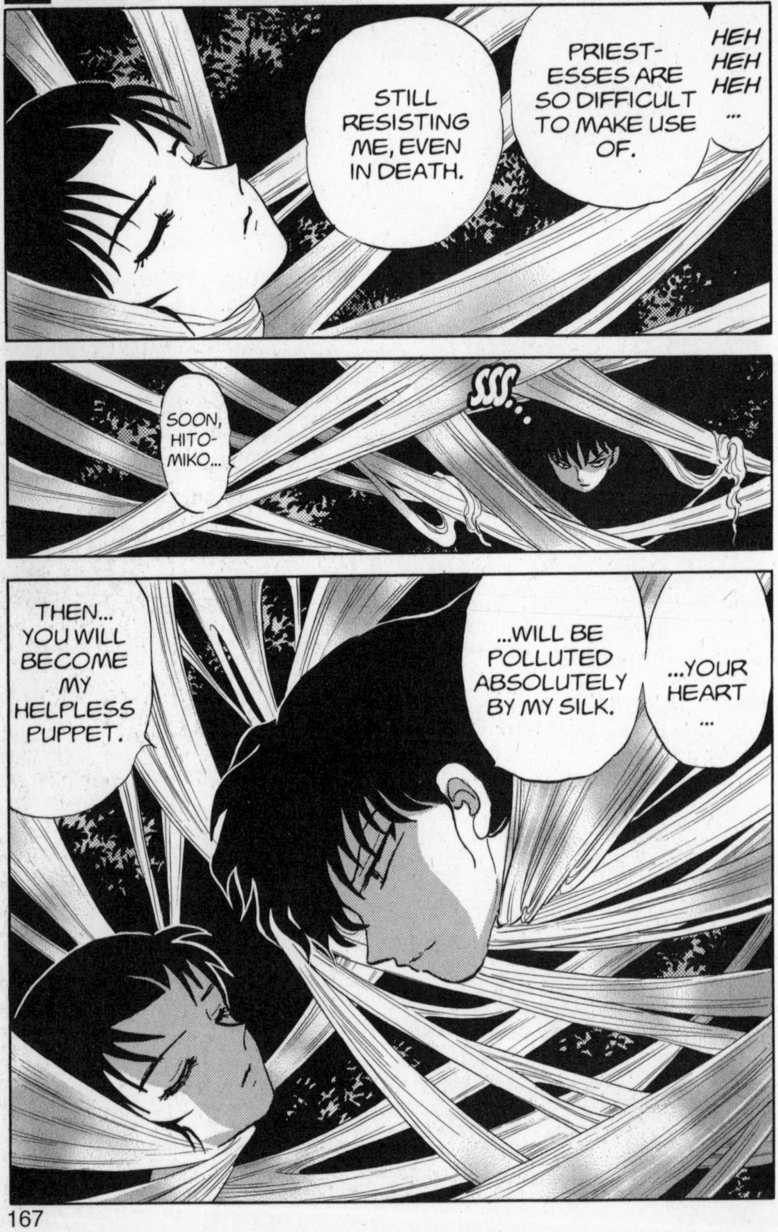
HEH HEH HEH ...
PRIEST-ESSES ARE SO DIFFICULT TO MAKE USE OF.
STILL RESISTING ME, EVEN IN DEATH.
SSS...
SOON, HITO-MIKO...
...YOUR HEART ...
...WILL BE POLLUTED ABSOLUTELY BY MY SILK.
THEN... YOU WILL BECOME MY HELPLESS PUPPET.

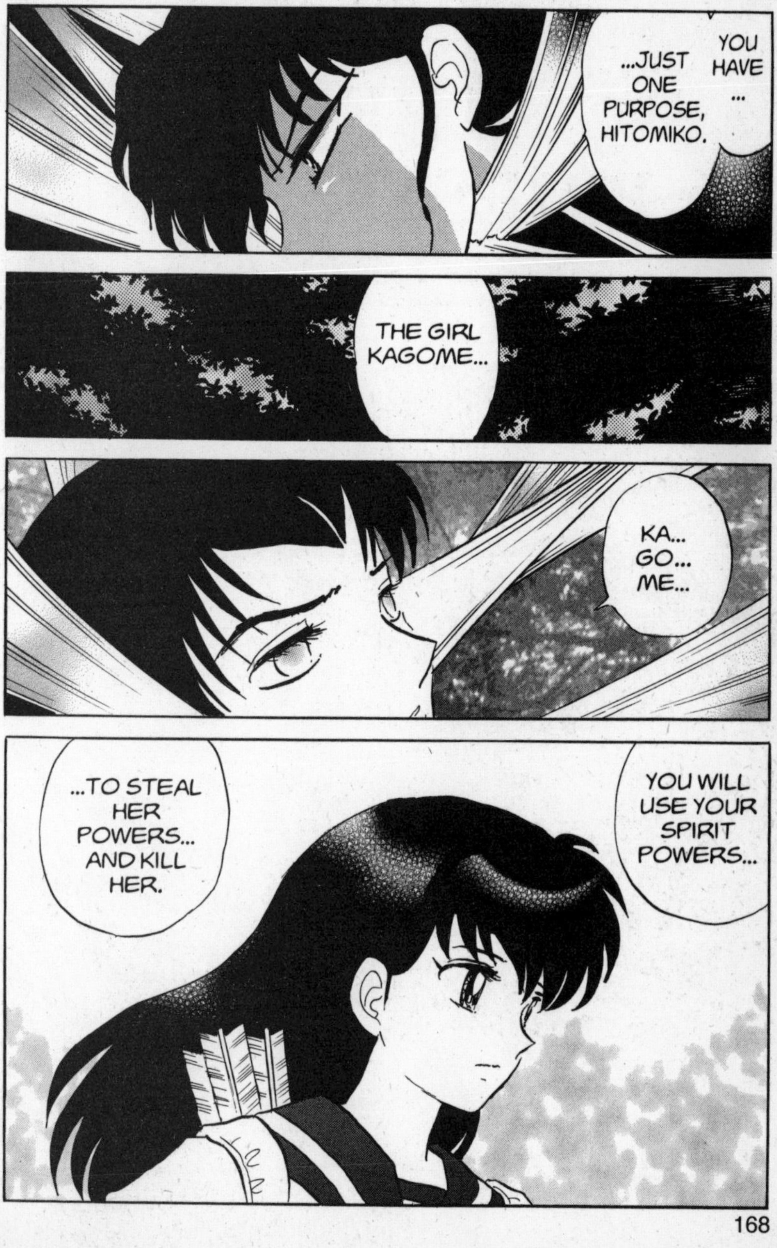
YOU HAVE ...
...JUST ONE PURPOSE, HITOMIKO.
THE GIRL KAGOME...
KA... GO... ME...
YOU WILL USE YOUR SPIRIT POWERS...
...TO STEAL HER POWERS... AND KILL HER.

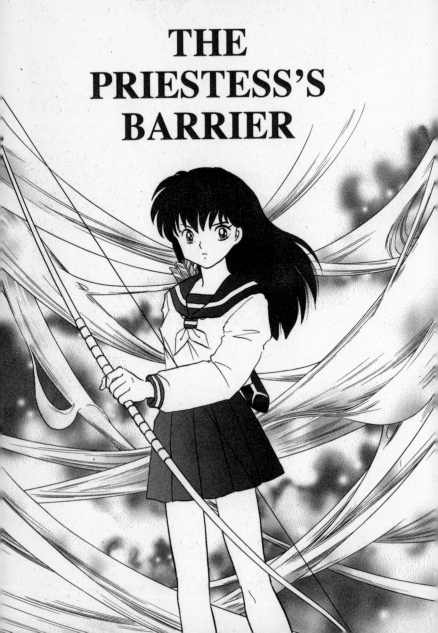

SCROLL 10

THE PRIESTESS'S BARRIER

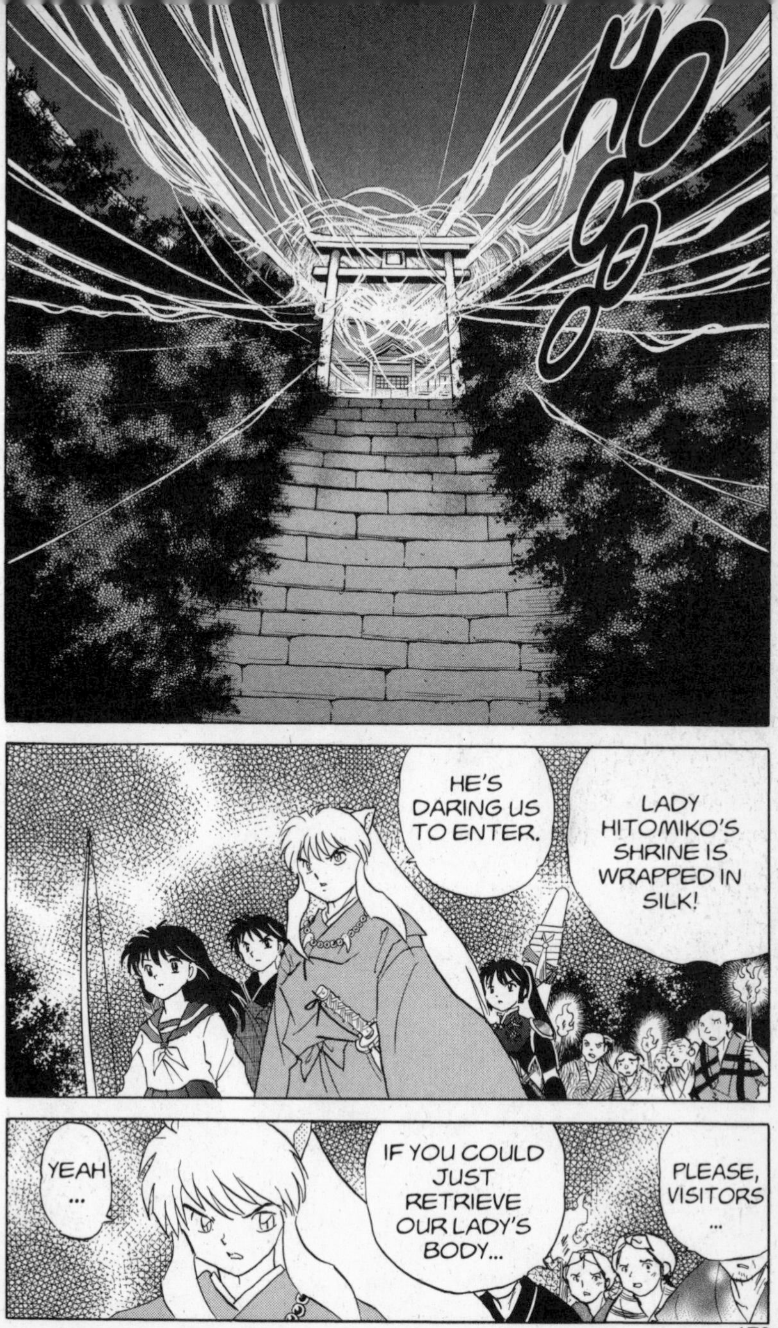
HOGOGO
LADY HITOMIKO'S SHRINE IS WRAPPED IN SILK!
HE'S DARING US TO ENTER.
PLEASE, VISITORS ...
IF YOU COULD JUST RETRIEVE OUR LADY'S BODY...
YEAH ...

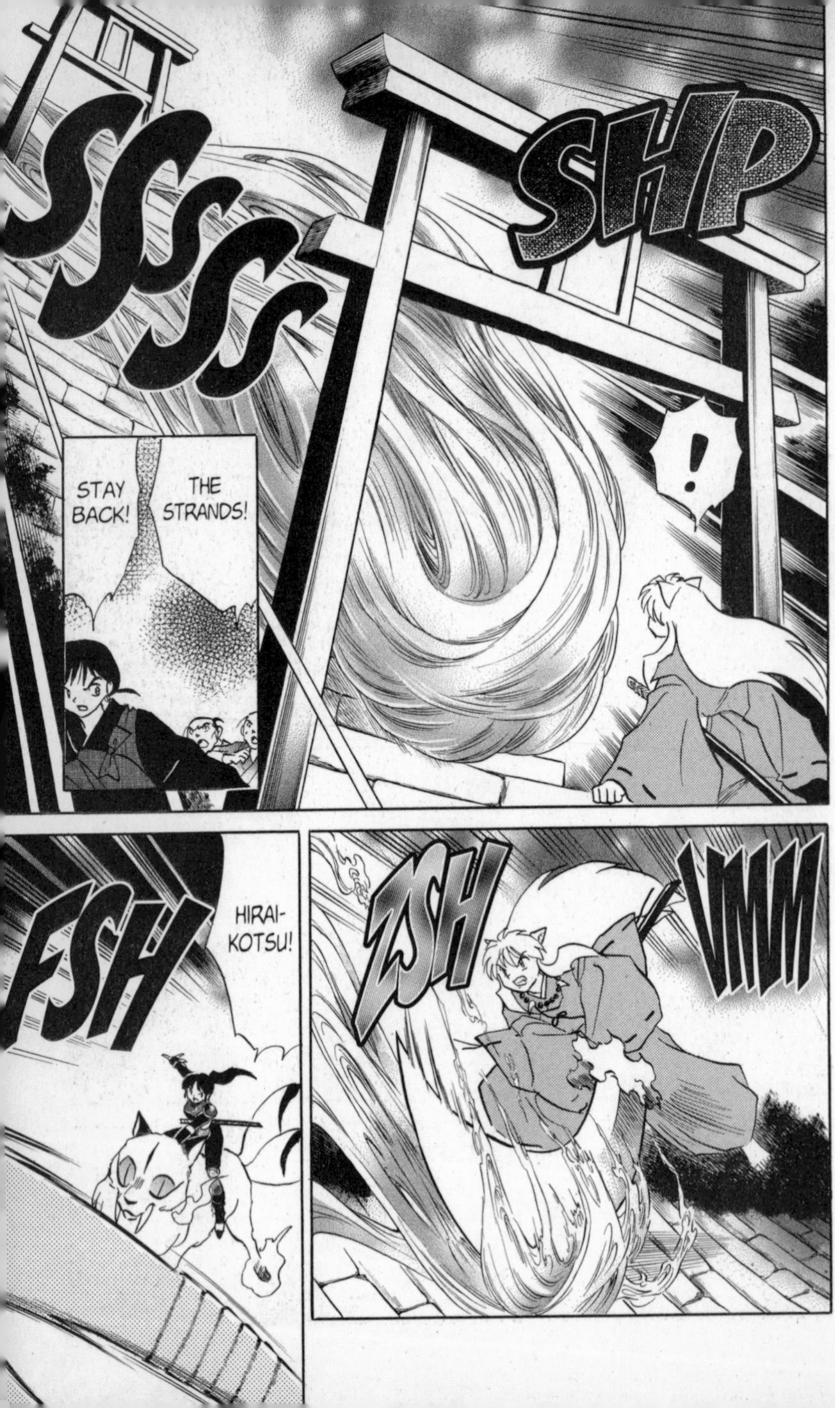
SHP
SSSSS
!
THE STRANDS!
STAY BACK!
VMM
ZSH
HIRAI-KOTSU!
FSH

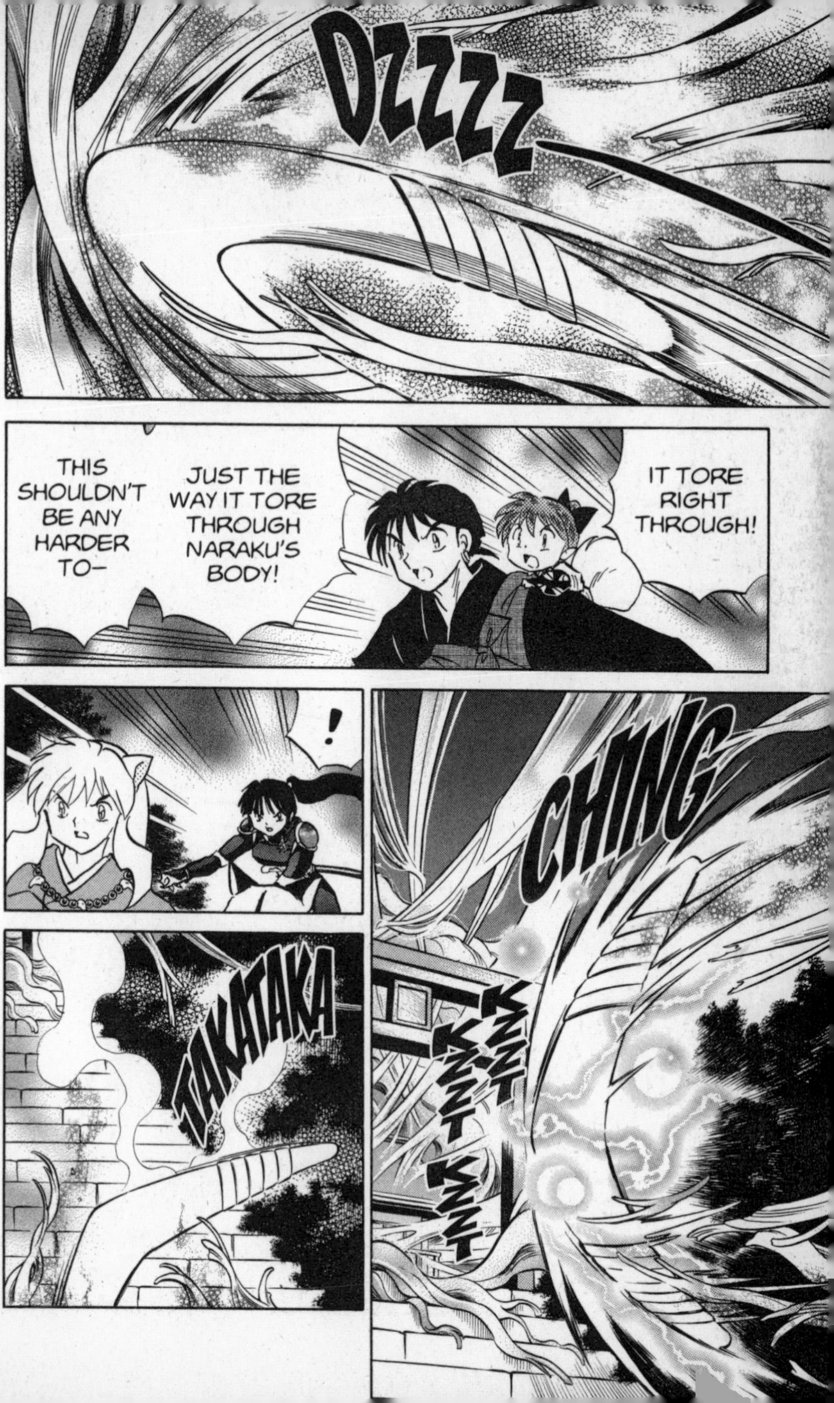
DZZZZZ
IT TORE RIGHT THROUGH!
JUST THE WAY IT TORE THROUGH NARAKU'S BODY!
THIS SHOULDN'T BE ANY HARDER TO–
CHING
KZZZT
KZZZT
KZZZT
!
TAKATAKA

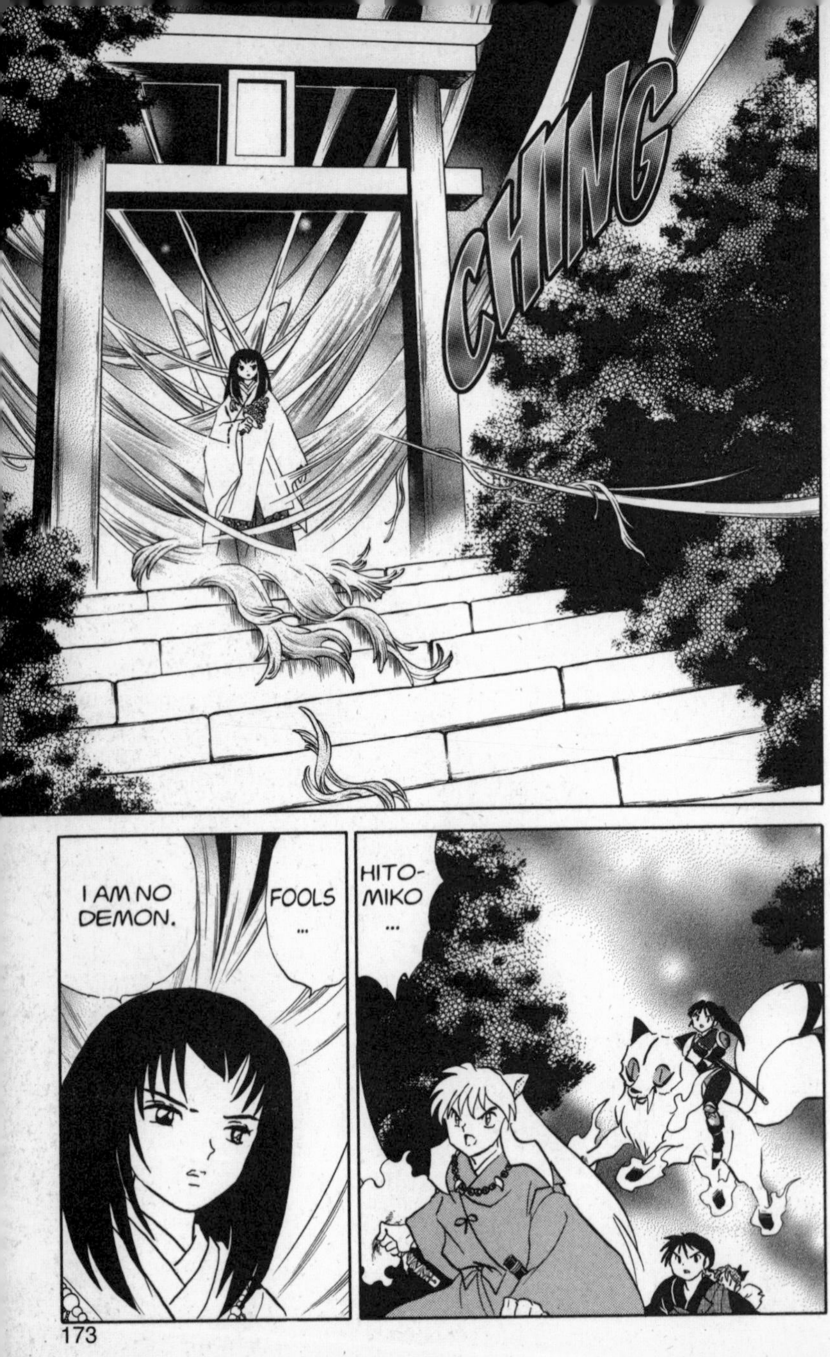
CHING
HITO-MIKO...
FOOLS...
I AM NO DEMON.

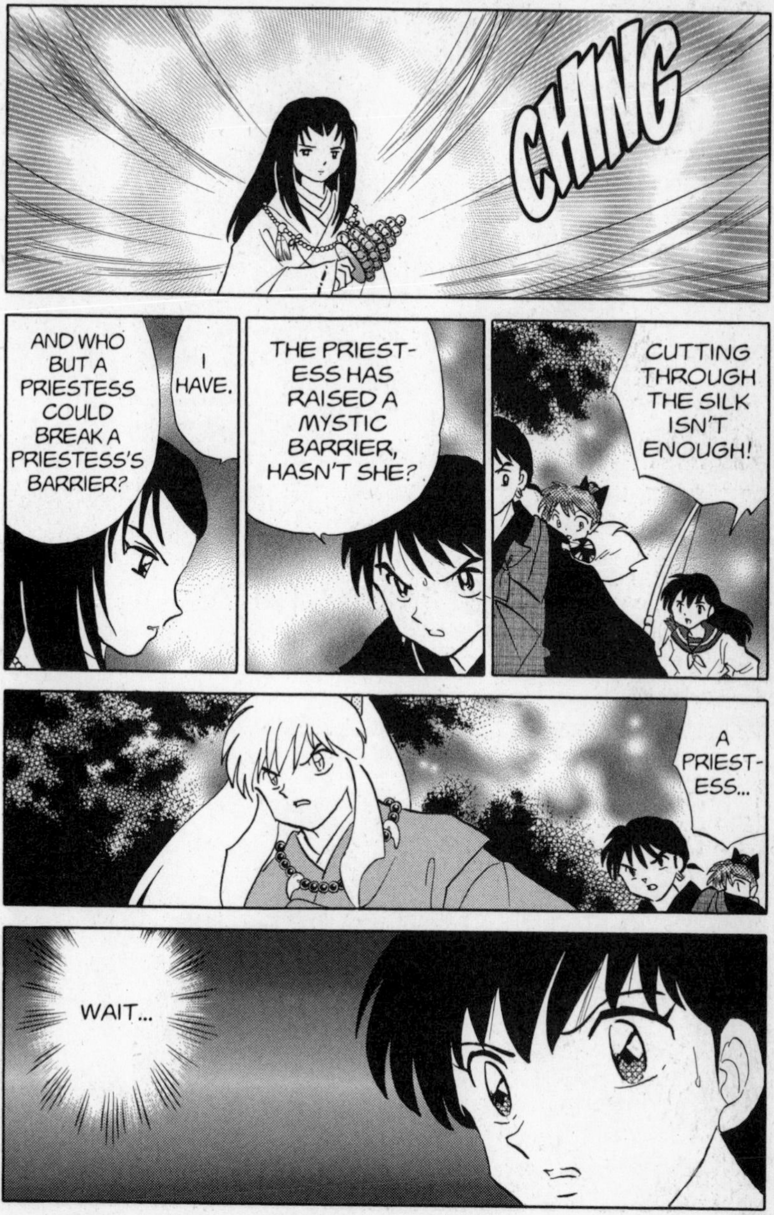
CHING
CUTTING THROUGH THE SILK ISN'T ENOUGH!
THE PRIEST-ESS HAS RAISED A MYSTIC BARRIER, HASN'T SHE?
I HAVE.
AND WHO BUT A PRIESTESS COULD BREAK A PRIESTESS'S BARRIER?
A PRIEST-ESS...
WAIT...

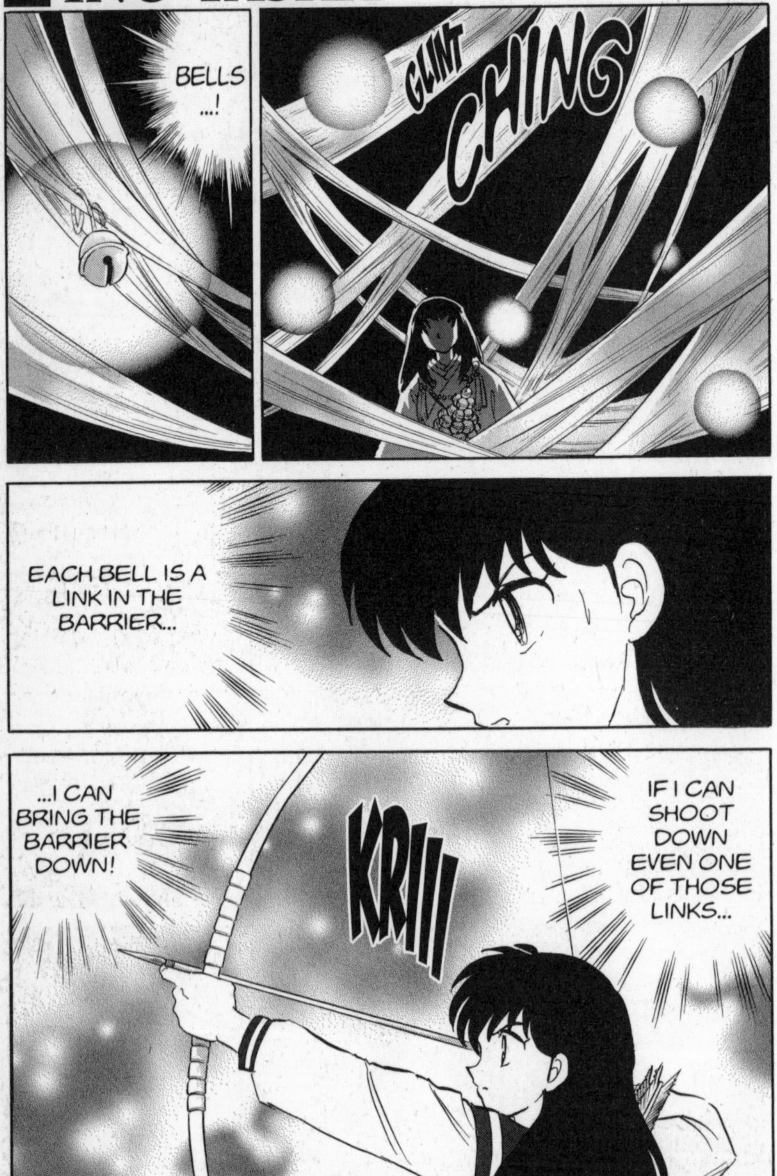
GLINT
CHING
BELLS ...!
EACH BELL IS A LINK IN THE BARRIER...
IF I CAN SHOOT DOWN EVEN ONE OF THOSE LINKS...
KRIII
...I CAN BRING THE BARRIER DOWN!

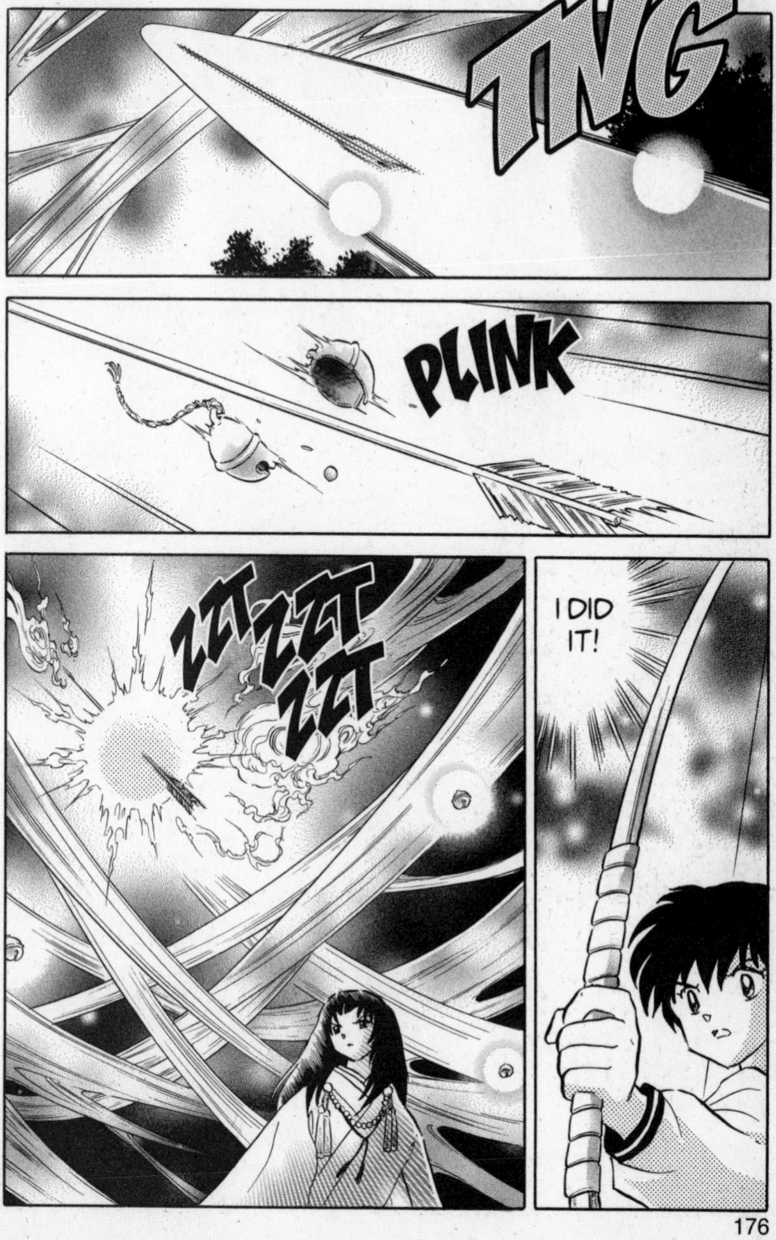
TNG
PLINK
I DID IT!
ZZT ZZT ZZT

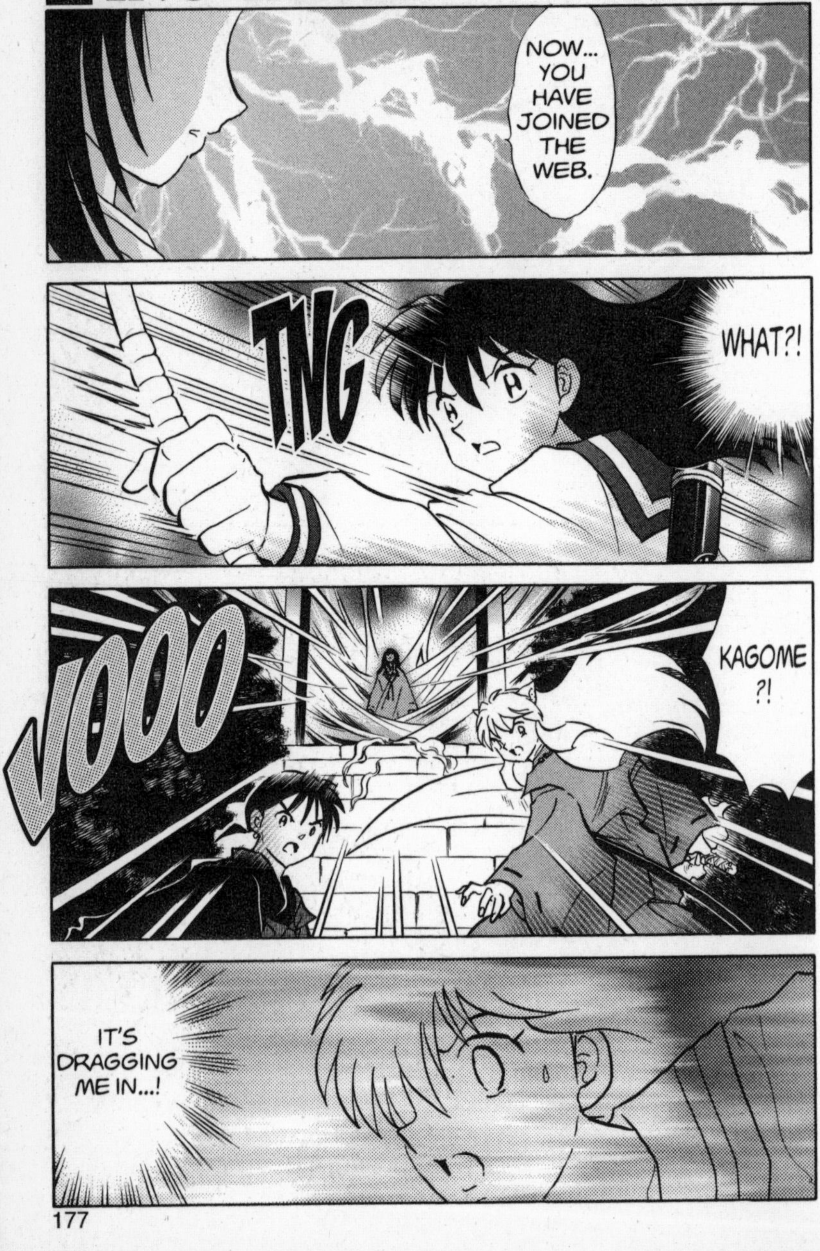
NOW... YOU HAVE JOINED THE WEB.
WHAT?!
TNG
KAGOME ?!
VOOO
IT'S DRAGGING ME IN...!

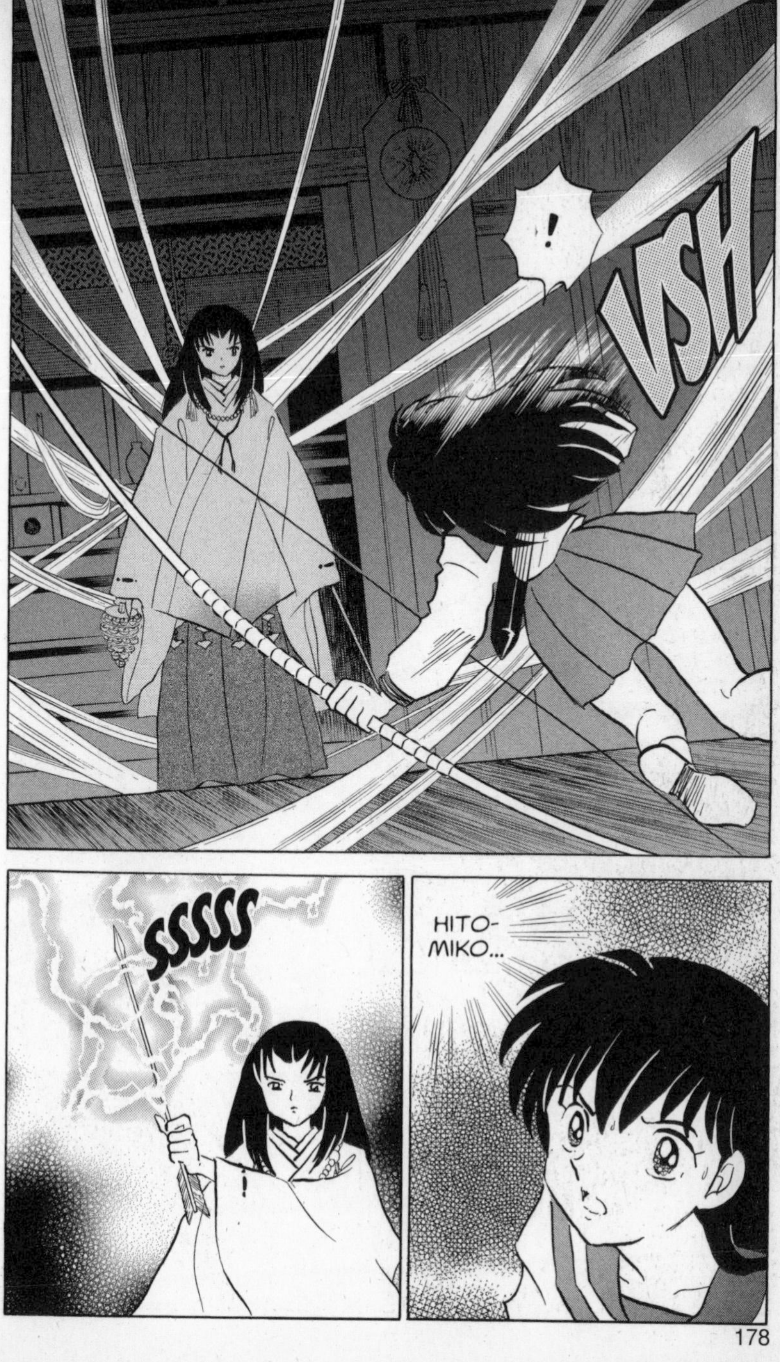
VSH
!
HITO-MIKO...
SSSSS
!

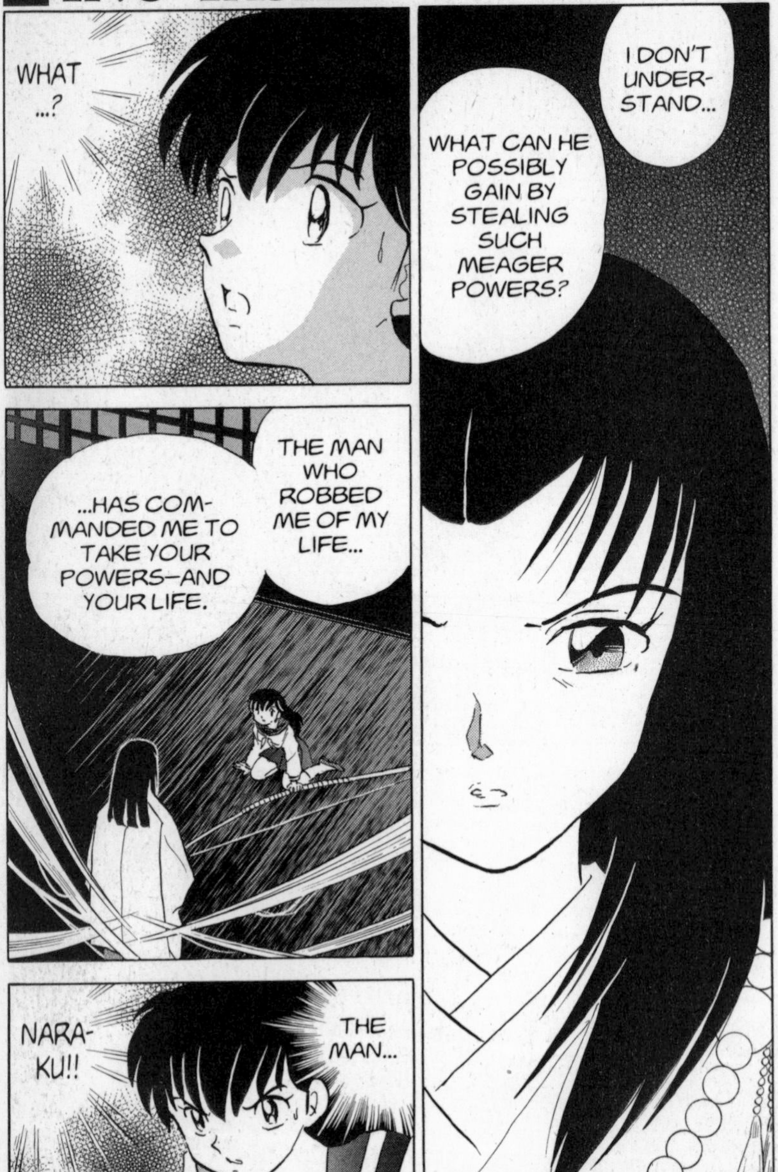
I DON'T UNDER-STAND...
WHAT CAN HE POSSIBLY GAIN BY STEALING SUCH MEAGER POWERS?
WHAT ...?
THE MAN WHO ROBBED ME OF MY LIFE...
...HAS COM-MANDED ME TO TAKE YOUR POWERS—AND YOUR LIFE.
THE MAN...
NARA-KU!!

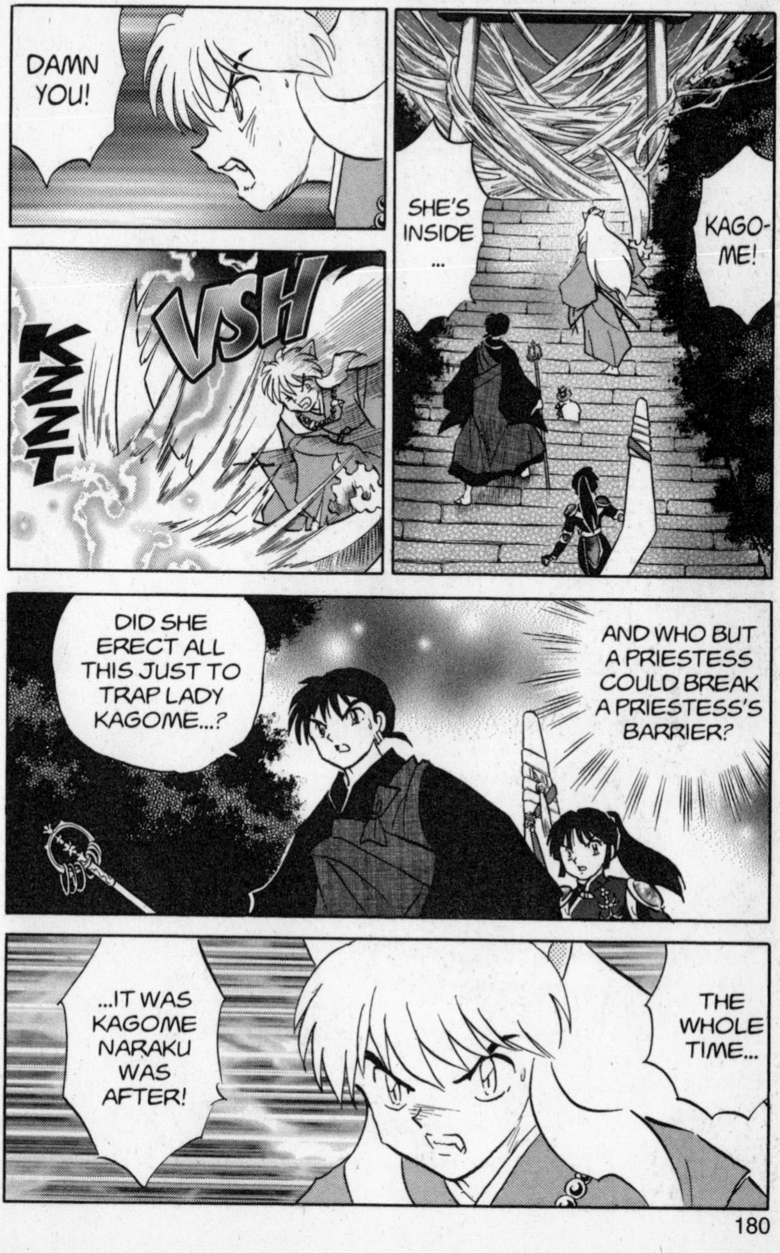
KAGO-ME!
SHE'S INSIDE ...
DAMN YOU!
VSH
KZZT
AND WHO BUT A PRIESTESS COULD BREAK A PRIESTESS'S BARRIER?
DID SHE ERECT ALL THIS JUST TO TRAP LADY KAGOME...?
THE WHOLE TIME...
...IT WAS KAGOME NARAKU WAS AFTER!

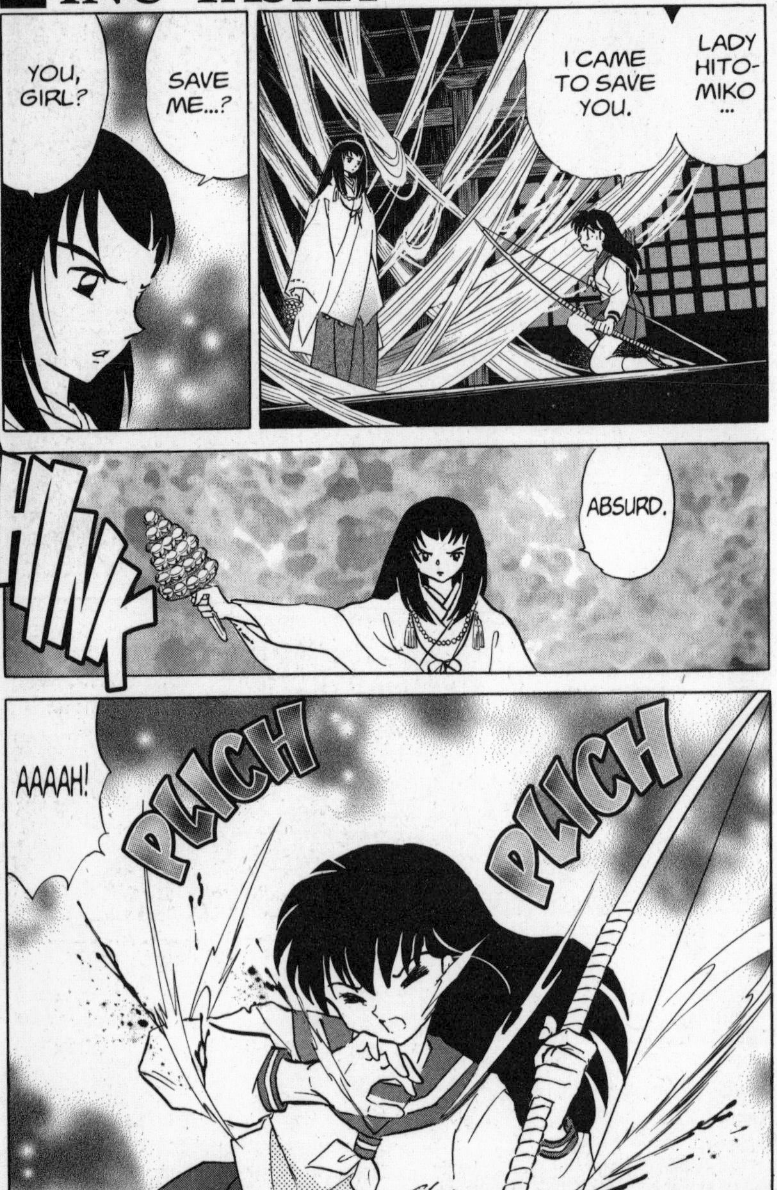
LADY HITO-MIKO ...
I CAME TO SAVE YOU.
SAVE ME...?
YOU, GIRL?
ABSURD.
CHINK
PLICH
PLICH
AAAAH!

SPTT
MY BLOOD...
YOUR BLOOD SHALL FORM YOUR CAGE.
YOU MAY NO LONGER STIR FROM THAT SPOT.
WHAT ...?
OH...
I CAN'T MOVE!
MNG...

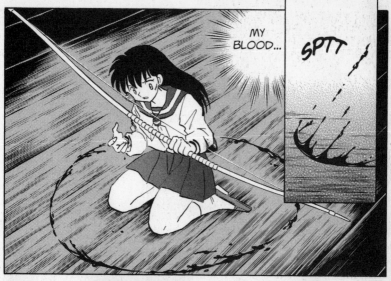

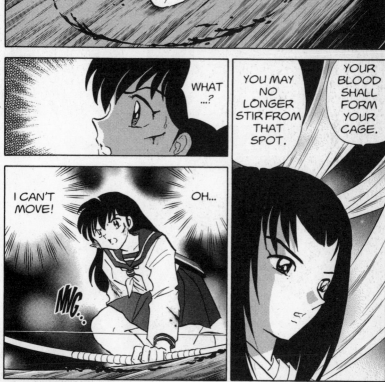

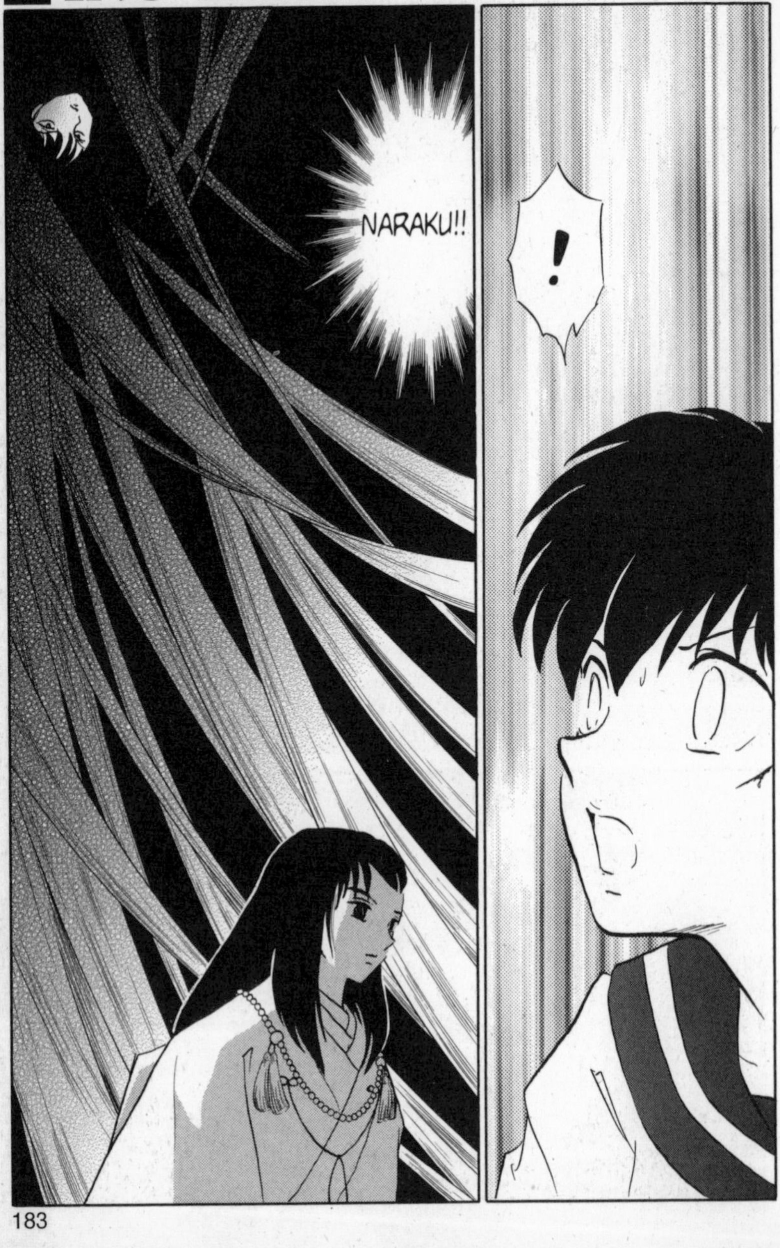
!
NARAKU!!

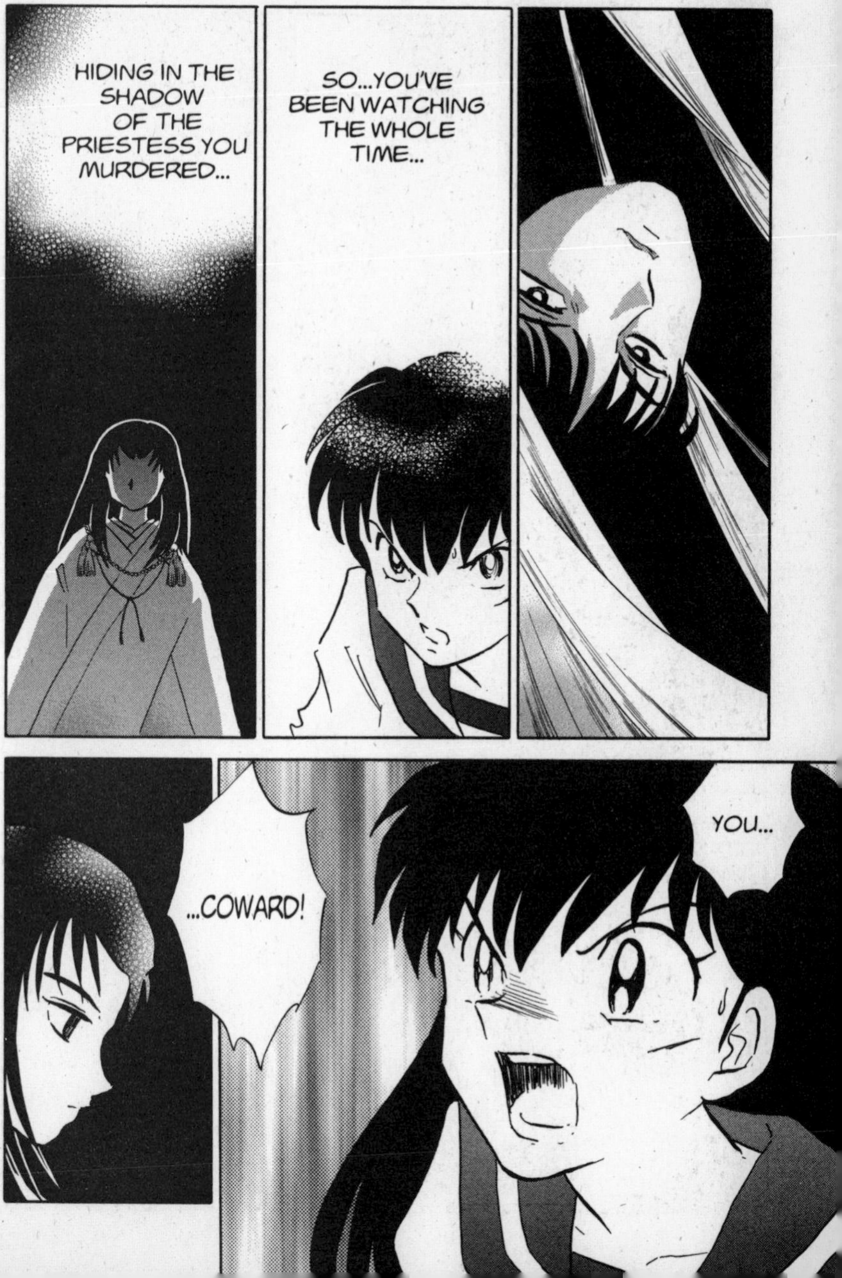
SO...YOU'VE BEEN WATCHING THE WHOLE TIME...
HIDING IN THE SHADOW OF THE PRIESTESS YOU MURDERED...
YOU...
...COWARD!

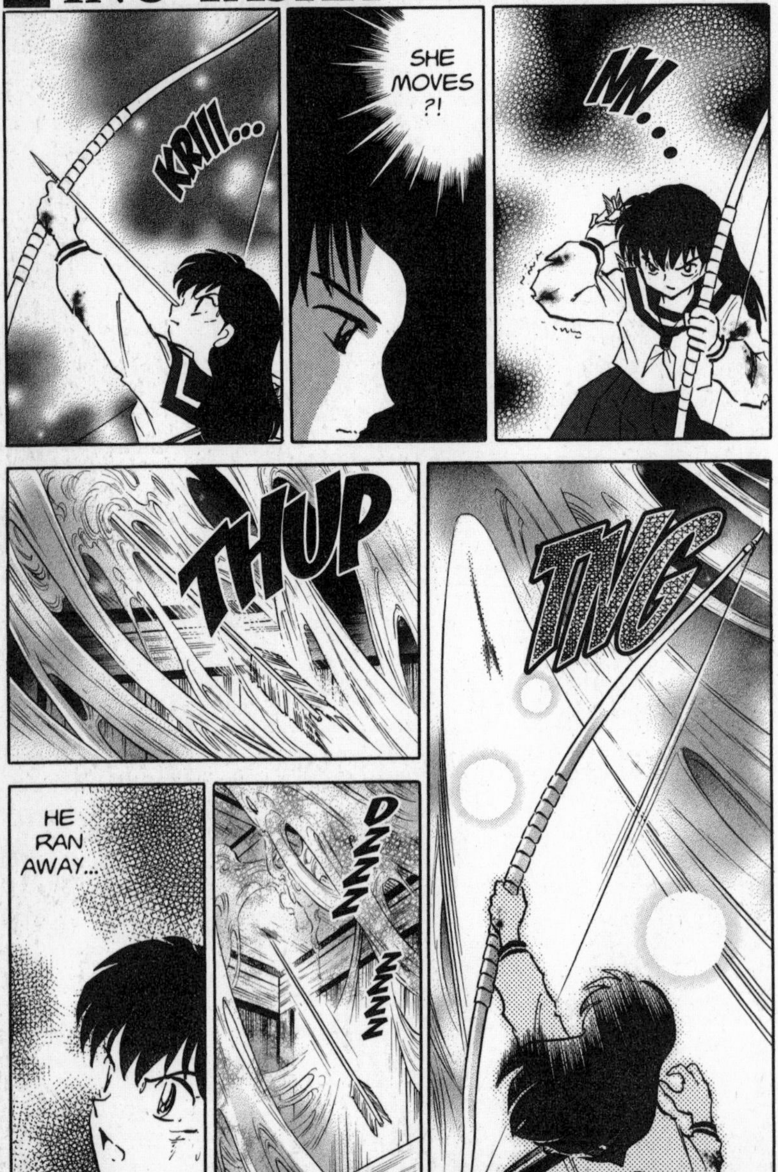
MN...
SHE MOVES ?!
KRIIII...
TWG
THUP
DZZZZ ZZZZZ
HE RAN AWAY...

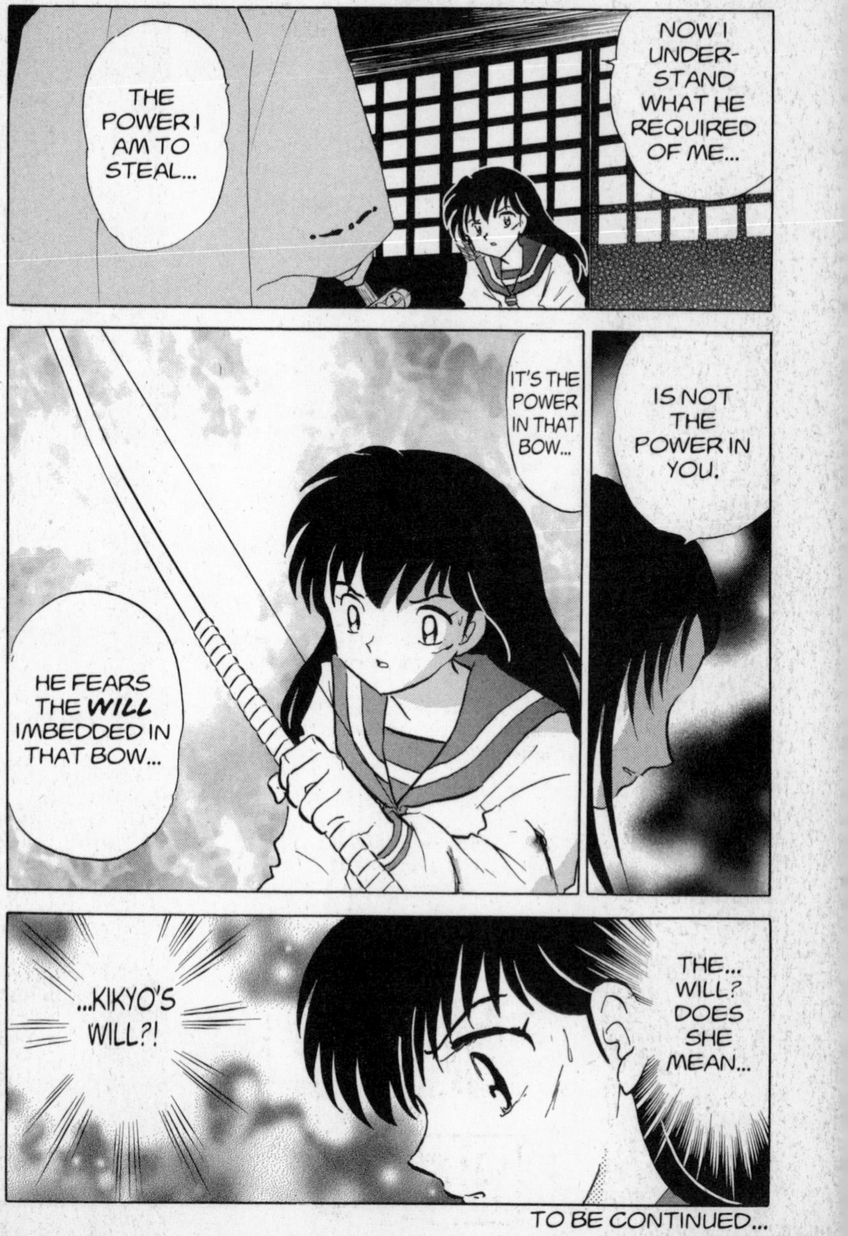
NOW I UNDER-STAND WHAT HE REQUIRED OF ME...
THE POWER I AM TO STEAL...
IS NOT THE POWER IN YOU.
IT'S THE POWER IN THAT BOW...
HE FEARS THE *WILL* IMBEDDED IN THAT BOW...
THE... WILL? DOES SHE MEAN...
...KIKYO'S WILL?!

TO BE CONTINUED...

INUYASHA

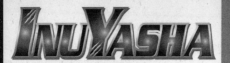

INUYASHA

VOL. 51

Shonen Sunday Edition

Story and Art by

RUMIKO TAKAHASHI

Original Japanese edition "INUYASHA"
published by SHOGAKUKAN Inc.

English Adaptation by Gerard Jones

Translation/Mari Morimoto
Touch-up Art & Lettering/Bill Schuch
Cover & Interior Graphic Design/Yuki Ameda
Editor/Annette Roman

VP, Production/Alvin Lu
VP, Sales & Product Marketing/Gonzalo Ferreyra
VP, Creative/Linda Espinosa
Publisher/Hyoe Narita

Printed in the U.S.A.

Published by VIZ Media, LLC
P.O. Box 77010
San Francisco, CA 94107

10 9 8 7 6 5 4 3 2 1
First printing, August 2010

RATED T+ FOR OLDER TEEN

PARENTAL ADVISORY
INUYASHA is rated T+ for Older Teen and is recommended for ages 16 and up. This volume contains violence.

ratings.viz.com

viz media — SHONEN SUNDAY

www.viz.com — WWW.SHONENSUNDAY.COM

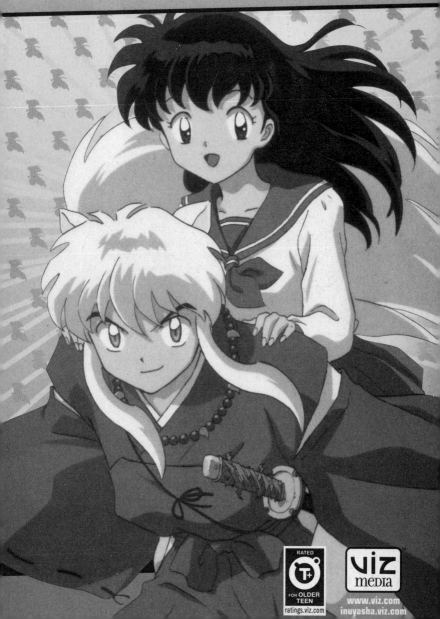

INUYASHA

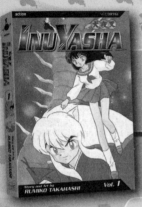

Read the action from the start with the original manga series

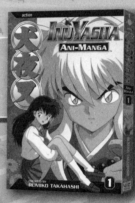

Full color adaptation of the popular TV series

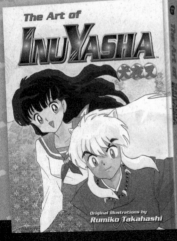

Art book with cel art, paintings, character profiles and more

TV SERIES & MOVIES ON DVD!

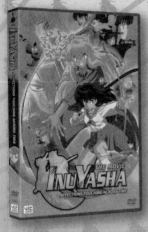

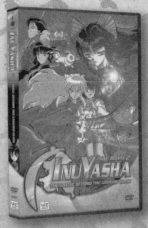

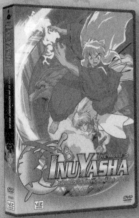

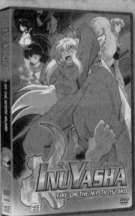

See more of the action in *Inuyasha* full-length movies

RATED
FOR
TEEN
ratings.viz.com

www.viz.com
inuyasha.viz.com

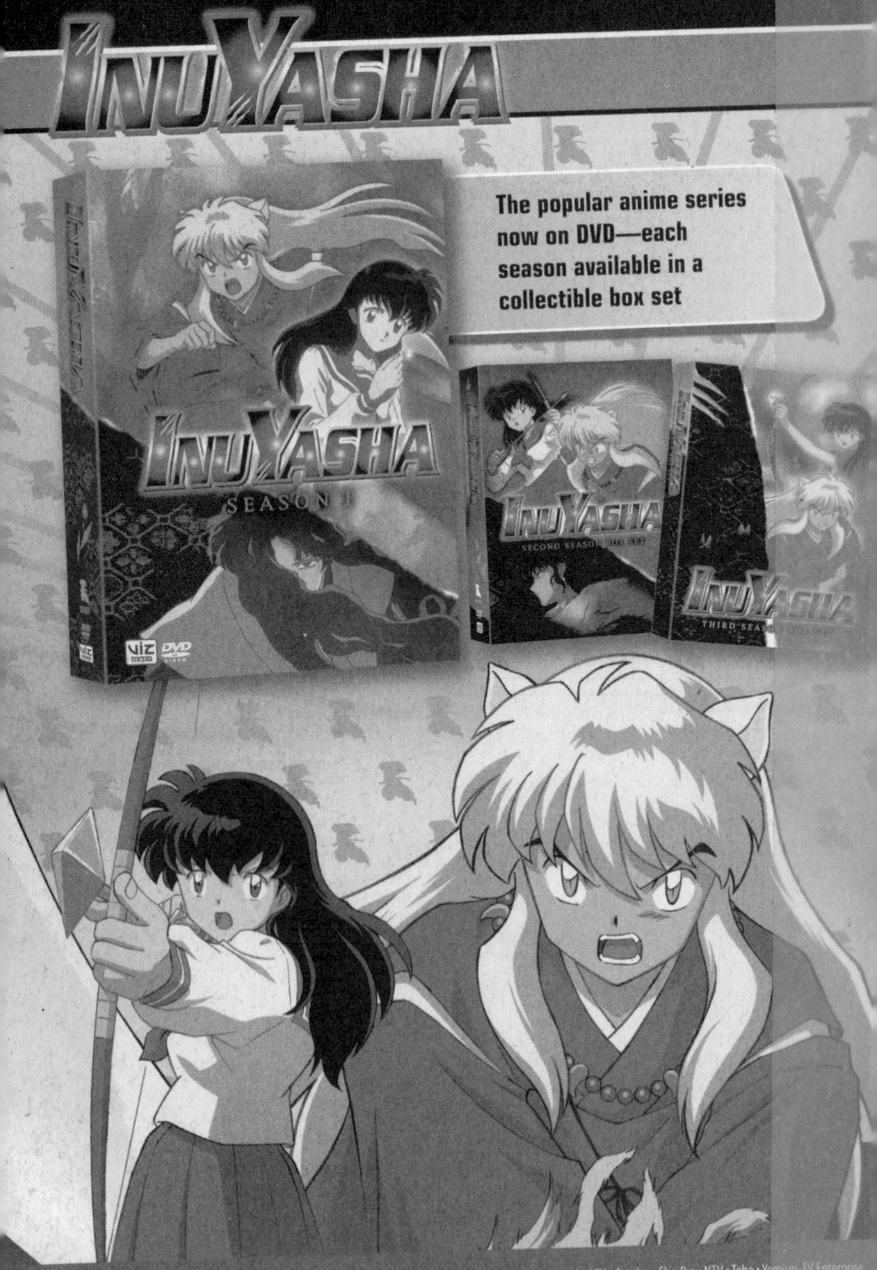
InuYasha
The popular anime series now on DVD—each season available in a collectible box set
InuYasha
Season 1
InuYasha
Second Season Box Set
InuYasha
Third Season

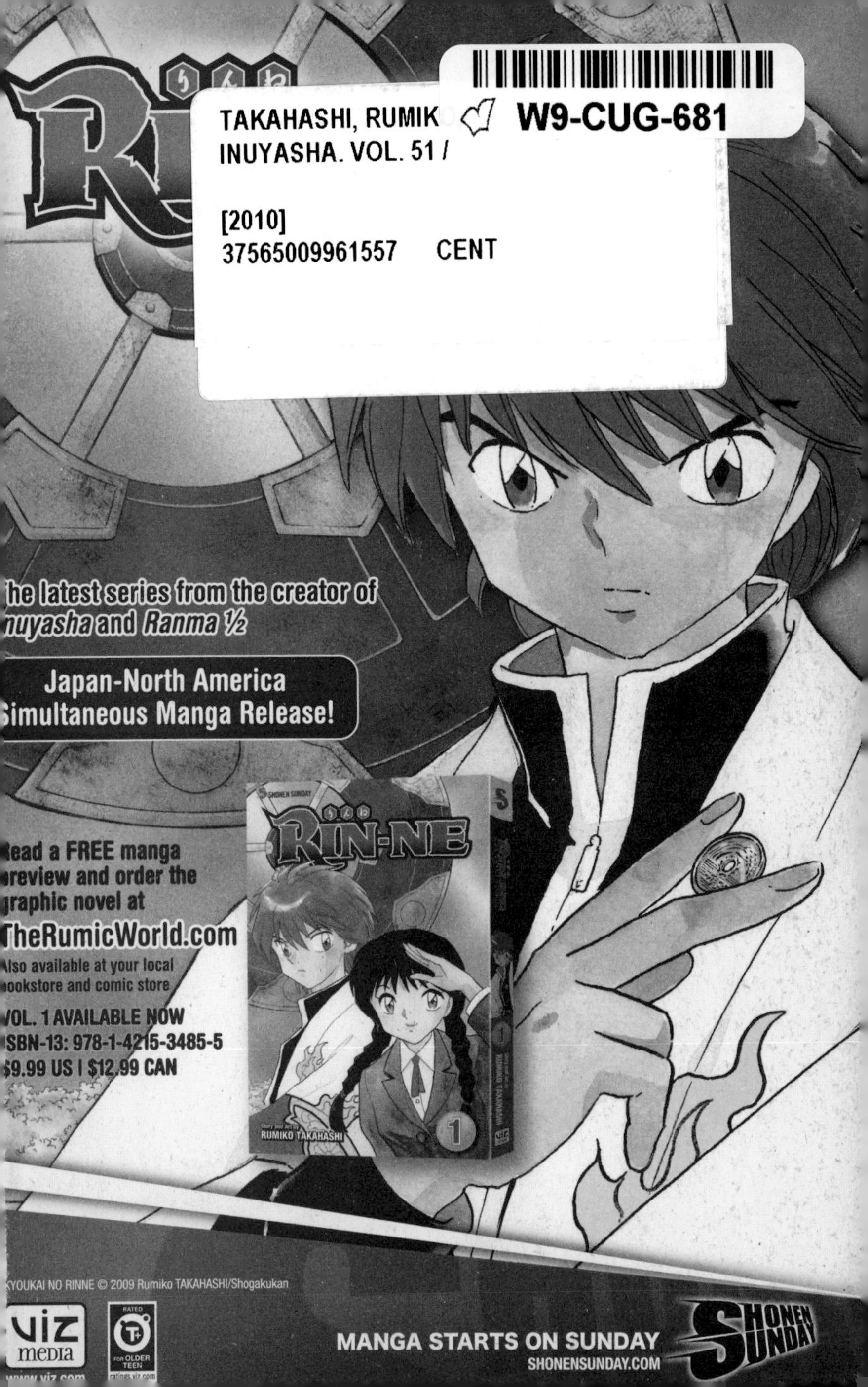
RIN-NE
he latest series from the creator of
nuyasha and Ranma ½
Japan-North America
imultaneous Manga Release!
ead a FREE manga
review and order the
raphic novel at
TheRumicWorld.com
lso available at your local
ookstore and comic store
OL. 1 AVAILABLE NOW
SBN-13: 978-1-4215-3485-5
$9.99 US | $12.99 CAN
SHONEN SUNDAY
RIN-NE
Story and Art by
RUMIKO TAKAHASHI
1
KYOUKAI NO RINNE © 2009 Rumiko TAKAHASHI/Shogakukan
viz media
RATED T+ FOR OLDER TEEN
ratings.viz.com
www.viz.com
MANGA STARTS ON SUNDAY
SHONENSUNDAY.COM
SHONEN SUNDAY